ARTURO TOSCANINI

Toscanini, c. 1937. *RCA*

Arturo Toscanini

THE NBC YEARS

by Mortimer H. Frank

with a foreword by Jacques Barzun

Amadeus Press
Portland, Oregon

Published in 2002 by
Amadeus Press (an imprint of Timber Press, Inc.)
The Haseltine Building
133 S.W. Second Avenue, Suite 450
Portland, Oregon 97204, U.S.A.

Reprinted 2002

Printed through Colorcraft Ltd., Hong Kong

Library of Congress Cataloging-in-Publication Data

Frank, Mortimer H.
     Arturo Toscanini : the NBC years / by Mortimer H. Frank ; with a
  foreword by Jacques Barzun.
          p.   cm.
     Includes videography (p.   ), discography (p.   ), bibliographical
  references (p.   ), and index.
     ISBN 1-57467-069-7
     1. Toscanini, Arturo, 1867–1957—Criticism and interpretation.
  2. NBC Symphony Orchestra. I. Title.

ML422.T67 F73 2002
784.2′092—dc21
[B]
                                                          2001035527

True ease . . . comes from art, not chance
As those move easiest who have learn'd to dance.

Pope, *An Essay on Criticism*

For Michael Gray and Anthony Paterno
who helped make this book possible

and for George Jellinek
who helped to make it readable

CONTENTS

Foreword: Toscanini Then and Now *by Jacques Barzun*   9

Preface   15
Acknowledgments   19

Chapter 1. NBC Comes to Toscanini   21
Chapter 2. The Broadcasts   41
Chapter 3. The NBC Repertory   115
Chapter 4. Reconstructing Toscanini   235

Appendix 1. Nonbroadcast Toscanini NBC Symphony Orchestra
             Concerts   261
Appendix 2. The NBC Symphony Orchestra Tours   265
Appendix 3. Works Performed by Toscanini at NBC Absent from His
             New York Philharmonic Programs   272
Appendix 4. Works Performed by Toscanini with the New York
             Philharmonic Absent from His NBC Symphony Orchestra
             Programs   276
Appendix 5. NBC Symphony Orchestra Personnel   278
Appendix 6. Preservation of the NBC Symphony Orchestra
             Broadcasts   282
Appendix 7. The Toscanini Videos   285
Appendix 8. Discography   289
Appendix 9. NBC Symphony Orchestra Broadcasts: The Other
             Conductors   318

Notes   345
Bibliography   352
Index   355

Foreword

TOSCANINI THEN AND NOW

Jacques Barzun

During the two closing decades of the twentieth century, Toscanini's name and fame have once again occupied the public mind. Books, articles, reviews, broadcasts, a film, *Toscanini the Maestro*, on an RCA videocassette have presented the man and his work, either in favorable terms or the reverse.

This surge of interest has occurred despite floating notions that Toscanini's star has permanently dimmed, because his influence on musical culture was harmful and because he was a dictatorial literalist concerned only with promoting himself. But evidently his memory is still vivid, and his work remains important for the very issues that it keeps raising. Surely since his death in 1957 he has not been promoting himself nor has he provoked the present controversy by performing. Hence his presence in our minds is the point to consider: why? And a parallel question demands an answer: where are the others, his rivals and his successors?

The conclusion is inescapable that he was—that he is—an inherently great figure who stands for perfectly definite ideas and who will remain an object of admiration and detraction, like all great artists. It is foolish to suppose that the masters—Bach, Shakespeare, Raphael—are adored by everybody for all time. It is only the lesser talents that earn unanimity, thanks to their smaller, undisturbing claims.

Toscanini's personality was of the kind that encourages the growth of legends. From the tale of his dalliance in Rio de Janeiro at the age of nineteen when he should have been just then at the opera conducting *Aida* to his incessant temper and physical assaults during rehearsals, they are congenial misrepresentations. In Rio he may well have been dallying, but he was not expected at the opera. He rushed there from his tryst to take the place of *two* conductors who, one after the other, had abandoned the podium. Toscanini was only the singing coach, but his conducting the opera from memory calmed the riotous audience and won their wholehearted ovation. As for bad temper, it was only occasionally displayed and its physical expression was visited on objects, not people. So much for legend.

Those whose memory goes back far enough will recall that Toscanini, already famous in Europe, emerged in New York from that curious underworld, the orchestra pit of an opera house. No doubt an opera conductor is visible—he is head and shoulders above the instrumentalists under him—but he has to appear full height, on a podium above the level of the eye, before the wider musical public is aware of his commanding presence. One reason is that for the opera buffs, the singers are all in all, whereas in the concert hall, the conductor is king. The truth is that on the East Coast Toscanini acquired a name that all must know only in the late 1920s, when he conducted the New York Philharmonic. He became a national figure when the NBC orchestra was founded for him in 1937.

Soon after that, "Toscanini" turned into a sort of generic term for conducting, as Michelangelo stands for painting and Einstein for science. The public needs these grand incarnations; they disburden the memory and simplify conversation: "take Shakespeare—" "take Toscanini—." This elevation was what his critics resented and still resent as if he himself had usurped the throne at the expense of other towering figures. It was the era when admiration for the victorious commander of 110 musicians turned to hero worship. In addition, some critics then and now maintain that Toscanini imposed and fastened on contemporary musical culture a number of regrettable features.

To admirers these features are positive qualities, of which some are not found in other conductors, or not found to the same degree. For it is true that in his time the musical scene was well supplied with great leaders of great orchestras: Bruno Walter, Furtwängler, Klemperer, Monteux, Ansermet, Beecham, Van Hoogstraten, and perhaps the finest and least adulated of them all, Erich Kleiber. Every one of these men had immense talent and the ability to project both music and personality. If Toscanini struck good judges as unique in power and scope, it must have been for reasons not arising from publicity.

His special virtue was conscience, principle expressed through both musicianship and moral energy. Toscanini's passionate devotion was to music first; other things came next, including self, authority, the love of women, and whatever else made up his individual humanity. The primacy of music and the rule of conscience meant absolute respect for the musical work. He had none of the egotism that teases public and reviewers into admiration with "my" Fifth Symphony, "my (startling) reading" of Schubert's "Unfinished." Toscanini's reading was of the score. In his own unassuming words, his task was "to come as close as possible to expressing the composer's ideas." He put on no misplaced modesty of manner, but he was humble when in face of the text. He sought out its minutest details; he coached and compelled the performers to see and observe them; his role was to reassemble them into a coherent whole—the composer's, not his.

This fidelity, to the extent that a human will could achieve it, was reflected in all he said, did, or demanded. It was implied in his soberness of gesture. He did not belong to the now reigning school of soulful gymnasts who (again) "interpret" the music to the audience physically. He disliked applause, that anti-musical noise, and he used a device to cut it short: he signaled to the concertmaster that he should get up and lead out the orchestra, whether the clapping had ceased or not. The creed of music paramount was evident likewise in his forbidding encores by opera singers, that anti-artistic practice par excellence.

A sample of his attention to detail I had the privilege of observing at first hand. In 1947 Toscanini had given with the NBC orchestra a performance of Berlioz's *Roméo et Juliette* symphony, complete. I had just then finished research for my biography of Berlioz and had present to my mind a discrepancy between the French and the German editions of the score. They differed in the placing of mutes on the strings at one point in the Love Scene. I had mentioned this detail to Bruno Zirato, Caruso's former secretary and now Toscanini's Man Friday. To my surprise, I was invited to tea at the Villa Pauline, Toscanini's house in Riverdale.

Toscanini questioned me closely as to the successive editions of the Berlioz score, the dates, the genesis of the work, the mood and intention of the passage affected, and the possible cause of the error in the score he had used, which was one edited in Germany forty years after Berlioz's death. Then we talked about music in general, Berlioz's instrumentation and harmonic practice, and finally he played for me a test pressing of the Queen Mab Scherzo from that same symphony. He stood close in front of me, listening intently and watching my facial expression at the delicate or difficult passages.

His hearing was clearly as acute as his eyesight was myopic, his sense of rhythm and tempo absolute. Some listeners questioned the tempos he chose for some movements in the Beethoven symphonies, but his choice was calculated and invariable. The result was a sharp-edged vitality that could not be matched. Nor was it due to tempo by itself. When Toscanini led rubato, one could be sure that on the return to strict time, not a beat had been lost or gained. This is a physical and intellectual pleasure.

Intellect in truth played a large role in Toscanini's conception of expressiveness. That last quality is usually ascribed to "right feeling," and it is true that many performers find right expression coming naturally, at least some of the time, out of what they call feeling. But the danger is great, as when a singer "feels" so deeply that he or she adds a sob to the vocal line that already expresses lament. But even with better judgment, what is felt spontaneously may be inappropriate dramatically or damaging to balance within the movement or the composition as a whole. Music is many-faceted and it takes mind to make sure that no element slights another. It was this total understanding that in rehearsal Toscanini labored to impart to his players. He used whatever words might convey the needed effect at that precise moment, and when repeated suggestion failed, he would lay down the baton and pointing to his head, he would shout "T'ink!"

The result was that clear-cut rendering of the music that listeners of various temperaments argued about. The music sounded like a stream of lava, slow or fast, and its bright clarity was that of polished steel. This pair of opposite qualities is what made Toscanini the perfect conductor of Berlioz—fire and ice at the same time and no sentimentality. Toscanini thus rescued Tchaikovsky from the wallowing languor other conductors imposed on him, and showed Boito's *Mefistofele* for the masterpiece that it is. And so it went for other Italian composers little appreciated here until done by the Toscanini method: expressing as far as possible "the composer's ideas."

With his recordings, Toscanini helped to bring about the enlargement of the repertoire that took place in the 1950s, thanks to the advent of the long-playing disk. It marked the escape from the narrow round of "the repertoire." Musical taste also improved by permitting immediate comparisons within a growing store of music that could be heard at will. Toscanini contributed his share of works, although he disliked recording sessions. He found tedious and painful the way they are run. The music is played in fragments, over and over, as the engineers discard them for acoustic reasons. No work is played from beginning to end, and this is purgatory for the mind that has conceived it as a whole and counts on the impetus of continuity.

One more word needs saying about the Toscanini conscience. Perhaps it could have been predicted that its controlling force would guide him far beyond the realm of music, but human character is not necessarily symmetrical. In Toscanini, it proved to be so. His stand against both the Fascist and the Nazi regimes is a matter of record. He gave up conducting at La Scala and Bayreuth. True, he had the advantage of fame and security that was denied to others; he could act fearlessly and signalize the turpitude of the oppressor. But he did not escape unscathed. In Bologna in 1931, aged sixty-two, he was mobbed and assaulted by Fascist youth for refusing to play the new national anthem, *Giovinezza*. He refused to conduct in his native land for fifteen years, during eight of which he was a self-exile.

When critics today deplore Toscanini's "arrogant, authoritarian methods," they are expressing a latter-day political attitude rather than assessing the facts. If Toscanini had not been a strong assertive character, he probably would not have stood up to Mussolini or resisted the Wagner family's entreaties. More important, conducting operas and orchestras cannot be done by looking for democratic consensus. Italian opera companies are notoriously anarchical and large orchestras, though more self-controlled, can do their best only by obedience to commands. The age of baroque music, when the first violin could from his desk gently lead the small band, is gone. In music since about 1800, the number and complexity of the efforts to be unified require a host of decisions by one mind. As on a ship, the course must be set by a single intelligent will.

What justifies a particular commander is, once again, the integrity of his aim and the merit of its result. When a great artist is a moral wretch or a self-centered scoundrel, we make allowances and forget the flaws for the sake of the art. When on the contrary the artist is guided by a lucid conscience, one finds that the term "great artist" or even "great man" is inadequate, perfunctory. One wants to say rather what Napoleon said after meeting Goethe: "Here is a man!"

PREFACE

Enough books have been written about Toscanini—more, quite likely, than any other conductor has inspired—to make one wonder if another is needed. Some of those books, however, were produced during the conductor's lifetime and consequently lack the perspective that time alone can provide. Moreover, none involves a close study of his seventeen years (1937–1954) at NBC, the last and longest professional association of his unprecedented sixty-eight-year career. Those years have, of course, been discussed. Sometimes they were excessively praised, other times they were deemed an inferior appendage to past triumphs, and often they were judged to be a period in which advancing years and declining powers left the conductor without the authority and control that he exerted during his preceding decade with the New York Philharmonic. Such specious views resulted mainly from a lack of access to transcriptions of the NBC Symphony Orchestra broadcasts made by the network's engineers.

The first change in this situation occurred in 1981 and grew out of the unfortunate razing of one of Toscanini's two Riverdale homes, the Villa Pauline. Many residents of the neighborhood, myself included, wanted to create a permanent memorial to the conductor in the area. With this in mind and as a professional critic, I approached Peter Sauer, the director of Wave Hill (Toscanini's other Riverdale home), which, after having been acquired by New York City in 1975, had evolved into a magnificent public garden and environmental center beautifully situated on a twenty-eight-acre estate overlooking the Hudson River. I suggested that Wave Hill might gain access to transcriptions of the NBC Symphony broadcasts and create an archive that could be used for study and public presentations. The suggestion was favorably received, and from it grew the Toscanini Collection at Wave Hill. The core of this collection comprised tapes of all the conductor's NBC Symphony broadcasts, most of them derived from primary sources such as transcription discs made by the network's engineers.

When I was appointed curator of the collection, I was able to realize a long-held desire to gain access to otherwise unavailable material. That desire sprang

from an interest in Toscanini initially stimulated thirty years earlier by his recordings of Beethoven's "Eroica" and "Pastoral" Symphonies. These in turn
led to my acquiring all of his recordings and reading as much about him as possible. That reading offered occasional suggestions that Toscanini's work before
an audience was often more compelling than his efforts in the recording studio.
Repeated hearings of those public performances, in addition to providing a
revealing walk into history, has confirmed those suggestions and enabled me to
refute many of the specious generalizations made about the conductor's NBC
years.

The deepened perspective on Toscanini's NBC career resulting from the
Wave Hill project was extended in 1991, when the New York Public Library
for the Performing Arts acquired the Toscanini family archive. Begun and maintained by the conductor's son, Walter, it is considerably broader than the Wave
Hill Collection. It includes all the NBC broadcasts and the rehearsals for them,
as well as concert performances Toscanini led with orchestras other than the
NBC Symphony. In addition, it houses his correspondence, annotated scores,
and a rich variety of iconography and other relevant documents. With the Wave
Hill Toscanini project suspended at this writing and NBC's own transcriptions
of the Toscanini broadcasts that were sent to the Library of Congress being
unavailable for auditioning, the New York Public Library remains the only
public institution where all of Toscanini's work at NBC may be heard. None of
the library's holdings may be copied, however, for private acquisition.

In preparing this book I have drawn mainly on the Wave Hill material,
supplementing it with research at the New York Public Library. Toscanini's
NBC performances and the production of his NBC broadcasts have been my
primary concerns. I have worked toward correcting some inaccurate generalizations and biased judgments that have infected Toscanini criticism during the
last two decades of the twentieth century. But I have not done so in an effort to
gain converts. Toscanini's work continues to speak for itself. Nor have I resurrected the childish allegations concerning ostensible adversarial positions that
existed between Toscanini and some of his most distinguished peers. Some critics, for example, continue to speak of Wilhelm Furtwängler as Toscanini's great
rival, implying that an ongoing conflict existed between them while ignoring,
for instance, the fact that Toscanini recommended Furtwängler in 1936 to be his
successor at the New York Philharmonic.

I hope that this volume will have value on two levels: as a critical evaluation
of Toscanini's work at NBC and as a reference tool that provides previously
unpublished information along with pertinent facts. Pursuing these aims has led
to some necessary redundancies. Toscanini's RCA recordings, for example, are
specified in both chapter 3 and the discography, the citations in the latter offering more detailed information. Special circumstances pertain to the broadcasts
of complete operas. Most exemplify Toscanini's only surviving performance of

a work, so one can never be sure how representative it may be. Then, too, these in-concert renditions were not subject to the limitations imposed by fully staged productions, especially in matters of pacing.

Finally, I do not consider this book the last word on Toscanini's NBC career. Particularly worthy of further study are his dress rehearsals, which often comprise uninterrupted performances that differ from their succeeding broadcast counterparts. But these deserve a book unto themselves.

ACKNOWLEDGMENTS

This book owes its existence to Michael Gray and Anthony Paterno. Both had access to primary sources of Toscanini broadcasts, which they shared with me before those broadcasts became available to the public. George Jellinek went far beyond what one can expect from a good friend, reading the entire (sometimes messy) typescript and providing innumerable helpful comments that have benefited this volume in many ways. I am also grateful to the late Martin Bernstein and to Harvey Sachs for reading portions of the manuscript and identifying shortcomings before they slipped into print.

Sachs's influence is evident throughout this book. His *Toscanini* remains the most objective, accurate, and richly documented biography of the conductor, and many of the quotations and a good deal of the factual information I have incorporated derive from his research. Although I have disputed some of the views of B. H. Haggin and Robert C. Marsh, their books on Toscanini remain valuable and have enriched this volume in a variety of ways.

A special debt is owed to Jacqueline Guttman. As performing arts director at Wave Hill, she was instrumental in establishing a Toscanini archive there and securing my position as its curator.

Many others helped in a variety of ways. To Richard Benson, Ray Burford, Robert Carlson, Christopher Dyment, Annette Goldman, Harris Goldsmith, Keith Hardwick, and Donald Carl Meyer I am grateful for providing printed material and listening sessions that I could not have had access to on my own. For encouragement and support I am indebted to Toscanini's grandson, Walfredo, and his wife, Elaine, and to Alan Steckler, who has always responded with enthusiasm to my writing about the maestro. Two grants from the Research Foundation of the City University of New York facilitated research that otherwise would have been difficult to pursue. To Eve Goodman of Amadeus Press goes my gratitude for making this volume more concise and coherent than it otherwise might have been. And Barbara Norton's many suggestions have contributed to its readability and accuracy.

I am especially indebted to my daughter-in-law, Amy Frank. In preparing this manuscript, she acted not merely as a word processor but as a collaborator, immersed in the book's sense and able to make sound professional judgments about problematic issues in the text.

The greatest (and certainly the longest) support has come from my wife, Carol, and son, Matt. Both have seen this book grow over a period of years from a loosely conceived idea to its present state, shared in my many exciting discoveries, and displayed ceaseless patience with what, at times, must have seemed my manic enthusiasm. And to Carol is due a special acknowledgment for taking on the burden of some of the most difficult and tedious aspects of proofreading. Her eye for accuracy and her critical judgment provided in many, many instances a needed corrective to my own.

1

NBC COMES TO TOSCANINI

On 29 April 1936 mounted police were summoned to Carnegie Hall to restrain a huge crowd that had gathered to obtain the few remaining standing-room tickets for what was then assumed to be Arturo Toscanini's farewell concert with the New York Philharmonic. A decade earlier Toscanini had made his first guest appearance with that orchestra and in 1929 had been named its principal conductor. In the fall of 1935 he declared his intention not to return to the Philharmonic for the 1936–37 season, and many believed that the United States was quite possibly seeing the last of him at that April farewell performance.

The decade Toscanini spent at the Philharmonic was a key period in his career, completing his transition from primarily a conductor of opera to an almost exclusively symphonic one. Indeed, the first decade of his career (1886–96) was spent solely in the opera house. On 20 March 1896 at Turin's Teatro Regio he directed his first symphonic concert. It included Schubert's Ninth Symphony, Tchaikovsky's *Nutcracker Suite* (then only four years old), the Italian premiere of the *Tragic* Overture by Johannes Brahms (who was still alive at the time), and the Entrance of the Gods into Valhalla from Wagner's *Rheingold*.

Subsequent symphonic ventures included concerts in Turin, Milan, and New York's Metropolitan Opera, as well as, during the 1920–21 season, a transcontinental tour of North America with the La Scala orchestra, when Toscanini made his first recordings. But prior to coming to the New York Philharmonic, Toscanini, like so many conductors of his time, spent most of his professional life in the theater: first in Italy, where his most prestigious positions involved three separate appointments as musical director of La Scala (1898–1903, 1906–8, and 1921–29), in New York as a principal conductor at the Metropolitan Opera (1908–15), and finally at two of Europe's most respected summer festivals, Bayreuth (1930–31) and Salzburg (1935–37). His Bayreuth appearances marked the first time a non-German had conducted there, and those at Salzburg the last time he conducted a staged opera in its entirety.

Had he never led a symphonic concert, Toscanini would have a secure place in the history of modern performance practice solely because of the many

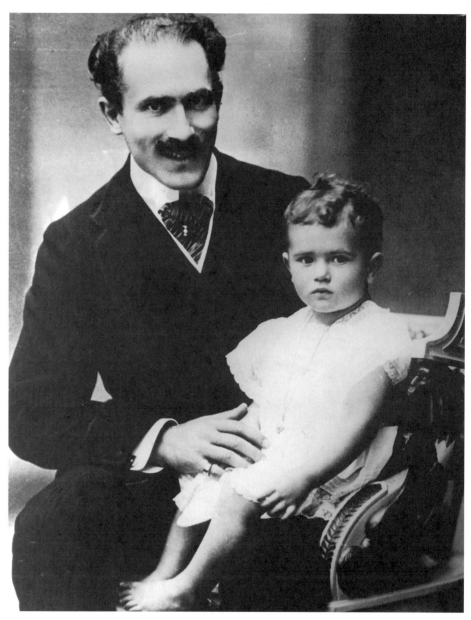

Toscanini with daughter Wanda, 1908. *RCA*

reforms he introduced in the theater and the many premieres he led there.[1] But he became best known to later generations primarily as a symphonic conductor, first at the New York Philharmonic and then during his seventeen years at NBC, his last and longest professional association (1937–54). The great majority of Toscanini's surviving work comes from his NBC period.

At the time of his retirement from the New York Philharmonic, the documentation of Toscanini's work was minimal. Nothing of his productions at La Scala or the Metropolitan Opera had been preserved, and the handful of recordings he had made by 1936—acoustic discs with the La Scala Orchestra and a more significant batch with the New York Philharmonic—were confined to orchestral pieces. Those few Philharmonic recordings certainly convey his extraordinary talent and give a reasonably good idea of the kind of sonority he favored. But their small number does not document the range and variety of his repertory. Were it not for the advent of radio, Toscanini's earliest recordings might well be the prime audible evidence of his work. Fortunately, NBC made it otherwise.

In the fall of 1936, David Sarnoff, president of the Radio Corporation of America, which owned the subsidiary Red and Blue networks of the National Broadcasting Company, proposed to Clarence Mackay, chairman of the board of directors of the New York Philharmonic, that Toscanini might cap his retirement with a transcontinental tour with the orchestra that NBC would broadcast. Nothing came of the proposal, but Sarnoff grasped the suitability of symphonic music to what was still called in 1936 "the miracle of broadcasting." Toscanini–New York Philharmonic performances of Beethoven's Ninth Symphony were carried over the air as early as 1927, and beginning in 1930, the Columbia Broadcasting System brought the Sunday afternoon concerts of that orchestra (many led by Toscanini) to a huge radio audience each week. Not long afterward, NBC began carrying the concerts of the Philadelphia Orchestra and Boston Symphony, and other stations were broadcasting live performances of less celebrated American symphony orchestras. What seems to have been clear to Sarnoff, who was not sophisticated musically, was that the symphonic repertory had a key place in the world of radio and that it would be to NBC's advantage not only to fill that place, but to fill it with a conductor generally acknowledged to be one of the most charismatic and possibly the most famous recreative musician alive.

When the plan for a Toscanini-led Philharmonic tour collapsed, Sarnoff embarked on a considerably bolder venture: organizing a new world-class symphony orchestra specifically for broadcasting and created expressly for Toscanini. In January 1937 Sarnoff sent Samuel Chotzinoff to Italy to explore the venture with the conductor. A pianist of more than passing accomplishment, Chotzinoff had accompanied a number of renowned singers, Alma Gluck among them, and instrumentalists, including Jascha Heifetz, whose sister he married. He also had been a music critic for two major newspapers in New York, the *Post* and the *World*. And of greatest importance, perhaps, in his criticism he had frequently voiced an unabashed admiration of Toscanini.

In his *Toscanini: An Intimate Portrait* (1956), Chotzinoff recalled the details of his meeting with Toscanini in terms so ludicrously melodramatic they make the conductor seem like an irascible child requiring the most delicate handling. As the book would have one believe, Chotzinoff spent two weeks in Italy without being able to bring himself to approach Toscanini about returning to the United States. Finally, in an after-dinner scene in which Toscanini allegedly was consuming brandy, Chotzinoff decided to be bold and make his move. Having done so, he "needed a climax" to crown his presentation. He quoted a magazine article that described how canaries "once sang the chorus of the Ninth Symphony" as a result of having heard it in a Toscanini-Philharmonic broadcast. This, according to Chotzinoff, convinced Toscanini of the potential of broadcasting and of the wide audience he could reach by conducting concerts for radio. But to think that Toscanini was sufficiently simple-minded to accept Sarnoff's proposal as a result of being told such nonsense is to believe that the conductor was a puerile fool devoid of sophistication.[2]

A somewhat more credible if still suspect account of what happened on Chotzinoff's mission is given in an unsigned article, "Toscanini on the Air," in the January 1938 issue of *Fortune*.[3] According to this article, Chotzinoff, armed with "six huge scrapbooks of letters from admiring radio listeners, raised the issue with Toscanini on his second day in Milan:

'Maestro, did you ever hear of the NBC?'
'No.'
'Did you ever hear of David Sarnoff?'
'No.'"[4]

After spending some time identifying Sarnoff and his NBC, Chotzinoff continued: "They want you in New York to conduct concerts for the radio or to be associated with them in any conceivable way you would consent to." Then, according to the article, Chotzinoff handed Toscanini a memorandum outlining various proposals ranging from a five-year contract to agreements covering considerably shorter periods. After reading them, Toscanini responded, "I do this": ten concerts to be broadcast in a season of ten weeks. But the conductor had one major qualification: the orchestra would have to be on par with the best in the United States—in other words, the New York Philharmonic, the Boston Symphony, and the Philadelphia Orchestra. If this condition was not met, Toscanini added succinctly, "I will not conduct."

Chotzinoff immediately phoned Sarnoff in New York, suggesting he come to Italy himself to close the deal. Sarnoff declined, preferring, as he told Chotzinoff, to take up the matter with NBC's board of directors to inform them of "what they are getting in for." "Tell them they may be getting in for millions,"

Caricature of Toscanini drawn c. 1910 by Enrico Caruso. *BMG Classics*

Chotzinoff countered. "Nothing but the world's greatest orchestra will do for him."[5]

NBC crowned its public announcement of the new venture with a four-page, quarto-sized folder printed on heavy glossy paper. Its front cover featured a large photograph of Toscanini, its back cover an NBC logo. Inside were two statements. On the right-hand page was a facsimile of a letter from Toscanini to Sarnoff written from Milan on 5 February 1937:

> I am very happy to accept your invitation to broadcast a series of symphonic concerts over the National Broadcasting Company networks. It is a great pleasure for me to think that I shall be able to put myself once more in touch with the radio public which gave in my last season with the Philharmonic the greatest proof of its appreciation and sympathy.

On the left-hand page was a considerably longer text headed "Mr. David Sarnoff's Statement to the Public":

> On behalf of the National Broadcasting Company and other members of the RCA family, I invited Maestro Arturo Toscanini, the world's greatest conductor, to return to America and broadcast a series of concerts with the National Broadcasting Company's Symphony Orchestra over its nationwide networks.
>
> In order to place before the Maestro the possibilities of this proposal and to discuss with him the matters involved in such an undertaking, I sent Mr. Samuel Chotzinoff, the celebrated music critic, and intimate friend and great admirer of the Maestro, to Milan, Italy, the home of the conductor.
>
> With the aid of modern means of communication, including the transoceanic radio and telegraph and radiotelephone systems, the negotiations were expedited and a contract has been signed covering the exclusive services of the Maestro in America for these radio concerts.
>
> The series of programs will be given the widest possible distribution over the air, and will be presented to the listening public as sustaining [unsponsored] broadcasts of the National Broadcasting Company.
>
> A good deal of planning and preparation must precede this effort, but the concerts will begin at the end of the present year [1937].
>
> We are delighted to be able to secure the return of Maestro Toscanini to America. His incomparable genius will further stimulate and enrich musical appreciation in our country.
>
> At NBC we are pursuing the policy of giving millions of our listeners the greatest artists the world has to offer.
>
> The opportunity to bring this message of music to the countless millions of American listeners has made a great appeal to the Maestro.

Despite its occasional superlative, this statement is reasonably restrained—more restrained, in fact, than Chotzinoff himself was. Certainly his estimate of

Toscanini with David Sarnoff at the time the maestro came to NBC. *BMG Classics*

the cost of the project was, to say the least, hyperbolic; it turned out to be far less than the "millions" he had cited to Sarnoff. Toscanini's fee for the ten broadcasts was to be $40,000, with his $5000 in income tax to be paid by NBC. The varying salaries of the orchestral musicians—ranging from a minimum scale of $105 per week paid to the majority of them to the $450 a week received by the concertmaster, Mischa Mischakoff—brought the total cost for each NBC-Toscanini broadcast to about $17,000. Theoretically, this figure might well have been reduced had a sponsor been involved. The Ford Motor Company, for example, had taken on sponsorship of the Detroit Symphony broadcasts, and in 1936 General Motors bought time on some CBS–New York Philharmonic broadcasts (for this occasion the orchestra was renamed "the General Motors Symphony").

But sponsorship entitled the corporation to a say in what was aired, and this would have run counter to the other details of Toscanini's NBC contract. He was to have exclusive rights in choosing programs and engaging soloists and choruses. He was also given the final word regarding orchestral personnel and permission to conduct the NBC Symphony in two additional concerts for which ticket sales would benefit causes of his choice. Finally, he required that Artur Rodzinski, whom he had come to admire in Salzburg and who was then director of the Cleveland Orchestra, be engaged by NBC to organize the new symphony and select its personnel. In return, it was agreed that for the ten weeks that Toscanini was working for NBC, the network was to retain exclusive rights to his services.

On the surface, it may seem surprising that Toscanini chose to return to New York so soon after his resignation from the Philharmonic. For one thing, he had a fifty-one-year career behind him, and he was no longer young. At the party in honor of his seventieth birthday in March 1937, he confided to Hugo Burghauser of the Vienna Philharmonic: "I am now an old man. And who knows; every new day is a gift from heaven, which I cannot even expect and hope for. I am not sick, but after seventy where are you? Should I even go out and conduct?"[6] This candid confession notwithstanding, there remained in him an almost desperate need to lead an orchestra. To live was to work, and life without work would have meant death. NBC's proposal fulfilled his needs while proving considerably less arduous than his schedule at the New York Philharmonic. He would have to conduct but one concert a week, rather than the four the Philharmonic required. He would have a world-class orchestra at his disposal that he could mold as he saw fit, and through radio, he would reach the largest audience possible. Little wonder that he accepted Sarnoff's proposal so quickly.

From Sarnoff's point of view, the agreement must have seemed equally beneficial. Even if the NBC Symphony failed to draw a sponsor, association with Toscanini's name was bound to lend prestige to the network. Surely that prestige would help lure prospective sponsors to other programs where they might reach the "select" audience of the kind NBC would be attracting. Put more bluntly, Sarnoff, whatever his public statements on the matter, was not motivated solely by high artistic ideals.

Perhaps the most remarkable among many remarkable aspects of this new venture was the speed and efficiency with which the NBC Symphony was assembled. John F. Royal, head of the programming department at NBC, arranged for the auditions that Rodzinski conducted. Applications for positions came from throughout the United States and from other countries as well. As it happened, however, thirty-one of the instrumentalists who ultimately passed the audition—almost exactly a third of the orchestra's final complement of ninety-two musicians—were already in the employ of NBC.

The creation of a world-class orchestra within eight months sent shock waves through the musical community. For one thing, it was viewed as a threat to other symphonic organizations still struggling under the burden of the depression. They felt their finest instrumentalists, attracted by the opportunity of being in New York and working with Toscanini, might be siphoned off by NBC.

Toscanini, holding a score of Bartók's *Music for Strings, Percussion, and Celeste*, with Artur Rodzinski in Salzburg, 1936. *BMG Classics*

And to some extent, that is exactly what happened. According to a promotional book published by NBC that provided sketches of each musician in the orchestra, "twenty-one of its members formerly held first-desk positions in other famous orchestras."[7] Among them were the oboist Robert Bloom of the Rochester Philharmonic; the violists Carlton Cooley of the Cleveland Orchestra and Arthur Granick of the National Symphony in Washington, D.C.; Mischakoff, concertmaster of the Chicago Symphony; the trombonist Armand Ruta, who held the position of principal in both Cleveland and Philadelphia; and the violinist Kalman Smit of the Cincinnati Symphony.

Complementing this seasoned group was another of relatively inexperienced players, many of them in string sections. One who gained great distinction was the cellist Alan Shulman, who carved out a career as a composer while in the orchestra and who, with his older brother Sylvan (also a charter member of the NBC Symphony), was to achieve renown in the Stuyvesant Quartet.

By September 1937 the orchestra was fully assembled and preparing for its first concert. Shortly thereafter, the entire project threatened to collapse. On 8 November—with the NBC Symphony having already made its broadcast debut under Rodzinski in what the network tagged a "dress rehearsal"—Toscanini received word that NBC, in order to maintain its newly formed orchestra, was discharging other employees, musicians among them.[8] A furious Toscanini called from Italy and announced his withdrawal from the project. Panic ensued at network central. For one thing, NBC had not been completely open with the conductor, as it had failed to inform him that the orchestra's personnel would have other musical duties at the network beyond those of the symphony broadcasts. This deceit was to prove disastrous when Toscanini ultimately discovered it three years later (see the discussion of the 1941–42 season in chapter 2). On the basis of what Chotzinoff originally told him, Toscanini believed the new orchestra was for his exclusive use or for the use of other conductors of whom he approved.

Chotzinoff cabled a reply to Toscanini's threatened withdrawal that expanded NBC's duplicity in the matter. It suggested that rather than discharging musicians, NBC was taking on many new ones in order to form the orchestra. To be sure, sixty-one new musicians were hired, who, along with the thirty-one retained by NBC from its staff orchestra, comprised the NBC Symphony. But many of those sixty-one were replacements for less skilled players. Toscanini, however, trusting Chotzinoff as a friend, withdrew his threatened resignation.

Prior to Toscanini's arrival, another problem occurred. His choice of Rodzinski to audition the personnel proved unwise—the younger conductor was temperamentally ill suited for this responsibility. Paranoid and unsure of himself, Rodzinski feared his selections would not please Toscanini. He took this fear out on the orchestra by constantly admonishing the younger players, "Wait till Toscanini comes." Alan Shulman recounted an incident in which Rodzinski was particularly hard on the oboist Robert Bloom, whom he accused of playing "out of tune." Ultimately, in frustration, Bloom retorted, "Maestro, was it sharp or flat?" Rodzinski was reduced to countering, "Adjust yourself."[9]

Most likely the problems generated by Rodzinski's abrasive personality led NBC to engage Pierre Monteux to lead the initial three broadcast concerts of the orchestra (on 13, 20, and 27 November).[10] The official word from NBC, however, was different: "Opening his own orchestra's season in Cleveland prevented Rodzinski from remaining in New York to conduct the NBC broadcast of 13 November 1937. Pierre Monteux, France's most distinguished conductor . . . presided at that historic event, remaining to conduct the first three weekly broadcasts."[11] Ultimately Rodzinski did return to lead three broadcasts (4, 11, and 18 December) that preceded Toscanini's debut with the orchestra on Christmas night, 1937.

Criticism has been made (especially by Joseph Horowitz in his book *Understanding Toscanini*) of the extremes to which NBC went to promote its new enterprise. The network printed postcards picturing the orchestra with inset portraits of Monteux, Rodzinski, and Toscanini. It produced press releases that

Charcoal drawing by Bettina Steinke for the promotional volume
The NBC Symphony Orchestra (1938). *BMG Classics*

may have set records for the number of superlatives they contained. Representative of the hype the new ensemble inspired was an article by Marcia Davenport titled "All Star Orchestra" that appeared in 1937 in *Stage*, a slick, glossy publication that defined itself as "the magazine of after-dark entertainment." Its intended readership was educated and affluent. Summarizing NBC's hiring of Toscanini for its new orchestra, Davenport noted:

> A train of unprecedented events, this twentieth-century gesture of Medici-like magnificence, carried through by an American business corporation for the benefit of millions of anonymous but powerful listeners. Only American audacity would dare to approach the god of all conductors, and having won him, proceed then to build an orchestra worthy of him.[12]

Such purple prose may well have offended in some quarters for its excesses, which ran counter to the more reserved style generally used to promote symphonic music.

But—and this is a key issue—the music on the broadcasts did not diverge in any way from the typical programs of major symphony orchestras. Nor was the style of the presentation of the broadcasts—in its comments about the music or in its supplementary commentary—any different from that used in New York Philharmonic broadcasts carried by CBS. In other words, it is essential to separate the promotion of the product from the product itself, a distinction those critical of the entire NBC-Toscanini venture have often failed to make.[13]

Admittedly, certain features of the NBC Symphony presentations departed from concert norms. This is because the network thought of them primarily as broadcasts and only secondarily as concerts, many of the details affecting their production being rooted in standards and customs that radio had generated. Paramount among them was the distribution of tickets. The law prohibited the sale of tickets for public broadcasts.[14] Instead, tickets were free and could be obtained for almost any program by a written request to the network. But a Toscanini concert was not *any* program, and for his first appearance with the orchestra NBC received fifty thousand requests for fourteen hundred available seats. Throughout Toscanini's NBC career, tickets for one of his broadcasts required either special access or the courage to go to the event in the hope that someone in the long line would have an extra ticket to give away. In Toscanini's third NBC broadcast (8 January 1938), this situation was obliquely acknowledged by the announcer when he noted that tickets for the conductor's 6 February benefit concert marked his "first appearance with the orchestra open to the general public"—in other words, the first for which tickets would be sold.

Also departing from concert-hall convention were NBC's printed programs. Rather than being provided in a playbill-like magazine, the three works comprising Toscanini's first concert were specified on a single sheet of satin.

Not mere ostentation but also practical considerations may have motivated such an exotic treatment. This was, after all, a broadcast, and broadcasting procedures dictated elimination of all extraneous noise. Conventionally printed programs rustled and rattled and consequently would not do. Satin, of course, was expensive and subsequently gave way to linen, which in turn proved too expensive and was replaced with unrustleable cork or cardboard. And on the programs was a printed admonition to the audience not to cough or produce other audible intrusions.

But what most set the NBC Symphony presentations apart from conventional concerts was the hall in which they took place—a large studio on the eighth floor of the RCA building in New York's Rockefeller Center that seated fourteen hundred.[15] Its identifying number—8H—was to become anathema in the world of symphonic music. Like all broadcasting studios, 8H was designed to absorb, not reflect, sound and thereby produce a resonance-free background that would promote clarity. For the spoken word, this is an ideal acoustic environment. But music's requirements are different, and the extreme acoustical deadness of 8H ran counter to musical needs. At its worst—as heard on some Victor recordings and over miles and miles of telephone lines through which NBC concerts were transmitted across the continent—the studio took on a surrealistic deadness that suggested the orchestra was performing in a padded closet. Indeed, many wondered why Toscanini tolerated the studio.

The most frequent explanation for Toscanini's acceptance of the acoustical shortcomings of 8H is that he liked the dryness of the hall for its clarity, which complemented the textural transparency he favored. Certainly the clipped, staccato effect he preferred on certain chords—so as to ensure that what followed them would be well defined—was more readily achieved in 8H than in a more resonant concert hall. Toscanini may also have accommodated himself to the sonic peculiarities of 8H because of a desire to reach the wide audience that the broadcasts attracted.

At the same time, Toscanini would probably not have tolerated anything like the dreadful sound that many people were hearing from their inexpensive AM radios. Far more likely is the assumption that 8H, for all its shortcomings, was not nearly so bad as it seemed when its acoustics were impaired by poor reproduction. Indeed, how one responded to 8H when in the hall may have been tied to how one responded to Toscanini. Virgil Thomson, for example, who was hostile to Toscanini, found everything about 8H offensive:

> The NBC hall is not a pleasant place to hear music. Not only are the acoustics, as is well-known, deplorable, but the manners of the staff are in no way encouraging to personal expansiveness. At every turn one is disciplined, guided, scolded, admonished. It is almost impossible to get into the place or out of it without being pushed around mentally or physically by someone in uniform. The "watchdogs of capital," as one

of my composer friends [Roy Harris] calls all this uniformed personnel, do not, with their police-like severity, create an atmosphere of welcome or of ease. They make it difficult, in fact, to listen to music with a free mind.[16]

Contrast this to comments made by Olin Downes, the senior music critic for the *New York Times* and a longtime admirer of Toscanini:

Another word should be spoken for the behavior of the audience [in 8H]. Think of it: an audience on time; no noise of late-comers; not a sound or rumble in the hall while the orchestra is playing. This is a new standard for listeners, and we would that it could be applied rigorously in other places than radio stations.

And in the same article, written as a review of the NBC Symphony's first broadcast concert under Pierre Monteux, Downes assessed 8H's acoustics:

The writer listened to the new orchestra from two different places. He wished to hear it in the performance of the Bach-Respighi C-minor organ passacaglia and the Mozart "Haffner" Symphony from a listening room where he could watch conductor and players and hear the music as it was heard presumedly by radio listeners in different parts of the country and the world. Afterward he heard the orchestra from a place in the concert hall in the performance of a movement from Cesar Franck's *Psyché* and three movements of Debussy's "Ibéria," and Richard Strauss's *Till Eulenspiegel*.

The sound of the music over the radio—no doubt with some of the best kind of receiving apparatus—was remarkable for the sonority and resonance of tone, and the cleanness with which, for the greater part of the time, all the inner parts as well as the main effects of the orchestra were revealed. Sometimes there was a slight preponderance of strings; a chord or two of wind instruments not perfectly balanced or at least edged so that the upper voice was entirely distinct. Sometimes there was too much brass. But these things, in all probability, were the result of the particular way in which the performance was transmitted.

Then came the opportunity for closer acquaintance with this orchestra in its concert hall or, as it is known in the NBC building, its studio. This studio . . . is made for broadcasting and it has not the resonance of a concert hall. . . . The result of this was that the orchestra was put to a very severe test. The strings, which were so vibrant when heard from the outside, are dryer in color in the studio. The same applies to the brass and in a lesser degree to the woodwind instruments.

So that one heard this orchestra with a lessened resonance, as if you listened to each instrument under a microscope. If a person who is a little near-sighted and sees all things rather soft-edged puts on a pair of good glasses, he gets something of the impression through the eyes that listening to the orchestra in the studio gives the ears. The orchestra must be a particularly good one, exceptionally accurate and well-trained to meet successfully these conditions.[17]

The concluding paragraph of this review might well be taken for attributes of the Toscanini style itself: the sharply focused clarity that Downes describes exemplified a key feature of Toscanini's performances, and this may be another reason Toscanini did not object to 8H. But the most plausible reason of all is that the studio, though it lacked resonance, was far better than it seemed when its acoustics were poorly reproduced. Most of the reference recordings made by NBC's engineers suggest that the sound of the studio, if quite dry and somewhat compressed, retained a clarity, impact, and naturalness of timbre greatly removed from the surreal, wooden deadness imposed by inferior radio reception and poorly microphoned commercially released recordings.

Owing to the studio's sonic peculiarities, microphone placement was critical, the difference of even a few feet often creating a marked difference in the overall sound. Even in reference discs the hall sometimes sounds painfully dead. The ideal placement was evidently just above and slightly behind the podium. This suggests that Toscanini was listening from an ideal acoustical point, a further explanation of why he did not object to 8H.

At the start of the third (1939–40) season, NBC experimented with artificially produced resonance injected into the broadcasts. Unlike the ugly, detail-covering, balance-altering electronic reverberation imposed by RCA on some of Toscanini's commercially released recordings, NBC's manipulations were tasteful and musical and suggested considerably more "air" around the sound. This practice was discontinued after two years because the studio was structurally modified to improve its acoustics. Although improvements did result from the modification, microphone placement remained extremely critical, since poor positioning caused the newly created resonance to lend the sound an opaque unpleasantness. But with the microphone well positioned, the acoustic was more than merely acceptable, as is attested by the studio 8H recording Toscanini made in 1945 for RCA of Gershwin's *An American in Paris*. And when the broadcasts were permanently transferred to Carnegie Hall in the fall of 1950 (studio 8H by then having been converted to a television studio), their sound was better still, even if the very close microphone placement favored there by NBC eliminated some of the hall's natural resonance. Indeed, Toscanini may well have preferred this placement for the clarity it engendered.

During the first four seasons, the broadcasts were aired on Saturday nights for an hour and a half, occasionally a bit longer when the music so demanded. They were similar, in both length and content, to most symphony orchestra concerts. In New York City the broadcasts were carried by NBC's Red and Blue networks and thus could be heard on either station WEAF or station WJZ. Many of them featured an intermission talk, which Samuel Chotzinoff, who

Toscanini conducting a rehearsal in Carnegie Hall. On the left is the
principal second violinist, Edwin Bachmann. *BMG Classics*

had been named general music director at the network, usually gave. There
were other speakers too, notably Olin Downes and Alistair Cooke. Sometimes
exceeding ten minutes, Chotzinoff's monologues were aimed at the musically
uninformed and never dealt with music in any technical way. If sometimes ver-
bose, they were intelligent and pointed, often placing the music being performed in a meaningful sociological or biographical context.

During the initial season, the commentary by the NBC announcer Howard Claney sometimes sounded pretentious; at other times it was extemporane-
ous, with patches of silence that would seem clumsy by today's standards. But as
the programs continued, the announcements became more polished.

Beginning with the 1941–42 season, the programs were shortened to an
hour. This remained the standard length, and longer broadcasts took place only
when required by the particular repertory. The day and hour of the programs
occasionally changed. Specific broadcast times are provided in the summaries of
individual seasons in chapter 2.

The notion sometimes promulgated that the broadcasts suffered from excessive commercial intrusion should be put to rest. Full-time sponsors were acquired for only five of the orchestra's seventeen seasons: General Motors for three, Socony Vacuum Oil for one, and a quartet made up of the House of Squibb, Whitehall Pharmaceutical, the Ford Motor Company, and RCA for another. Reynolds Metals bought air time for three telecasts. The only other commercial intrusions—and they were oblique—occurred during the two seasons following General Motors' abandonment of the programs. In such instances it was noted that "while these programs are sustaining," the purchase of products of companies sponsoring "other" NBC broadcasts would help "to keep the NBC Symphony on the air."

In the light of the considerable hype used to promote the creation of the orchestra and the return of Toscanini to the United States, the opening commentary for his NBC debut stands as a welcome corrective of taste and restraint:

> Christmas greeting to those in the United States and Canada and those in other parts of the world who might be listening by shortwave. The National Broadcasting Company is proud to present the incomparable conductor Arturo Toscanini, who tonight directs for the first time the National Broadcasting Company Symphony Orchestra in its regular Saturday evening concert. Mr. Toscanini's program this evening will consist of three works.

The announcer went on to discuss briefly the opening work, Vivaldi's Concerto Grosso in D Minor, Op. 3 No. 11, noting that "very little is known about Vivaldi" (a comment that reveals how far we have advanced musicologically in the last half century). The entire opening statement lasted only two minutes and twenty-three seconds and was confined to a few words about Vivaldi and an introduction of the first-desk soloists in the concerto.

The program that evening—the Vivaldi, Mozart's Symphony No. 40, and Brahms's Symphony No. 1—bespeaks the seriousness with which Toscanini approached this new venture: each work comes from a distinct period in the history of Western music, each is in a minor key, and each is starkly dramatic. Listener response to the program proved favorable far beyond NBC's high expectations. Letters poured into the network, and during the third of Toscanini's broadcasts NBC indulged itself, taking the opportunity to quote some of that mail on the air and to read some of the accolades that had appeared in many newspapers. One typical quote from an unidentified paper declared, "Radio is to be congratulated for doing what radio does best."

Near the conclusion of Toscanini's first season, he was so pleased with his orchestra—and NBC so pleased with the series—that he signed a new three-year contract with the network calling for sixteen concerts in each of those three seasons. He also agreed to add an eleventh broadcast to the first season. It took

Toscanini and the NBC Symphony receiving applause at the conclusion of the last broadcast of the orchestra's first season, 5 March 1938. *BMG Classics*

place on 5 March 1938, and Thomas Mann was one of many distinguished people in the audience. The opening announcement for the broadcast was more
flamboyant than that of Christmas night, colored by such extravagant locutions
as "momentous" and "gala" to describe the all-Wagner program that was about
to ensue. During the intermission, Samuel Chotzinoff spoke in praise of Toscanini. David Sarnoff then read a prepared statement that included these words
from the conductor:

> Having reached the end of these eleven weeks of concerts I am over-
> come with sadness at the parting from my dear and capable collabora-
> tors who with a deep devotion and admirable cooperation have greatly
> contributed to the beautiful artistic success of this series of concerts. I
> trust that the vast radio audience was satisfied and that these concerts
> carried joy and serenity to remote regions and to the humblest abodes.
> When I think of this, my sadness diminishes. And when I think that
> next October I shall be able to resume my work with the magnificent
> orchestra of the NBC for an even longer period, the sadness changes to
> joy.

Sarnoff's own words contained an interesting point:

> The National Broadcasting Company is an American business. It has
> employees and it has stockholders. It serves their interests best when it
> serves the public best. We believe in this principle and maintain it as our
> guiding policy. That is why we organized the NBC Symphony Or-
> chestra and invited the world's greatest conductor to direct it.

This statement cuts two ways. On the one hand, it states that NBC feels a duty
to bring quality broadcasting to the public. On the other, it implies that the
network's business is business—that the organization has economic responsi-
bilities to itself and the people who work for it.

However one views Sarnoff's statement, it should not color one's judgment of the series his venture produced: seventeen seasons of orchestral concerts
broadcast to a vast audience and preserved in generally superb transcriptions
that stand as an unprecedented and detailed record of the work of an extraordinary artist as he shaped, modified, and reevaluated his conceptions of some of the
monuments of Western music. What is more, in recording all the broadcasts of
the NBC Symphony directed by conductors other than Toscanini—a group
that included such luminaries as Pierre Monteux, Artur Rodzinski, Bruno Walter, George Szell, Leopold Stokowski, Fritz Reiner, Dimitri Mitropoulos, Erich
Kleiber, Ernest Ansermet, and Guido Cantelli, among others—NBC left a
priceless documentation of performance practice.[18] Whatever Sarnoff's motives,
he gave the world a treasure.

2

THE BROADCASTS

Only in the last three decades of the twentieth century have major symphony orchestras come to recognize the importance of preserving their history by creating a systematic archive of recordings of their concert performances. Some ensembles, to be sure, were more alert than others to such a necessity, the Boston Symphony, for example, having a richer record of its past than the New York Philharmonic. There were, of course, isolated instances of foresight that produced invaluable documents, a notable case in point being a 1940 Beethoven cycle led by Willem Mengelberg with the Amsterdam Concertgebouw Orchestra. But in 1937, when the NBC Symphony Orchestra was created, such documentation, if it existed at all, was random and sporadic. It is thus all the more remarkable that each of the seventeen years of the orchestra's broadcasts has been preserved with unique completeness.

Were the listings provided here of the programs Toscanini conducted for the network only a list, it would command interest simply as important raw information about the longest professional association of his career. But with all those broadcasts recorded in what are, in the main, sonically superior transcriptions, the list becomes a guide to resurrectable history. Entering into that history and studying those broadcasts leave no doubt about the inaccuracy of the allegation sometimes made that Toscanini's NBC years were a comparatively second-rate appendage to his extraordinary career—and furthermore, as the allegation goes, one in which his powers suffered a marked decline. More than a few inferior readings occurred in these concerts, and some of them must have been an embarrassment to Toscanini. But many magnificent ones were also given that attest to a conductor in full control and to a thinking artist who is modifying his views of a particular work from one presentation to another. Indeed, with Toscanini having used NBC's recordings of his broadcasts for study, the concerts survive not only as a document of his work but also as a record of his own response to it. Then, too, his NBC years include performances of works that he never conducted before coming to the network. And as chapter 3 makes clear, Toscanini's NBC years produced readings of many scores for which he left no approved recording.

The years I have spent listening and relistening to these broadcasts have left no doubt in my mind that the conductor James Levine (commenting in a video biography of the conductor, available on RCA cassette 60341-3-RG) was fully justified in claiming, "Toscanini was the most consistently great conductor of our century. He conducted outstanding performances of a vast international repertoire at a time when many conductors were concentrating on their own national repertoires." Even if one does not share Levine's primary view of Toscanini's greatness, the NBC broadcasts alone substantiate Levine's claim about Toscanini's international repertory. They also reveal his special favorites: Beethoven and Brahms (the only composers to whom he devoted cycles), Verdi (whom he had known personally), and Wagner. Also, certain works occurred with unusual frequency, notably the "Eroica" and "Pastoral" Symphonies of Beethoven, the prelude to *Die Meistersinger von Nürnberg* and the Rhine Journey from *Götterdämmerung* by Wagner, Berlioz's Queen Mab Scherzo, and Debussy's *La mer*. Still, the notion sometimes propounded that Toscanini's repertory, if large in terms of numbers, is narrow in terms of range does not withstand scrutiny. Neither does the ill-judged belief that he was inimical to "modern" music. Issues of this ilk are dealt with in chapter 4.

This second chapter is divided into seventeen sections, one for each of Toscanini's years at NBC. Because chapters 3 and 4 deal mainly with musical interpretation, comments about individual broadcasts, where appropriate at all, are mostly limited to other matters: the peculiarity of the concerts or their promotion purely as broadcasts, the special relevance of a program in Toscanini's career, and unusual occurrences such as (in two instances) his stopping a performance and beginning it anew.

I have resisted the temptation to specify timings for each performance. With the advent of the compact disc, it has become a fashionable (and often thoughtless) practice to use timings as a guide to the character of an interpretation. But duration, of itself, is often misleading. Identical timings for the performance of a given movement, for example, may not indicate identical or even similar readings.

I have also rejected indicating which of these broadcast performances has been released on unauthorized CDs, mainly because many of these discs move in and out of the catalog with a rapidity that makes them hard to track. Appendix 8, however, does offer an overview of them. And I have gone out of my way to avoid in most instances (in this and successive chapters) what may be termed the "best-version" syndrome. Among Toscanini's admirers are those who feel the need to single out his finest performance of a given work, similar to the way one might seek out the best refrigerator or washing machine. But the re-creation of a work of art is not an appliance. It is a living thing that defies superlatives. The need for a "best" friend, after all, usually passes with adolescence. Most of all, I hope the information provided here will prove useful, add to what is known of Toscanini's years at NBC, and, in so doing, correct a number of misconceptions about them.

First Season (1937–38)

Perhaps there is no better indication of the effect Toscanini had upon the newly formed NBC Symphony Orchestra than the response of Samuel Antek, a charter member of the ensemble, who later pursued a career as a conductor:

> I was a violinist in that orchestra, and we were awaiting the first appearance of our conductor. There was no audience. The men, instruments in hand, sat nervously rigid, scarcely breathing. Suddenly, from a door on the right side of the stage, a small, solidly built man emerged. Immediately discernible were the crowning white hair and impassive, squat, high-cheekboned mustached face. He was dressed in a severely cut black alpaca jacket, with a high clerical collar, formal striped trousers, and pointed, slipperlike shoes. In his hand he carried a baton. In awed stillness we watched covertly as he walked up the few steps leading to the stage.
>
> As he stepped up to the podium, by prearranged signal, we all rose, like puppets suddenly propelled to life by a pent-up tension. We had been warned in advance not to make any vocal demonstration and we stood silent, eagerly and anxiously staring.
>
> He looked around, apparently bewildered by our unexpected action, and gestured a faint greeting with both arms, a mechanical smile lighting his pale face for an instant. Somewhat embarrassed, we sat down again. Then, in a rough hoarse voice he called out, "Brahms!" He looked at us piercingly for the briefest moment, then raised his arms. In one smashing stroke, the baton came down. A vibrant sound suddenly gushed forth from the tense players like blood from an artery.
>
> With each heart-pounding timpani stroke in the opening bars of the Brahms First Symphony his baton beat became more powerfully insistent, his shoulders more strained and hunched as though buffeting a giant wind. His outstretched left arm spasmodically flailed the air, the cupped fingers pleading like a beseeching beggar. His face reddened, his muscles tightened, eyes and eyebrows constantly moving.
>
> As we in the violin section tore with our bows against our strings, I felt I was being sucked into a roaring maelstrom of sound—every bit of strength and skill called upon and strained into being. Bits of breath, muscle, and blood, never before used, were being drained from me. Like ships torn from their mooring in a stormy ocean, we bobbed and tossed, responding to these earnest, importuning gestures. With what a fierce new joy we played!
>
> "So! So! So!" he bellowed, "Cantare! Sostenere!" His legs were bending slightly as he braced himself for his violent movements, which

were becoming larger, more pile-driving, as the music reached its first
great climax. "Cantare! Sostenere!" I was to hear these words often in the
years to come. "Sing! Sustain!" Toscanini's battle cry! This was the first
time they were flung at us, and for seventeen years we lived by them.

This passage has been quoted often by both Toscanini's admirers and his
detractors to underscore their respective viewpoints. Whatever ambiguity it
might contain is eradicated, however, in another passage, where Antek adds:

> Playing with Toscanini was a musical rebirth. The clarity, intensity,
> and honesty of his musical vision—his own torment—was like a cleans-
> ing baptismal pool. Caught up in his force, your own indifference was
> washed away. You were not just a player, another musician, but an
> artist once more searching for long forgotten ideals and truths. You
> were curiously alive, and there was a purpose and self-fulfillment in
> your work. It was not a job, it was a calling.[1]

The initial impact of Toscanini on Antek and doubtless on many other
members of the NBC Symphony is obvious in the remarkably committed quality that stamps nearly every performance directed by the conductor during his
first year with the orchestra. B. H. Haggin has contended it was not until the
NBC Symphony's transcontinental tour of 1950 "that it began to exhibit the
precise, finished, and sensitive execution, the blending, refinement, and beauty
of tone of a first-rate orchestra."[2] To some extent this may be true, but it may
also be argued that some performances of Toscanini's later NBC years suffered,
in part, from the conductor's and orchestra having developed excessive familiarity with each other. This may have neutralized some of the mutual stimula-
tion that existed between Toscanini and the musicians during their early association. In addition, the personnel of the orchestra underwent some key changes
during its middle and later years, when some of its finest musicians—the oboist
Robert Bloom, the flutist John Wummer, and the cellist Leonard Rose, among
others—left for other posts or for careers as soloists.

Beyond question, many of the performances given during the first season
command special interest: the stylish (for its time) Vivaldi Concerto Grosso,
Op. 3 No. 11; the first two Brahms symphonies, played with exceptional rhythmic elasticity; a richly atmospheric *La mer* of Debussy; a Borodin Second Symphony boasting a striking blend of lilt, grace, and power; and a Cherubini *Anacréon* Overture that transforms an often seemingly rambling minor score into a
taut miniature masterpiece.

With the exception of two benefit concerts (6 February and 4 March 1938),
which took place in Carnegie Hall, all the broadcasts emanated from studio 8H.
To judge from surviving sources, NBC's engineers had not as yet found an optimum placement for the microphone in 8H, so that the orchestra sounded
cramped and bass deficient, much of its weight absorbed by the anechoic hall.

Still, some of the broadcasts are preserved with wider frequency response than that present in the first Victor recordings Toscanini made in 8H. Unless otherwise noted, all programs were aired on Saturdays from 10:00 to 11:30 P.M.

25 Dec. 1937 Vivaldi: Concerto Grosso in D Minor, Op. 3 No. 11
Mozart: Symphony No. 40 in G Minor, K. 550
Brahms: Symphony No. 1 in C Minor, Op. 68

1 Jan. 1938 Schubert: Symphony No. 9 in C Major, D. 944
Beethoven: String Quartet in F Major, Op. 135: Lento;
Scherzo
R. Strauss: *Death and Transfiguration*, Op. 24

8 Jan. 1938 Mozart: *The Magic Flute*: Overture
Beethoven: Symphony No. 6 in F Major, Op. 68,
"Pastoral"
Saint-Saëns: *Danse macabre*, Op. 40
Debussy: *La mer*

15 Jan. 1938 Brahms: *Tragic* Overture, Op. 81
Sibelius: Symphony No. 2 in D Major, Op. 43
Busoni: *Rondo arlecchinesco*, with Jan Peerce, tenor
Tommasini: *Carnival of Venice*

22 Jan. 1938 Cherubini: *Anacréon*: Overture
Haydn: Symphony No. 98 in B-flat Major
Brahms: Serenade No. 2 in A Major, Op. 16
Wagner: *Die Meistersinger von Nürnberg*: Prelude

29 Jan. 1938 Rossini: *La scala di seta*: Overture
Schumann: Symphony No. 3 in E-flat Major, Op. 97,
"Rhenish"
Paganini-Toscanini: *Moto perpetuo*
Mussorgsky-Ravel: *Pictures at an Exhibition*

5 Feb. 1938 Scarlatti-Tommasini: *The Good Humored Ladies*: Ballet Suite
Mendelssohn: Symphony No. 4 in A Major, Op. 90,
"Italian"
Berlioz: *Roméo et Juliette*, Op. 17: Queen Mab Scherzo
Rossini: *Semiramide*: Overture

The WRVR rebroadcast of this concert (see Appendix 6) substituted (without so specifying) Toscanini's 1948 broadcast performance of the Rossini overture for the one given on this broadcast of a decade earlier.

6 Feb. 1938 Beethoven
Symphony No. 1 in C Major, Op. 21
Symphony No. 9 in D Minor, Op. 125, with Vina
Bovy, soprano; Kerstin Thorborg, contralto; Jan
Peerce, tenor; and Ezio Pinza, bass

In order to preserve the "benefit" status of this concert, which required the sale of tickets, the First Symphony was not broadcast. The beneficiary was to have been the Salzburg Festspielhaus, where Toscanini was planning to return for the summer of 1938. Hitler's annexation of Austria, however, was increasingly likely and the future of the Salzburg Festival, as a result, increasingly in jeopardy. Toscanini canceled his summer plans and designated the Italian Welfare League the beneficiary of this concert, which took place on Sunday evening.

12 Feb. 1938   Weber: *Euryanthe*: Overture
                      Brahms: Symphony No. 2 in D Major, Op. 73
                      Wagner: *Siegfried Idyll*
                      Dukas: *The Sorcerer's Apprentice*

A few minor but exposed technical slips from individual instrumentalists probably would have led Toscanini to withhold his approval of these magnificent readings of the Weber and Brahms works.

19 Feb. 1938   Handel: Concerto Grosso in B Minor, Op. 6 No. 12
                      Haydn: Symphony No. 88 in G Major
                      Roussel: *The Spider's Feast*: Suite
                      Weber-Berlioz: *Invitation to the Dance*, Op. 65
                      Martucci: *Tarantella*

26 Feb. 1938   Wagner: *The Flying Dutchman*: Overture
                      Borodin: Symphony No. 2 in B Minor
                      Brahms: *Variations on a Theme by Haydn*, Op. 56a
                      Smetana: *The Moldau*

4 Mar. 1938   Verdi: Requiem, with Zinka Milanov, soprano; Bruna
                           Castagna, contralto; Charles Kullman, tenor; and
                           Nicola Moscona, bass

Sources for this concert—broadcast only in shortwave to audiences outside the United States—are afflicted with high-frequency distortion and cross talk from what is apparently a telephone line, and the conversing voices occasionally create an obtrusive counterpoint to the music. Like the concert of 6 February, this one was originally intended to benefit the Salzburg Festspielhaus. Again Toscanini changed the beneficiary, this time specifying that the proceeds go to the Casa di Riposo in Milan, a home for elderly and indigent musicians. The concert took place on Friday evening.

5 Mar. 1938   Wagner
                          A Faust Overture
                          Lohengrin: Prelude to Act I; Prelude to Act III
                          Tannhäuser: Overture
                          Tristan und Isolde: Prelude and Liebestod
                          Parsifal: Prelude to Act I

> Wagner-Toscanini: *Götterdämmerung*: Dawn and Siegfried's
>   Rhine Journey
> Wagner: *Die Walküre*: Ride of the Valkyries

This broadcast exceeded the usual ninety minutes by more than a quarter of an hour, not only because of the great number of works on the program, but also as a consequence of talks given by Samuel Chotzinoff and David Sarnoff. The concert received front-page coverage from the *New York Times*.

Second Season (1938–39)

After leading the NBC Symphony in two sessions (on 7 and 8 March 1938) in which he recorded Haydn's Symphony No. 88, part of Mozart's Symphony No. 40, and the two movements of the Beethoven String Quartet, Op. 135, that he had performed earlier in the season, Toscanini left for Europe. As his second season drew near, his return to America was threatened. From Italy he had traveled to Palestine to lead—without fee—the newly formed Palestine Symphony (now the Israel Philharmonic), made up of many European Jewish refugees, just when Mussolini was embracing Hitlerlike anti-Semitism. Upon his return to Italy, Toscanini was branded an "Honorary Jew" by the press. His passport was revoked, adding to the humiliation he had been suffering for some time as a result of having his phone tapped by the Fascists. (Indeed, owing to this intrusion the word of his initial agreement with NBC spread quickly.) And it was from this tap that Mussolini learned that Toscanini considered the Fascist anti-Semitic stance "medieval stuff." With visitors to the Toscanini home having their license plates recorded by the police and with the more extreme element of the Fascist press demanding "Toscanini should be shot," his position in Italy was becoming extremely dangerous.

The pressure to return Toscanini's passport placed on Mussolini by the international press and by Joseph Kennedy, who was then the American ambassador to England, may have saved the conductor's life. Confronted by world outrage, Mussolini relented and returned the conductor's passport shortly before he was due to leave for New York, where he arrived five days prior to his first NBC concert.

As he walked into his initial rehearsal for the season, the orchestra rose, not only to acknowledge his stand against Hitler and Mussolini, but also in awareness of the danger he had narrowly escaped. An ovation of several minutes ensued. Toscanini tried to stop it but could not, perhaps the only time the orchestra felt it had every right to ignore his wishes.

For this second season, the NBC Symphony was expanded from ninety-two to ninety-four musicians, and additional changes in personnel were made–twenty in all. Although Harvey Sachs admits to not knowing "whether any of these departures were involuntary," a conversation I had in 1978 with the cellist Alan Shulman indicates this may have been the case in at least one instance.[3] It involved a violinist who also sat in a quartet that bore his name. At a rehearsal break during the first season, this violinist, according to Shulman, walked up to Toscanini, clicked his heels, bowed, and introduced himself. The conductor's displeasure at such behavior was evident from his lack of response to it and may have prompted the violinist's contract not being renewed.

The excitement of the first season must have carried over to the second, as Toscanini and his orchestra continued to collaborate exclusively in repertory that they had yet not performed together. Toscanini directed sixteen broadcasts, divided into two series of eight. In between, in December, Artur Rodzinski led four broadcasts, while Toscanini made out-of-town appearances with the orchestra, one in Newark on 13 December, the other in Baltimore on 27 December. Shortly after returning for his second series of broadcasts, which began on 7 January, he took the NBC Symphony to Boston (10 January), Chicago (31 January), Pittsburgh (1 February), and Providence (7 February). None of these concerts was broadcast.

During this season, Samuel Chotzinoff began to appear on the broadcasts as an intermission speaker. The uneven quality of sound of the NBC reference discs suggests that the engineers were still seeking the optimum placement of the microphone. Their best efforts, though, marked a significant improvement over those of the previous year: the ambience was less boxy and benefited from a slightly wider frequency response and dynamic range, resulting in greater presence and definition.

For this second season, Gene Hamilton became the program announcer, a position he was to hold for three years. His smooth, euphonious delivery was a big improvement over Howard Claney's stilted style, and the overall commentary became far more polished and professional, free of the previous season's awkward silences and clumsy improvisations.

Toscanini's repertory for this season was more adventurous and varied than that of the year before, ranging from Bach's Second Brandenburg Concerto to the world premieres of Samuel Barber's *Adagio for Strings* and *Essay No. 1 for Orchestra*, and including one extraordinary curiosity: the overture to Giacomo Meyerbeer's opera *Dinorah*, a thirteen-and-a-half-minute work requiring a chorus as well as an orchestra. And there were several performances that exemplify Toscanini's finest work at NBC, notably those of Mozart's Symphony No. 35, Schubert's Symphony No. 2, Dvořák's Symphony No. 9, and Wagner's overtures to *Rienzi* and *The Flying Dutchman*. All of the broadcasts continued to emanate from studio 8H and to be aired on Saturdays from 10:00 to 11:30 P.M.

After his final appearance of the season and continuing intermittently for six weeks (during which time the broadcasts were directed by Bruno Walter), Toscanini led five sessions (on 27 February; 1, 7, and 29 March; and 17 April) in which he completed his recordings of Mozart's Symphony No. 40 and recorded the Beethoven Fifth and Eighth Symphonies, Rossini's *William Tell* Overture, and Paganini's *Moto perpetuo*, the last in the arrangement used for his broadcast presentation of the previous year. On 14 March he took the NBC Symphony to Washington, D.C., for a nonbroadcast concert. This concluded his American activities for the season.

15 Oct. 1938 Vaughan Williams: *Fantasia on a Theme by Thomas Tallis*
Brahms: Symphony No. 3 in F Major, Op. 90
Martucci: *Notturno*; *Noveletta*
Tchaikovsky: *Romeo and Juliet*: Fantasy Overture

22 Oct. 1938 Rossini: *La Cenerentola*: Overture
R. Strauss: *Don Quixote*, Op. 35, with Emanuel
Feuermann, cello
Beethoven: Symphony No. 5 in C Minor, Op. 67
This concert features the only NBC performance Toscanini led of *Don Quixote* in which the soloist was not the orchestra's principal cellist, Frank Miller.

29 Oct. 1938 Bach: Brandenburg Concerto No. 2 in F Major, BWV
1047
Haydn: Symphony No. 31 in D Major, "Hornsignal"
Tchaikovsky: Symphony No. 6 in B Minor, Op. 74,
"Pathétique"
The harpsichordist in the performances of the Bach and Haydn works is Erich Leinsdorf. This account of the Tchaikovsky marked the first time Toscanini had played it since initially conducting it in 1898.

5 Nov. 1938 Graener: *The Flute of Sans-Souci*
Barber: *Adagio for Strings*
Essay No. 1 for Orchestra
Debussy: *Images*: "Ibéria"
Dvořák: Symphony No. 9 in E Minor, Op. 95 ("From the
New World")

12 Nov. 1938 Beethoven: *Coriolan* Overture, Op. 62
Schubert: Symphony No. 2 in B-flat Major, D. 125
Franck: *Les éolides*
Meyerbeer: *Dinorah*: Overture, with the Metropolitan
Opera Chorus

19 Nov. 1938 Schumann: *Manfred*, Op. 115: Overture
Mendelssohn: Symphony No. 5 in D Major, Op. 107,
"Reformation"
Wagner: *Die Meistersinger*: Prelude to Act III (played in
memory of Clarence H. Mackay)
Berlioz: *Roméo et Juliette*, Op. 17: Love Scene
Rossini: *William Tell*: Passo a sei

26 Nov. 1938   Smetana: *The Bartered Bride*: Overture
                    Martucci: Symphony No. 1 in D Minor, Op. 75
                    Liszt: *Orpheus*
                    Ravel: *Daphnis et Chloé*: Suite No. 2

Prokofiev's *Russian* Overture, Op. 72, and dances by Kurt Atterberg were originally programmed for this concert. Neither of these selections ever entered Toscanini's repertory.

3 Dec. 1938   Beethoven: Symphony No. 3 in E-flat Major, Op. 55,
                    "Eroica"
                    Wagner: *Siegfried*: Forest Murmurs
                       Götterdämmerung: Siegfried's Death and Funeral Music
                       Rienzi: Overture

7 Jan. 1939   Mozart: Symphony No. 35 in D Major, K. 385, "Haffner"
                    Brahms-Rubbra: *Variations and Fugue on a Theme by Handel*,
                       Op. 24
                    Loeffler: *Memories of My Childhood*
                    Wagner: *Die Meistersinger von Nürnberg*: Prelude

14 Jan. 1939   Bazzini: *Saul*: Overture
                    Shostakovich: Symphony No. 1 in F Minor, Op. 10
                    Franck: *Psyché*: Psyché's Slumber; Psyché and Eros
                    Strauss, R.: *Salome*: Dance of the Seven Veils

Although Toscanini had conducted the overture to Vittorio Alfieri's play *Saul* by Antonio Bazzini (1818–97) on several occasions in Italy prior to Mussolini's rise to power, his inclusion of it on this concert may have been motivated as much by political as by musical reasons because the drama, based on Old Testament themes, was anathema in Mussolini's Italy. By performing it, Toscanini may have been trying to call attention to what he felt was Mussolini's noxious effect on the arts.

21 Jan. 1939   Berlioz: *Harold in Italy*, Op. 16, with William Primrose,
                       viola
                    Catalani: *La Wally*: Prelude to Act IV
                       Loreley: Dance of the Water Nymphs
                    Ravel: *Boléro*

Originally programmed for this concert was the prelude to Act II of Karl Goldmark's *Queen of Sheba*. During this season William Primrose shared the NBC Symphony's first-viola stand with Carlton Cooley.

28 Jan. 1939   Gluck-Wagner: *Iphigenia in Aulis*: Overture
                    Beethoven: Symphony No. 8 in F Major, Op. 93
                    de Falla: *El amor brujo*, with Josephine Burzio, contralto
                    Rossini: *William Tell*: Overture

4 Feb. 1939   Mozart: Symphony No. 38 in D Major, K. 504, "Prague"
                    Respighi: *The Fountains of Rome*

Weber-Berlioz: *Invitation to the Dance*, Op. 65
Elgar: *Enigma Variations*, Op. 36

11 Feb. 1939   Brahms: Symphony No. 4 in E Minor, Op. 98
Liebeslieder Waltzes, Op. 52, with Erich Leinsdorf and
    Joseph Kahn, piano
Academic Festival Overture, Op. 80

18 Feb. 1939   Sibelius: Symphony No. 2 in D Major, Op. 43
Lemminkainen Suite, Op. 22: "The Swan of Tuonela"
En Saga, Op. 9
Finlandia, Op. 26

25 Feb. 1939   Wagner: *The Flying Dutchman*: Overture
Tannhäuser: Prelude to Act III (original version);
    Overture and Bacchanale
Tristan und Isolde: Prelude and Liebestod
Wagner-Toscanini: *Götterdämmerung*: Dawn and Siegfried's
    Rhine Journey
Wagner: *Die Walküre*: Ride of the Valkyries

The prelude to Act III of *Tannhäuser* performed on this broadcast is an earlier version that Wagner later shortened for the opera house. Its selection by Toscanini was vigorously promoted by NBC prior to the broadcast as a "premiere," with prebroadcast publicity noting that the orchestral parts were copied from a manuscript discovered in the Library of Congress. A young associate professor of music at New York University, Martin Bernstein (who had played in the New York Philharmonic under Toscanini and was later to gain distinction as a Wagner scholar), tried to save NBC embarrassment by meeting with Samuel Chotzinoff to point out that this earlier version had already been published by Novello and had been discussed by Sir Donald Tovey in volume 4 of his *Essays in Musical Analysis*.[4] Chotzinoff, evidently eager to have the Toscanini broadcast hailed as a premiere, ignored Bernstein's information and—according to what Bernstein told me in 1988—abruptly dismissed him. One wonders, too, about Toscanini's awareness of this publicity. As an admirer of Tovey, he quite likely knew of the Tovey essay, which cites the Novello score. The incident characterizes the ignorance and poor judgment of NBC officials. Significantly, when Toscanini gave his next performance of the work, the network billed it simply as the "original" version.

Third Season (1939–40)

With his successful second NBC season behind him, Toscanini was again off to Europe, leading the BBC Symphony in London through a Beethoven cycle during May 1939. It included all the symphonies, seven familiar overtures, the Missa Solemnis, and the two movements from the String Quartet, Op. 135, that he had recorded. During the summer he was in Lucerne for a festival that attracted a number of renowned musicians who, like Toscanini, were boycotting Salzburg, among them Pablo Casals, Sir Adrian Boult, Bronislaw Huberman, Adolf and Hermann Busch, and Vladimir Horowitz. Toscanini's contribution to the festival comprised seven concerts. They included two performances of the Verdi Requiem, the Brahms Piano Concerto in B-flat Major with Horowitz, and a performance for specially invited guests (Friedelind Wagner among them) featuring a small ensemble in the *Siegfried Idyll* at the Triebschen villa, where the work had first been performed sixty-nine years earlier. Three days after the last concert in Lucerne, Germany invaded Poland. Toscanini would not return to Europe until the war's end.

Now in exile in New York City, Toscanini moved from the Astor Hotel (where he had lived since coming to NBC) to the Villa Pauline, a mansion in the Riverdale section of the Bronx, which he rented. He led sixteen broadcasts, again broken into two groups of eight each, fourteen of which took place in studio 8H. The high point of the season was a six-week Beethoven cycle. Those familiar with it consider it one of his great achievements at NBC.

During the week that preceded Toscanini's second group of broadcasts, three guest conductors appeared: Désiré Defauw led four concerts, Bernardino Molinari and Bruno Walter, five each. The Walter appearances are especially interesting in that they featured works with which he was not ordinarily associated and for which he left no studio recordings: D'Indy's *Istar Variations*, Ravel's *Rapsodie espagnole*, Tchaikovsky's Fifth Symphony, and Debussy's *Prelude to the Afternoon of a Faun*.

While the guests were appearing, Toscanini remained active. On 29 December 1939 he led a benefit concert for the Chatham Square Music School in which he directed a chamber orchestra that included Jascha Heifetz, Nathan Milstein, Emmanuel Feuermann, Adolph Busch, and William Primrose in Mozart's *Musical Joke* and Gillet's *Loin du bal*. He also took the NBC Symphony to Newark on 21 February 1940 for a second concert (not broadcast) made up of works drawn from NBC programs given that season. And on 10 March, he recorded the Beethoven Violin Concerto with Heifetz, a collaboration renewed from Toscanini's days with the New York Philharmonic. Six days later he began his second series of concerts.

It was during this season that NBC, fully aware of the acoustical problems posed by studio 8H, started injecting artificially produced reverberation into the broadcasts. The practice was initially tentative and not used in all of Toscanini's first series of concerts. But for the second series it was employed more often to very good effect. Samuel Chotzinoff was now a more frequent intermission speaker, and the programs continued (except as noted here) to be aired from 10:00 to 11:30 P.M. on Saturday evenings, with Gene Hamilton as the principal announcer. On 9 May, three days after Toscanini's last concert of the

On the lawn of the Villa Pauline, c. 1948. *RCA*

regular season, he recorded the Brahms B-flat Piano Concerto with Horowitz. Badly stung by some abysmal recordings produced in studio 8H, RCA held the sessions in Carnegie Hall. The recording became one of the all-time bestsellers in the classical record market. An unscheduled broadcast was added for 14 May, shortly after which Toscanini and the orchestra departed for an extended tour of South America.

14 Oct. 1939   Schubert: Symphony No. 8 in B Minor, D. 759, "Unfinished"
R. Strauss: *Don Juan*, Op. 20
Haydn: *Sinfonia concertante* in B-flat Major, Op. 84, with Mischa Mischakoff, violin; Frank Miller, cello; Robert Bloom, oboe; and William Polisi, bassoon
Bach-Respighi: Passacaglia and Fugue in C Minor, BWV 582

All of the soloists in the Haydn were first-desk players.

21 Oct. 1939   Prokofiev: Symphony No. 1 in D Major, Op. 25,
                    "Classical"
                    Brahms: Double Concerto in A Minor, Op. 102, with
                        Mischa Mischakoff, violin, and Frank Miller, cello
                    Strong: *Die Nacht*
                    Wagner: *Parsifal*: Good Friday Spell
                    Die Meistersinger von Nürnberg: Prelude

The unusual length of this broadcast (an hour and three-quarters) was caused by
a last-minute insertion of the *Parsifal* excerpt, played as a memorial to the critic
Lawrence Gilman, who had died a month earlier. The soloists in the Brahms
were first-desk musicians.

23 Oct. 1939   Beethoven Cycle 1
                    Fidelio: Overture
                    Symphony No. 1 in C Major, Op. 21
                    Symphony No. 3 in E-flat Major, Op. 55, "Eroica"

4 Nov. 1939   Beethoven Cycle 2
                    Symphony No. 2 in D Major, Op. 36
                    Symphony No. 4 in B-flat Major, Op. 60
                    Leonore Overture No. 3, Op. 72a

11 Nov. 1939   Beethoven Cycle 3
                    Coriolan Overture, Op. 62
                    Symphony No. 6 in F Major, Op. 68, "Pastoral"
                    Symphony No. 5 in C Minor, Op. 67

18 Nov. 1939   Beethoven Cycle 4
                    Egmont, Op. 84: Overture
                    Septet for Woodwinds, Horn, and Strings in E-flat
                        Major, Op. 20
                    Symphony No. 7 in A Major, Op. 92

25 Nov. 1939   Beethoven Cycle 5
                    Leonore Overture No. 1, Op. 138
                    The Creatures of Prometheus, Op. 43: Adagio and
                        Allegretto
                    Symphony No. 8 in F Major, Op. 93
                    String Quartet in F Major, Op. 135: Lento and Vivace
                    Leonore Overture No. 2, Op. 72

2 Dec. 1939   Beethoven: Cycle 6
                    Fantasy in C Minor for Piano, Chorus, and Orchestra,
                        Op. 80, with Ania Dorfmann, piano, and the
                        Westminster Choir, directed by John Finley
                        Williamson
                    Symphony No. 9 in D Minor, Op. 125, with Jarmila
                        Novotna, soprano; Kerstin Thorborg, contralto;

Jan Peerce, tenor; Nicola Moscona, bass; and the
Westminster Choir

This concert took place in Carnegie Hall and was a benefit for the Junior League Welfare Fund. This may have been the only time Toscanini conducted the Choral Fantasy. He had considered another presentation with the Philharmonia Orchestra of London in 1952 but dropped the idea.

16 Mar. 1940 Schumann: Symphony No. 3 in E-flat Major, Op. 97,
"Rhenish"
R. Strauss: *Till Eulenspiegel's Merry Pranks*, Op. 28
Harris: Symphony No. 3
Paganini-Toscanini: *Moto perpetuo*
Rossini: *William Tell*: Overture

23 Mar. 1940 Schubert: Symphony No. 2 in B-flat Major, D. 125
Wagner: *Parsifal*: Prelude to Act I; Good Friday Spell; other
excerpts

The "other excerpts" comprise a curiosity: a kind of orchestral synthesis (probably made by Toscanini) of music from Acts II and III. Included are references to the preludes of both acts, Klingsor's Magic Garden (up to the appearance of Kundry), passing quotations from the Good Friday Music, and the closing scene of the opera. Without voices, these excerpts prove cumulatively dull. Toscanini may have felt the same, which would explain why he never programmed them again.

30 Mar. 1940 Castelnuovo-Tedesco: *The Taming of the Shrew*: Overture
Martucci: Symphony No. 2 in F Major, Op. 81
Verdi: *Aida*: Overture (premiere; see chapter 3)
Respighi: *Roman Festivals*

6 Apr. 1940 Tchaikovsky: Symphony No. 6 in B Minor, Op. 74,
"Pathétique"
The Nutcracker Suite, Op. 71A
Romeo and Juliet: Fantasy Overture

13 Apr. 1940 Debussy: *Marche écossaise*
Debussy-Ravel: *Danse*
Debussy: Nocturnes: *Nuages*; *Fêtes*
Images: "Ibéria"
La damoiselle élue, with Jarmila Novotna, soprano, and
Hertha Glaz, contralto
La mer

20 Apr. 1940 Elgar: *Introduction and Allegro for Strings*, Op. 47
Mozart: Symphony No. 41 in C Major, K. 551, "Jupiter"
Dvořák: *Scherzo capriccioso*, Op. 66
Mussorgsky-Ravel: *Pictures at an Exhibition*

Gene Hamilton's comments introducing the Mozart are telling: "Mr Toscanini will not use the full body of strings [employed] in the Elgar, so as . . . to avoid giving the work a heaviness not in keeping with the music."

27 Apr. 1940 Grieg: *Holberg Suite*, Op. 40
          Sibelius: Symphony No. 4 in A Minor, Op. 63
          Franck: *Les éolides*
          Ravel: *La valse*

RCA recorded the performances of the Sibelius and Ravel works, and Toscanini approved both for release. Although unauthorized CDs of both have appeared, neither was issued by RCA.

6 May 1940 Brahms: Serenade No. 1 in D Major, Op. 11: first
             movement
          Piano Concerto No. 2 in B-flat Major, Op. 83, with
             Vladimir Horowitz
          Symphony No. 1 in C Minor, Op. 68

This concert was a benefit for the greater New York Fund and took place on a Monday evening in Carnegie Hall. It was broadcast at 9:00 P.M.

14 May 1940 Smith: "The Star-Spangled Banner"
          Brahms: Symphony No. 1 in C Minor, Op. 68
          Beethoven: *Egmont*, Op. 84: Overture
          Barber: *Adagio for Strings*
          Fernandez: *Reisado do pastoreio*: Batuque
          R. Strauss: *Don Juan*, Op. 20
          Ravel: *La valse*

This concert aired at the unusual time of Tuesday from 10:15 P.M. to 12:15 A.M. and took place in Constitution Hall in Washington, D.C. It was arranged at the request of the United States government for members of the Pan American Scientific Congress and was probably intended as a promotional launch of Toscanini's tour of South America with the NBC Symphony. Leo S. Rowe, director of the General Pan American Union, was the intermission speaker.

Fourth Season (1940–41)

At the end of May 1940, Toscanini and the NBC Symphony sailed to Brazil for the orchestra's South American tour. To make the tour financially possible, all the musicians and the conductor agreed to reduce their usual fees. Framing the trip were opening and closing concerts in Rio de Janeiro on 13 June and 9 July, the latter transmitted in part to the United States by shortwave. At the end of the tour, Toscanini wrote to his orchestra: "You have never played so well, so inspired. We have never been so linked before."[5]

The orchestra was inactive for the remainder of the summer. Its fall season began on 13 October with the first of six concerts directed by William Steinberg, who had been engaged by Toscanini as an assistant. During the season,

NBC began experimental FM transmission of the broadcasts and continued to use tastefully applied synthetic reverberation on over-the-air transmissions to improve the ambience of studio 8H.

Toscanini's first appearance of the season yielded one of his most compelling NBC performances—a stirring Verdi Requiem—and the last of his initial five concerts comprised an equally compelling account of Beethoven's Missa Solemnis.

At the rehearsal for the Missa an incident occurred (discussed in detail in the introduction to the fifth season) that sparked Toscanini's resignation in the spring of 1941 as director of the NBC Symphony. After a four-week hiatus in January, during which Alfred Wallenstein (first cellist in the New York Philharmonic under Toscanini) directed the orchestra, Toscanini returned to lead four concerts in February, after which another four were led by George Szell.

During Szell's preparation of Beethoven's "Eroica," which was to be broadcast on 22 March, Toscanini—who had become a frequent visitor to the rehearsals of guest conductors at NBC—exploded over Szell's incessant stopping of the orchestra. Alan Shulman recounted the incident:

> After the first movement, Harvey Shapiro [another cellist in the orchestra] and I put a sheet of paper alongside our music and marked on it every time the guest conductor [Szell] stopped in the second movement. It was fifty-seven times! Maestro had come in after the first fifteen or twenty minutes and sat in the balcony of 8H; and after a while he began to pace back and forth, but by the time we reached the end of the "Eroica" he was running—he was so furious and angry. And we heard later that he went to the dressing room and gave the guest conductor hell for wearing out the orchestra needlessly.[6]

Toscanini's behavior on this occasion was not atypical and exemplified an unprofessional and far from admirable side of his response to certain conductors who displeased him. Two seasons earlier, he had walked out in disgust of a rehearsal of Mozart's Symphony No. 40 directed by Bruno Walter. This type of incident has led Toscanini's detractors to denigrate him for a general intolerance toward other conductors. To so view him, however, is to ignore his coexisting generosity toward the many conductors he admired, even when their view of a given work diverged from his. Furthermore, his displeasure with Walter and Szell did not cause him to block either from returning for subsequent guest appearances with the NBC Symphony.

While Szell was directing four broadcasts, Toscanini and the orchestra met for three recording sessions (24 February and 10 and 17 March) devoted to snippets of Wagner, Verdi, and the Brahms First Symphony. All were produced in Carnegie Hall, and the Brahms, one of the conductor's favorite works, was issued the following year as a commemorative of Toscanini's seventy-fifth birthday.

With Szell's guest stint completed, Toscanini returned to conduct four more broadcasts, the high points of which were his only NBC presentations of Mendelssohn's Third Symphony ("Scottish"), the overture to Berlioz's *Les francs-juges*, and a breathtakingly virtuosic, exhilarating, yet tautly controlled account of the overture to Rossini's *La gazza ladra*. The broadcasts continued to be aired on Saturday evenings, but after Toscanini's all-Verdi concert of 23 November (which, as in the past, ran from 10:00 P.M. to 11:30 P.M.), air time was moved to 9:35 P.M., with most of the programs concluding at 11:00. A few, however, ran slightly longer.

After his final appearance on 19 April, Toscanini had led only thirteen broadcasts (nine from studio 8H, four from Carnegie Hall) rather than the sixteen his NBC contract specified. Whether this reduced number resulted from his anger with the network is not clear. Although the season's conclusion had produced his resignation from NBC, he appeared in Carnegie Hall on 6 and 14 May to lead two more recording sessions devoted to Johann Strauss, Tchaikovsky (the Piano Concerto No. 1 in B-flat Minor, with Vladimir Horowitz), and Wagner. A recording of the Rákóczy March from Berlioz's *Damnation of Faust* was also produced but not approved by Toscanini for release. With these sessions concluded, Toscanini and NBC effected a mutually agreed upon divorce. World War II, ironically, would shortly revive the marriage.

23 Nov. 1940 Verdi: Te Deum
                Requiem, with Zinka Milanov, soprano; Bruna
                Castagna, contralto; Jussi Björling, tenor; Nicola
                Moscona, bass; and the Westminster Choir, directed
                by John Finley Williamson
This concert, which took place in Carnegie Hall, was an Alma Gluck memorial benefiting Roosevelt Hospital.

7 Dec. 1940 Sibelius: Symphony No. 2 in D Major, Op. 43
                Pohjola's Daughter, Op. 49
                Lemminkäinen Suite, Op. 22: "The Swan of Tuonela";
                "Lemminkäinen's Return"
The critic Olin Downes, who was a staunch Sibelius admirer, gave the intermission talk on this broadcast.

14 Dec. 1940 Franck: Symphony in D Minor
                Vieuxtemps: Ballade
                Franchetti: *Cristoforo Colombo*: Nocturne, with William
                Horne, tenor
                Enesco: Romanian Rhapsody No. 1

23 Dec. 1940 Beethoven: Missa Solemnis, Op. 123, with Zinka Milanov,
                soprano; Bruna Castagna, contralto; Jussi Björling,
                tenor; Alexander Kipnis, bass; and the Westminster
                Choir, directed by John Finley Williamson

This concert took place in Carnegie Hall and was a benefit for the National Conference of Christians and Jews.

1 Feb. 1941 Mozart: *The Magic Flute*: Overture
Haydn: Symphony No. 99 in E-flat Major
R. Strauss: *Ein Heldenleben*, Op. 40

A curiosity of this broadcast (perhaps a coincidence) is that the entire program is in E-flat.

8 Feb. 1941 Gluck-Wagner: *Iphigenia in Aulis*: Overture
Brahms: Symphony No. 3 in F Major, Op. 90
Liszt: *From the Cradle to the Grave*
Kodály: *Marosszék Dances*
Martucci: *Tarantella*

15 Feb. 1941 Leopold Mozart: *Toy* Symphony
W. A. Mozart: *Sinfonia concertante* in E-flat Major, K. 364,
   with Mischa Mischakoff, violin, and Carlton Cooley,
   viola
Schubert-Joachim: Grand Duo, D. 812
J. Strauss: *Voices of Spring*
   Tritsch-Trastch Polka

22 Feb. 1941 Wagner: *Lohengrin*: Prelude to Act I
Tannhäuser: "Dich, teure Halle," with Helen Traubel
Die Walküre: Act I, Scene 3, with Helen Traubel,
   soprano, and Lauritz Melchior, tenor
Götterdämmerung: Prologue, Dawn, Brünnhilde and
   Siegfried's Duet, and Siegfried's Rhine Journey, with
   Traubel and Melchior
Siegfried: Siegfried's Death and Funeral Music
Götterdämmerung: Brünnhilde's Immolation and Finale,
   with Traubel

This concert took place in Carnegie Hall and was a benefit for the Lenox Hill Foundation.

29 Mar. 1941 Wagner: *A Faust Overture*
Schumann: Symphony No. 2 in C Major, Op. 61
Martucci: *Canzone dei ricordi,* with Bruna Castagna, contralto
Tommasini: *Carnival of Venice*

5 Apr. 1941 Rossini: *Il Signor Bruschino*: Overture
Mendelssohn: Symphony No. 3 in A Minor, Op. 56,
   "Scottish"
Berlioz: *Les francs-juges*: Overture
   Roméo et Juliette, Op. 17: Love Scene; Queen Mab
   Scherzo
The Damnation of Faust: Rákóczy March

12 Apr. 1941   Beethoven: Symphony No. 6 in F Major, Op. 68,
                        "Pastoral"
                    Wagner: *Parsifal*: Prelude and Good Friday Spell
                    Sinigaglia: *Piedmont Suite*: Over the Fields and Woods;
                        Rustic Dance
                    Rossini: *La gazza ladra*: Overture

19 Apr. 1941   Tchaikovsky: *Voyevoda*: Overture
                        Symphony No. 6 in B Minor, Op. 74, "Pathétique"
                        Piano Concerto No. 1 in B-flat Minor, Op. 23, with
                        Vladimir Horowitz

This concert took place in Carnegie Hall and was a benefit for the Junior League
Welfare Fund.

Fifth Season (1941–42)

Everything about this season was different from the four preceding ones. The
broadcasts were shortened to an hour and moved to Tuesday evenings. No
longer did they emanate from studio 8H; instead, they took place in what was
then called the Cosmopolitan Opera House but later became better known as
the Mecca Temple or City Center. And to defray the costs of renting that house,
NBC sold, rather than gave away, tickets for the broadcasts. But the biggest
change of all was the appointment of Leopold Stokowski to replace Toscanini,
who had resigned his NBC position. Rumors that Toscanini might not return
to the orchestra had been circulating since well before the end of the previous
season and were confirmed in a letter of 30 April 1941 that the conductor sent
to David Sarnoff:

> My dear Sarnoff:
>   First of all I have to make my apology for having delayed so many
> times and for a long while to answer your letter of February 24th.
>   If in that time it was hard and painful for me to take a conclusive
> decision about to accept or not your proposal to conduct next season
> the NBC orchestra, today things are not at all changed and I feel that I
> am in the same state of mind as before. However, I have to come to an
> end making free you and me of the nightmare which weighs upon us
> since February.
>   My old age tells me to be high time to withdraw from the militant
> scene of Art. I am tired and a little exhausted—the dreadful tragedy
> which tears to pieces unhappy humanity saddens me and makes me
> crazy and restless:—how can I find peace, heart, wish, and strength in
> order to meet with new responsibility and new work? As for me, it is
> impossible . . . so that my Dear David don't be hesitating any longer
> and make up at once your plan for the next season. . . . Later on if my
> state of mind, health, and rest will be improved and you will judge my

cooperation advantageous enough for the NBC call me and I shall be glad to resume once more my work. Believe me dear Sarnoff I am sad at heart to renounce the joy to conduct that very fine orchestra you formed for me and gave me so great satisfaction!

My deepest gratitude for you will be never lessened. . . . Many thanks for the cooperation you gave me in my task as well as the facilities you placed at my disposal.

Affectionately yours,

Arturo Toscanini[7]

Toscanini's decision was rooted in several factors. For one, he was, as the letter to Sarnoff suggests, depressed by the world scene and the complicity of his native Italy in the calamitous events of the time. But more to the point were key occurrences that ruptured his relationship with NBC. The major one had its source in the network's duplicity in failing to acknowledge that the personnel of the NBC Symphony would have other duties beside those involving Toscanini. The conductor had become increasingly puzzled over why, on some occasions, the musicians would play with great commitment at rehearsals and, on others, like tired old men. Gradually it became apparent that on these latter occasions they were coming to him spent from having had to play for other broadcasts. The situation reached a ludicrous and ugly climax during the rehearsal in Carnegie Hall for the Missa Solemnis performance of 28 December 1940. Alan Shulman recalled the incident:

> On a Friday in December [27] 1940 we were scheduled to rehearse from 5 to 7:30 in Carnegie Hall for a performance of the *Missa Solemnis* the next night. There was a concert of the Chicago Symphony in Carnegie Hall that afternoon, after which the platform had to be set up on the stage for the chorus in the *Missa*: so the rehearsal didn't start until 5:30, which meant it would go on to 8. But thirty-five men of the orchestra had to play with Frank Black in the Cities Service program in Studio 8H at 8; and they had to leave at 7:30 if they were to pack their instruments, get to 8H, change their clothes, and be ready for the broadcast at 8. And since this was the first time we were doing the *Missa* with the maestro he was really out to work. So 7:30 came, and he kept right on working; then it was 7:32 and 7:33 and at that point the personnel manager stood behind the maestro and signaled to them one by one to sneak out; and it was only after a number of men had done this that the Old Man's eye caught the movement of the bassoon that one of the men was holding as he crawled out, and he discovered what was going on. He was so infuriated that he threw down his stand and walked out. He conducted the performance the next night and finished the season; but a couple of months later when the conductors for the 1941–42 season were announced he was not among them, and we learned that Stokowski was going to conduct us instead.[8]

Contrary to Shulman's implication, this was not the only cause of Toscanini's resignation. To be sure, he must have been offended by NBC's insensitive stupidity in the whole affair. Obviously it would have been more prudent for the network to assign other musicians to Frank Black and permit those in the symphony to continue the rehearsal. And who could think that Toscanini, despite his notorious myopia, could fail to notice musicians crawling away right under his nose? He could only view this occurrence as an expression of contempt.

Such contempt was apparent in other network actions as well, one of which involved Hugo Burghauser, who, as a member of the Vienna Philharmonic, had been instrumental in securing Toscanini's guest appearances with that orchestra in the 1930s. Burghauser had fled Austria at the time of the *Anschluss*, and Toscanini recommended him for a position with the NBC Symphony. But Burghauser was told by Chotzinoff and H. Leopold Spitalny, the orchestra's personnel manager, that although Toscanini had the right to reject players, he was not empowered to hire them. Obviously, in rejecting Burghauser, NBC thrust another affront in Toscanini's face.

Still another distasteful matter concerned the hiring, for the summer of 1941, of a guest conductor whom Toscanini considered incompetent. Most likely this was Charles O'Connell, who had been the producer for some of Toscanini's recordings and whose musical views clashed with Toscanini's. (One wonders, too, how the septuagenarian Toscanini must have felt about NBC's engaging for that summer the eleven-year-old Lorin Maazel to conduct an orchestra of seasoned professionals.) According to Marek, Toscanini attended the rehearsals of the conductor to whom he strongly objected, and "what he heard so infuriated him, he went tearing down the hall shouting, 'This is not my orchestra, what has that man done to my orchestra. He is a disgrace. *Vergogna! Vergogna!*'" [shame, shame!].[9]

As Toscanini's letter of resignation to Sarnoff implies, he was not closing the door on a possible future association with NBC. Sarnoff must have recognized this and did not permit the conductor's withdrawal to end the life of the orchestra created for him. Instead, he hired Stokowski as a new director. It was at Stokowski's insistence that the concerts were transferred from studio 8H to the Cosmopolitan Opera House. And while the orchestra was playing there, 8H, also at Stokowski's instigation, was undergoing structural modifications to enliven its acoustics.

During this season Toscanini was far from inactive. He moved from the Villa Pauline to another mansion, Wave Hill, located one block farther south in Riverdale. In the summer of 1941 he returned to South America for the last time, where he led several performances of the Verdi Requiem and Beethoven's Ninth with the Teatro Colón orchestra in Buenos Aires. In November 1941 and January and February 1942 he conducted the Philadelphia Orchestra in several concerts and recording sessions. And in the spring of 1942, as part of the New

Toscanini at Wave Hill, his Riverdale residence from 1941 to 1945. *Wave Hill*

York Philharmonic's centenary celebration, he returned to that orchestra to direct a six-week Beethoven cycle that included all the symphonies, several overtures, the Triple Concerto, and the Missa Solemnis.

But it was the world crisis, which on the one hand had caused Toscanini so much grief, that led to his return to NBC. Asked by the Department of the Treasury to conduct the NBC Symphony in two broadcasts to promote the sale of defense bonds (soon to become war bonds), Toscanini readily acceded. Discovering in the process that the orchestra had not been damaged by incompetent leadership and clearly enjoying working with it, he agreed to conduct three more broadcasts for the Department of the Treasury. These, in effect, opened the door to his return and to his leading in the summer of 1942 the American premiere of Shostakovich's Seventh Symphony.

Harvey Sachs suggests that by this time NBC was finding Stokowski "as hard to handle as Toscanini" and, using Toscanini's son, Walter, as an intermediary, tried winning him back. Always the pragmatist, Toscanini probably recognized that it would be in his best interests to return so long as Chotzinoff and Spitalny "should not show their faces in the studio during rehearsals."[10] One oddity of the season: Stokowski as the new director led a total of only eight concerts. Toscanini, who was at that time not even a "guest" conductor, led a total of six.

Unlike the programs directed by Stokowski and guest conductors, those Toscanini led were aired on Saturday evenings from 9:30 to 10:30. Deems Taylor was the narrator for each, and although an audience was present, no applause was permitted. To judge from the excellent quality of the recordings produced by the NBC engineers, the programs emanated from a refurbished studio 8H. Present on some of those recordings is the applause of orchestral members at the close of the programs after radio transmission had stopped. It seems they were glad to have their maestro back.

On 11 December 1941 and 19 March 1942 Toscanini recorded some shorter works with the NBC Symphony: Johann Strauss's *On the Beautiful Blue Danube*, Barber's *Adagio for Strings*, Thomas's *Mignon* Overture, the Prelude and Liebestod from Wagner's *Tristan und Isolde*, and "The Star-Spangled Banner." Shortly thereafter, a ban on recordings was imposed by the American Federation of Musicians. It would be three years before Toscanini would make another recording for commercial release.

6 Dec. 1941   Beethoven: Septet for Woodwinds, Horn, and Strings in
                          E-flat
                    Major, Op. 20
                    Wagner: *Parsifal*: Good Friday Spell
                    J. Strauss: *On the Beautiful Blue Danube*

This broadcast opened with a talk by the secretary of the treasury, Henry Morgenthau, who, in making an appeal for the purchase of defense bonds, avoided use of the word "war."

13 Dec. 1941   Barber: *Adagio for Strings*
Smetana: *The Moldau*
Dvořák: Symphony No. 9 in E Minor, Op. 95, "From the New World"

24 Jan. 1942   Mendelssohn: *A Midsummer Night's Dream*, Op. 21: Overture
Schubert: Symphony No. 8 in B Minor, D. 759, "Unfinished"
Barber: *Essay No. 1 for Orchestra*
Verdi: *I vespri siciliani*: Overture

14 Mar. 1942   Thomas: *Mignon*: Overture
Mendelssohn: Symphony No. 4 in A Major, Op. 90, "Italian"
Copland: *El salón México*

4 Apr. 1942   Bach: Suite No. 3 in D Major for Orchestra, BWV 1068: Air
Haydn: Symphony No. 101 in D Major, "Clock"
Wagner: *Parsifal*: Prelude and Good Friday Spell

This broadcast concluded with a brief talk by David Sarnoff promoting the sale of war bonds.

19 July 1942   Shostakovich: Symphony No. 7 in C Major, Op. 60, "Leningrad"

The radio commentary accompanying this American premiere was unusually extensive. It begins with opening remarks by Ben Grauer noting that the broadcast is dedicated to Russian War Relief. Following is a brief statement by Edward C. Cartier, at the time president of that organization, incorporating his reading of a telegram from Shostakovich that expresses the hope that this performance will "benefit" a group that " is doing so much for my people." Grauer then returns to explain how three thousand pages of score and parts of the symphony were brought from Russia after being transferred to microfilm. Another (unidentified) announcer then reads a "radiogram" from Shostakovich, after which Toscanini conducts "The Star-Spangled Banner."

The symphony follows a brief introduction from Grauer. After the music's conclusion, Cartier returns to speak about Russia's role in the "battle against barbarism" and the "Hitler hordes." A closing announcement from Grauer appeals to all listeners to pledge 10 percent of their income to the purchase of war bonds and notes that every member of the NBC Symphony has made such a pledge. If all this sounds rather extreme, it must be taken in the context of the time and the ethos generated by World War II.

Much has been written about the exchange between Toscanini and Stokowski over who would lead this American premiere.[11] Both wanted it. Stokowski ultimately settled for a later performance, which—perhaps to appease him—was billed as the first "concert-hall presentation" of the score. Toscanini prepared the work only one more time in a series of concerts he gave in October 1942 with the New York Philharmonic. In studying the score, which he received only ten days prior to the broadcast, he found that one of the pages had been printed upside down. Years later, while listening to his NBC performance of the work, he allegedly asked, "Did I really learn and conduct such junk?"[12] Years later, too, Shostakovich finally heard this NBC performance and Toscanini's account of his First Symphony. He allegedly pronounced both "worthless." Perhaps this was simply a case of war producing strange bedfellows. But it may be that Shostakovich was not nearly so contemptuous of Toscanini as has been alleged. According to the composer's son, Maxim, when he asked his father whose recordings he should use as a model, the response was "Toscanini's."[13]

Sixth Season (1942–43)

Toscanini was now sharing the NBC spotlight with Stokowski. Toscanini's willingness to do so provides further indication of his pragmatism regarding his own best interests. Although the two conductors had exchanged podiums in 1930, when Stokowski was director of the Philadelphia Orchestra and Toscanini of the New York Philharmonic, Toscanini had developed a growing antipathy for his colleague's work, which he felt had become tasteless and vulgar. Alan Shulman, recounting a visit he made to Toscanini's home in the fall of 1941, noted that in the course of that visit Toscanini asked: "Did you hear the Philharmonic yesterday? . . . I listened and heard the Franck Symphony [conducted by Stokowski]. I was so angry I wrote a letter. I didn't mail it, of course. But the first sentence was 'Blessed are the arts which can survive without interpreters'." Shulman went on to note, "This to me is a classic, because it represents his [Toscanini's] whole philosophy as a musician."[14]

During the winter season, Stokowski and Toscanini each led twelve broadcasts, with Toscanini directing two additional benefit concerts. For the second of these, which took place on 25 April 1943 in Carnegie Hall, tickets could be obtained only through the purchase of war bonds. Ticket sales raised $10 million, and an additional million was gained at an intermission auction of the manuscript of Toscanini's orchestration of "The Star-Spangled Banner." During the summer, Toscanini led four more broadcasts to promote the sale of war bonds and a fifth to mark Mussolini's downfall.

Highly active though he now was at NBC, Toscanini did not confine his activities to the network. Prior to his first appearance with the orchestra, he returned to the New York Philharmonic to lead two series of concerts. The initial one featured the first American performance in the twentieth century of

Berlioz's *Roméo et Juliette*, the second, his last presentation of the Shostakovich Seventh. Then, after his two initial NBC appearances, he returned to the Philharmonic for a single all-Wagner program on 30 November to benefit the Red Cross. And the following February, he made guest appearances in Cincinnati and Philadelphia.

In the course of the NBC winter season, when neither Toscanini nor Stokowski was conducting, the orchestra was led by Désiré Defauw, Erich Leinsdorf, and Nicolai Malko. Having planned a six-week Brahms cycle, Toscanini asked Stokowski not to program any of the composer's works, a request that was honored perhaps reluctantly, Brahms being a Stokowski favorite. Stokowski, in fact, was the first conductor to record all the Brahms symphonies, having completed the cycle for Victor in 1933.[15]

Mutual antipathies notwithstanding, the simultaneous presence of Toscanini and Stokowski at NBC made for refreshingly diverse programs. Those of Toscanini generally centered on more familiar fare, while Stokowski offered key works that Toscanini never performed, notably Holst's *Planets*, Hindemith's Symphony in E-flat Major, Prokofiev's *Alexander Nevsky*, and Vaughan Williams's Symphony No. 4. And on 13 December, Stokowski also directed the Shostakovich Seventh Symphony.

The broadcasts were now moved to Sunday afternoons at 5:00. With the New York Philharmonic concerts broadcast from 3:00 to 5:00 P.M. by CBS, radio audiences had three consecutive hours of live music on Sunday afternoons. Except when unusually long works were performed, the NBC programs were limited to an hour. Ben Grauer became the regular announcer for the series, a position he would continue to hold for the duration of the orchestra's existence, and talks by Samuel Chotzinoff—now given as opening comments—were occasionally featured. The reconstruction of studio 8H generated some resonance, but sound quality remained exceptionally sensitive to microphone placement. To judge from NBC's reference discs, engineers experimented extensively with microphone placement, the least desirable location yielding a cramped, boxy deadness lacking in bass and as sonically deficient as some of the poorest efforts of the prerenovation years.

1 Nov. 1942   Loeffler: *Memories of My Childhood*
Creston: *Choric Dance No. 2*, Op. 17b
Gould: *A Lincoln Legend*
Gershwin: *Rhapsody in Blue*, with Benny Goodman, clarinet, and Earl Wild, piano

8 Nov. 1942   Rossini: *Il Signor Bruschino*: Overture
Kabalevsky: Symphony No. 2 in C Minor, Op. 19
Mendelssohn: Symphony No. 5 in D Major, Op. 107, "Reformation"

The Kabalevsky was an American premiere.

20 Dec. 1942   Brahms Cycle 1
                   Variations on a Theme by Haydn, Op. 56a
                   Symphony No. 3 in F Major, Op. 90

27 Dec. 1942   Brahms Cycle 2
                   Liebeslieder Waltzes, Op. 52, with Pierre Luboshutz and
                       Genia Nemenoff, piano
                   Serenade No. 2 in A Major, Op. 16

3 Jan. 1943   Brahms Cycle 3
                   Tragic Overture, Op. 81
                   Symphony No. 2 in D Major, Op. 73

10 Jan. 1943   Brahms Cycle 4
                   Symphony No. 4 in E Minor, Op. 98
                   Academic Festival Overture, Op. 80
                   Hungarian Dance No. 1 in G Minor

17 Jan. 1943   Brahms Cycle 5
                   Serenade No. 1 in D Major, Op. 11: first movement
                   Symphony No. 1 in C Minor, Op. 68

24 Jan. 1943   Brahms Cycle 6
                   A German Requiem, Op. 45, with Vivian della Chiesa,
                       soprano; Herbert Janssen, baritone; and the
                       Westminster Choir, directed by John Finley
                       Williamson

To accommodate this work, the usual one-hour broadcast was extended by fifteen minutes. The performance was sung in English.

31 Jan. 1943   Verdi: *La forza del destino*: Overture
                   Nabucco: Act III: "Va, pensiero," with the Westminster
                       Choir, directed by John Finley Williamson
                   I Lombardi: Act III: Trio, "Qui posa il fianco . . . Qual
                       volutta," with Vivian della Chiesa, soprano; Jan
                       Peerce, tenor; and Nicola Moscona, bass
                   La traviata: Prelude to Act III
                   Otello: Act III: Ballet Music
                   Hymn of the Nations, with Jan Peerce and the
                       Westminster Choir

Hymn of the Nations received its American premiere on this broadcast.

7 Feb. 1943   Gilbert: *Comedy Overture on Negro Themes*
                   Kennan: *Night Soliloquy*
                   Griffes: *The White Peacock*
                   Grofé: *Grand Canyon Suite*

24 Mar. 1943   Brahms: Symphony No. 1 in C Minor, Op. 68
                   Beethoven: Symphony No. 1 in C Major, Op. 21

Wagner: *Lohengrin*: Prelude to Act III
Tristan und Isolde: Prelude and Liebestod
Die Meistersinger von Nürnberg: Prelude

This concert took place in Carnegie Hall and was a benefit for infantile paralysis research. NBC's printed records state that the Wagner portion of this concert was broadcast, but listings in the *New York Times* do not confirm this.

4 Apr. 1943 Hérold: *Zampa*: Overture
Rossini: *William Tell*: Overture; Passo a sei
Boccherini: Minuet in A Major
Hoffstetter (formerly attrib. Haydn): Serenade in F Major
Mussorgsky: *Boris Godunov*: Act III: Introduction and Polonaise
Ponchielli: *La Gioconda*: Act III: Dance of the Hours
Lizst: Hungarian Rhapsody No. 2
Sousa: "The Stars and Stripes Forever"

Ben Grauer introduced the Sousa march as the "very embodiment and symbol of the fighting spirit of a democratic America."

11 Apr. 1943 Bach: Suite No. 3 in D Major for Orchestra, BWV 1068: Air
Kabalevsky: *Colas Breugnon*: Overture
Beethoven: Symphony No. 1 in C Major, Op. 21
Debussy: *La mer*

The Kabalevsky was an American premiere. This final broadcast of the winter season concluded with a talk delivered by Frank Mullin, an NBC vice president, noting that Toscanini and Stokowski would return to the orchestra the following season. Probably because of the inclusion of this talk, the Bach Air was not broadcast.[16]

25 Apr. 1943 Tchaikovsky: Symphony No. 6 in B Minor, Op. 74, "Pathétique"
The Nutcracker Suite, Op. 71A
Piano Concerto No. 1 in B-flat Minor, Op. 23, with Vladimir Horowitz

For this war bond concert given in Carnegie Hall, the symphony was not broadcast. During the performance of its second movement, the cellist Oswaldo Mazzucchi suffered a sudden onset of abdominal pain and collapsed. With the aid of an NBC official, Al Walker, and the flutist Harry Moscowitz, Mazzucchi was carried from the stage while the performance continued without interruption.

20 June 1943 Donizetti: *Don Pasquale*: Overture
Haydn: Symphony No. 94 in G Major, "Surprise"
Handel: Minuet from Concerto Grosso in D Major, Op. 6 No. 5
Bolzoni: Minuet in B Major

Debussy: *Prelude to the Afternoon of a Faun*
Dukas: *The Sorcerer's Apprentice*
This broadcast included an intermission talk by Colonel Oveta Culp Hobby to promote the Women's Army Corps. It was also the first of four summer concerts that Toscanini directed to encourage purchase of war bonds.

18 July 1943   von Suppé: *Poet and Peasant*: Overture
                       Massenet: *Scènes alsaciennes*
                       Bolzoni: *Medieval Castle*
                       J. Strauss: *Voices of Spring*
                       Nicolai: *The Merry Wives of Windsor*: Overture
An intermission talk was given by Robert Patterson, the acting secretary of war.

25 July 1943   Verdi: *Luisa Miller*: Overture; "Quando le sere," with Jan
                             Peerce, tenor
                       Don Carlo: "O don fatale," with Nan Merriman, mezzo-
                             soprano
                       Un ballo in maschera: "Eri tu," with Frank Valentino,
                             baritone
                       La forza del destino: "Pace, pace, mio Dio," with
                             Gertrude Ribla, soprano
                       Rigoletto: Act III, with all of the above and Nicola
                             Moscona, bass
It was during this broadcast that Mussolini's downfall was announced. Harvey Sachs has described what occurred in the studio:

> Toscanini and soprano Gertrude Ribla had just left the stage when an announcement was broadcast into the hall and over the air: Benito Mussolini had been deposed. Toscanini, beside himself, rushed back on the stage, clasped his hands and gazed heavenwards, in a sign of thanksgiving, while the audience, equally beside itself, applauded, cheered, screamed, and all but tore the studio to pieces.[17]

None of this bedlam could have been apparent to those listening on the radio. Two announcements of Mussolini's deposition went over the air, the first in an intermission talk carried by shortwave from the Pacific given by Admiral Harold R. Stark. It was probably during this talk that the audience erupted. After Stark concluded, the broadcast switched to the NBC newsroom, where a "roundup of the important events of the day from Italy" was given that included a second announcement of the deposition. When Ben Grauer then returned to introduce Act III of *Rigoletto*, no audience reaction was evident.

9 Sept. 1943   Beethoven: Symphony No. 5 in C Minor, Op. 67: first
                             movement
                      Rossini: *William Tell*: Overture
                      Olivieri: "Garibaldi's War Hymn"
                      Smith-Toscanini: "The Star-Spangled Banner"

This was the first of three unscheduled broadcasts, each meant to mark a key event in the evolving Allied victory in World War II. It ran for only half an hour and celebrated Mussolini's downfall. Toscanini's playing of only the first movement of the Beethoven was symbolically intended to underscore the incompleteness of the Allied triumphs. (On 18 May 1945, he broadcast the entire symphony to mark Germany's surrender.)

Today the propaganda voiced on this program seems ludicrous. Certainly keeping a straight face is difficult when the announcer notes, "These are times of stealthy comings and goings." Those who lived through the war, however, may better understand the excesses and absurdities it sometimes generated.

This performance of "The Star-Spangled Banner" was the first time Toscanini's own arrangement—with its canonic middle section—was aired. This broadcast was transmitted by shortwave to Italy.

19 Sept. 1943 Bizet: *Fair Maid of Perth*: Suite (excerpts)
L'Arlésienne: Suites 1 and 2 (excerpts)
Bizet-Toscanini: *Carmen*: Suite

The excerpts from the *Arlésienne* suites include the Prelude, Minuet, and Adagietto from No. 1; the Pastorale from No. 2; and, to conclude, the Carillon from No. 1. From *Perth* Toscanini played the Prelude, Serenade, March, and Gypsy Dance. At the outset of this broadcast, Ben Grauer said that any listener pledging purchase of a $1000 war bond would receive an autographed picture of Toscanini.

Seventh Season (1943–44)

This season differed from the previous six in two ways. For one, no major guest conductor was engaged. Prior to Toscanini's first broadcast of the winter season on 31 October, Frank Black, the director of music at NBC, led five concerts and subsequently all the others that neither Toscanini nor Stokowski conducted. But the biggest change was in NBC's having acquired the first sponsor for the series, the General Motors Corporation (GM). The programs, which continued to air at 5:00 P.M. on Sundays, were renamed "The General Motors Symphony of the Air." And the name Symphony of the Air was adopted by the NBC Symphony when it attempted to survive on its own after Toscanini's retirement.

During World War II the production of cars and other GM products had ceased while the corporation, like many others, devoted itself to the war effort. Consequently, commercial messages on the broadcasts centered upon reiterated admonitions to "back the attack" by purchasing war bonds and maintaining production of weapons at a high level.

With GM's sponsorship came the end of commentary by Samuel Chotzinoff and the advent of intermission talks by C. F. Kettering, as he was always introduced. Charles F. Kettering was a vice president at General Motors and, I have been told by people who knew him, a person of exceptional charm, grace, and wit. None of these characteristics emerged in his little homilistic chats, which were aimed at the war effort, the marvels of American initiative, and the virtues of individualism and creative thinking, traits he often illustrated by tracing the life of a significant figure in American industry. Kettering was clearly ill at ease before the microphone and spoke in a stiff, sometimes stumbling style made all the more awkward by his gravelly voice. With broadcasting styles having become more polished and streamlined and audiences more sophisticated (and cynical), Kettering's talks—copies of which were available to listeners on request—seem embarrassingly naive.[18]

Toscanini led twelve and Stokowski eleven of the winter season's concerts. Two benefit concerts were added in April, both led by Toscanini. During the summer he conducted four more broadcasts to promote the sale of war bonds. As in the previous season, the programs of Stokowski and Toscanini provided welcome contrast, those of the former featuring the Fourth Symphony of Howard Hanson, Hindemith's *Nobilissma visione*, Butterworth's *A Shropshire Lad*, and —with Eduard Steuermann as soloist—the world premiere of Schoenberg's Piano Concerto.

Taken as a whole, Toscanini's performances were uneven, many suffering from a breathless, even crude intensity. The war, which isolated him from his country and from his daughter Wally, was doubtless taking its toll on him as it was on his orchestra, as some of its finest instrumentalists had entered the armed forces. Possibly owing to wartime pressure, Toscanini made but one guest appearance during the year, leading the Philadelphia Orchestra in a Beethoven program. It was the last time he conducted that distinguished ensemble. On 8 and 20 December 1943, he recorded the overture to Verdi's *Forza del destino* and *Hymn of the Nations* for an Office of War Information propaganda film. In 1988 it was released on videocassette by the Library of Congress. This performance of the *Hymn* is the only one he directed that included the "Internationale" (see entry in chapter 3).

31 Oct. 1943   Mozart: *The Magic Flute*: Overture
                    Haydn: Symphony No. 104 in D Major, "London"
                    Beethoven: Symphony No. 8 in F Major, Op. 93
This program ran beyond the scheduled hour and was cut off the air while the finale of Beethoven was still in progress. Toscanini was allegedly furious when he discovered the broadcast had been terminated. Perhaps it was this uproar that led to an NBC policy elevating him to a position held at the time only by President Roosevelt: both were to be free from network time restrictions.

7 Nov. 1943   Degeyter: "The Internationale"
                   Liadov: *Kikimora*
                   Glinka: *Jota aragonesa*
                   Kalinnikov: Symphony No. 1 in G Minor

Ben Grauer's opening comments explain the rationale for this program: "Today Arturo Toscanini salutes a fighting ally. He devotes his concert to Russian music in tribute to the magnificent courage of the Russian army and the intrepid spirit of the Russian people."

14 Nov. 1943 Cimarosa: *Il matrimonio segreto*: Overture
Debussy: *Images*: "Ibéria"
Mignone: *Fantasia brasileira*
Gershwin: *An American in Paris*

21 Nov. 1943 Rossini: *The Barber of Seville*: Overture
Atterberg: Symphony No. 6 in C Major, Op. 31
Ravel: *La valse*

28 Nov. 1943 Wagner: *Die Meistersinger von Nürnberg*: Prelude to Act III
Tannhäuser: Overture and Bacchanale
Tristan und Isolde: Prelude and Liebestod
Die Walküre: Ride of the Valkyries

5 Dec. 1943 Mozart: *The Marriage of Figaro*: Overture
Piano Concerto No. 27 in B-flat Major, K. 595, with
Mieczyslaw Horszowski
Symphony No. 35 in D Major, K. 385, "Haffner"
This performance included Toscanini's corrections of a then-standard text lacking seven measures in the opening *tutti* of the concerto. At the end of the first movement's cadenza, he lost concentration and required a gratuitous cadential flourish from Horszowski to bring in the return of the orchestra.[19]

5 Mar. 1944 Beethoven: *The Creatures of Prometheus*, Op. 43: Overture;
Adagio and Allegretto
Symphony No. 6 in F Major, Op. 68, "Pastoral"

12 Mar. 1944 Mussorgsky: *Khovanschina*: Prelude to Act I
Tchaikovsky: *The Tempest: Symphonic Fantasy after
Shakespeare*, Op. 18
Shostakovich: Symphony No. 1 in F Minor, Op. 10

19 Mar. 1944 Weber: *Oberon*: Overture
Haydn: Symphony No. 92 in G Major, "Oxford"
Respighi: *The Pines of Rome*

26 Mar. 1944 Castelnuovo-Tedesco: *The Taming of the Shrew* Overture
Schubert: Symphony No. 2 in B-flat Major, D. 125
Berlioz: *Roméo et Juliette*, Op. 17: Queen Mab Scherzo
Smetana: *The Moldau* (performed but probably not
broadcast)

2 Apr. 1944 Mignone: *Four Brazilian Sketches*
Gershwin: Piano Concerto in F Major, with Oscar Levant

9 Apr. 1944   Wagner: *Parsifal*: Prelude and Good Friday Spell
                   Mendelssohn: Violin Concerto in E Minor, Op. 64, with
                       Jascha Heifetz
According to Nicholas Moldovan, a violist in the NBC Symphony, Heifetz
plunged into the finale of the Mendelssohn at a far faster tempo than he had chosen in rehearsal, and "the Old Man [Toscanini] didn't try to hold him back."[20]

18 Apr. 1944   Smith: "The Star-Spangled Banner"
                   Brahms: Symphony No. 1 in C Minor, Op. 68
                   Tchaikovsky: Symphony No. 6 in B Minor, Op. 74,
                       "Pathétique"
                   Beethoven: Symphony No. 5 in C Minor, Op. 67
This concert took place on a Tuesday evening in Carnegie Hall and was given
to promote the sale of war bonds. Six and a half million dollars were raised from
this exceptionally long program, which the *New York Times* critic Olin Downes
called "gigantic." It is not clear how much, if any, of it was broadcast: NBC's
records claim that Tchaikovsky and Beethoven were aired, but the *New York
Times* does not confirm this in its listing of broadcasts for this date.

25 May 1944   Wagner: *Tannhäuser*: Overture
                   Wagner-Toscanini: *Götterdämmerung*: Dawn and Siegfried's
                       Rhine Journey
                   Wagner: *Die Walküre*: Ride of the Valkyries
                   Verdi: *Rigoletto*: Act III, with Zinka Milanov, soprano; Nan
                       Merriman, mezzo-soprano; Jan Peerce, tenor;
                       Leonard Warren, baritone; and Nicola Moscona, bass
                   Hymn of the Nations, with Jan Peerce, tenor, and the
                       600-voice All City High School Glee Club
                   Sousa: "The Stars and Stripes Forever"
This benefit concert took place on a Friday evening in the old Madison Square
Garden (between Forty-ninth and Fiftieth Streets) and featured a combined
NBC Symphony and New York Philharmonic. It raised $100,000 for the Red
Cross and an additional $10,000 during an intermission auction—conducted
by Mayor Fiorello LaGuardia—of Toscanini's baton. NBC's records suggest
the concert was broadcast, but the *New York Times*'s listings do not confirm this.
It is possible, though, that the auction was aired by the city-owned radio station
WNYC.

25 June 1944   Prokofiev: Symphony No. 1 in D Major, Op. 25,
                       "Classical"
                   Mancinelli: *Venetian Scenes*: Flight of the Lovers
                   Waldteufel-Toscanini: *The Skaters Waltz*
                   Tchaikovsky: *The Nutcracker Suite*, Op. 71A
                   Rossini: *La gazza ladra*: Overture

2 July 1944 Haydn: Symphony No. 99 in E-flat Major
Franck: *Les éolides*
Puccini: *Manon Lescaut*: Act II: Minuet; Act III: Intermezzo
Brahms: Hungarian Dances No. 17 in F-sharp Minor, No.
 20 in E Minor, and No. 21 in E Minor

An intermission talk by Admiral John Hall could not be transmitted as planned by shortwave; its text was read instead by a studio announcer.

27 Aug. 1944 Hérold: *Zampa*: Overture
Boccherini: Minuet in A Major
Hoffstetter (attrib. Haydn): Serenade in F Major
Sibelius: *Lemminkäinen Suite*, Op. 22: "The Swan of
 Tuonela"
Tchaikovsky: *Eugene Onegin*, Op. 24: Waltz
Sousa: "Semper Fidelis"
 "El Capitan"

3 Sept. 1944 Bossi: *Intermezzi Goldoniani*
Mozart: Symphony No. 29 in A Major, K. 201
de Falla: *El amor brujo*: Ritual Fire Dance and Dance of
 Terror
Goldmark: Symphony in E-flat Major, Op. 26, "Rustic
 Wedding": In the Garden; Serenade
Glinka: *Jota aragonesa*

The Goldmark excerpts were a replacement for the Nocturne and Scherzo from Mendelssohn's *Midsummer Night's Dream,* which were originally programmed for this broadcast.

Eighth Season (1944–45)

With Leopold Stokowski's departure, Toscanini was now the sole principal conductor of the NBC Symphony. For a seventy-seven-year-old, he had a busy season, leading sixteen scheduled broadcasts and an additional one on 18 May 1945 in which, as promised, he performed the Beethoven Fifth in its entirety to mark the surrender of Germany. He also led two concerts that were not broadcast: an Italian potpourri on 31 October 1944 made up of the overture to Rossini's *The Barber of Seville,* excerpts from Verdi operas, and the Dance of the Hours from Ponchielli's *La Gioconda;* and a benefit concert in Carnegie Hall on 19 February 1945 comprising the overture to Weber's *Der Freischütz,* Ravel's *La valse,* Mussorgsky's *Pictures at an Exhibition,* and (with Vladimir Horowitz) the Brahms B-flat Piano Concerto. On 13 January 1945 he returned for the last time to the New York Philharmonic, directing a pension-fund concert that duplicated the program for his first appearance with that orchestra on 14 January 1926: Haydn's "Clock" Symphony, Respighi's *Pines of Rome,* Sibelius's "Swan of Tuonela," Siegfried's Death and Funeral Music from Wagner's *Götterdäm-merung*, and the overture to Weber's *Euryanthe*. In April he visited Los Angeles, making his only guest appearance with that city's orchestra—a favor, perhaps, to Alfred Wallenstein, the principal cellist in the New York Philharmonic under Toscanini and, in 1945, the director of the Los Angeles Philharmonic.

Toscanini in 1945 in Los Angeles, where, at Alfred Wallenstein's invitation, he conducted a pension-fund concert of the Los Angeles Philharmonic.
Otto Rothschild; Walfredo Toscanini

In September 1945 Toscanini added a postscript to the NBC season with three additional broadcasts, one of them on the first of the month marking the surrender of Japan. On 25 September he led an all-Beethoven program in a nonbroadcast Carnegie Hall benefit for war orphans and Italian welfare societies; the centerpiece of the concert was the Ninth Symphony and featured the soloists Norma Andreotti, Nan Merriman, Jan Peerce, and Lorenzo Alvary.

The union ban having been lifted, Toscanini agreed to make recordings again. In December 1944 he recorded in studio 8H three works by Beethoven: the *Creatures of Prometheus* and *Leonore* No. 3 Overtures and the Second Symphony, the last of which he refused to approve for release. In May and June he returned to 8H, recording Gershwin's *An American in Paris*, Haydn's Symphony No. 98, Sousa's "Stars and Stripes Forever," and the Scherzo from Mendelssohn's String Octet in an orchestration by the composer that included winds. Sonically, these proved to be some of the best recordings made in that studio, providing a further illustration of what could be achieved there with a judiciously placed microphone. The engineer in charge at the time was an exceptionally capable man named Robert Johnson, who may well have grasped better than anyone else how to solve the auditorium's peculiar acoustic problems.

Given the more-than-acceptable quality of these recordings, it is surprising that RCA elected to hold additional sessions in Carnegie Hall in June, July, and August. Sonically, they were all disappointing—save that devoted to the Beethoven First Piano Concerto (with Ania Dorfmann)—and inferior to what had just been produced in 8H. In addition to the concerto, the recordings included a handful of Rossini overtures, Mozart's "Jupiter" Symphony, the overture to Verdi's *La forza del destino*, and (not approved by Toscanini) the Beethoven Seventh. In a hall noted for its fine acoustics, especially its presence and full bass, RCA's engineers produced recordings lacking weight and blurred by resonance that masked the detail that was a feature of Toscanini's transparent sonority. Indeed, some of these efforts were inferior to what RCA had achieved nine years earlier in Carnegie Hall in Toscanini's last recordings with the New York Philharmonic.

During Toscanini's absence from the NBC Symphony, the orchestra was led by Eugene Ormandy and the then-unknighted Malcolm Sargent, both of whom programmed works outside Toscanini's repertory, among them Stravinsky's *Firebird* Suite and Dvořák's Seventh Symphony.[21] All the summer concerts were composed of pops fare led by Frank Black.

With General Motors continuing its sponsorship, NBC now published a monthly newsletter for the radio audience summarizing the orchestra's forthcoming programs. Titled "Symphony Notes," printed on glossy quarto-sized paper, and illustrated with photographs, it promoted the broadcasts and provided music appreciation for the layman. Because it may be difficult today to recall the extraordinary way in which the phonograph, especially after the advent of the long-playing record, broadened the perspective and awareness of a musically untrained audience, these notes may now seem trivial and simplistic. But they were also filled with relevant comments, as this passage written by David Hall (a member of the production staff for the broadcasts) about the Beethoven Seventh should make clear:

> By seizing a single rhythmic figure, as in the first and the last movements, and driving it relentlessly onward through every melodic, harmonic, and tone-color variant, Beethoven achieves . . . the effect of enormous energy and momentum as well as unparalleled instrumental richness. Yet his orchestra is no larger than that required for . . . a Mozart symphony: woodwinds and brasses in two, the usual strings, and no trombones.[22]

To be sure, the "usual" number of strings used by Toscanini (and other major conductors of the time) was doubtless larger than that employed in Beethoven's day. Nonetheless, Hall's comments clarify some of the work's compelling features.

Theoretically, the nine-week Beethoven Festival (as it was tagged) that comprised Toscanini's initial group of appearances with the orchestra would seem to be the season's highlight. But some of the performances in the series are rigid and rushed and thus inferior to those he led in his 1939 Beethoven cycle. And unlike most other Beethoven cycles, this one omitted four symphonies (Nos. 4, 5, 6, and 9). The broadcasts continued to be aired on Sunday afternoons at 5:00 P.M., with intermission talks again given by C. F. Kettering.

22 Oct. 1944   Beethoven Festival 1
                    Symphony No. 1 in C Major, Op. 21
                    Symphony No. 8 in F Major, Op. 93

29 Oct. 1944   Beethoven Festival 2
                    Leonore Overture No. 1, Op. 138
                    The Creatures of Prometheus, Op. 43: Adagio and
                        Allegretto
                    Piano Concerto No. 3 in C Minor, Op. 37, with Artur
                        Rubinstein

5 Nov. 1944   Beethoven Festival 3
                    Symphony No. 3 in E-flat Major, Op. 55, "Eroica"
The broadcast opened with an extensive talk by Alan Orth, introduced as "an associate of C. F. Kettering."

12 Nov. 1944   Beethoven Festival 4
                    Egmont, Op. 84: Overture
                    String Quartet in F Major, Op. 135: Lento and Vivace
                    Piano Concerto No. 1 in C Major, Op. 15, with Ania
                        Dorfmann

Cover of *Symphony Notes* for 28 October through 2 December 1945, published to complement the NBC Symphony broadcasts. *RCA*

This performance of the concerto, unlike the one Dorfmann and Toscanini recorded the following August, features a rarely heard first-movement cadenza by Reinecke.

19 Nov. 1944   Beethoven Festival 5
                   Symphony No. 7 in A Major, Op. 92
                   Leonore Overture No. 2, Op. 72

26 Nov. 1944   Beethoven: Festival 6
                   Coriolan Overture, Op. 62
                   String Quartet in B-flat Major, Op. 130: Cavatina
                   String Quartet in C Major, Op. 59 No. 3: Finale
                   Piano Concerto No. 4 in G Major, Op. 58, with Rudolf
                   Serkin

Because the finale of Op. 59 No. 3 follows the preceding movement without pause, Toscanini, to provide a suitable opening, prefaced the finale with the slow introduction that opens the work's first movement.

3 Dec. 1944   Beethoven Festival 7
                   Septet for Woodwinds, Horn, and Strings in E-flat
                   Major, Op. 20: first, fourth, and sixth movements
                   Symphony No. 2 in D Major, Op. 36

10 Dec. 1944   Beethoven Festival 8
                   Fidelio: Act I, with Rose Bampton (Leonore), Eleanor
                   Steber (Marzelline), Herbert Janssen (Pizarro), Sidor
                   Belarsky (Rocco), Joseph Laderoute (Jaquino), and
                   chorus directed by Peter Wilhousky

For this and the following week's broadcast a Kettering talk was omitted so as to permit each of the opera's two acts to be presented within the confining hour of the program. And although this was an unstaged, concert presentation, it is possible that time limitations also dictated the omission of nearly all the opera's dialogue.

17 Dec. 1944   Beethoven: Festival 9
                   Fidelio: Act II, cast as above, with Jan Peerce (Florestan)
                   and Nicola Moscona (Don Fernando)

21 Jan. 1945   Kabalevsky: *Colas Breugnon*: Overture
                   Tchaikovsky: *Manfred* Symphony, Op. 58

28 Jan. 1945   Dvořák: *Scherzo capriccioso*, Op. 66
                   Cello Concerto in B Minor, Op. 104, with Edmund Kurtz

4 Feb. 1945   Cherubini: *Anacréon*: Overture
                   Mozart: Symphony No. 41 in C Major, K. 551, "Jupiter"
                   Berlioz: *Roméo et Juliette*, Op. 17: Queen Mab Scherzo
                   Wagner: *Die Meistersinger von Nürnberg*: Prelude

11 Feb. 1945   Debussy: *Images*: "Ibéria"
                    Prelude to the Afternoon of a Faun
                    La mer

18 Feb. 1945   Schumann: Symphony No. 3 in E-flat Major, Op. 97,
                    "Rhenish"
                    Mendelssohn: String Octet in E-flat Major, Op. 20:
                    Scherzo
                    Gershwin: *An American in Paris*

25 Mar. 1945   Haydn: Symphony No. 98 in B-flat Major
                    Kabalevsky: Symphony No. 2 in C Minor, Op. 19

Mozart's overture to *The Marriage of Figaro* was to be the opening work on this
program, but it was omitted for lack of time.

1 Apr. 1945   Gluck: *Orfeo ed Euridice*: Act II, with Nan Merriman,
                    mezzo-soprano; Edna Phillips, soprano; and chorus
                    directed by Peter Wilhousky
                    Bach: *St. Matthew Passion*: Closing chorus (sung in English)

18 May 1945   Beethoven: Symphony No. 5 in C Minor, Op. 67

This special half-hour broadcast, tagged "Victory, Part II," was given to mark
Germany's surrender. The overly dramatic announcements that accompanied
Toscanini's 1943 broadcast marking Mussolini's downfall are absent from this
presentation.

1 Sept. 1945   Beethoven: Symphony No. 3 in E-flat Major, Op. 55,
                    "Eroica"
                    Smith: "The Star-Spangled Banner"

This special forty-eight-minute broadcast—"Victory, Part III"—marked the
surrender of Japan. Like its predecessor, it was an ad hoc affair that took place in
8H without the usual audience present. Preceding the playing of "The Star-
Spangled Banner" was a plea from the announcer for "no more war."

2 Sept. 1945   Smith: "The Star-Spangled Banner"
                    Foroni: Overture in C Minor
                    Grofé: *Grand Canyon Suite*
                    Berlioz: *The Damnation of Faust*: Rákóczy March

9 Sept. 1945   Cherubini: *Anacréon*: Overture
                    Smetana: *The Moldau*
                    Mendelssohn: Symphony No. 5 in D Major, Op. 107,
                    "Reformation"

Ninth Season (1945–46)

Five broadcasts directed by Frank Black preceded Toscanini's initial appearance
for this season. Again, he led sixteen concerts, this time in three groups of six, six,

and four. The second of these groups concluded with a pair of one-hour broadcasts featuring a concert presentation of Puccini's *La bohème* that marked the fiftieth anniversary of its premiere in Turin's Teatro Regio, a premiere Toscanini had led.

The two most prominent guest conductors for this season were Dimitri Mitropoulos and Erich Kleiber, each directing four concerts between the two intervals of Toscanini's three sets. Kleiber's programming included familiar fare—the Beethoven "Pastoral" Symphony and a group of Wagner's works—that reflected Toscanini's tastes. But they also featured works from the classical period—Mozart's Symphony No. 33 and Schubert's Symphony No. 3—that Toscanini never played and Kleiber never recorded. Also included in Kleiber's programs was Ravel's *Mother Goose* Suite.

An exponent of twentieth-century music, Mitropoulos offered more avant-garde fare: Vaughan Williams's *London* Symphony, Schoenberg's Second String Quartet, and Berg's Violin Concerto (with Joseph Szigeti). It is important to be aware of this because it corrects the misconception that Toscanini refused to tolerate other conductors who would permit his orchestra (in the words of one critic) to "be scarred by Schoenberg's 'wrong notes'."[23] Granted, Toscanini was utterly confounded by the modern Viennese school. As he readily admitted toward the end of his life: "I don't know—I think I have an excellent memory, and in fact I don't experience any difficulty in studying a score; but with *Wozzeck*, which isn't part of my spirit, I give up after a couple of pages. And I can't understand how Mitropoulos is able to knock that stuff into his head."[24]

Obviously, these remarks, made in old age, reflect a musical temperament out of step with serialism. But—and this is the central issue—Toscanini, whatever his taste, did not permit it to interfere with choosing guest conductors such as Mitropoulos whose programs contained repertory to which he, Toscanini, was incapable of responding.

During this season Toscanini made no guest appearances and led only two recording sessions, both held in Carnegie Hall. On 11 March 1946 he recorded three works by Wagner (the prelude to *Die Meistersinger*, *Siegfried Idyll*, and Ride of the Valkyries), and on 8 April he recorded the Air from Bach's Suite No. 3, Tchaikovsky's *Romeo and Juliet* Fantasy Overture, and the overture to Kabalevsky's *Colas Breugnon*.

World War II having ended, General Motors turned its commercial messages to the promotion of its automobiles, with the first broadcast of the season being devoted to the top-of-the-line Cadillac. The concerts continued to be aired on Sundays from 5:00 to 6:00 P.M., and C. F. Kettering remained a weekly intermission speaker.

28 Oct. 1945   Brahms: *Tragic* Overture, Op. 81
                    Symphony No. 4 in E Minor, Op. 98

4 Nov. 1945   Mendelssohn: *Hebrides* Overture, Op. 26
Berlioz: *Roméo et Juliette*, Op. 17: Romeo Alone;
    Celebration at the Capulets; Love Scene; Queen Mab
    Scherzo
Glinka: *Jota aragonesa*

11 Nov. 1945   Rossini: *Il Signor Bruschino*: Overture
Schubert: Symphony No. 9 in C Major, D. 944
Originally scheduled for this broadcast (in place of the Rossini) was Schubert's overture to *Des Teufels Lustschloss*, D. 84. The idea behind this programming was to present Schubert's first and last orchestral works, a practice Toscanini had applied to Mozart at the New York Philharmonic, where he programmed on the same concert that composer's Symphonies Nos. 1 and 41.

18 Nov. 1945   Vaughan Williams: *Fantasia on a Theme by Thomas Tallis*
Wolf-Ferrari: *Le donne curiose*: Overture
Elgar: *Enigma Variations*, Op. 36
A breakdown in the ensemble at the beginning of the fourth variation of the Elgar produced a scrambled mess.

25 Nov. 1945   Castelnuovo-Tedesco: *A Fairy Tale* Overture
Rieti: Symphony No. 4, "Sinfonia tripartita"
Creston: *Frontiers*
Siegmeister: *Western Suite*
With the exception of *Frontiers*, every work on this program was a premiere.

2 Dec. 1945   Bellini: *Norma*: Introduction and Druids' Chorus
Verdi: Te Deum
Boito: *Mefistofele*: Prologue
This program featured the Peter Wilhousky Chorus (in the Boito), the Edoardo Petri Boys Choir, and Nicola Moscona, bass.

6 Jan. 1946   Wagner: *Tannhäuser*: Prelude to Act III
    Siegfried Idyll
Wagner-Toscanini: *Götterdämmerung*: Dawn and Siegfried's
    Rhine Journey
Wagner: *Die Meistersinger von Nürnberg*: Prelude
The prelude to Act III of *Tannhäuser* was introduced here simply as "the original version" (see the entry for the broadcast of 25 February 1939).

13 Jan. 1946   Humperdinck: *Hansel und Gretel*: Prelude
Prokofiev: Symphony No. 1 in D Major, Op. 25,
    "Classical"
Liadov: *Kikimora*
Mancinelli: *Venetian Scenes*: Flight of the Lovers
Enesco: Romanian Rhapsody No. 1, Op. 11
J. Strauss: *Voices of Spring*

Exceptionally inaccurate execution at the beginning of the Mancinelli required that Toscanini stop the orchestra and start the piece again. When the Toscanini Society issued this broadcast on LP, the fault was excised.

20 Jan. 1946   Wolf-Ferrari: *The Secret of Suzanne*: Overture
                      Busoni: *Rondo arlecchinesco*, with Andrew McKinley, tenor
                      Martucci: Piano Concerto No. 1 in B-flat Minor, Op. 66,
                           with Glauco d'Attily

27 Jan. 1946   Mozart: *Don Giovanni*: Overture
                           Symphony No. 40 in G Minor, K. 550
                      Verdi: String Quartet in E Minor: third and fourth
                           movements
                           Otello: Act III Ballet Music
                           La forza del destino: Overture

3 Feb. 1946   Puccini: *La bohème*: Acts I and II, with Licia Albanese
                           (Mimi), Ann McKnight (Musetta), Jan Peerce
                           (Rodolfo), Francesco Valentino (Marcello), Nicola
                           Moscona (Colline), George Cehanovsky (Schaunard),
                           Salvatore Baccaloni (Benoit and Alcindoro), the Peter
                           Wilhousky Chorus, and the Edoardo Petri Boys
                           Choir

10 Feb. 1946   Puccini: *La bohème*: Acts III and IV, with cast as above
At the conclusion of Act IV, the brasses entered ever so slightly early. Backstage afterward, Toscanini, according to Chotzinoff, "abandoned himself to an elemental rage more devastating than any I had ever witnessed," which culminated in his summoning the offending players, whom he called "porci" (pigs), and giving them a severe reprimand.[25] For the RCA recording of the broadcast, the offending passage was replaced with the corresponding portion of the dress rehearsal.

17 Mar. 1946   Schumann: Symphony No. 2 in C Major, Op. 61
                      R. Strauss: *Till Eulenspiegel's Merry Pranks*, Op. 28

24 Mar. 1946   Scarlatti-Tommasini: *The Good Humored Ladies*
                      Franck: Symphony in D Minor

31 Mar. 1946   Wagner: *The Flying Dutchman*: Overture
                      Brahms: Symphony No. 3 in F Major, Op. 90

7 Apr. 1946   Kabalevsky: *Colas Breugnon*: Overture
                      Roussel: *The Spider's Feast*: Suite
                      Roger-Ducasse: Sarabande, with offstage chorus directed
                           by Peter Wilhousky
                      Tchaikovsky: *Romeo and Juliet*: Fantasy Overture

Tenth Season (1946–47)

Two weeks after his 7 April 1946 broadcast, Toscanini departed for Italy, returning to his native country for the first time since 1938. There he led the La Scala
orchestra in a number of concerts. The first of these (on 11 May 1946) marked
the reopening of La Scala, which had been rebuilt after sustaining severe damage
during the war by Allied bombs. (A sonically poor recording of that concert—
made up of works by Rossini, Verdi, Puccini, and Boito—has circulated on LP
and CD.) Subsequent concerts with the orchestra were given in Italy and
Switzerland throughout the summer. A few of these performances also had limited circulation on LP and included some of Toscanini's finest surviving accounts
of Beethoven's First Symphony and the prelude to Wagner's *Die Meistersinger*.

During Toscanini's stay in Italy the NBC Symphony was led by a variety of
conductors, including Frank Black, Franco Autori, Efrem Kurtz, Alexander
Smallens, Robert Shaw, Fabien Sevitzky, Hans Schweger, and Wilfrid Pelletier.
Vladimir Golschmann also directed two broadcasts, one of which featured the
Beethoven Second Piano Concerto performed by William Kapell, a collabora-
tion that subsequently produced a memorable studio recording of the work.
And two concerts were led by the twenty-eight-year-old Leonard Bernstein, the
first devoted to Marc Blitzstein's *Airborne* Symphony, the second to the Haydn
Symphony No. 102 and the Ravel Piano Concerto, with the conductor dou-
bling as soloist.

This season also marked (on 25 March 1947) Toscanini's eightieth birthday,
but he gave no sign of cutting back on his NBC activities. He again led sixteen
concerts, this time broken into two groups of seven and nine. The first of these
concluded with two broadcasts devoted to a complete concert presentation of
Verdi's *La traviata*. The second opened with two broadcasts featuring a complete
performance of Berlioz's dramatic symphony *Roméo et Juliette*. Between Toscanini's two series were eight other concerts, four led by Fritz Reiner, four by
Eugen Szenkar (a Hungarian who fled the Nazis and built a career in Brazil,
where he may have met Toscanini). Both conductors' programs were filled
almost exclusively with standard fare, the most radical works being Hindemith's
Mathis der Maler and the suite from Bartók's *Miraculous Mandarin* (both led by
Reiner).

Throughout the season Toscanini was active in the recording studio, participating in five sessions that produced splendid accounts of the Schumann
Manfred Overture and excerpts from Berlioz's *Roméo et Juliette*. He also made his
second recording (but first to be released) of the Schubert Ninth Symphony
and his only studio recording of Wagner's *Faust Overture*. (In 1990 EMI released
a 1935 live Toscanini BBC Symphony account of the work on CD.) With the
exception of the initial recording session, which was held in NBC studio 3A (a
smaller version of 8H with even drier acoustics), all took place in Carnegie Hall.

Many failed to gain Toscanini's approval. He rejected outright those of Debussy's *La mer*, the prelude to Wagner's *Parsifal*, and the Queen Mab Scherzo from Berlioz's *Roméo et Juliette*. He was also reluctant to approve the recording made in 3A of Mozart's "Haffner" Symphony, an attitude one can readily understand after hearing the superiority of the three broadcast performances of the work that he gave at NBC.

The broadcasts continued to be aired on Sunday evenings between 5:00 and 6:00 P.M. from studio 8H, but General Motors gave up its sponsorship of the series. On the first broadcast of the winter series, Ben Grauer noted that these were now "sustaining programs" and asked the radio audience to support them by purchasing products advertised on other NBC broadcasts. With the loss of a sponsor and the resulting absence of C. F. Kettering's talks, more time became available for music and for Grauer's comments about it. These remained, in general, models of brevity and good taste. During the year, Grauer frequently called attention to the lack of sponsorship, stating on Toscanini's final broadcast (6 April 1947) that "these concerts are made possible through advertising received from NBC sponsors of other programs throughout the week."

27 Oct. 1946   Wagner: *A Faust Overture*
                    Berlioz: *Harold in Italy*, Op. 16, with William Primrose

3 Nov. 1946   Mozart: *The Magic Flute*: Overture
                    Divertimento in B-flat Major, K. 287
                    Symphony No. 35 in D Major, K. 385, "Haffner"
According to B. H. Haggin, Toscanini turned his attention to K. 287 after hearing what he felt was an especially unstylish performance of the work led by Serge Koussevitzky.[26]

10 Nov. 1946   Schumann: *Manfred*, Op. 115: Overture
                    Tchaikovsky: *Manfred* Symphony, Op. 58
It was during a rehearsal for this performance of the *Manfred* Symphony that Toscanini delivered to the orchestra an extraordinarily personal digression:

> E *passione, dolore*—sorrow, passion Entusiasmo—*ma* no Sleep when you play! Put *entusiasmo* like me! I don't enjoy to conduct—no, no, I 'ate to conduct, I 'ate! Because I suffer too much—Troppo! What— you look at me? Why? You are aston-ed? You think that I am crazy? No, no. Sensitive, yes. Don't look at me in this way.[27]

17 Nov. 1946   Smetana: *The Bartered Bride*: Overture
                    Humperdinck: *Königskinder*: Prelude to Act III
                    Brahms: *Variations on a Theme by Haydn*, Op. 56a
                    R. Strauss: *Death and Transfiguration*, Op. 24

24 Nov. 1946   Beethoven: *Coriolan* Overture, Op. 62
                       Piano Concerto No. 3 in C Minor, Op. 37, with
                       Myra Hess

Wagner-Toscanini: *Götterdämmerung*: Dawn and Siegfried's
Rhine Journey

Toscanini admired Myra Hess for her bravery during World War II, when, in
the face of frequent German bombings of London, she continued her recitals at
the National Gallery. He invited her to New York to perform Beethoven's
"Emperor" Concerto, and that was the work announced for this program on the
previous week's broadcast. But at their first meeting, the pianist found the tempo
too fast, and Beethoven's Third Concerto was substituted. At the final rehearsal
of the work, Toscanini miscued the orchestra in the second movement. Recognizing his memory lapse, he later told Hess, " I say terrible things about those
other conductors, but I cannot conduct myself."[28]

1 Dec. 1946   Verdi: *La traviata*: Act I and Act II, Scene 1, with Licia
                   Albanese (Violetta), Jan Peerce (Alfredo), Robert
                   Merrill (Germont), Maxine Stellman (Flora), John
                   Garris (Gastone), George Cehanovsky (Douphol),
                   Paul Dennis (d'Obigny), Arthur Newman (Grenvil),
                   Johanne Moreland (Annina), and the Peter
                   Wilhousky Chorus

8 Dec. 1946   Verdi: *La traviata*: Act II, Scene 2, and Act III; cast as above

9 Feb. 1947   Berlioz: *Roméo et Juliette*, Op. 17: Parts 1 and 2, with Gladys
                   Swarthout, mezzo-soprano; John Garris, tenor;
                   Nicola Moscona, bass; and the Peter Wilhousky
                   Chorus

16 Feb. 1947   Berlioz: *Roméo et Juliette*, Op. 17: Part 3, cast as above
                   The Damnation of Faust, Op. 24: Scene 7, with Mack
                   Harrell, bass

Gladys Swarthout sang in these performances with a broken knee incurred early
in the first week of February.

23 Feb. 1947   Sinigaglia: *Le baruffe chiozzotte*: Overture
                   Schubert: Symphony No. 9 in C Major, D. 944

2 Mar. 1947   Franck: *Rédemption*: Symphonic Interlude
                   Dukas: *Ariane et Barbe-bleu*
                   Debussy: *La mer*

9 Mar. 1947   Brahms: *Tragic* Overture, Op. 81
                   Serenade No. 1 in D Major, Op. 11: Minuets 1 and 2
                   Symphony No. 2 in D Major, Op. 73

16 Mar. 1947   Beethoven: *Consecration of the House* Overture, Op. 124
                   The Creatures of Prometheus, Op. 43: Adagio and
                   Allegretto
                   Symphony No. 6 in F Major, Op. 68, "Pastoral"

This was probably Toscanini's first performance of the overture.

23 Mar. 1947   Cherubini: Symphony in D Major
                    Catalani: *La Wally*: Prelude to Act IV
                    Loreley: Dance of the Water Nymphs
                    Respighi: *The Fountains of Rome*

During the rehearsal of the *La Wally* excerpt, Toscanini—in one of his most famous eruptions—lashed out at the orchestra: "Are you stupid? Don't you know what in Italian means andante?"

30 Mar. 1947   Mendelssohn: String Octet in E-flat Major, Op. 20
                    Symphony No. 5 in D Major, Op. 107, "Reformation"

6 Apr. 1947   Wagner: *Parsifal*: Prelude and Good Friday Spell
                    Die Walküre: Act I, Scene 3, with Rose Bampton and
                    Set Svanholm

Eleventh Season (1947–48)

During May and June 1947 Toscanini directed two recording sessions of four performances: two of Berlioz's Queen Mab Scherzo, the prelude to Wagner's *Parsifal*, and the first movement of Haydn's "Clock" Symphony. Rejecting everything for release save the Haydn, Toscanini returned to Italy, where he spent an inactive summer. During his absence, several guest conductors led the NBC Symphony: Hans Lange and Alfred Wallenstein (both of whom had worked with Toscanini at the New York Philharmonic), Hans Schweger (director of the Kansas City Philharmonic), Izler Solomon (director of the Columbus Philharmonic), and Frank Black. Milton Katims, a violist in the NBC Symphony, whom Toscanini admired and who went on years later to become director of the Seattle Symphony, also made the first of his several appearances as a conductor in front of his colleagues.

Prior to the beginning of the 1947–48 winter series, Toscanini, who had returned to New York in August, led his orchestra on two occasions. One was a nonbroadcast concert in Ridgefield, Connecticut, on 6 September, with Wagner's *Siegfried Idyll* and Beethoven's First Symphony as the major works. On 21 September he directed one of his last concerts in the orchestra's summer series, described here because of its proximity to the forthcoming winter season.

With the official opening of the new season on 25 October, NBC moved the broadcast to Saturdays from 6:30 to 7:30 P.M. Harvey Sachs suggests that this shift was necessitated by the network's failure to acquire a sponsor for the prime late-Sunday-afternoon hour the concerts had been filling. As he goes on to note:

> NBC . . . moved Toscanini to Saturday at 6:30 when vast numbers of Americans were eating supper and/or preparing to go out. Toscanini, however, was told by NBC that more people would be able to listen to the broadcasts at that hour; and people close to him, who knew better, allowed him to believe this.[29]

Toscanini's appearances for the season fell into two eight-week series. Between them were eight other broadcasts, four led by Erich Kleiber, four by Ernest Ansermet. Kleiber directed mostly standard fare—the Schubert Fifth, the Tchaikovsky Fourth, and the Borodin Second Symphonies, and a magnificent account of Beethoven's "Eroica." Ansermet's programs were less conservative: Debussy's *Jeux* and *Gigues*, Martinů's Fifth Symphony, and Frank Martin's *Petite symphonie concertante*, among other works. One of them, Ravel's *La valse*, elicited a significant response from Toscanini: "Ansermet is good musician. When he play [sic] *La Valse* is different from my *La Valse* . . . but is good."[30] Whatever Toscanini's intolerance of the work of some conductors, he remained open to interpretive views that diverged from his own and treated them with respect.

In what was a generally distinguished season for Toscanini, three events stand out: the concert performance (given in two broadcasts) of Verdi's *Otello* and the first two of ten broadcasts that the network (and Toscanini) ultimately elected to televise.

Between 27 October and 16 December, Toscanini led six recording sessions, three in studio 8H, three in Carnegie Hall. He rejected a Beethoven Seventh, a Debussy *La mer*, a Dance of the Sylphs from Berlioz's *The Damnation of Faust*, and "Ye spotted snakes" from Mendelssohn's *Midsummer Night's Dream*. Among those he approved, the most successful were the Mozart Divertimento K. 287 and the Tchaikovsky "Pathétique" Symphony. Neither, however, matched his best broadcast accounts. The same is even truer of the recordings he made of Beethoven's *Consecration of the House* Overture and excerpts from Mendelssohn's *Midsummer Night's Dream*.

After the last broadcast of the winter season, Toscanini led one more concert with the NBC Symphony, a nonbroadcast benefit for the New York Infirmary Fund given in Carnegie Hall on 25 April. It was devoted to Verdi's Te Deum and Requiem and featured the soloists Herva Nelli, Nan Merriman, William McGrath, and Norman Scott. It remains one of his finest accounts of the Requiem.

21 Sept. 1947 Kabalevsky: *Colas Breugnon*: Overture
        Beethoven: Symphony No. 1 in C Major, Op. 21
        Smetana: *The Moldau*
        Gillis: Symphony No. 5½

25 Oct. 1947 Beethoven: *Consecration of the House* Overture, Op. 124
        String Quartet in F Major, Op. 135: Lento and Vivace
        Symphony No. 7 in A Major, Op. 92

1 Nov. 1947 Mendelssohn: *Die schöne Melusine* Overture, Op. 32
        String Quintet No. 2 in B-flat Major, Op. 87: third
        movement

>Music for *A Midsummer Night's Dream*, Opp. 21 and 61:
Overture; Scherzo; Nocturne; Intermezzo; Wedding
March; "Ye Spotted Snakes"; Finale; with Edna
Phillips, Genevieve Warner, and the Peter Wilhousky
Chorus

This concert commemorated the centenary of Mendelssohn's death.

8 Nov. 1947   Mozart: *The Marriage of Figaro*: Overture
>Bassoon Concerto in B-flat Major, K. 191, with Leonard
Sharrow
Divertimento in B-flat Major, K. 287
The Magic Flute: Overture

According to Alan Shulman, the cadenza Sharrow played in the bassoon concerto was composed by Toscanini. Shulman correctly observed that "it had
nothing to do with the work but just ambled on and on."[31]

15 Nov. 1947   Prokofiev: Symphony No. 1 in D Major, Op. 25,
>"Classical"
Tchaikovsky: Symphony No. 6 in B Minor, Op. 74,
"Pathétique"

22 Nov. 1947   Bach: Suite No. 3 in D Major for Orchestra, BWV 1068
>Vivaldi: Violin Concerto in B-flat Major, with Mischa
Mischakoff
Handel: Concerto Grosso in B Minor, Op. 6 No. 12
Bach-Respighi: Passacaglia and Fugue in C Minor, BWV
582

What is striking about this broadcast—aside from the rarity (for the time) of a
major conductor leading an all-baroque program—is the contrast in performance styles it encompasses. The Bach-Respighi, with its grandiose orchestration of this familiar organ work, obviously views the composer from an early-
twentieth-century perspective. But the other works are performed with a small
orchestra having a transparent texture, relatively little vibrato in the strings, and
a harpsichord to provide continuo support. The Vivaldi was announced as an
American premiere. It is not one of his more inspired works.

29 Nov. 1947   Wolf-Ferrari: *Le donne curiose*: Overture
>Kodály: *Háry János*: Suite
Debussy: *La mer*

6 Dec. 1947   Verdi: *Otello*: Acts I and II, with Ramón Vinay (Otello),
>Herva Nelli (Desdemona), Giuseppe Valdengo (Iago),
Nan Merriman (Emilia), Virginio Assandri (Cassio),
Leslie Chabay (Roderigo), Arthur Newman
(Montano), Nicola Moscona (Lodovico), the Peter
Wilhousky Chorus, and the Edoardo Petri Boys
Choir

13 Dec. 1947 Verdi: *Otello*: Acts III and IV, cast as above
Each of the *Otello* broadcasts began at 6:15 P.M. and ran for seventy-five minutes.

14 Feb. 1948 R. Strauss: *Don Juan*, Op. 20
Berlioz: *Roméo et Juliette*, Op. 17: Queen Mab Scherzo
Mussorgsky-Ravel: *Pictures at an Exhibition*

21 Feb. 1948 Brahms: *Variations on a Theme by Haydn*, Op. 56a
Symphony No. 3 in F Major, Op. 90

28 Feb. 1948 Glinka: *Jota aragonesa*
Tchaikovsky: *Manfred* Symphony, Op. 58

6 Mar. 1948 Haydn: *Sinfonia concertante* in B-flat Major, Op. 84, with
Mischa Mischakoff, violin; Frank Miller, cello; Paul
Renzi, flute; and Leonard Sharrow, bassoon
Mozart: Symphony No. 39 in E-flat Major, K. 543
Beethoven: *Leonore* Overture No. 3, Op. 72a

13 Mar. 1948 Donizetti: *Don Pasquale*: Overture
Mancinelli: *Venetian Scenes*: Flight of the Lovers
Busoni: *Berceuse élégiaque*
Martucci: *Novelletta*
Verdi: *Otello*: Act III: Ballet Music
Rossini: *Semiramide*: Overture

This concert was dedicated to Radio Centro Musical, the newly formed Cuban
network, which was to carry the NBC Symphony broadcasts. During the concluding commentary, in which the content of the following week's all-Wagner
program was announced, nothing was mentioned about NBC's plans to televise
the concert. This was probably because of an existing ban by the American Federation of Musicians on televising symphonic concerts. The ban was lifted on 18
March, two days before the planned telecast was to take place.

20 Mar. 1948 Introductory talk by David Sarnoff
Wagner: *Lohengrin*: Prelude to Act III
Tannhäuser: Overture and Bacchanale
Siegfried: Forest Murmurs
Wagner-Toscanini: *Götterdämmerung*: Dawn and Siegfried's
Rhine Journey
Wagner: *Die Walküre*: Ride of the Valkyries

David Sarnoff's introductory talk celebrates the coming of live symphonic music
to television, noting that the total number of people who had seen Toscanini
since the inception of the NBC Symphony was but one-tenth the number that
would be seeing him this evening on television. The talk did not claim, however, that NBC was the first network to televise a symphonic concert, and with
good reason: NBC and CBS had been competing for such a groundbreaking

premiere, and CBS ultimately beat NBC by an hour and a half, televising the
Philadelphia Orchestra under Eugene Ormandy at 5:00 P.M.

27 Mar. 1948   Debussy: *Images*: "Ibéria"
                    Prelude to the Afternoon of a Faun
                    Nocturnes: *Fêtes*
                    La mer

According to Haggin, Toscanini planned to include Debussy's *Rondes de print-
emps* on this broadcast but then changed his mind.[32]

3 Apr. 1948   Beethoven: Symphony No. 9 in D Minor, Op. 125, with
                    Ann McKnight, soprano; Jane Hobson, contralto;
                    Irwin Dillon, tenor; Norman Scott, bass; and the
                    Collegiate Chorale, directed by Robert Shaw

This, the second of ten Toscanini telecasts, featured considerably better camer-
awork than did the first. It is the only one of Toscanini's five NBC presentations
of the Ninth to take place in studio 8H instead of Carnegie Hall. It also marked
the first broadcast performance in which the chorus was prepared by Robert
Shaw, whom Toscanini considered the finest choral conductor he worked with
at NBC. William Horne was originally announced as the tenor for this performance, and his name appeared on the printed program. Irwin Dillon was his
replacement.

Twelfth Season (1948–49)

A month after his 3 April 1948 performance of the Ninth Symphony, Toscanini
left for Italy, where in June he appeared at La Scala in a performance marking the
thirtieth anniversary of Boito's death. What set this program apart from any
other postwar Toscanini appearance was its featuring excerpts from the composer's *Mefistofele* and *Nerone* in *staged* presentations. In effect, Toscanini was
again conducting in-theater opera, if only excerpts, and this would be the last
time stage directions would concern him. Aside from one additional concert at
La Scala in September, the conductor spent the remainder of the summer away
from the podium.

     During Toscanini's absence from New York, the NBC Symphony was led
by a variety of guests: Erich Leinsdorf, Milton Katims, Hans Schweger, Alexander Hilsberg (associate conductor of the Philadelphia Orchestra), Hans Lange,
and Massimo Freccia (who three years later would be appointed director of the
Baltimore Symphony). Toscanini returned to NBC at the end of October and
opened the season with a magnificent six-week Brahms cycle, the second of
two he led with the orchestra. In all, he conducted sixteen concerts, divided into
two groups of eight each. Separating the two series were guest appearances by
Ernest Ansermet and a young Italian named Guido Cantelli. Toscanini, having

heard Cantelli in Italy, was greatly impressed. He invited the young conductor to New York, and after his first NBC appearance wrote to Cantelli's wife:

> I am happy and moved to inform you of Guido's great success and that I introduced him to my orchestra which loves him as I do. This is the first time in my long life that I have met a young man so gifted. He will go far, very far. Love him well, because Guido is also good, simple and modest. His departure will leave a great gap here.[33]

Cantelli, of course, did go far, and at the time of his untimely death in a plane crash in November 1956—less than two months before Toscanini died—he was about to be appointed principal conductor of the New York Philharmonic, a position that went instead to Leonard Bernstein. How different the history of musical life in the United States might have been had that disaster at Orly airport not occurred!

Cantelli's programs were eclectic, ranging from Haydn's Symphony No. 93 to Hindemith's *Mathis der Mahler* (both of which he recorded with the orchestra). Neither, incidentally, was in Toscanini's repertory. And the music Ansermet presented covered two centuries, from Bach's Third Orchestral Suite to Honegger's *Horace victorieux*. Ansermet also performed Bartók's *Music for Strings, Percussion, and Celeste* and Schubert's Ninth Symphony, the latter being especially significant as a work Ansermet never recorded.

Air time for the broadcasts remained 6:30 to 7:30 P.M. on Saturdays. Owing to a knee injury, Toscanini made no recordings during this season. He did, however, consent to the additional strain of four telecasts, the last two of which—concert performances of *Aida*—marked the conclusion of the winter season. One more concert followed: a nonbroadcast benefit for City College in Carnegie Hall on 20 April devoted to Beethoven (the *Creatures of Prometheus* Overture and "Eroica" Symphony) and Wagner (the *Tannhäuser* Overture and Bacchanale, and Act I, Scene 3, of *Die Walküre*, with Rose Bampton and Set Svanholm). All of the broadcasts emanated from 8H. Toscanini had planned to leave for Italy immediately after his benefit performance, but a rib injury sustained in a bathtub fall delayed his departure for a month.

In retrospect, this season ranks as one of Toscanini's finest, exhibiting a standard of excellence maintained throughout each broadcast. Almost all of these concerts are free of the overwrought intensity that infected some of his wartime efforts, and none displays the slackening tension that was to emerge from time to time in the seasons to come. Indeed, the Beethoven "Eroica," Brahms Fourth, Schubert "Unfinished," and Strauss *Till Eulenspiegel* of this season shine as some of his most commanding performances. To be sure, more distinguished performances were to come in the years that followed, but never with the unflagging consistency Toscanini maintained in this, his twelfth NBC season.

23 Oct. 1948 Brahms Cycle 1
              Serenade No. 1 in D Major, Op. 11: first movement
              Piano Concerto No. 2 in B-flat Major, Op. 83, with
                  Vladimir Horowitz

30 Oct. 1948 Brahms Cycle 2
              Tragic Overture, Op. 81
              Symphony No. 1 in C Minor, Op. 68

6 Nov. 1948 Brahms Cycle 3
              Academic Festival Overture, Op. 80
              Serenade No. 1 in D Major, Op. 11: Minuets 1 and 2
              Symphony No. 2 in D Major, Op. 73

In the development section of the finale of the Second Symphony a glaringly
exposed wrong entrance breaks Toscanini's concentration, after which the line
slackens. The movement's coda lacks the cumulative force usually heard in Toscanini's presentations of this work.

13 Nov. 1948 Brahms Cycle 4
              Double Concerto in A Minor for Violin and Cello, Op.
                  102, with Mischa Mischakoff, violin, and Frank
                  Miller, cello
              Liebeslieder Waltzes, Op. 52, with Joseph Kahn and
                  Arthur Balsam, piano; chorus prepared by Walter
                  Preston
              Hungarian Dance No. 1 in G Minor

This concert was the first of the season's four telecasts. It also remains a prime illustration of the occasional eccentricities of Toscanini's programming: the orchestra
had to reassemble at the end of the waltzes, which were performed with but two
pianos and chorus, for a three-minute work of no great consequence.

Speaking about RCA's first LP release of this performance of the Double
Concerto, the cellist, Frank Miller, complained of the recording's poor balance
and about not having the opportunity "to correct one bad mistake" in the
finale.[34]

20 Nov. 1948 Brahms Cycle 5
              Variations on a Theme by Haydn, Op. 56a
              Symphony No. 3 in F Major, Op. 90

27 Nov. 1948 Brahms Cycle 6
              Gesang der Parzen for Chorus and Orchestra, Op. 89, with
                  the Robert Shaw Chorale
              Symphony No. 4 in E Minor, Op. 98

4 Dec. 1948 Mozart: Symphony No. 40 in G Minor, K. 550
              Dvořák: *Symphonic Variations*, Op. 78
              Wagner: *Tannhäuser:* Overture

This concert was the second telecast of the season, and it is interesting, near the end of the Wagner, to see the cellist, Frank Miller, and Benar Heifetz glance at each other with looks that suggest (and this is admittedly speculative) a difficulty had been successfully negotiated. Originally announced for this program instead of the *Tannhäuser* Overture was the prelude to Wagner's *Die Meistersinger*.

11 Dec. 1948   Mendelssohn: *Die schöne Melusine* Overture, Op. 32
Liadov: *Kikimora*
R. Strauss: *Don Quixote*, Op. 35, with Frank Miller, cello

12 Feb. 1949   Berlioz: *Roman Carnival* Overture, Op. 9
Roméo et Juliette, Op. 17: Queen Mab Scherzo
Harold in Italy, Op. 16, with Carlton Cooley, viola

19 Feb. 1949   Beethoven: *Coriolan* Overture, Op. 62
Symphony No. 3 in E-flat Major, Op. 55, "Eroica"

26 Feb. 1949   Kabalevsky: Symphony No. 2 in E Minor, Op. 19
Sibelius: *En Saga*, Op. 9
Wagner-Toscanini: *Götterdämmerung*: Dawn and Siegfried's
Rhine Journey

5 Mar. 1949   Rossini: *La scala di seta*: Overture
Schubert: Symphony No. 8 in B Minor, D. 759,
"Unfinished"
Franck: *Les éolides*
R. Strauss: *Till Eulenspiegel's Merry Pranks*, Op. 28

12 Mar. 1949   Haydn: Symphony No. 99 in E-flat Major
Weber-Berlioz: *Invitation to the Dance*, Op. 65
Mendelssohn: Symphony No. 4 in A Major, Op. 90,
"Italian"

19 Mar. 1949   Beethoven: *Consecration of the House* Overture, Op. 124
The Creatures of Prometheus, Op. 43: Adagio and Allegretto
Symphony No. 6 in F Major, Op. 68, "Pastoral"
In the fourth movement of the symphony, the timpanist Karl Glassman, apparently miscounting measures, made two intrusive wrong entrances.

26 Mar. 1949   Verdi: *Aida*: Acts I and II, with Herva Nelli (Aida), Eva
Gustavson (Amneris), Teresa Stich-Randall
(Priestess), Richard Tucker (Radames), Giuseppe
Valdengo (Amonastro), Norman Scott (Ramfis),
Virginio Assandri (Messenger,) Dennis Harbour
(King), and the Robert Shaw Chorale

2 Apr. 1949   Verdi: *Aida*: Acts III and IV, cast as above
This and the previous week's broadcast were televised. Each was extended by fifteen minutes beyond the usual hour to accommodate the opera.

Thirteenth Season (1949–50)

Toscanini remained inactive throughout most of the summer of 1949, not appearing in public until 3 September, when he led a concert with the La Scala Orchestra that inaugurated Venice's twelfth contemporary music festival. The most modern work on Toscanini's program was Richard Strauss's *Don Juan*, composed in 1888. A few days later he conducted two concerts at La Scala, returning shortly thereafter to New York.

During his absence from NBC the orchestra was led by several guests ranging from Sigmund Romberg and Arthur Fiedler to Fritz Reiner, Dimitri Mitropoulos, Antal Dorati, Wilfrid Pelletier, and Milton Katims, all favoring programs of relatively light fare. On 7 October Toscanini returned to his orchestra for a nonbroadcast concert given in Ridgefield, Connecticut. His NBC season began three weeks later and again consisted of sixteen concerts divided into two series of eight each. The broadcasts continued to be aired on Saturdays from 6:30 to 7:30 P.M.

His knee having improved, Toscanini returned to the recording studio, participating in a total of eleven sessions between 7 November 1949 and 19 March 1950. The first involved a start on the Beethoven Second Symphony (the recording was not completed until 1951). Also recorded was the Beethoven "Eroica," which RCA had scheduled for the previous year but had had to bypass because of Toscanini's painful knee. The first six sessions were held in Carnegie Hall, the remainder in studio 8H. Two of the performances preserved in those 8H sessions—Schubert's "Unfinished" Symphony and Dukas's *Sorcerer's Apprentice*—marked the last of the Toscanini recordings to be issued in the 78 rpm format.

The highlights of the season included magnificent accounts of Tchaikovsky's "Pathétique" Symphony and Schumann's "Rhenish" Symphony, a remarkably idiomatic and expressive performance of the little-known C Minor Requiem of Cherubini, and a complete concert performance of Verdi's *Falstaff*. Shortly thereafter, Toscanini and the orchestra embarked on a transcontinental tour of the United States, after which two recording sessions took place in 8H on 1 and 2 June.

The 1950 transcontinental tour in the spring of 1950 was surely among the peaks for both conductor and orchestra in their seventeen-year association. They were acclaimed everywhere during their six weeks in twenty cities in a tour that stretched over 8600 miles. Not since its South American trip a decade earlier had the orchestra been at Toscanini's exclusive disposal. Moreover, it was performing primarily in concert halls (not all of them, to be sure, acoustically ideal) rather than in the more claustrophobic confines of 8H. It is thus not surprising that the violinist Samuel Antek claimed: "The performances all along were undoubtedly the finest I have ever heard the orchestra give. No wonder Toscanini 'was delighted and pleased as I never saw him before'."[35]

Son Walter and maestro Toscanini on NBC tour, 1950. *RCA*

In many ways, the tour was a model of its kind. The orchestra had its own train, the last car of which comprised an apartment for Toscanini. Concerts were given less frequently than on most other tours so that the musicians were not worn out, and twenty-eight works were prepared to ensure variety. (Oddly, one work, the overture to Rossini's *La Cenerentola*, had been programmed on only a single Toscanini broadcast—22 October 1938.) In effect, the tour train formed a society in microcosm, having, among other things, its own stationery and laundry lists. And Toscanini, delighting in the opportunity to see the country, remained relaxed yet extraordinarily energetic throughout. He took in local attractions, fraternized with the musicians in ways that were impossible in the more formal confines that existed in New York, and responded warmly and gratefully to the intense enthusiasm with which he and the orchestra were received by playing encores, usually "The Stars and Stripes Forever" in the North and "Dixie" in the South. The tour proved a huge success, with concerts in every city sold out. Two days after the last stop of the trip (27 May, in Philadelphia), Toscanini gave a large party for the entire orchestra

From left to right: RCA executive Frank Falson, Walter Toscanini, the maestro,
and David Sarnoff during the 1950 NBC tour. *RCA*

at his home, the Villa Pauline in Riverdale, to which he had returned at the end
of World War II.

29 Oct. 1949   Berlioz: *Roméo et Juliette*, Op. 17: Romeo Alone; Fêtes at
                   the Capulets; Queen Mab Scherzo
                   Debussy: *La mer*

5 Nov. 1949   Beethoven: Symphony No. 2 in D Major, Op. 36
                   Elgar: *Enigma Variations*, Op. 36

12 Nov. 1949   Cimarosa: *Il matrimonio per raggiro*: Overture
                   Schumann: Symphony No. 3 in E-flat Major, Op. 97,
                   "Rhenish"
                   Tchaikovsky: *Romeo and Juliet*: Fantasy Overture

Originally announced for this broadcast but replaced by the Tchaikovsky work
was the Suite No. 2 from Ravel's *Daphnis et Chloé*, which was reprogrammed for
the following week.

Toscanini directing a mock orchestra of NBC musicians at a cookout in Sun Valley, California, during the NBC Symphony tour of 1950. *BMG Classics*

19 Nov. 1949   Boccherini: String Quartet in D Major, Op. 6 No. 1
Haydn: Symphony No. 98 in B-flat Major
Ravel: *Daphnis et Chloé*: Suite No. 2

26 Nov. 1949   Mozart: *The Magic Flute*: Overture
Beethoven: Symphony No. 3 in E-flat Major, Op. 55,
"Eroica"

3 Dec. 1949   Cherubini: *Ali Baba*: Overture
Tchaikovsky: *Manfred* Symphony, Op. 58

10 Dec. 1949   Giordano: *Siberia*: Prelude to Act III
Il Re: Dance of the Moor
Puccini: *Manon Lescaut*: Prelude to Act III
Busoni: *Berceuse élégiaque*
Rondo arlecchinesco, with Samuel Gallu, tenor
Respighi: *Roman Festivals*

The Puccini "Prelude" is the same work identified as "Intermezzo" on the broadcast of 2 July 1944.

17 Dec. 1949   Wagner: *Parsifal*: Prelude and Good Friday Spell
Wagner-Toscanini: *Götterdämmerung*: Dawn and Siegfried's
    Rhine Journey
Wagner: *Siegfried*: Siegfried's Death and Funeral Music
    Die Walküre: Ride of the Valkyries

18 Feb. 1950   Cherubini: *Medea*: Overture
Requiem in C Minor

25 Feb. 1950   Brahms: *Variations on a Theme by Haydn*, Op. 56a
Symphony No. 4 in E Minor, Op. 98

4 Mar. 1950   Kabalevsky: *Colas Breugnon*: Overture
Glinka: *Jota aragonesa*
Tchaikovsky: Symphony No. 6 in B Minor, Op. 74,
    "Pathétique"

11 Mar. 1950   Mozart: Symphony No. 40 in G Minor, K. 550
Schubert: Symphony No. 8 in B Minor, D. 759,
    "Unfinished"
Smetana: *The Moldau*

18 Mar. 1950   Dvořák: Symphony No. 9 in E Minor, Op. 95, "From the
    New World"
Dukas: *The Sorcerer's Apprentice*
Wagner: *Die Meistersinger von Nürnberg*: Prelude

25 Mar. 1950   Prokofiev: Symphony No. 1 in D Major, Op. 25,
    "Classical"
Debussy: *Images*: "Ibéria"
Saint-Saëns: *Danse macabre*, Op. 40
R. Strauss: *Don Juan*, Op. 20

1 Apr. 1950   Verdi: *Falstaff*: Act I; Act II, Scene 1; with Giuseppe
    Valdengo (Falstaff), Antonio Madasi (Fenton), Frank
    Guarrera (Ford), Gabor Carelli (Dr. Caius), John
    Carmen Rossi (Bardolph), Norman Scott (Pistola),
    Herva Nelli (Alice), Teresa Stich-Randall (Nanetta),
    Nan Merriman (Meg), Cloe Elmo (Mistress Quickly),
    and the Robert Shaw Chorale

8 Apr. 1950   Verdi: *Falstaff*: Act II (completion); Act III; cast as above
To accommodate the opera, broadcast time was extended by five minutes on 1 April and fifteen minutes on 8 April.

Fourteenth Season (1950–51)

Anything coming after the exceptionally successful NBC Symphony tour of 1950 might have seemed anticlimactic, but the 1950–51 season that followed proved especially frustrating and disappointing for Toscanini. Returning to Italy after two recording sessions in early June, he led the Verdi Requiem at La Scala on 17 June. At about this time the problem with his knee recurred; the condition became painful and was apparently serious. In addition, NBC decided to convert studio 8H to a television studio and gave Toscanini a choice of Carnegie Hall or the Manhattan Center as a new home for the orchestra. The latter, with its hollow resonance and blurred, harsh acoustics, was in some respects worse than 8H, and it was anathema to the conductor. Carnegie Hall was thus his unequivocal preference. When he expressed it to NBC, he was told that the hall, because of scheduling difficulties, was unavailable. Thus, as the summer drew to a close, he was faced not only with a problematic knee that threatened his career but also with the prospect of having to perform—if, indeed, he could—in a hall that he deemed totally unacceptable.

Ultimately NBC secured Carnegie Hall for the broadcasts, but pain led Toscanini to cancel his commitments for the fall. The new season began officially on 23 October 1950, with Fritz Reiner making the first of three consecutive appearances. Jonel Perlea then led two broadcasts and Erich Leinsdorf one, after which Guido Cantelli led the orchestra for the ensuing eight weeks. All of these programs aired on Monday evenings from 10:00 to 11:00 P.M. They were sponsored by Whitehall Pharmaceutical and RCA Victor.

When Toscanini finally returned after the new year, air time was shifted to the old hour of 6:30 to 7:30 P.M. on Saturdays, and the House of Squibb became the sole sponsor of the programs. Because difficulties with his knee remained, Toscanini conducted with a special railing built around the podium. Save for his first appearance—a benefit for the Casa di Riposo—the broadcasts were given before a small audience, which was requested not to applaud, most likely so as to expedite Toscanini's entrance and departure.

Upon his belated return the conductor had planned to lead a series of six concerts, but pain forced his withdrawal after the fourth. His replacements for the two succeeding broadcasts were Bruno Walter and Wilfrid Pelletier. Physical incapacity also limited Toscanini's recordings to a single session on 10 January 1951 devoted to Richard Strauss's *Don Juan*.

27 Jan. 1951   Verdi: Te Deum
                    Requiem, with Herva Nelli, Fedora Barbieri, Giuseppe
                    di Stefano, Cesare Siepi, and the Robert Shaw
                    Chorale
The Te Deum was not broadcast. Ralph Hunter, who prepared the chorus for this performance, told me that after the first full rehearsal Toscanini decided

that the chorus was too small and wanted it augmented by about thirty voices, no easy task on such short notice, especially for a weekend performance during the height of the season. Ultimately the requisite number was found, but this last-minute urgency may well have been one of the factors contributing to the uncommon sloppiness in parts of the performance.

3 Feb. 1951   Beethoven: *The Creatures of Prometheus*, Op. 43: Overture
            Symphony No. 4 in B-flat Major, Op. 60
            Leonore Overture No. 3, Op. 72a

An intermission talk was given on this broadcast by the prominent radio personality John Nesbit, introduced as "the American storyteller." The concert was taped by NBC for delayed broadcast. Unfortunately, a loose connection, causing a ground loop, imposed a hum on the tape, necessitating that low frequencies be filtered in order to make the audio acceptable for broadcast. This filtering deprived the sound of the orchestra of requisite weight and presence.

10 Feb. 1951   Mendelssohn: *A Midsummer Night's Dream*, Op. 21:
             Overture
             Brahms: Symphony No. 2 in D Major, Op. 73

17 Feb. 1951   Debussy: *Prelude to the Afternoon of a Faun*
             Respighi: *The Fountains of Rome*
             Elgar: *Enigma Variations*, Op. 36

Having canceled the two concerts that were to follow this one, Toscanini believed that he might be directing his last performances on this broadcast. As a result, he took special pains in preparing each work, particularly the Debussy, as is attested by rehearsal recordings.

Fifteenth Season (1951–52)

Shortly after he withdrew from the previous season, Toscanini, on the advice of his doctor, tried to strengthen his problematic knee by exercising on a stationary bicycle. Throwing himself into the therapy with characteristic intensity, he overdid it and incurred a minor stroke. Although he recovered quickly, he knew he had received an ominous warning, one that prevented him from fulfilling his hope of conducting staged opera at a Verdi festival in Busseto and from appearing at the opening of the Royal Festival Hall in London. To make things worse, his wife, whose illness had prevented her from coming to New York for the 1950–51 season, had a heart attack in April of 1951, and Toscanini returned immediately thereafter to be with her. On 23 June she died.

The death of his wife and Toscanini's own physical deterioration doubtless contributed to his prevailing depression. Although he had agreed to return to NBC for the 1951–52 season, his emotional condition raised questions about his ability to get through an entire season. As Harvey Sachs noted:

Toscanini arriving in Milan after the 1950–51 NBC Symphony Season. On the left, his daughter Wally; on the right, her daughter Emanuela. *BMG Classics*

Toscanini's grief, insomnia, abstinence from food, and general mental state caused serious worry in his family for several weeks. Then he made a decision: he had long ago promised to make some recordings with the Scala Orchestra, the sale of which would benefit Casa Verdi [Casa di Riposo]. Now he felt that this would be an opportunity—away from the public eye—to see whether he could go on.[36]

Three works by Verdi were recorded—the overture to *I vespri siciliani* and the two familiar preludes from *La traviata*—and although Toscanini rejected the overture for release, it seemed clear that not only was he capable of working, he would be rejuvenated by it.

And so he was. Toscanini returned to New York in September 1951 and between 29 September and 29 October led five recording sessions prior to opening the season on 3 November. In all, he participated in an astonishing (for an eighty-five-year-old man) twenty recording sessions between his initial September effort and 1 April 1952. He also conducted twelve broadcasts during the winter season, four of which were televised, and he led an additional two broadcasts (originally unscheduled) during the summer of 1952. Moreover, he retained sufficient energy for recording sessions shortly after each of those summer programs. In short, after having been despondent, apathetic, and physically unable to work, Toscanini was, in effect, resurrected.

With the exception of three of the telecasts, all the programs remained unsponsored, and all aired from 6:30 to 7:30 P.M. on Saturdays. Guido Cantelli made the greatest number of guest appearances, seven in all, and two each were made by Peter Herman Adler, Massimo Freccia, Milton Katims, and Alexander Hilsberg. Eugene Ormandy and Fritz Reiner each led a single concert.

3 Nov. 1951   Weber: *Euryanthe*: Overture
                   Brahms: Symphony No. 1 in C Minor, Op. 68
This concert was televised, the only one among the four telecasts not to be sponsored. Originally planned for inclusion on this broadcast was the overture to Meyerbeer's *Étoile du nord*. The decision to exclude it was evidently made at the last minute; an uninterrupted dress rehearsal of the performance survives.

10 Nov. 1951   Prokofiev: Symphony No. 1 in D Major, Op. 25,
                   "Classical"
                   Berlioz: *Roméo et Juliette*, Op. 17: Queen Mab Scherzo
                   Beethoven: Symphony No. 7 in A Major, Op. 92
A few serious flaws in execution affect the Beethoven, most notably an exposed wrong note from the horn in the first-movement coda. Originally announced for this program was the Andante con moto from Raff's String Quartet No. 5. It is worth noting that Toscanini, unable to procure the timpani part, wrote it out from memory. After the work was canceled, that handwritten recollection was filed in the NBC library. Some time later, Edwin Bachmann, the orchestra's

principal second violinist, compared Toscanini's recollection to the printed text and discovered only two very minor discrepancies. In his eighty-sixth year, the maestro's photographic memory remained in full focus.

17 Nov. 1951 Tchaikovsky: *The Nutcracker Suite*, Op. 71A
Dvořák: *Symphonic Variations*, Op. 78
Rossini: *Semiramide*: Overture

24 Nov. 1951 Beethoven: Septet for Woodwinds, Horn, and Strings in E-flat Major, Op. 20
Wagner: *Die Meistersinger von Nürnberg*: Prelude
Wagner-Toscanini: *Götterdämmerung*: Dawn and Siegfried's Rhine Journey

22 Dec. 1951 Cherubini: *Anacréon*: Overture
Beethoven: Symphony No. 1 in C Major, Op. 21
Respighi: *The Pines of Rome*
Brahms: Symphony No. 4 in E Minor, Op. 98

The two initial works on this lengthy benefit concert (which raised $28,000 for the Italian Welfare League) were not broadcast.

29 Dec. 1951 Wagner: *Lohengrin*: Prelude
Siegfried: Forest Murmurs
Tristan and Isolde: Prelude and Liebestod
Götterdämmerung: Siegfried's Death and Funeral Music
Die Walküre: Ride of the Valkyries

This concert was televised and sponsored "as a public service" by the Reynolds Metals Company. The well-known actress Helen Hayes gave an intermission talk in support of the Girl Scouts of America.

5 Jan. 1952 Weber: *Der Freischütz*: Overture
Franck: *Psyché*
Rossini: *William Tell*: Passo a sei
Elgar: *Enigma Variations*, Op. 36

12 Jan. 1952 Beethoven: *Leonore* Overture No. 2, Op. 72
Symphony No. 6 in F Major, Op. 68, "Pastoral"

8 Mar. 1952 Kabalevsky: *Colas Breugnon*: Overture
Cherubini: Symphony in D Major
R. Strauss: *Death and Transfiguration*, Op. 24

Toscanini called an extra rehearsal of the Strauss work for a Sunday morning. Many of the musicians resented this unscheduled weekend assignment, but the rehearsal proved to be one of their great experiences in the orchestra.[37]

15 Mar. 1952 Franck: *Rédemption*: Symphonic Interlude
Sibelius: *En Saga*, Op. 9
Debussy: Nocturnes: *Nuages*; *Fêtes*
Rossini: *William Tell*: Overture

This, the third of the season's telecasts, was again sponsored "as a public service" by the Reynolds Metals Company. This "service," it should be noted, did not preclude commercial messages for the company.

22 Mar. 1952   Beethoven: Symphony No. 5 in C Minor, Op. 67
                   Respighi: *The Pines of Rome*

The last of the season's telecasts was again presented " as a public service" under the sponsorship of Reynolds Metals Company. Intermission talks were given by E. Roland Harriman (president of the American Red Cross) and the celebrated actress Katharine Cornell in support of the American Red Cross. An exposed faulty viola entrance in the Fifth Symphony was corrected in the LP, CD, and videotape editions of this performance.

29 Mar. 1952   Beethoven: Symphony No. 1 in C Major, Op. 21
                   Symphony No. 9 in D Minor, Op. 125, with Eileen
                         Farrell, soprano; Nan Merriman, mezzo-soprano;
                         Jan Peerce, tenor; Norman Scott, bass; and the
                         Robert Shaw Chorale

This concert (a benefit in which the First Symphony was not broadcast) raised $64,000 for the Building Fund of the New York Infirmary, at the time the largest amount ever taken in at the Carnegie Hall box office.

In the first movement of the Ninth Symphony, the brass made their initial entrance too quickly, and this exposed flaw at the very outset of the performance apparently caused Toscanini to lose interest and concentration throughout the first two movements. To accommodate the Ninth Symphony, the broadcast began fifteen minutes earlier than usual at 6:15 P.M.

26 July 1952   Thomas: *Mignon*: Overture
                   Liadov: *Kikimora*, Op. 63
                   Wagner: *Siegfried Idyll*
                   Ponchielli: *La Gioconda*: Dance of the Hours
                   Sibelius: *Finlandia*, Op. 26

Nothing indicated Toscanini's rejuvenation better than his last-minute decision to lead this and the following week's broadcast in NBC's *Summer Symphony* series, which normally emanated from the Belasco Theater. When the audience for this concert lined up outside that theater, it was taken by bus to Carnegie Hall to hear this concert led by Toscanini. Richard Korn, who was originally scheduled to conduct at the Belasco, was given an on-the-air promise of another concert later in the summer season, a promise NBC honored.

2 Aug. 1952   Hérold: *Zampa*: Overture
                  Catalani: *La Wally*: Prelude to Act IV
                        Loreley: Dance of the Water Nymphs
                  Bizet-Toscanini: *Carmen*: Suite
                  Humperdinck: *Hänsel und Gretel*: Prelude
                  Weber: *Oberon*: Overture

Sixteenth Season (1952–53)

After his two summer broadcasts of 1952, Toscanini left New York for Italy. On 19 September he appeared for the last time at La Scala, conducting an all-Wagner program. Less than a week later he was off to London to prepare a two-concert Brahms cycle with the Philharmonia Orchestra, a farewell to a favorite city he had not visited since 1939. According to Harvey Sachs, the conductor's fee for each concert was £1800 (about $7000), "the largest sum ever paid to a musician up to that time in Britain."[38] While in England Toscanini met with Sir Laurence Olivier, and the two are said to have discussed, among other things, the differences between Shakespeare's *Othello* and Verdi's *Otello;* that exchange might well have been as worthy of preservation as the finest work of either of the two artists.

With Toscanini in Europe for the remainder of the summer, the NBC Symphony resumed its Belasco Theater programs with guest conductors Massimo Freccia, Frank Miller (the orchestra's principal cellist), Walter Hendl, Richard Korn, Thomas Schippers, Milton Katims, and Jonel Perlea. Toscanini inaugurated the regular winter season on 1 November and directed fourteen broadcasts broken into three series of appearances. Between each, Guido Cantelli was the sole guest conductor, leading eight broadcasts. During these guest appearances, the orchestra was Cantelli's exclusively; the ten recording sessions that Toscanini directed took place during the periods in which he was also leading concerts. Cantelli, incidentally, programmed Britten's *Sinfonia da requiem*, a work then only twelve years old.

In many respects this season stands out among Toscanini's last years. There were, to be sure, occasional signs of age, most evident in slackening tension and increased imprecision. But in addition to producing several fine recordings (one of which, Debussy's *Prelude to the Afternoon of a Faun*, he rejected for release), many of his live performances took on a repose and concentration that had been less evident in the years immediately preceding. Certainly his accounts of Gluck, Mozart, Mussorgsky, Verdi, Debussy, and Wagner stand out, and the season concluded with a major undertaking—a benefit concert featuring a single work, Beethoven's Missa Solemnis. Possibly no one except, perhaps, Toscanini was aware that with the exception of a few works by Wagner, everything in this season's programs was being prepared by the conductor for the last time. All of his broadcasts save the last continued to be aired from 6:30 to 7:30 P.M. on Saturdays, and all took place in Carnegie Hall.

1 Nov. 1952   Brahms: Symphony No. 3 in F Major, Op. 90
Strauss: *Till Eulenspiegel's Merry Pranks*, Op. 28

8 Nov. 1952   Beethoven: Symphony No. 8 in F Major, Op. 93
Wagner: *Tannhäuser:* Overture and Bacchanale
Verdi: *La forza del destino:* Overture

In the printed programs for the previous week's concert, Haydn's Symphony No. 31 was specified for this broadcast. But the decision to substitute the Beethoven Eighth was evidently made fairly early, since Ben Grauer's closing remarks on 1 November specified the Beethoven for this broadcast. Because the concert would otherwise have exceeded its hour's time, it was necessary to scrap the first-movement repeat in the Beethoven, the only one of Toscanini's NBC performances of the work in which this was done. Some of the musicians (or possibly Toscanini) forgot about this, erroneously producing an unwanted first ending at the conclusion of the exposition that, along with other instances of careless execution, scarred the performance.

15 Nov. 1952   Rossini: Sonata No. 3 for Strings
Saint-Saëns: Symphony No. 3 in C Minor, Op. 78, with
Joseph Kahn, piano, and George Crook, organ

The sonata was billed as an American premiere and was a last-minute replacement for the Bach-Respighi Passacaglia and Fugue in C Minor.

22 Nov. 1952   Gluck-Wagner: *Iphigenia in Aulis*: Overture
Gluck: *Orfeo ed Euridice*: Act II, with Nan Merriman
(Orfeo), Barbara Gibson (Euridice), and the Robert
Shaw Chorale, prepared by Ralph Hunter

The chaconne from *Orfeo ed Euridice* was announced on the previous week's broadcast for this program but was replaced by the overture.

10 Jan. 1953   Berlioz: *Roman Carnival* Overture
Tchaikovsky: *Manfred* Symphony, Op. 58

17 Jan. 1953   Beethoven: *Egmont*, Op. 84: Overture
Martucci: Piano Concerto No. 1 in B-flat Minor, Op. 66,
with Mieczyslaw Horszowski

24 Jan. 1953   Haydn: Symphony No. 94 in G Major, "Surprise"
Mussorgsky-Ravel: *Pictures at an Exhibition*

31 Jan. 1953   Schumann: *Manfred*, Op. 115: Overture
Rossini: *William Tell*: Passo a sei
Dvořák: Symphony No. 9 in E Minor, Op. 95, "From the
New World"

The close of the third movement of the Dvořák is marred by an exposed error from the violins.

7 Feb. 1953   Schubert: Symphony No. 9 in C Major, D. 944
Wagner: *Die Meistersinger von Nürnberg*: Prelude

14 Feb. 1953   Debussy: *Images*: "Ibéria"
Prelude to the Afternoon of a Faun
La mer

7 Mar. 1953 Wagner: *Lohengrin*: Prelude
Siegfried Idyll
Siegfried: Siegfried's Death and Funeral Music
Tristan and Isolde: Prelude and Liebestod
Die Walküre: Ride of the Valkyries

14 Mar. 1953 Schubert: Symphony No. 5 in B-flat Major, D. 485
Smetana: *The Moldau*
Respighi: *The Pines of Rome*
This was probably Toscanini's first performance of the Schubert.

21 Mar. 1953 Cherubini: *Anacréon*: Overture
Mozart: Symphony No. 40 in G Minor, K. 550
Tchaikovsky: *Romeo and Juliet*: Fantasy Overture
This broadcast included an appeal by Leroy Lincoln on behalf of the American Red Cross.

28 Mar. 1953 Beethoven: Missa Solemnis, Op. 123, with Lois Marshall, soprano; Nan Merriman, mezzo-soprano; Eugene Conley, tenor; Jerome Hines, bass; and the Robert Shaw Chorale, prepared by Ralph Hunter
This concert, a benefit for the Hospitalized Veterans Music Service, was broadcast in its entirety. Owing to the length of the Missa, it began at 5:45 P.M., forty-five minutes earlier than usual. The organ malfunctioned in the Kyrie and was useless thereafter.

Seventeenth Season (1953–54)

At the conclusion of the previous season, Toscanini remained in his Riverdale home until the beginning of the summer, when he returned to Italy. The NBC Symphony continued in his absence with an extended "summer" series, the first part of which ran through 30 June in Carnegie Hall with guest conductors Milton Katims, Frank Brieff (an NBC Symphony violist and later conductor of the New Haven Symphony), Walter Hendl, and Don Gillis (producer of the NBC Symphony broadcasts) leading programs made up of repertory staples and lighter works. Beginning on 5 July, the broadcasts moved to NBC's studio 6A in Rockefeller Center and aired on Sunday evenings from 5:00 to 6:00 P.M. Also consisting of a mixture of pops and standard repertory, these concerts continued until 20 September, after which the broadcast time reverted to the usual Saturday slot for five weeks until Toscanini's first appearance was to take place.

Toscanini did not appear on 8 November as scheduled, but the reason for his failing to do so may well have gone beyond the official excuse of incapacity. Two opposing pressures must have been exerting themselves on him at the same time. On the one hand, he needed to conduct: "work I must, otherwise life is unbearable,"[39] he had written to his daughter Wally during the 1952–53 season.

Then, too, he must have realized that should he decide to resign from NBC, his departure would almost surely signal the end of the orchestra created for him. Thus it is quite possible that he continued as long as he did not only to satisfy his own needs, but also out of a sense of responsibility to the musicians he deeply respected.

On the other hand, he could not deny time's debilitating effects. Shortly after conducting the previous season's Missa Solemnis he wrote, "I am old, very old [86]. I can stand it no longer [and am] in very bad humor."[40] Then, two months later, in another letter: "I am not well, and no one believes me, the asses, but I am not the same as I was. My eyes have worsened so much that I can no longer find glasses which can help me. My legs and memory fail me. I sleep little and badly and am tormented by tragic, commonplace or fearful dreams. All in all, a poor, unhappy man—and they have forced me to accept another year [1953–54] of concerts. And I, imbecile that I am, and tired of having myself bother, have given in."[41]

This letter makes clear Toscanini's awareness of his need to retire. Alan Shulman was one of several musicians in the orchestra who believed that the conductor's resignation was imposed by NBC, the network having decided that Toscanini and his orchestra were no longer affordable in an age in which broadcasting was increasingly dominated by television.[42] But Harvey Sachs notes: "We know that in the spring of 1953 Toscanini had signed a contract for the following season and then regretted having done so, and that he stated explicitly during the summer that the coming season would be his last."[43]

If Toscanini had any inclination to continue beyond his last year at NBC it may have been nullified when he was about to prepare for two broadcasts devoted to a concert presentation of Verdi's Un ballo in maschera. He had known the work since childhood, but "just before the first rehearsal . . . he could no longer remember the words of the opera."[44] For Toscanini, with his almost freakish photographic memory, such an experience must have been terrifying. Fortunately, his memory returned, and the opera was done. But after the second broadcast Toscanini said: "This is my last opera performance. . . . From now on I'll do what I can: short symphonic concerts and, so far as operas are concerned, overtures at most."[45]

Although this statement suggests Toscanini was undecided about retirement, it does not preclude his having come to realize that a regular seasonal commitment to NBC had become impossible. Sachs's view is that the "full story" of Toscanini's retirement—whether self-imposed or an outgrowth of an NBC fiat—"will never be known." As Sachs notes, Toscanini's daughter Wally spoke with direct simplicity about her father's resignation: "He realized that he was very old and thought it was time to stop."[46]

During this last season, ironically, NBC acquired a sponsor for the series, the Socony Vacuum Oil Company, and commercial messages returned. Ironic, too, was the network's decision to move the programs to the preferred air time of Sunday evenings from 5:30 to 6:30 P.M. With Toscanini "indisposed," Pierre Monteux led the first two programs of the winter series. Toscanini returned on 22 November and, according to some witnesses with whom I have spoken, looked "ashen." He led eleven broadcasts, some of which—considering the extreme pressures of the last season—are astonishing in their control and power. Other, however, clearly bespeak a conductor losing his grip. Guest appearances (aside from Monteux's two) were made almost exclusively by Guido Cantelli, who led eight programs. But Charles Munch conducted on 28 March, filling in for Toscanini, who, possibly owing to the mounting emotional strain of the moment, was unable to appear.

No recording sessions were held for this season, but two months after his last concert, Toscanini returned to the orchestra on 3 and 4 June to remake brief portions of the broadcast of *Aida* and *Ballo*, both of which RCA intended to release. He never conducted again. Alan Shulman spoke of Toscanini at these sessions: "he came in like a house afire. It was incredible, and we said, 'My God, he's a rejuvenated man'."[47] This apparent rejuvenation may well have led Shulman and others in the orchestra to wonder if the lapses and other problems that Toscanini experienced during the season were indeed caused by advancing years or by the knowledge that NBC intended, in effect, to fire him. Surely a memory failure at his last concert must have had some connection to the tension of the moment. But the speculations of Shulman and others do not take into account Toscanini's self-doubt and the growing awareness of failing powers he himself expressed. Given his stature and eminent position, the conductor, had he so wished, most likely could have continued his career, even were it to be more restricted. That he did not do so seems almost certainly to have been a decision of his own.[48]

22 Nov. 1953   Brahms: *Tragic* Overture, Op. 81
                   R. Strauss: *Don Quixote*, Op. 35, with Frank Miller, cello,
                        and Carlton Cooley, viola
There were errors in execution in both of these performances, particularly that of the Strauss.

29 Nov. 1953   Wagner: *Tannhäuser*: Prelude to Act III
                   Berlioz: *Harold in Italy*, Op. 16, with Carlton Cooley, viola
The prelude to Act III of *Tannhäuser* was not identified on the air (as it should have been) as Wagner's original version. See comments for the broadcast of 25 February 1939.

6 Dec. 1953   Beethoven: *Coriolan* Overture, Op. 62
                  Symphony No. 3 in E-flat Major, Op. 55, "Eroica"
The overture is marred by a faulty entrance at its close. At the dress rehearsal for this concert, Toscanini asked the orchestra to repeat the Funeral March of the

"Eroica" after having gone through it in splendid fashion. "Once more," he implored, "just for me." This may well have been a self-indulgence rooted in his knowledge that he would never again be preparing the Beethoven symphony he had probably played more frequently than any other.

13 Dec. 1953   Mussorgsky: *Khovanschina*: Prelude
Franck: *Les éolides*
Weber-Berlioz: *Invitation to the Dance*, Op. 65
Mendelssohn: Symphony No. 5 in D Major, Op. 107, "Reformation"

17 Jan. 1954   Verdi: *Un ballo in maschera*: Act I, with Jan Peerce (Riccardo), Robert Merrill (Renato), Herva Nelli (Amelia), Claramae Turner (Ulrica), Virginia Haskins (Oscar), George Cehanovsky (Silvano), Nicola Moscona (Samuel), Norman Scott (Tom), John Carmen Rossi (Judge and Servant), and the Robert Shaw Chorale

24 Jan. 1954   Verdi: *Un ballo in maschera*: Acts II and III, cast as above
This and the previous week's broadcasts were extended beyond an hour to accommodate the opera. Jan Peerce was a replacement for Jussi Björling, who had to withdraw from the production ten days before the first of the two broadcasts.

28 Feb. 1954   Mendelssohn: Symphony No. 4 in A Major, Op. 90, "Italian"
R. Strauss: *Don Juan*, Op. 20
Weber: *Oberon*: Overture
A brief intermission talk was given by President Dwight D. Eisenhower. The impassioned account of the Strauss is spoiled by a few untidy passages.

7 Mar. 1954   Beethoven: *Leonore* Overture No. 2, Op. 72b
Symphony No. 6 in F Major, Op. 68, "Pastoral"
The "Pastoral" was the first Beethoven symphony Toscanini played at NBC. With this performance, it became the last and the one most frequently programmed exclusively for broadcast. The *Leonore* No. 2 is marred by a glaring gratuitous appoggiatura from the solo trumpet just before the coda.

21 Mar. 1954   Rossini: *The Barber of Seville*: Overture
Tchaikovsky: Symphony No. 6 in B Minor, Op. 74, "Pathétique"
The performance of the Tchaikovsky sounds like a first run-through of an unfamiliar work by a highly skilled ensemble. As one musician in the orchestra said to B. H. Haggin, "He [Toscanini] was all there in the rehearsal, but not at the performance."[49] Doubtless the pressure of imminent retirement was taking its toll.

4 Apr. 1954   Wagner: *Lohengrin*: Prelude
                      Siegfried: Forest Murmurs
                      Wagner-Toscanini: *Götterdämmerung*: Dawn and Siegfried's
                          Rhine Journey
                      Tannhäuser: Overture and Bacchanale
                      Die Meistersinger von Nürnberg: Prelude

So much has been written about this last concert that anything further might seem redundant. Still, some issues require clarification. Contrary to Samuel Chotzinoff's comments, Toscanini's loss of concentration and possible memory lapse during the *Tannhäuser* Bacchanale did not result in the orchestra's having "stopped playing and the house [being] engulfed in darkness."[50] As a stereophonic tape of the concert, recorded in the hall rather than from a broadcast transmission, makes clear, the orchestra continued playing when Toscanini momentarily stopped conducting. Some critics, in fact, evidently not that familiar with the Bacchanale, did not even mention the few moments of resulting ensemble disarray. NBC's recording of the broadcast preserves Ben Grauer's interruption of the Bacchanale, which cited "technical difficulties" that ostensibly required Toscanini's recording of the Brahms First Symphony to be suddenly substituted for the live performance. This substitution was prompted by Guido Cantelli, who, along with Chotzinoff, was in the control room and became fearful that Toscanini might not be able to continue.

When Toscanini's baton stopped during the Bacchanale, the principal cellist, Frank Miller, picked up the beat, but the conductor quickly recovered and finished the piece. At its conclusion, he began to leave the podium but was reminded that the *Meistersinger* prelude remained to be played. Conducting swiftly (yet not as blandly as in his 1950 broadcast of the work), he finished the program. As the last C major chords of the prelude resounded, he dropped his baton and walked off the stage, never again to appear before a live audience. Applause continued for several minutes, Grauer finally noting: "The audience attendant, the orchestra silent, we hope for one more reappearance of Maestro Toscanini." With these words the broadcast concluded.

Immediately following its transmission, an NBC news "bulletin" announced Toscanini's retirement. At the conductor's request, Grauer said nothing on the air about the retirement, although everyone in Carnegie Hall had been given a copy of the resignation Toscanini had sent David Sarnoff on 25 March. Sarnoff accepted it, but a copy of Toscanini's letter in the NBC files is marked "not for release until April 4."

It is hardly surprising that all of the performances on this program, given the strain of the moment, fell short of Toscanini's best. Indeed, it is remarkable that some of them remain impressive. As Toscanini himself said later that evening, "I conducted as if it had been a dream. It almost seemed to me that I wasn't there."[51]

Toscanini had originally planned for this concert to consist exclusively of the Brahms *German Requiem*, but as the season progressed, he realized that he was not up to preparing it. Thus this still-longer-than-usual Wagner program (running from 6:15 to 7:30 P.M.) was substituted.

Tension mounted at the final rehearsal, with Toscanini erroneously blaming the timpanist, Karl Glassman, for an incorrect entrance in the Rhine Journey, an outburst that caused the rehearsal to be cut short. And the conductor's discomfort at the concert is suggested by his having launched into Forest Murmurs before Grauer's introductory comments were finished. For anyone who cares about Toscanini—and certainly for the conductor himself—this concert was not so much a "dream" as a nightmare.

Epilogue (1954–63)

For nine years after Toscanini's retirement, the NBC Symphony struggled to maintain itself as an independent ensemble. Rechristened the Symphony of the Air (the name taken from the subtitle of the NBC Symphony broadcasts when sponsored by General Motors), the orchestra gave its initial concert on 27 October 1954 in Carnegie Hall. I was present at this extraordinary event.[52] Most of the Toscanini sonority and discipline were still evident, but the maestro's retirement was dramatized by an empty podium: the conductorless orchestra was "led" with the briefest and fewest possible signals from the concertmaster, Daniel Guilet.

As perhaps intended, the event made all too painfully clear the need for a governing baton. Indeed, this concert, made up of staples from Toscanini's repertory, indirectly revealed one of the most striking but (as Jacques Barzun has noted) least acknowledged aspect of his style—rhythmic subtlety and flexibility. If all the performances bore something of the conductor's stamp, each at the same time mummified it, rhythmic rigor mortis having imposed a mechanical deadness on the characteristic Toscanini vitality.

The orchestra had cabled Toscanini in Italy, inviting him to return as a guest conductor or, if possible, in a more involved fashion, but he was unable to accept. Increasing numbers of key personnel left the ensemble, the first-desk players in particular accepting offers from major orchestras. Despite one successful tour, the Symphony of the Air never became what might be termed a full-time group, and its ranks were increasingly depleted by the musicians' need for regular employment. As a result, its survival became more and more tenuous. That the group, which billed itself "the orchestra that refused to die," managed —as an increasingly hollow shell of what it once was—to survive for nine years seems, in retrospect, miraculous.[53]

3

THE NBC REPERTORY

In a review of Toscanini recordings reissued in 1990, Joseph McLellan noted that during the conductor's lifetime some critics began to complain that he played everything "the same way." McLellan went on to claim that such an opinion may have been "an exaggeration, but one rooted in reality."[1] At the core of this specious judgment is an ignorance that has colored a good deal of Toscanini criticism. Journalists have been ready to generalize about the conductor without having considered all his work. Such generalizations miss a crucial point that is often ignored, especially by critics hostile to the conductor: that few of his studio recordings exemplify his "typical" view of a given work for the simple reason that—more often than not—he had no such view.

In this lies the source of the importance of the performances discussed in this chapter. Time and again they reveal a recreative artist whose interpretive vision was constantly in flux. Toscanini's many accounts of a given work may share some features, but one is almost never a clone of another. Such differences suggest how often the maestro was rethinking and revising his conception of a score.

This endless reevaluation, this "relentless self-dissatisfaction," as the conductor's biographer Harvey Sachs has so aptly termed it, is strikingly underscored by the performances considered in this chapter. Studying them brings to mind two obvious but sometimes overlooked issues. The first relates to the ambiguity central to all great art. Surely if a piece of music had only one meaning and there were only one correct way to interpret it, the composition would fail to fascinate, for the same underlying reasons that *King Lear* or *Moby-Dick* defies a single "correct" interpretation. When this is forgotten, another key issue may be passed over: that a musician's commercially released recording will, in most instances, not exemplify a fixed conception of the work at hand for the simple reason that the sensitive, intelligent performer, aware of great music's multileveled ambiguity, knows the impossibility of having such a conception.

The phonograph has provided ample evidence of this point. Wilhelm Furtwängler's three studio recordings of Beethoven's Fifth Symphony, for example, differ from each other in many ways. And his preserved concert accounts of the work uncover even more differences. A great number of live performances given by celebrated musicians make clear that their best work was not always done in the recording studio. With Toscanini, the differences between studio recording and live performance are often especially marked. Thus, to examine his broadcast performances, despite the duplication of repertory they often involve, is neither pointless nor redundant. Quite the contrary, they serve as a reminder of the discoveries to be gleaned in studying and restudying a masterpiece.

Then there are works of which Toscanini approved no studio recording or broadcast performance for release. These are especially valuable for enriching his profile. Some of these works, to be sure, are ephemera, such as Luigi Mancinelli's "Flight of the Lovers" or grander but nonetheless minor scores such as the symphonies of Giuseppi Martucci. Others, however, include major compositions such as the Brahms *German Requiem* or, as in the case of the overture to Meyerbeer's *Dinorah*, a cogent example of an evanescent tradition.

For his time, Toscanini recorded extensively: his official discography totals roughly 125 hours of music. The completion of RCA's eighty-two-CD *Toscanini Collection* in 1992 marked the first occasion all of his recordings for that company (which includes every one he made with the NBC Symphony) were available simultaneously. That collection (discussed in Appendix 8) should stand for some time as a central point of reference providing important glosses on his live performances, which in turn often lead one to view the studio products in a new light.

The material in this chapter is organized alphabetically by composer. Dates of broadcast performances are given so that the frequency with which Toscanini prepared a given work can be readily ascertained. Also provided are the catalog numbers and recording dates (the latter in boldface type) for those works that are part of RCA's *Toscanini Collection*. Included, too, are the few pieces that Toscanini recorded with the NBC Symphony but never prepared for broadcast. For clarity, I have divided the listings of repertory under each composer's heading into three categories: (1) "unissued repertory," comprisisng works not represented in Toscanini's "official" discography that have never been issued in any commercial form; (2) "unofficially issued repertory," comprising broadcasts never sanctioned for release by Toscanini or his heirs of works absent from his official discography; and (3) "officially issued repertory," comprising works for which a performance approved by Toscanini or members of his family has been issued. All of RCA's Toscanini Collection falls into this last category. ("Unofficial" releases that involve scores for which Toscanini is represented by an "official" one are cited in Appendix 8.) Because, as noted in chapter 2, the unofficial items are often produced in very small numbers and have, in addition to their poor distribution, a limited shelf life, I have not cited record numbers for them in this chapter. The best and most widely circulated items among them are identified in Appendix 8.[2]

Atterberg, Kurt (1887–1974)

Unofficially Issued Repertory
Symphony No. 6 in C Major, Op. 31 (21 Nov. 1943)

Although a prolific composer, Kurt Atterberg was hardly known outside his native Sweden; the brief international attention he gained was the result of his having won the Schubert Prize in 1928 for this symphony. Sponsored by England's Columbia Graphophone Company, the prize was originally to be given for completing Schubert's "Unfinished" Symphony. But many felt that this made no more sense than putting arms on the Venus di Milo, and so an original composition was sought as a way of honoring the centennial of Schubert's death. The composer of the winning score was to receive $10,000, and the work itself would be recorded.

For years it was assumed that Atterberg's prizewinning work was a hoax. It allegedly contained deliberate borrowings from several composers, some of whom were on the prize-determining jury. In an interview with John W. Freeman, Atterberg made clear that no hoax was intended or carried out. The article containing that interview also relates how Toscanini came to the music:

> One day in the spring of 1943 during a visit from Toscanini (occasioned by his having rented my parents' house [Wave Hill] for several years . . .) the Maestro spotted the score [of the Atterberg Sixth Symphony] artfully laid out on the piano and wanted to know what it was. I asked if he remembered the critical ruckus over the Schubert Prize, and his reply was typical: "Never mind all that nonsense, is the music any good?" After a few minutes scrutinizing he asked to borrow it. The following fall, when I had begun to wonder how to retrieve the score tactfully, a telegram at boarding school announced that Toscanini was going to perform the symphony.

Eighteen years after that performance, Atterberg finally had an opportunity to hear it when Freeman brought him a tape from Toscanini's son, Walter. The composer's response was enthusiastic: "an excellent performance—clear and exactly in the tempos as I like to hear it."[3]

Freeman also told me that at the time Toscanini was studying the score, he listened to the recording of the work made by Sir Thomas Beecham and felt the tempos were wrong. Toscanini tried to obtain the only other recording of the piece, one made by the Berlin Philharmonic under Atterberg's direction, but no copy of what was then a very rare set was to be found in New York. With Atterberg's own performance requiring one fewer 78 rpm disc than Beecham's, it seems probable that the composer's tempos were faster than that conductor's and thus possibly closer to Toscanini's. He was most likely drawn to the work by its craftsmanship, economy, and masterful orchestration, traits emphasized in the conductor's animated, carefully shaped reading.

Bach, Johann Sebastian (1685–1750)

Unofficially Issued Repertory

Brandenburg Concerto No. 2 in F Major, BWV 1047 (29 Oct. 1938)
Passacaglia and Fugue in C Minor, BWB 582, orch. Respighi (14 Oct. 1939, 22 Nov. 1947)
Suite for Orchestra No. 3 in D Major, BWV 1068 (22 Nov. 1947)
St. Matthew Passion, BWV 244: "Wir setzen uns mit Tränen nieder" (sung in English) (1 Apr. 1945)

Officially Issued Repertory

Suite for Orchestra No. 3 in D Major, BWV 1068: Air (1 Apr. 1942); RCA 60308 **(8 Apr. 1946)**

These works make up but a tiny fraction of Toscanini's repertory. Yet owing to their controversial and starkly contrasting interpretive styles, they reveal a good deal about performance practices of the period and ways in which he departed from some of them.

The great C Minor Passacaglia receives the kind of big-orchestra inflation in this Respighi arrangement that typified the bloated Bach of Leopold Stokowski and Serge Koussevitzky, among many conductors of the period. But Toscanini brings greater rhythmic steadiness to Bach than does Stokowski, with a well-defined bass strengthened in its reiterations by a firmly maintained tempo. Both broadcast accounts, if overblown in terms of sonority, are highly structured and build to a mighty climax.

In overall performance style, the Second Brandenburg is utterly different: the orchestra is small, a harpsichord is clearly audible, and the texture is exceptionally well defined, with tempos—typical of today's authentically styled presentations—lively in outer movements and with a middle (slow) movement that is never permitted to drag. This is a far cry from the Brandenburg No. 2 recorded a decade earlier by Stokowski with members of the Philadelphia Orchestra. There, tempos are considerably slower, and the overall sonority is muddled with textures made all the more colorless by a solo trumpet transposed down an octave. Toscanini, to be sure, was not always the purist either. When he performed the work in 1936 with the New York Philharmonic, the difficulty of the trumpet part led him to have it played on an E-flat clarinet. And in this NBC presentation, the trumpeter, Bernard Baker, was permitted to transpose a few passages, mostly down an octave, but on one occasion at the work's close, down a fourth, this latter practice breaking Bach's melodic line and the pointed effect of the high F at the end of the piece. Still, for its time, this is a remarkably stylish, if far from perfectly executed, performance—a harbinger of the kind that became relatively common two decades later, but one that was rarely given by symphonic conductors in the late 1930s.

The same holds true for the only NBC presentation that Toscanini gave of the Third Orchestral Suite and the closing chorus from the *St. Matthew Passion*. In the latter, textures are transparent and the bass line clear without being excessively weighty. And the tempo, if not quite so quick as that employed by today's purveyors of "authenticity," is free of the lugubrious, dirgelike breadth favored by some of Toscanini's peers.

In the suite, Toscanini's tempos for the dances are animated, his pacing of the Air in all of his performances of it lacking even a hint of sentimentality and having, again, a light yet well-defined bass line. But what is most interesting is his treatment of the French overture with which the work opens. Today, of course, it is played even by symphony orchestras with the baroque practice of double-dotting or at least overdotting its dotted configurations. In 1947 such practices, if familiar to scholars, were not in vogue. Yet Toscanini's bracing tempo for the movement (played with all its repeats ignored) suggests he understood the need to inflect it with the forward thrust that extended dotted values provides. As in the Second Brandenburg, a small orchestra is used, and a harpsichord is audible. In the main, Toscanini's Bach shows the conductor straddling two worlds: on the one hand, he reflected nineteenth-century traditions, but on the other, he recognized when they needed to be swept away.

Barber, Samuel (1910–81)

Unissued Repertory
Essay No. 1 for Orchestra (5 Nov. 1938, 24 Jan. 1942)

Officially Issued Repertory
Adagio for Strings (5 Nov. 1938, 14 May 1940, 13 Dec. 1941): RCA CD
        60307 **(19 Mar. 1942)**

The two performances of the *Essay No. 1 for Orchestra* are almost identical: lean in sonority, aptly austere, with the music's contrapuntal sections bound together by a firmly maintained pulse. The later of the two accounts seems more colorful and slightly better balanced, but this is probably an illusion created by its superior recording. At the 1938 performance, a world premiere, Barber was called to the stage twice. The four accounts of the *Adagio for Strings* are remarkably similar. Toscanini was especially responsive to music of this character, taming its potential lushness while highlighting its melodic richness without permitting the piece to cloy.

Bazzini, Antonio (1818–97)

Unissued Repertory

Saul: Overture (14 Jan. 1939)

Bazzini, one of Puccini's teachers, composed only one opera; this overture is a concert piece inspired by a popular play by the Italian tragedian Count Vittorio Alfieri (1749–1803). When Mussolini inaugurated his anti-Semitic policies, *Saul* —which dealt with the king's unification of the Hebrew nation—was banned. Toscanini's NBC performance of the overture was, at least in part, a political statement. But he also must have admired the work, as it entered his repertory well before Mussolini's noxious policies were executed. The overture had its premiere in London in 1877. It is a thoroughly professional score of no great imagination, one that might well pass for second-rate Verdi. Toscanini's chiseled, forward-pressing reading conveys a unity that might be wanting in a less tautly organized performance.

Beethoven, Ludwig von (1770–1827)

Unofficially Issued Repertory

The Creatures of Prometheus, Op. 43: Adagio and Allegretto (25 Nov. 1939, 5 Mar. 1944, 29 Oct. 1944, 16 Mar. 1947, 19 Mar. 1949)
Fantasia in C Minor for Piano, Chorus, and Orchestra, Op. 80, "Choral Fantasy" (2 Dec. 1939)
String Quartet in C Major, Op. 59 No. 3: Finale (26 Nov. 1944)
String Quartet in B-flat Major, Op. 130: Cavatina (26 Nov. 1944)

Officially Issued Repertory

Piano Concertos:
  No. 1 in C Major, Op. 15 (12 Nov. 1944): RCA 60268 (**9 Aug. 1945**)
  No. 3 in C Minor, Op. 37 (29 Oct. 1944, 24 Nov. 1946): RCA 60261 (broadcast of **29 Oct. 1944**)
  No. 4 in G Major, Op. 58 (26 Nov. 1944): RCA 60268 (broadcast of **26 Nov. 1944)**
Violin Concerto in D Major, Op. 61, with Jascha Heifetz (no broadcast performance): RCA CD 60261 (**11 Mar. 1940)**
Fidelio, Op. 72 (Act I, 10 Dec. 1944; Act II, 17 Dec. 1944): RCA 60273, 2 CDs (includes **10** and **17 Dec. 1944**, with the exception of Leonore's Act I "Abscheulicher" and "Komm Hoffnung," which were drawn from a recording session of **14 June 1945**).
Missa Solemnis (18 Dec. 1940, 28 Mar. 1953): RCA 60272; 2 CDs **(30 Mar. 1953, 31 Mar. 1953, 2 Apr. 1953)**
Overtures:
  Consecration of the House, Op. 124 (16 Mar. 1947, 25 Oct. 1947, 19 Mar. 1949): RCA 60267 **(16 Dec. 1947)**

Coriolan, Op. 62 (12 Nov. 1938, 11 Nov. 1939, 26 Nov. 1944, 24 Nov. 1946, 19 Feb. 1949, 6 Dec. 1953): RCA 60267 **(1 June 1945)**

The Creatures of Prometheus, Op. 43 (5 Mar. 1944, 3 Feb. 1951): RCA 60267 **(18 Dec. 1944)**

Egmont, Op. 84 (18 Nov. 1939, 14 May 1940, 19 Nov. 1944, 17 Jan. 1953): RCA 60267 (from broadcast of **18 Nov. 1939)**, RCA 60270 **(19 Jan. 1953)**

Fidelio, Op. 72b (28 Oct. 1939, 29 Oct. 1944). The only recording is that drawn from the broadcast of the complete opera cited above.

Leonore No. 1, Op. 138 (25 Nov. 1939, 29 Oct. 1944). No RCA–NBC Symphony recording was made; see Appendix 8.

Leonore No. 2 (25 Nov. 1939, 19 Nov. 1944, 12 Jan. 1952, 7 Mar. 1954): RCA 60267 (from broadcast of **25 Nov. 1939)**

Leonore No. 3, Op. 72a (4 Nov. 1939; 17 Dec. 1944, in *Fidelio*; 6 Mar. 1948, 3 Feb. 1951): RCA 60255 (from broadcast of **4 Nov. 1939)**, RCA 60267 **(1 June 1945)**

String Quartet in F Major, Op. 135: Lento and Vivace (1 Jan. 1938, 25 Nov. 1939, 12 Nov. 1944, 25 Oct. 1947): RCA 60267 **(8 Mar. 1938)**

Septet for Woodwinds, Horn, and Strings in E-flat Major, Op. 20 (18 Nov. 1939; 6 Dec. 1941; 3 Dec. 1944, 1st, 4th, and 6th movements only; 24 Nov. 1951): RCA 60270 **(26 Nov. 1951)**

Symphonies:

No. 1 in C Major, Op. 21 (28 Oct. 1939, 11 Apr. 1943, 1 Sept. 1947): RCA 60252 **(21 Dec. 1951)**

No. 2 in D Major, Op. 36 (4 Nov. 1939, 3 Dec. 1944, 5 Nov. 1949): RCA 60253 **(7 Nov. 1949** and **5 Oct. 1951)**

No. 3 in E-flat Major, Op. 55, "Eroica" (3 Dec. 1938, 28 Oct. 1939, 5 Nov. 1944, 1 Sept. 1945, 19 Feb. 1949, 26 Nov. 1949, 6 Dec. 1953): RCA 60269 (broadcast of **28 Oct. 1939)**; RCA 60252 (broadcasts of **28 Nov.** and **5 Dec. 1949)**; RCA 60271 (broadcast of **6 Jan. 1953)**

No. 4 in B-flat Major, Op. 60 (4 Nov. 1939, 3 Feb. 1951): RCA 60254 (broadcast of **3 Feb. 1951)**

No. 5 in C Minor, Op. 67 (22 Oct. 1938; 11 Nov. 1939; 18 Apr. 1944, possibly not broadcast; 18 May 1945; 22 Mar. 1952; 1st movement only 9 Sept. 1943): RCA 60270 **(27 Feb.** and **1 Mar. 1939)**; RCA 60255 (broadcast of **22 Mar. 1952)**

No. 6 in F Major, Op. 68, "Pastoral" (8 Jan. 1938, 11 Nov. 1939, 12 Apr. 1941, 5 Mar. 1944, 16 Mar. 1947, 19 Mar. 1949, 12 Jan. 1952, 7 Mar. 1954): RCA 60254 **(14 Jan. 1952**, with several portions drawn from the broadcast of **12 Jan. 1952)**

No. 7 in A Major, Op. 92 (18 Nov. 1939, 19 Nov. 1944, 25 Oct. 1947, 10 Nov. 1951): RCA 60253 **(9 Nov. 1951**, with several portions drawn from the broadcast of **10 Nov. 1951)**

No. 8 in F Major, Op. 93 (28 Jan. 1939, 25 Nov. 1939, 31 Oct. 1943,

22 Oct. 1944, 8 Nov. 1952): RCA 60269 (**17 Apr. 1939**); RCA
60255 (**10 Nov. 1952**)

No. 9 in D Minor, Op. 125 (6 Feb. 1938, 2 Dec. 1939, 3 Apr. 1948,
29 Feb. 1952): RCA 60256 (**31 Mar.** and **1 Apr. 1952**)

With the possible exception of Verdi, no other composer inspired the passion
Beethoven ignited in Toscanini. Throughout the conductor's career, his music
remained at the core of Toscanini's repertory. The few works not represented
in his official discography command more than passing interest.

The Adagio and Allegretto from Beethoven's only ballet, *The Creatures of
Prometheus*, comprise the most trivial music by the composer that Toscanini ever
programmed. Indeed, one wonders why he played it with such relative frequency. Perhaps it had something to do with these excerpts being the only
music in all of Beethoven's output to call for a harp. Interestingly, too, three of
the five performances occurred on broadcasts that featured the composer's "Pastoral" Symphony.

The Choral Fantasy is another matter. It is, of course, an important work,
not only because it has some musical merit, but also as an effort that was, most
likely, a trial run for the finale of the Ninth Symphony. At the time Toscanini
gave his only NBC performance of the fantasy, pairing it on the program with
the Ninth, it was not nearly so well known as it is today. No recording had
been made in the 78 rpm era, and a lack of familiarity may have led one reviewer
of the performance to claim that the pianist (Ania Dorfmann) "played not only
with admirable spirit and feeling, but almost as if M. Toscanini himself had
guided and controlled her fingers."[4] At best, however, the performance is ragged
and uneven, pianist and conductor sometimes not together, with Dorfmann
smearing passages, perhaps as a result of Toscanini's tempos sometimes being too
fast to permit clean articulation. Certainly the nervous intensity of some of the
pacing neutralizes the music's improvisational charm. This fault notwithstanding, Toscanini's shaping of a few of the work's weaker moments lends it a point
and expressivity rarely encountered in other performances.

With the concertos the discrepancy between commercially released recordings and concert performances is minimal for the simple reason that of the three
commercially released piano concertos, those of Nos. 3 and 4 are taken from
broadcasts; in the case of the violin concerto, no broadcast performance took
place. But there is a discrepancy between all of RCA's extended-play editions
of the violin concerto and its original 78 rpm release. All, to be sure, suffer from
the cramped, dry acoustic of studio 8H. Nevertheless, the original 78s have a
fullness and presence that subsequent editions never duplicated. With the loss of
that presence comes a parallel loss of subtlety, rhythmic inflection, and dynamic
gradation, all less apparent in the extended-play transfers than in the original
discs. Still, there is no denying the continuity and freedom from affectation that
distinguishes Toscanini's collaboration with Heifetz, and the technical wizardry

of the violinist himself. From his treacherously exposed entrance in octaves, one never doubts his sureness of intonation, the uncloying richness of his tone, and his firm grasp of line and structure.

In the First Piano Concerto, one finds marked differences between the performance Toscanini and Dorfmann recorded in August 1945 and their broadcast collaboration of the previous November. Although neither displays the color, inflection, and wit that the finest pianists have brought to the music, the studio effort sounds bland and glib, conductor and pianist performing as if they wanted to get through the piece as expeditiously as possible. By contrast, their work on the broadcast is far more expansive and nuanced, especially in the more broadly paced opening movement, where Dorfmann plays a relatively unfamiliar (and unstylish) cadenza by Reineke rather than the well-known third of three cadenzas composed by Beethoven that she favored in the subsequent recording.

For many years the partnership with Artur Rubinstein in the Third Piano Concerto came under fire, in part because of the dreadful sound of the original 78s and of their subsequent LP transfer. But with sonically superior NBC acetates having been used for the CD edition, the performance becomes more attractive.

Rubinstein's recollection of the rehearsals for the broadcast is revealing. It has often been claimed—with some justification—that Toscanini was averse to performing concertos and did so only when he could exert complete authority over the performance. Rubinstein's experience with the conductor, however, suggests something different. After some unsatisfactory run-throughs in which pianist and conductor were seemingly at odds about several details, Toscanini turned to Rubinstein and asked, "Would you kindly repeat the first movement?" A skeptical Rubinstein agreed, and as the pianist put it, "a miracle happened":

> The tempo was right this time and the tutti sounded with all the nuances required. Toscanini did not miss one tiny detail. He was right there, and we finished every phrase beautifully together. He respected all my dynamics, held up the orchestra where I made the tiniest rubato, came in after the cadenza on the dot, and we finished the movement with a flourish. The second movement went smoothly . . . because the music is a wonderful dialogue between the piano and the orchestra. The third movement was worked out very professionally and with bravura by the Maestro.[5]

Two often-overlooked qualities of Toscanini as an accompanist emerge here: flexibility and rapidity in assimilating a soloist's conception. Moreover, when he found that conception to be musical, he would go along with it, even when it differed from his own. It is likely that Toscanini's collaboration with Myra Hess in the same work on the NBC broadcast two years later comes closer to his view, especially in the first movement, which is taken at a quicker tempo. One senses Hess working hard to keep up, but she manages to stay with the conductor, the part-exchanges between piano and orchestra emerging with welcome clarity. Moreover, Hess projects the slow movement with a sustained breadth that makes the earlier Rubinstein account seem comparatively superficial.

The broadcast performance of the Fourth Concerto with Rudolf Serkin lacks the delicacy and repose that he and Toscanini produced in 1936 when Serkin was a soloist with the New York Philharmonic (his American debut with an orchestra), a performance preserved in an air check of an AM broadcast and once available from the old Toscanini Society on LP.

Fidelio entered Toscanini's repertory relatively late, his first performance of the opera having been given in 1927 at La Scala. The RCA recording preserves nearly all of the two broadcasts that comprised an unstaged performance shorn of virtually all dialogue. Aside from the two substitutions cited in the headnote for this entry, RCA also substituted a 1945 studio recording of the *Leonore* No. 3 for the 1944 broadcast account in the LP editions of the complete opera that appeared about a year after its initial release in the mid-1950s. With the reissue of the opera on compact disc, the 1944 *Leonore* has been restored. It is a less tidy, less well recorded reading, but one that is more rhetorical and expressive.

The performance of the E major *Fidelio* Overture from the 10 December broadcast is far more matter-of-fact than the account from Toscanini's 1939 Beethoven cycle, which boasts a wider parameter of tempos, greater breadth in its sustained introduction, and an overpowering climax not matched in 1944. Indeed, it is such differences that feed speculation that this concert presentation may have differed from a staged *Fidelio* that Toscanini led at the Salzburg Festival in 1935, a production some have hailed as the opera performance of the century. Unlike Toscanini's other Salzburg productions, this one is not preserved on an in-house recording, all that has apparently survived of it being a wretched-sounding shortwave air check of a good portion of the first act. Comparing that air check to the NBC production, Harvey Sachs notes:

> It is quite unlike the concert version; the pacing is generally broader . . . the singing is better, and the playing does not have the tenseness which the NBC betrays; but above all else there is a sustained, monumental dramatic power (no doubt helped by the fact that it comes directly from the theater) which one experiences with astonishment.[6]

It seems safe to say that despite many fine things in the 1944 broadcasts, they may not exemplify Toscanini's best efforts with a work that he had come to love deeply.

The Missa Solemnis came even later than *Fidelio* to Toscanini's repertory, his first performance being with the New York Philharmonic in 1934. Thereafter it was more or less a staple in that repertory: he led it with the Vienna Philharmonic in 1937, with the BBC Symphony in 1939, and with the New York Philharmonic in 1935 and 1942. In short, in a twenty-year span between Toscanini's first performance and his retirement, he prepared the work seven times for concerts, crowning them with a recording made shortly after the second NBC broadcast of the score. When one considers how rarely the Missa is mounted, such frequent performance seems extraordinary. Perhaps he came to share the view expressed by Beethoven, who called it "my greatest composition." Owing to especially relevant features, the three NBC accounts and that of 1935 with the New York Philharmonic are discussed in chapter 4.

Of the nine Beethoven overtures that Toscanini performed, only that of *King Stephan* was excluded from his NBC programs. Among the other eight, four—*The Creatures of Prometheus, Egmont,* and *Leonore* Nos. 2 and 3—gained RCA releases typical of Toscanini's best work. All save *Prometheus* comprise accounts recorded during the conductor's 1939 Beethoven cycle. As originally issued on 78 rpm discs, those 1939 performances were mummified by a bass-deficient exaggeration of the dry acoustics of studio 8H. Indeed, all three were so technically dreadful that none was issued in the United States, their initial release being restricted to English HMV discs. Since 1992, however, the performances can be heard to much better advantage in RCA's *Toscanini Collection,* where, save for the *Egmont* Overture, the sonically superior NBC reference discs have replaced the inferior RCA recordings of the concerts as a source.

Among the four other Beethoven overtures that Toscanini turned to at NBC, *Consecration of the House* deserves special comment, mainly because it owes to him in part its modern popularity. For some inexplicable reason, the work was relatively ignored during the first half of the twentieth century. Only two recordings (Felix Weingartner's and Arthur Fiedler's) appeared before Toscanini's, and such widely admired Beethoven interpreters as Wilhelm Furt-wängler and Bruno Walter evidently never turned to it. In 1947, when the work entered Toscanini's repertory, his tempo for the main fugal section seemed uncommonly fast when judged against the two available recordings. Subsequently, however, many conductors have adopted a pace close or equal to his.

Toscanini's most rhythmically flexible, tightly controlled, and dramatically potent accounts of the *Leonore* No. 1 and *Fidelio* Overtures comprise his first NBC broadcasts of each, both available in unofficial releases. Conversely, his most convincing account of *Coriolan* is that of his last season. Among all the Beethoven overtures, he may have found this one the most problematic. As he once noted, "I have never succeeded in playing it as I felt it."[7] Typical of his willingness to face a challenge, he programmed it more frequently than any other Beethoven overture during his NBC tenure. What sets his last performance of the work apart from all its predecessors is a slightly broader tempo that permits better integration of the striking unspecified rallentando that Toscanini imposed at corresponding points of the exposition and recapitulation—a rhythmic distension more redolent of Willem Mengelberg. Here one feels that, for the first time, the conductor may have come close to playing the work as "he felt it."

The practice of performing quartet movements with a string orchestra supported by double basses was fairly common in Toscanini's day. Some conductors, notably Dimitri Mitropoulos, even directed entire quartets with a symphony orchestra's strings. (Influenced in part by Mitropoulos, Leonard Bernstein, in the mid-1970s, performed and recorded in their entirety Beethoven's quartets Opp. 131 and 135 with members of the Vienna Philharmonic.)

Toscanini loved the Beethoven quartets, especially Op. 59 No. 3 and the last ones (Opp. 127, 130, 131, 132, and 135). It was the Op. 59 No. 3 that four members of the NBC Symphony played for him at the Villa Pauline two weeks before his death. His broadcast of its fugal finale must have struck many as unusually quick. Yet more recently ensembles such as the New Music and Juilliard Quartets have favored a similar tempo, as did the Busch Quartet in Toscanini's day. The Cavatina from Op. 130 received a performance of touching directness and apt simplicity, free of exaggeration or mannerism.

Toscanini's interest in the Beethoven quartets delighted the NBC string players, as it gave them an opportunity to perform familiar fare under a brand of direction they had never previously experienced. The violinist Joseph Gingold spoke of the matter:

> I remember in those first few weeks [of the 1937–38 season] a wonderful experience in the two movement of Beethoven's Quartet Op. 135, which Toscanini played with a string orchestra and in which I've never heard any quartet approach him. The way he worked out every detail in the Largo [Lento] and the fire in the Scherzo. And those complicated string crossings, that he worked out with the violins alone.[8]

Gingold might have added that the sharply contrasted dynamics of the Vivace are clarified with a stark abruptness rarely achieved by string quartets. Among all five of Toscanini's surviving performances, the Lento in the studio recording stands alone in its exceptional breadth, lending the movement an almost mystical stasis.

When asked why he conducted Beethoven's Septet, Toscanini said that it was the first score he bought with his own money and that its balances never seemed right to him in the original version. The first and second broadcasts of the work are studies in contrast, the earlier one relaxed and infused with frequent application of portamento, the later one more rapid, rhythmically stricter, and purged of portamento. When Toscanini returned to the work for the last time (in 1951 for a broadcast and subsequent recording), he adhered in the main to the tempos in his stricter account but modified them with reversions to some of the portamento and flexibility of his first NBC presentation.

Toscanini at his Riverdale home, the Villa Pauline, a few weeks before he died. On the left is the NBC Symphony's second concertmaster, Daniel Guilet; on the right, Metropolitan Opera conductor Wilfrid Pelletier. Another NBC Symphony member, the violist Emanuel Vardi, is between Guilet and Toscanini. That evening four string players from the orchestra visited to perform Beethoven quartets for the maestro.
Rose Bampton, Wave Hill

By the time he came to NBC, Toscanini had gained recognition as a pre-eminent Beethoven interpreter. It is thus not surprising that he was one of the earliest conductors to complete a recorded cycle of the nine symphonies.[9] Despite the many splendid things this traversal contains, it is not wholly representative of what Toscanini could achieve with the music, a shortcoming underscored by the superiority of many of his broadcast performances.

Walter Legge, for many years the most influential classical-record producer for EMI and the person responsible for bringing Toscanini to London in 1952 to lead the Philharmonia Orchestra in a Brahms cycle, claimed he told Toscanini that some of his tempos for *La traviata* were "too fast." According to Legge, Toscanini admitted that his work at NBC might have benefited from such criticism.[10] To a certain extent, this applies to the conductor's recordings of the Beethoven symphonies that have gained the widest circulation and consequently become the best known. Most notable in this regard are the NBC studio recordings of Nos. 1, 2, and 7 and the second NBC recording (from a 1952 broadcast) of No. 5. All typify many of the most admirable aspects of Toscanini's Beethoven: continuity, clarity, structural integrity, and textural transparency. But all, in varying degrees, lack the control, rhythmic suppleness, and dramatic impact of alternative performances he gave with the NBC Symphony or with other orchestras.

With Symphonies Nos. 4 and 6, however, the issue is not so clear cut. Here the familiar RCA-NBC recordings demonstrate Toscanini's admirable approach to each. But other NBC performances offer a few instances of greater nuance, closer attention to detail, or more disciplined execution than is evident in the RCA releases. Particularly noteworthy are the inclusion of a first-movement exposition repeat in the 1939 broadcast of No. 4 and Toscanini's care at the end of the finale of No. 6 in bringing out Beethoven's "crescendo, subito piano" indication, an effect that emphasizes the passage's remarkable tenderness and is best realized in the 1939 broadcast performance. Constant in all Toscanini's performances, though, is his equally striking treatment of the C major chord that occupies the entire fourth measure of the first movement. Beethoven indicates its elongation with a fermata, a specification that some conductors acknowledge with minimal rhythmic distension. Toscanini, however, not only holds the chord long enough to freeze the pulse, he adds further emphasis by playing it with an unspecified diminuendo, thereby suggesting an apt and almost magical repose. Such details are important because they exemplify a pointed (sometimes overlooked) care and subtlety that characterize most of Toscanini's Beethoven. Significantly, too, the "Pastoral" was the first and the last of Beethoven's symphonies that Toscanini presented at NBC and the one he broadcast most frequently, eight times in all.[11] This and the special affection his performances convey suggest that it may well have been his favorite among the nine.

With the Third, Eighth, and Ninth Symphonies, Toscanini has been well served by RCA. The company's release of three different performances of the "Eroica"—two from NBC broadcasts (1939 and 1953) and one from a 1949 recording session—are especially remarkable for the great variety of interpretive features they encompass. Each differs from the others in terms of tempo, application of rubato, and clarification of detail. Yet each is like the others in suggesting the young lion of a composer, playing the upstart in creating a pathbreaking work that is still considered the doorway to nineteenth-century style. For all the symphony's revolutionary traits, however, it remains tied to the eighteenth century, most notably in its orchestra, which departs from the traditional one favored by Haydn and Mozart only to the extent of calling for a third horn. And the textural transparency of Toscanini's readings, where winds and brass are given their due and never swamped by the strings, reflects his grasp of this revolutionary work's roots in an earlier style.

One unique feature of Toscanini's approach occurs at the conclusion of the first movement's coda, where, in a grand peroration, the score's opening theme is repeated four times. Like many conductors, he favored a revision of Beethoven's *Urtext* in having the last repetition played throughout (rather than partially) by trumpets. And beginning with his 1939 NBC performance, he had the trumpets execute that theme with a sustained legato line unmatched in the work of the more than fifty other conductors whose performances of the music I have heard and reviewed. Not only is the dramatic power of this practice overwhelming, it is aesthetically right, echoing the phrasing of the theme when it is first stated by the cellos and clarifying how, in sonata-form movements, themes undergo radical changes of character.

The 1952 NBC recording of the Eighth Symphony is one of the prizes of Toscanini's discography, partly because it offers very fine sound for its vintage. This recording and the sloppily played broadcast performance from the same year also mark the first time that Toscanini dispensed with an awkward alteration of the text in the onset of the recapitulation of the first movement. Here in this little giant of a symphony Beethoven affectionately mocks eighteenth-century tradition in a number ways. In the passage in question he quite literally turns tradition upside down, putting the main theme in the lower voices, the harmony in the upper ones. In all but his 1952 accounts, Toscanini, following a recommendation made by Felix Weingartner, reinforced the buried melody with uncalled-for timpani, thereby partially neutralizing the effect of Beethoven's humorous stroke.[12] In returning to the *Urtext*, he must have come to recognize this practice as flawed.

Writing in 1947, George Bernard Shaw noted that performances of the Ninth Symphony were "events separated by years."[13] This infrequency should be kept in mind if one is to appreciate Toscanini's position as one of the symphony's foremost proponents. When he led his first performance of the work (on 20 April 1902 in Milan), it marked but the fourth time the music was heard in that city. And in his ten years with the New York Philharmonic, he prepared the score five times. Moreover, during the last twenty-seven years of his career, he mounted seventeen performances of the Ninth, five of them at NBC.

This abundance bespeaks not only Toscanini's affection for the music, but the challenges it posed for him as well. Indeed, after performing the first movement for the last time in recording sessions that took place two days after his 1952 broadcast of the work, he claimed, "I still don't understand that music." Toscanini's admirers often cite this comment as an example of his humility, but it is partly an accurate admission. Among all of Beethoven's orchestral works, the first movement of the Ninth Symphony may be the one whose mysteries he never satisfactorily penetrated.

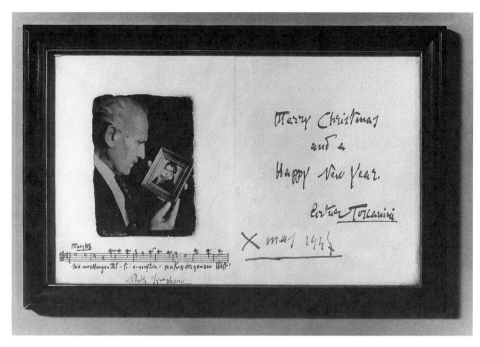

Toscanini's 1947 Christmas card. The musical quotation is from the finale
of Beethoven's Ninth Symphony. *BMG Classics*

From its tempo specification of "Allegro ma non troppo, un poco mae-
stoso" to its harmonically undefined initial rumblings and ironic D major recapitulation, the movement abounds in ambiguity. It loses some of its requisite
mystery in Toscanini's occasionally overwrought intensity. But this is partly the
result of overamplification in the broadcasts and recording of the movement's
hushed beginnings. Toscanini often complained about his careful dynamics having been distorted in the control room, but by 1952 he may have come to view
such distortion as an inevitable concomitant of electronic sound reproduction.
What one does hear to better advantage in the RCA recording than in any of the
broadcasts is the remarkable detail exposed at the movement's beginning, detail
that, in its own way, conveys the eerie void out of which a grand tonal universe
is to emerge. And however one reacts to the first movement in the 1952 recording, it stands as Toscanini's most expansive, most rhythmically secure, and most
pointedly inflected account of the music.

Unfortunately, the finale in the studio recording sometimes sounds rushed,
bespeaking the many takes and retakes Toscanini required before being satisfied.
Anyone who has worked before a microphone (whether recording speech or
music) will know that the more repetitions there are, the greater the tendency

to accelerate. If one compares the 1952 broadcast of the finale to the studio product of three days later, it is immediately clear that the conductor's conception, while essentially the same in both, has an ease before an audience that gave way to comparative tension when recording.

Ultimately, the shortcomings of Toscanini's Ninth may be inevitable. More than any other Beethoven symphony, it defies a completely satisfying reading. Whatever the conductor failed to grasp in the music, he understood many of its interpretive problems: how the first movement must remain rhythmically taut to suggest majesty and remain free of pretension; how both repeats must be observed in the second movement to preserve balance and proportion; how the third movement will become sentimental if unduly protracted; and how the finale's coda must be stable and unrushed so as to avoid any hint of frenzy.

What attracted Toscanini so strongly to Beethoven and made him such a convincing interpreter of the composer? In good measure, it may well have been intense identification. Both men embodied fascinating contradictions. Gentle and tender, both were also brash, radical, passionate, and driven—compulsive in their respective quests for artistic perfection. Both spoke defiantly of tradition, yet each absorbed it and honored it. And both gave vent to their most intense emotions, while subjecting them to the tightest of artistic reins. From such paradoxes came a dialectic—a tension between tradition and innovation, passion and intellect. It is this tension that lends Beethoven's music and Toscanini's finest performances of it clarity, unity, and shattering dramatic power.

Bellini, Vincenzo (1801–35)

Unofficially Issued Repertory
Norma: Introduction and Druids' Chorus (2 Dec. 1945)

That Toscanini had exceptionally high and rigid standards when it came to staging *Norma* is suggested by the very few performances of the opera that he conducted and by his refusal to present it at either La Scala or the Metropolitan. Tullio Serafin, who was an assistant to Toscanini at La Scala, noted that Toscanini kept changing the cast when preparing a performance of *Norma* there, and then, after three rehearsals, canceled the production because none of the singers met his requirements.[14] This NBC performance of the opera's opening is the only one of Bellini's music that Toscanini gave in the United States and is characterized by a tender, delicate elegance.

Berlioz, Hector (1803–1869)

Unofficially Issued Repertory
The Damnation of Faust, Op. 24: Scene 7 (16 Feb. 1647)
Les francs-juges, Op. 3: Overture (5 Apr. 1941)

Officially Issued Repertory

The Damnation of Faust: Rákóczy March (5 Apr. 1941, 2 Sept. 1945): RCA
60322 (broadcast of **2 Sept. 1945**)

Harold in Italy, Op. 16 (21 January 1939, 27 Oct. 1946, 12 Feb. 1949, 29
Nov. 1953; the first two performances with William Primrose, the
second two with Carlton Cooley): RCA 60275 (dress rehearsal of
28 Nov. 1953 and broadcast of **29 Nov. 1953**)

Roman Carnival Overture, Op. 9 (12 Feb. 1949, 10 Jan. 1953): RCA 60322
(**19 Jan. 1953**)

Roméo et Juliette, Op. 17: Complete score (9 Feb. 1947, 16 Feb. 1947): RCA
60274 (broadcasts of **9** and **16 Feb. 1947**; Queen Mab Scherzo
from broadcast of **10 Nov. 1951**)

Love Scene (19 Nov. 1938, 5 Apr. 1945, 29 Oct. 1949): RCA 60275
(**17 Feb. 1947**)

Festivities at the Capulets (4 Nov. 1945, 29 Oct. 1949): RCA 60275
(**17 Feb. 1947**)

Queen Mab Scherzo (5 Feb. 1938, 5 Apr. 1941, 26 Mar. 1944, 4 Feb.
1945, 14 Feb. 1948, 12 Feb. 1949, 10 Nov. 1951): RCA 60322
(broadcast of **10 Nov. 1951**)

At a talk given at the Morgan Library in New York City in November 1989, the
historian and Berlioz biographer Jacques Barzun noted that the resurgence of
interest in the composer that intensified in the second half of the twentieth century owed much to the efforts of Toscanini, who turned to Berlioz at a time
when most conductors were ignoring him. Granted, Toscanini directed but a
small number of Berlioz's works, but even those he turned to were rarities at the
time. More than a decade before *Harold in Italy* received its first recording, for
example, Toscanini included it on a 1929 concert with the New York Philharmonic.[15] And his 1943 performance with that orchestra of *Roméo et Juliette*
marked its first complete twentieth-century presentation in the United States.[16]
The Berlioz works that Toscanini led at NBC comprise most but not all of the
composer's music in his repertory, which included *The Damnation of Faust*, the
overture to *Benvenuto Cellini*, and the fourth and fifth movements of *Symphonie
fantastique*.

The performance of the overture to *Les francs-juges* is one of the prizes of
Toscanini's NBC years—a reading combining soaring lyricism and climactic
impact. The *Damnation of Faust* excerpt comprises the portion that bridges the
reveling in Auerbach's cellar and Faust's wooing of Marguerite; Faust (who does
not appear in this excerpt) and Méphistophélès (sung in this performance by
Mack Harrell) open the scene with "Voici des roses," which is followed by the
Chorus of Gnomes and Sylphs and the Dance of the Sylphs. Toscanini prefaced the aria with the orchestral close of Scene 6, but this preface was deleted
from a recording of the performance released in an unofficial Music and Arts CD
set. Toscanini had great admiration for the entire work, which he had per-

formed in Milan, Buenos Aires, Montevideo, and Turin, and it is unfortunate that he did not present it at NBC. This brief excerpt exhibits a delicacy and gentleness that typifies an important but often overlooked side of Toscanini's recreative style.

The second of Toscanini's two broadcast performances of the Rákóczy March was issued by RCA. In May 1941, a little over a month after giving the first of those performances, Toscanini recorded it, but he rejected that effort for release. Clearly, even with such relatively uncomplicated music, he exerted the same rigorous standards that he brought to the more demanding works of Beethoven and Brahms.

Toscanini's four NBC performances of *Harold in Italy* (the first two with William Primrose, the latter pair with Carlton Cooley) differ in some relatively small details, but, in varying ways, each boasts the kind of continuity that was pointedly noted by B. H. Haggin:

> It was the mercurial finale in Toscanini's performance around 1930 [probably that of 1929] that had me following the operation of Berlioz's mind with new understanding and delight; and the performance of . . . the entire work remained essentially the same—although more rigid in 1946 than in 1939, more relaxed again in 1953—and unequalled by any of the others I heard. It owes its effectiveness to its accuracy—especially its accuracy of tempo. Toscanini once pointed out to me the necessity of obeying Berlioz's metronome directions that Koussevitzky, for one, grandly ignored. They produced tempos which integrated not only the section of a movement (notably the third) but the movements within the entire work—making the recurring viola melody, for example, move at the same pace in each movement.[17]

Here, in one of his most perceptive comments, Haggin hit upon Toscanini's basic conception of the work: the unity he achieved in his grasp of the importance of clarifying tempo relationships. Little wonder that he could say after hearing the mannered Koussevitzky-Primrose recording of *Harold*, "Poor Primrose! Next year [1946] he come [*sic*] to play this piece with me again, and he must play correct! This is not correct."[18]

The Koussevitzky performance offers a *Harold* pulled out of shape as if it were taffy, with many uncalled-for shifts in tempo. Moreover, his way with the finale barely suggests the orgiastic abandon conveyed by Toscanini. At the time Primrose gave his performance of the work with Toscanini in 1939, he was still with the NBC Symphony, sharing its first-viola stand with Carlton Cooley. By 1946 he had left the orchestra, and his tone had become somewhat less opulent. Moreover, despite Toscanini's objection to Koussevitzky's freedom, the 1946 collaboration with Primrose is somewhat freer than in 1939, with the tempo of the finale also having become slightly slower. Both of Primrose's performances with Toscanini are very much those of a soloist.

In contrast, the two with Cooley are more the work of a member of the orchestra playing a prominent part. The earlier one is more precisely executed and benefits from inclusion of the first-movement repeat, observed in both accounts with Primrose but omitted in the 1953 broadcast. However, the best of the later Toscanini *Harold*s may be the dress rehearsal of 1953 (the main source for the RCA release, but not properly attributed until its appearance in the company's *Toscanini Collection*). Here the first-movement repeat is observed, and Cooley's tone, if less ripe than Primrose's, may be better suited to a part that Berlioz himself thought of as an obbligato to a symphony.

When Toscanini conducted the *Roméo et Juliette* in 1947, it marked the first time the entire work was aired, his 1942 New York Philharmonic presentation not having been broadcast. In 1965 RCA released the 1947 performances, substituting a more precisely executed Queen Mab Scherzo from the NBC broadcast of 10 November 1951. Despite a few flaws in the playing and singing, this pioneering performance captures the bold originality, intense passion, and melodic and harmonic daring that define so much of the Berlioz style. And, possibly of greatest significance, it preserves a historic event that gave a vast audience its first contact with a major masterpiece that in recent years—and owing surely to Toscanini's efforts—has deservedly become more familiar.

Those who readily (and inaccurately) dismiss Toscanini's repertory as "narrow" seem to forget his effort on behalf of Berlioz. One critic, in fact, lumped *Roméo et Juliette* with other minor "novelties" that Toscanini performed.[19] It was, of course, a novelty in 1947, but it was hardly a minor work. And for Toscanini it was not novel. He had a long familiarity with the score, having performed many orchestral excerpts from it. He called the Love Scene "the most beautiful music in the world," and all of his NBC performances of this music boast a sustained tenderness, intimacy, and sensuousness that were as much a part of the Toscanini recreative temperament as his more widely recognized insistence on precision, flair for drama, and skill in promoting integrity and generating powerful climaxes.[20]

Revealing in another way is the conductor's recurrent programming of the Queen Mab Scherzo, which he performed more frequently at NBC than he did any symphony by Beethoven or Brahms. He was probably attracted to the music's elfin, gossamer lightness, its darting rhythm, and its originality of texture, qualities that contribute to the way in which Berlioz, almost magically, conveys Mercutio's fantasy of "the fairies' midwife . . . / In shape no bigger than an agate stone / . . . Drawn with a team of little atomies / Athwart men's noses as they lie asleep." What also must have appealed to Toscanini was the challenge of the music's exceptionally virtuosic demands. Every detail is exposed, requiring each note to be precisely in place. And it is the degree to which that precision was obtained that sets off one Toscanini performance from another, their overall conception being among his most unvarying. But even his most careful efforts could be sabotaged: the close miking of the 1951 performance issued by RCA excessively magnified the delicacy of the antique cymbals and thus deprived them of their delicacy. Interestingly, too, Toscanini's 1942 Philadelphia Orchestra recording of the piece, while preserving the basic approach of his NBC account, does not quite match the flitting lightness of the best of them.

In the Festivities at the Capulets, Toscanini managed to project the music's unbridled exuberance without sacrificing its textural clarity. The same might be said for his three surviving accounts of the *Roman Carnival* Overture, each displaying a dazzling lightness and colorful transparency. Here is another instance in which there is little, if anything, to distinguish one performance from another.

Given Toscanini's affinity for Berlioz, his never having turned to the composer's Requiem is surprising. Still, his advocacy of Berlioz is striking when viewed in its historical place—a time, for example, when one eminent historian and critic could write that Berlioz failed to produce "one finished work."[21] Today, thanks in part to Toscanini, we know better.

Bizet, Georges (1838–1875)

Unofficially Issued Repertory
The Fair Maid of Perth: Suite: Serenade, March, and Gypsy Dance (19 Sept. 1943)

Officially Issued Repertory
L'Arlésienne: Suite: Overture, Minuet, Pastorale, Carillon (19 Sept. 1943): RCA 60274 (broadcast of **19 Sept. 1943**)
Carmen: Suite, arr. Toscanini (19 Sept. 1943, 2 Aug. 1952): RCA 60274 (**5 Aug. 1952**)

Toscanini admired Bizet's music, especially *Carmen*, which he led many times in the theater. His arrangement of the suite from the opera differs from Bizet's Suite No. 1 in the sequence of the selections it draws upon and the use of the Toreador's music as heard in the final act rather than in the opera's prelude. It also includes a harp cadenza composed by the maestro. The 1952 broadcast and subsequent recordings are as identical as two performances can be and differ from the earlier presentation in their occasionally faster tempos.

The performances of the *Arlésienne* and *Fair Maid of Perth* Suites offer prime examples of Toscanini's ability to project a work with unaffected, straightforward simplicity. Quite possibly his attraction to the former was rooted in its original orchestration, which included the first use of a solo saxophone by a major composer and the deployment of harp, horn, and plucked strings to suggest bells. These and other details emerge in sharp focus under Toscanini's direction.

Boccherini, Luigi (1743--1805)

Unissued Repertory
String Quartet in D Major, Op. 6 No. 1 (19 Nov. 1949)
String Quintet in E Major, Op. 13 No. 5: Minuet (11 Apr. 1943, 8 Aug. 1944)

In both performances of the Minuet, Toscanini achieved an intimacy that suggests chamber music, the muted NBC strings having a gossamer daintiness that suits the music perfectly. In the quartet (probably Toscanini's only performance of the work) the sonority is weightier than anything a string quartet might produce, yet the texture never sounds thick. Those who believe that Toscanini was unresponsive to eighteenth-century music should hear this sensitive and stylish reading, one that in its poised, relaxed, cantabile breadth makes clear that Toscanini and classicism could be eminently compatible.

Boito, Arrigo (1842–1918)

Officially Issued Repertory
Mefistofele: Prologue (2 Dec. 1945, 14 Mar. 1954): RCA 60276 (broadcast of **14 Mar. 1954**)

Aside from one in 1904 at the Metropolitan Opera House, these two performances (the latter one comprising the RCA release) mark Toscanini's only concert-hall presentation of this music in the United States. Both are essentially identical in concept, but the commercially released account, in addition to benefiting from Carnegie Hall acoustics, is free of the occassionally imprecise ensemble of the earlier rendition.

The 1954 broadcast towers as one of Toscanini's most remarkable achievements of his last years. His fabled control, which seemed to be ebbing in his final season, is fully evident here. The shape, dramatic contrasts, and stunning climax that he produced are astonishing, especially when judged in the context of what must have been the strain of the approaching end of an activity he could not live without. It is as if, for a brief hour, a younger conductor were in charge.

Toscanini's association with Boito was long and rooted in deep mutual admiration, the composer being one of the conductor's staunchest advocates when Toscanini was offered his first appointment as music director of La Scala in 1898. As a memento of their association and of Toscanini's admiration of Boito, this performance is an important document. Of greater significance, it is a moving experience.

Bolzoni, Giovanni (1841–1919)

Unissued Repertory
Minuet in B Major (20 June 1943)
Medieval Castle: Serenade (18 July 1943)

Admired as a skilled conductor by Verdi, Bolzoni gained further distinction as a violinist and pedagogue. He composed operas, orchestral works, and chamber music, all virtually forgotten today. Though both of these brief pieces attest to Bolzoni's skill as an orchestrator, they embody the faceless, relatively unimaginative Italian music that Toscanini was criticized for playing. The minuet remained a popular trifle well into the twentieth century.

Borodin, Alexander (1833–87)

Unofficially Issued Repertory
Symphony No. 2 in B Minor (19 Feb. 1938)

When Toscanini led this performance during his first NBC season, this symphony was far more of a repertory staple than it had become by the close of the twentieth century. In fact, in the 78 rpm era, when many major masterpieces were not recorded, the work gained five versions on disc. Toscanini took special pains to solve the technical problems in the music, especially that of securing accurate intonation in exposed unison passages. And he treated the score as if it were classically styled, emphasizing clarity and unity, while building impressive climaxes with tempos that were a bit broader than the norm.

Bossi, Enrico (1861–1925)

Unissued Repertory
Intermezzo Goldoniani (3 Sept. 1944)

A virtuoso organist and conductor, Bossi was also a prolific composer of chamber, orchestral, and sacred organ and vocal music. These three brief intermezzos demand virtuoso execution that does credit to the NBC Symphony's strings. But given the music's emptiness, one wonders what purpose this virtuosity serves.

Brahms, Johannes (1833–97)

Unofficially Issued Repertory
A German Requiem, Op. 45 (24 Jan. 1943)
Serenade No. 1 in D Major, Op. 11: first movement (6 May 1940, 17 Jan. 1943, 23 Oct. 1948); Minuet (9 Mar. 1947, 6 Nov. 1948)

Variations and Fugue on a Theme by Handel, Op. 24, orch. Rubbra (17 Jan. 1939)

Officially Issued Repertory

Piano Concerto No. 2 in B-flat Major, Op. 83 (6 May 1940, 23 Oct. 1948): RCA 60319 (**9 May 1940**)

Double Concerto in A Minor for Violin and Cello, Op. 102 (21 Oct. 1939, 13 Nov. 1948): RCA 60259 (broadcast of **13 Nov. 1948**)

Gesang der Parzen for Chorus and Orchestra, Op. 89 (27 Nov. 1948): RCA 60260 (broadcast of **27 Nov. 1948**)

Hungarian Dances: No. 1 in G Minor (10 Jan. 1943, 13 Nov. 1948); No. 17 in F-sharp Minor, No. 20 in E Minor, No. 21 in E Minor (2 July 1944): RCA 60257 (**17 Feb. 1953**; includes all four dances)

Liebeslieder Waltzes, Op. 52 (11 Feb. 1939, 27 Dec. 1942, 13 Nov. 1948): RCA 60260 (broadcast of **13 Nov. 1948**)

Overtures:

    Academic Festival, Op. 80 (11 Feb. 1939, 10 Jan, 1943, 6 Nov. 1948): RCA 60257 (broadcast of **6 Nov. 1948**)

    Tragic, Op. 81 (15 Oct. 1938, 3 Jan. 1943, 28 Oct. 1945, 9 Mar. 1947, 30 Oct. 1948, 22 Nov. 1953): RCA 60258 (broadcast of **22 Nov. 1953**)

Serenade No. 2 in A Major, Op. 16 (22 Jan. 1938, 27 Dec. 1942): RCA 60277 (broadcast of **27 Nov. 1942**)

Symphonies:

    No. 1 in C Minor, Op. 68 (25 Dec. 1937, 6 May 1940, 14 May 1940, 17 Jan. 1943, 18 Apr. 1944, probably not broadcast; 30 Oct. 1948, 3 Nov. 1951): RCA 60277 (**10 Mar.** and **11 Dec. 1941**); RCA 60257 (**6 Nov. 1951**)

    No. 2 in D Major, Op. 73 (12 Feb. 1938, 3 Jan. 1942, 9 Mar. 1947, 6 Nov. 1948, 10 Feb. 1951): RCA 60258 (**11 Feb. 1952**)

    No. 3 in F Major, Op. 90 (15 Oct. 1938, 8 Feb. 1941, 20 Dec. 1942, 31 Mar. 1946, 21 Feb. 1948, 20 Nov. 1948, 1 Nov. 1952): RCA 60259 (**4 Nov. 1952**)

    No. 4 in E Minor, Op. 98 (11 Feb. 1939, 10 Jan. 1943, 28 Oct. 1945, 27 Nov. 1948, 26 Feb. 1950, 22 Dec. 1951): RCA 60260 (**3 Dec. 1951**)

Variations on a Theme by Haydn, Op. 56a (26 Feb. 1938, 20 Dec. 1942, 7 Nov. 1946, 21 Feb. 1948, 20 Nov. 1948): RCA 60258 (**4 Feb. 1952**)

Among all the composers in Toscanini's repertory, Brahms generated the most varied responses. Nowhere are there to be found such striking examples of the conductor's constant self-criticism and his constant rethinking of familiar works. In such a context, his Brahms performances, especially those of the symphonies, cannot be viewed as typical, yet each, in divergent ways, is often commanding and indicative of a significant aspect of Brahms's creative personality.

It is regrettable that the only surviving Toscanini performance of *A German Requiem* is the lone presentation of the work that he led at NBC. Not that it is an inferior account; quite the contrary, it is magnificent. But we can never know whether or not, as with other Brahms works, it embodies a Toscanini view that was subject to constant revision. It does, however, illustrate his often-repeated credo, "Tradition is nothing but the last bad performance."

One might cite this performance (among many) to refute the inaccurate generalization that Toscanini's tempos were almost invariably faster than those of other conductors. Indeed, some of his tempos here are considerably slower than the norm. The effect of this approach is to strip away the halo of Victorian sobriety that has hung over many accounts of this score and that may have led George Bernard Shaw to find it "so execrably and ponderously dull that the very flattest of funerals would seem like a ballet or at least a *danse macabre* after it."[22] Sections that usually sound grimly broad become more animated under Toscanini. Conversely, the second section is more expansive than usual, an intense, powerful dirge with great cumulative force. And throughout, the textures, both choral and orchestral, have far greater focus and clarity. Particularly noteworthy is the Westminster Choir, trained by John Finley Williamson, a choral conductor who favored a rounded, blended, almost woolly vocal tone that was readily accepted by other conductors, notably Bruno Walter. Toscanini would have none of it, which contributed to his scrubbing this score clean. In every way, this *German Requiem* shines as one of his major achievements at NBC. The performance was sung in English, possibly a nod to the strong anti-German wartime ethos.

When Toscanini performed the entire Serenade No. 1 with the New York Philharmonic in 1935, it was not a repertory piece. No complete recording of the work was produced on 78 rpm discs, and even today it does not appear frequently on orchestral programs, doubtless owing to its relatively intimate scoring. No conductor I have heard matched Toscanini's tempo for the first movement—an intense, propulsive allegro molto that, if almost shockingly untraditional, seems absolutely right for this youthful, spirited work, which is sometimes ponderous under less sympathetic direction. The earliest of the three performances is the freest—propelled more fiercely than the later ones at some points, but more expansive at others. All are extraordinary. Both performances of the minuet are stated with relaxed, unaffected simplicity.

Were Edmund Rubbra's orchestration of the Handel variations less showy and more in the style of Brahms, Toscanini's account might command more interest. The conductor loved this work. Nevertheless—as revealed in an undated private journal kept by Toscanini and shown to me by RCA's John Pfeiffer—the conductor was fully aware of the shortcomings of Rubbra's unstylish effort, which received its premiere in this performance. Toscanini brought to the score the same sensitivity to classical variation style that stamped his long-admired way with Brahms's *Variations on a Theme by Haydn*: a clarification of the harmonic underpinnings that unify the work and of the wide emotional range that provides needed contrast from one variation to another. The conception is admirable, but clothed as it is in Rubbra's garish arrangement, it seems akin to putting chocolate sauce on filet mignon.

Probably Toscanini's most unvarying work in a major Brahms score is found in the two broadcasts and studio recording of the B-flat Major Piano Concerto with Vladimir Horowitz. The 1948 broadcast makes the strongest impression, since the 1940 Carnegie Hall studio recording suffers from one of RCA's most disappointing CD transfers. But all three project the same con-trolled vitality, long lines, and tautly structured unity. The first movement is direct and unmannered, the second appropriately stormy, the third tender with-out being sentimental, and the finale pointedly playful. Among Toscanini's col-laborations with soloists at NBC, those with Horowitz stand out, not only for their shared viewpoint, but also for the way they clarify the Brahms B-flat Major Piano Concerto as a carefully structured classical concerto very much in the Mozart-Beethoven mold.

The Double Concerto provides a different situation, with the two NBC performances, both featuring the same first-desk soloists, contrasting markedly. As issued by RCA on LP, the second of the two broadcasts was almost unlis-tenable: shrill, thin, and painfully cramped. Transferred onto compact disc (and videocassette), the performance sounds far more musical: the shrillness has been eliminated, the orchestra has been given more weight, and the overall ambience seems less cramped. As a result, the musical virtues—veiled in the original LP—have become more apparent, notably the way in which tightly knit organization and a steady pulse underscore the work's suggestion, with opposition of paired soloists against larger tutti forces, of the concerto grosso style. Brahms, it should not be forgotten, was a first-class musicologist who had edited Handel (among others) and was thoroughly familiar with the baroque concerto idiom, as Tos-canini's 1948 performance reminds us.

The 1939 broadcast comprises a considerably more improvisational reading, rhythms being less rigid and melodic lines lingered over more caressingly. None of this, however, violates good taste or the music's integrity. Indeed, it is a prime example of Toscanini's (and the soloists') command of rubato. In short, this is a performance that adds considerable dimension to Toscanini's Brahms.

The sole NBC performance of *Gesang der Parzen* is Toscanini's only Amer-ican presentation of the work and possibly the only one he conducted. Written for chorus and orchestra, it remains to this day a relatively unknown score, and Toscanini's inclusion of it in his 1948 Brahms cycle stands as one of his most imaginative strokes of programming. At the time of the performance, no record-ing of the work had been made. Toscanini's reading—in its rock-steady rhythm, colorful orchestral transparency, and sensitivity to the harmonic richness char-

From left to right: Toscanini, Vladimir Horowitz, David Sarnoff,
and Bruno Walter. *RCA*

acteristic of Brahms—suggests that the work deserves more frequent performances. As reproduced in the RCA CD transfer, the sound is especially good for
its vintage. Here is one of many examples typifying a little-acknowledged side
of Toscanini's repertory: its inclusion of forgotten works worthy of resurrection.

The four Hungarian Dances—the only ones Toscanini conducted in the
United States—boast the same precision and care he brought to the composer's
symphonies, but without the relaxed charm other conductors have suggested.
The studio recordings of 1953 provide virtual clones of the few NBC broadcast
performances.

For his three NBC presentations of the *Liebeslieder Waltzes*, Toscanini used
a chorus of sixteen voices rather than the one-voice-to-a-part scoring Brahms
specifies. This is one of the few instances among Toscanini's Brahms performances where hardly any variation exists from one presentation to the next. For
many tastes, his relatively unyielding, uninflected readings may seem too cool
and lacking in sensuousness. However, the conductor's style may appeal to those

Toscanini in Denver, Colorado, during the 1950 tour of the NBC Symphony. On the left is the NBC Symphony concertmaster, Mischa Mischakoff; on the right, the principal cellist, Frank Miller. *Fred. M. Mazzulla; Walfredo Toscanini*

who find the music sentimental, diluting as it does the music's potentially cloying spirit. It should be noted that the last of the three broadcasts, the one released by RCA on CD, is also visible on videocassette. And it is very much worth viewing: on Toscanini's face can be seen a variety of expressions, ranging from smiles to pleading glances, that he rarely displayed in concert performances.

The three broadcasts of the *Academic Festival* Overture (the last, from 1948, issued by RCA) are unorthodox, mainly in their prevailing breadth. It is this trait that has led even some of Toscanini's most fervent admirers to react unfavorably to his approach, which Robert C. Marsh, for example, found lacking in "humor and charm."[23] Marsh based his opinion on the 1948 performance, similar in its general style to the earliest of the three but better controlled. Had he heard the 1943 reading, he might have changed his mind: generally more relaxed, it is arguably more impish and humorous. But the 1948 performance, more than either of the others, clarifies the remarkable sonata structure Brahms built out of familiar student songs. Unfortunately, RCA's CD transfer of that performance remains as painfully shrill and unmusical as its previous LP release.

When it came to the *Tragic* Overture, Toscanini was of two minds, each expressed in his two earliest surviving performances of the work: a 1935 broadcast account with the New York Philharmonic and a 1937 studio recording with the BBC Symphony, the former expansive and weighty, the latter more aggressive and slightly lighter in sonority. In Toscanini's six NBC presentations of the work, these extremes are mirrored. Those of 1938, 1945, 1947, and 1948 are fleet and fierce, almost to the point of sounding angry. The 1943 performance is more suggestive of the Philharmonic account, albeit somewhat more precipitous and not as weighty. Closest to that 1935 reading is Toscanini's broadcast performance from his final season, issued by RCA.

For those who did not know the Philharmonic account, the 1953 broadcast, in its exceptional breadth, must have come as a shock, for it was totally unlike the familiar 1937 recording or any of Toscanini's other NBC performances of the work. Here, in his last performance of a score that had appeared on his first orchestral program fifty-seven years earlier, while Brahms was still alive, Toscanini directed a reading in which the composer's crabbed polyphony emerged in sharply focused texture, generating an austere tension. It is as if the conductor had completely rethought the work, possibly reaching back into the well of memory to recreate the kind of performance he had given in 1935, but one modified by a freshly conceived notion of sonority lacking the weight of the Philharmonic account. RCA's decision to issue the performance was surely wise. One wishes, though, that use had been made of some dress-rehearsal material to correct a lapse in precision.

The two broadcasts of the Serenade No. 2 are a study in contrast. That of 1938, in its unorthodox expansive tempos, sounds almost dreary at times, but it also has moments of beauty and grace absent from the considerably faster, more intense performance of 1942 released by RCA. Both performances have merit, but on balance, the earlier one is more interesting.

The most intriguing instances of Toscanini's fluctuating views are with the symphonies. Here, too, are examples of his willingness to depart from the literalness of the score. Thus one finds not only occasional disregard for Brahms's tempo indications, but also some instances of radical revisions in orchestration. Even before he came to NBC, Toscanini's view of the Brahms First was evidently in flux. B. H. Haggin's comments are telling:

> When he [Toscanini] had first played the Brahms First in New York [presumably the performance given in November 1930], he had decided that the Poco sostenuto of the introduction to the first movement must be the same [tempo] as the similar passage at the end of the movement. This turned out to be too fast for the proper effect of the introduction; nevertheless, in all the performances of the symphony that year, Toscanini stuck to this consistency at the cost of effectiveness; but when he played the work again in a later season, he took the introduction to the first movement at its traditional pace.[24]

Among all Toscanini's preserved NBC accounts of the First Symphony, the three earliest are the freest, especially in the first movement. In 1937 (his NBC debut), the rhythm was unusually free, with a liberal application of rubato that the conductor never duplicated. Like his last performance of the *Tragic* Overture, this account of the symphony suggests that he had reached into his past to resurrect the kind of Brahms First he might have led earlier.

In 1940 the first movement's pulse became less varied. Although many inflections from the reading of three years earlier remain, the line is tauter, the overall unity greater. With slashing accents, a pointed motivic profile, and remarkable cumulative tension, Toscanini produced on this occasion one of his most magnificent NBC achievements. In its combination of soaring lyricism, rhythmic control, and freedom from sentimentality and unwanted pomp, the performance clarifies Brahms's position as the inheritor of the classical symphonic tradition of Beethoven.

With the possible exception of the 1943 broadcast of the First Symphony, which comes close to matching the marvels of 1940, Toscanini's subsequent performances of the work (including his 1941 and 1951 studio recordings) prove less interesting. Aside from their quicker tempos and more stringent rhythm, their overall emotional range is considerably narrower: he took fewer interpretive risks, resulting in lower dramatic peaks and a less forceful impact. Nevertheless, taken of themselves, they are distinguished by their clarity and unity and as prime examples of how Toscanini reacted against the tasteless extremes of tempo and rhythmic freedom that disfigured the Brahms First offered by some other conductors.

Of all the Brahms symphonies, the Second may pose the fewest interpretive problems. Not surprisingly, then, it is the Brahms symphony in which one encounters the fewest changes in approach from one Toscanini reading to another. The main differences among them center on the pacing for the finale: sometimes relatively expansive, as in the magnificent 1952 studio recording, other times swift. The 1938 broadcast features a blend of both approaches. And common to all of Toscanini's surviving accounts is his refusal to accelerate in the movement's coda, where the lullabylike second subject is transformed into a festive peroration for full orchestra.

As in the Brahms First, Toscanini's way with the Second Symphony is distinguished by a prevailing freedom from sentimentality. Neither of the first two movements is unduly protracted, and both benefit from an exceptional clarity of texture and firmness of pulse, with rubato, if often evident, subtly applied. In both movements surging dynamics and arching phrases suggest the ebb and flow of the sea that Brahms knew so well and that clearly influenced his music. And in all of Toscanini's performances the third movement is a model of unaffected, straightforward simplicity.

Among all of Toscanini's studio recordings, that of the Brahms Third Symphony may well be the least representative. The interpretive problems the score poses—particularly in the shifting meters of its first movement—make it the most difficult of the composer's symphonies to perform convincingly. Toscanini must have recognized this, for, delighting in challenges, he performed it more frequently at NBC than any of the other Brahms symphonies. Furthermore, when he ultimately came to record the work (three days after his last NBC broadcast of it), he asked to hear all of his previous broadcast presentations in an effort to distill from them an ideal conception. According to Robert C. Marsh, this distillation comprised the first and fourth movements from the broadcast of 15 October 1938, the second movement from 31 March 1946, and the third movement from 20 November 1948. Marsh goes on to observe: "The 'ideal' version is consistently taut, hard-driven, and intense. [The recording] is slower and suffers . . . from both a lack of continuity and changes in rhythmic pulse and scanning of phrases."[25]

Everything Marsh claims for the recording is true. It is the slowest, most rhythmically slack of all Toscanini's surviving performances of the work. Worse yet, it is compromised by inferior reproduction in which an excessively close microphone placement flattens perspective and gives the NBC Symphony an immediacy that makes it sound like a small-scale toy orchestra. One may admire Toscanini's handling of individual details and the resulting clarity it yields, but the overall effect is, at best, that of caricature.

Contrary to what Marsh says, the ideal conception that Toscanini formulated from earlier broadcasts, if "intense," is not "hard driven." The outer movements from 1938, for instance, faster and considerably tauter than in the studio effort, also feature a breadth, grandeur, and repose absent from Toscanini's atypically fleet broadcast of 1941 and his slightly streamlined yet strongly accented and aptly majestic account of February 1948. Toscanini's vacillating approach to the Third Symphony was evidently not confined to NBC. His view was in transition earlier with the New York Philharmonic, and a preserved 1935 performance with that orchestra suggests an occasional shapelessness that crept into some of the NBC readings.[26]

Possibly because of his awareness of the many problems this symphony presents, Toscanini made more adjustments and revisions in its orchestration than in any other Brahms work. These have been detailed by Harris Goldsmith and include doublings to highlight melodic lines, redistribution of voices, and the addition of instruments to insure clarity or to suggest a specific ethos.[27] Perhaps the most striking instance of the last is the insertion of timpani "thwacks," as Goldsmith puts it, at measures 172–77 of the finale. Here Toscanini, inferring what he believed to be an effect Brahms desired at this point, wrote "violento" in his score. Possibly the oddest of Toscanini's emendations is his prefacing of the symphony's closing measures with thirty-second-note acciaccaturas, a practice that makes the final chords seem less conclusive and slightly ragged.

Unlike the recording Toscanini made of the Third Symphony, his 1951 studio account of the Fourth is superb: transparent, fluid, but unhurried, and preserved in monaural sound that often exposes more detail and color than can be heard in digitally engineered stereo. One wonders how much more revelatory the performance might be had it been captured with more modern technology. Nonetheless, it comprises one of Toscanini's superior efforts for RCA, both musically and sonically.

Yet fine as that performance is, the broadcast account of 1948 is even greater, possibly Toscanini's most striking surviving performance of the work. The clarity and color of other readings is present, but the expression is enriched by slightly broader tempos in outer movements and a modulated but firmly controlled rhythm that he never duplicated in other accounts. Yet in the finale, the tempo is maintained with a remarkable strictness that seems absolutely right for the movement. The dramatic power of this passacaglia should grow from the contrast between a constantly reiterated melody of eight notes and the succession of variations counterpointed to it. To clarify the melody and sustain tension, it is necessary to adhere to a relatively steady pulse. All of Toscanini's surviving performances do this, and it is one of his great contributions to Brahms interpretation that they thereby clarify the movement's structure. But the performance of 1948, with its slightly greater breadth, does so with greater control that yields a more potent intensity and a greater cumulative impact.

A few additional features of Toscanini's approach to the Fourth Symphony deserve comment. The first movement was never permitted to cloy as result of being unduly protracted. The *Luftpausen* favored by many German conductors (even by one as disdainful of mannerisms as Otto Klemperer) in the first and third movements never infected a Toscanini performance. And it is probably safe to say that in this work Toscanini, more than any other conductor, extracted a transparency of texture that dispels the once-frequent allegation that Brahms produced "thick" orchestrations. In fact, Toscanini was especially sensitive to the composer's imaginative and original use of the orchestra. A prime case in point occurs in the opening of the second movement. Here Brahms withholds bowed strings for thirty-nine measures, producing an unrelieved repetition of woodwind and pizzicato tone until the *arco* violins enter at measure 40. Under Toscanini, the tonal radiance of that entry gives compelling evidence of the expressive power of timbre.

Compared to Toscanini's changing views of the Brahms symphonies, his many surviving accounts of the *Haydn Variations*—five NBC broadcasts, two studio recordings (the first with the New York Philharmonic), and a concert performance with the Philharmonia Orchestra from 1952—display a consistent view, but one that was in many ways unconventional, its most striking feature being a wide range of tempos from one variation to the next. The figurations at the core of Variation 5, for instance, were always tossed off with a dashing élan that in Toscanini's most successful performances is remarkable for its virtuosity and piquant wit. The Poco più animato of Variation 1 is more expansive than is customary. Variation 2 is somewhat faster than the norm, the shaping of its staccato execution creating uncommon vibrance and sharpness of motivic profile. The horns in Variation 6 snarl rather than purr, producing a suitably biting astringence. And Variation 7 was always played more slowly than the norm, projecting a gentle grazioso ethos absent from most other performances.

Toscanini's treatment of the finale—a remarkable set of variations within the larger set—is also distinctive. As in the finale of the Brahms Fourth, it boasts a well-defined bass that clarifies its passacaglia structure without creating an unduly heavy sonority. Featured, too, is a slightly broader than orthodox tempo that permits the bucolic woodwind theme on which the work is built to return at its close in a dramatic transformation of uncommon splendor. And occasional shortcomings in execution aside, every one of Toscanini's performances of this score has an expressive range, flair for drama, and prevailing unity unmatched in the surviving work of any of his peers. Clearly this was a Toscanini specialty.

Toscanini once commented to B. H. Haggin that "Brahms's symphonies are first after Beethoven['s]." Such admiration was doubtless rooted in many factors. Brahms was, after all, a contemporary voice who composed some of his most notable masterpieces (such as the Double Concerto and the Clarinet Quintet) when Toscanini was professionally active. Then, too, the rich inventiveness of Brahms's music—its harmonic boldness, melodic ripeness, and masterful orchestration—must have appealed to him. But most of all, Toscanini's performances acknowledge his delight in the music's classicism, its self-contained freedom from excess, in which the boldness of Brahms's imagination acquired expressive power through his command of form and structure. In its clarification of that command, Toscanini's Brahms was at once stylish, emotionally gripping, and a welcome alternative to the overly lush, rhythmically slack, sometimes self-indulgent performances of some of his peers.

Busoni, Ferruccio (1866–1924)

Unofficially Issued Repertory
Berceuse élégiaque (3 Nov. 1948, 10 Dec. 1949)
Rondo arlecchinesco (15 Jan. 1938, 20 Jan. 1946, 10 Dec. 1949)

Toscanini first heard the *Berceuse* in 1911 when it was played by the New York Philharmonic under Gustav Mahler. According to Busoni, Toscanini was "charmed" by it. After the performance Busoni met Toscanini and wrote that the conductor "is the most intelligent musician I have met up to now (with perhaps the exception of [Richard] Strauss)."[28] Toscanini's way with these pieces exemplifies his ability to convey mood—the sustained, elegiac spirit of the *Berceuse* and the tart, dissonant wit in the *Rondo*. Neither work, however, can be considered among Busoni's more important or radical achievements.

Castelnuovo-Tedesco, Mario (1895–1968)

Unissued Repertory
A Fairy Tale Overture (12 Nov. 1945)
The Taming of the Shrew Overture (30 Mar. 1940, 3 Mar. 1944)

The Italian-born Castelnuovo-Tedesco was one of a handful of musicians who remained loyal to Toscanini when the conductor was under Mussolini's surveillance. As a Jew, the composer was ultimately forced out of Italy in 1939, settling in the United States. The overture to *The Taming of the Shrew* is the first of seven concert overtures based on Shakespeare that Castelnuovo-Tedesco composed between 1931 and 1942. Both are charming but conservative scores that Toscanini plays with conviction and clarity.

Catalani, Alfredo (1854–93)

Officially Issued Repertory
Loreley: Dance of the Water Nymphs (21 Jan. 1939, 23 Mar. 1947, 2 Aug. 1952)
La Wally: Prelude to Act IV (21 Jan. 1939, 23 Mar. 1947, 2 Aug. 1952): both works RCA 60309 (**5 Aug. 1952**)

The history of Italian opera might well have been different had Catalani not died so young. Toscanini became an early champion of the composer and made his Italian conducting debut directing Catalani's *Edmea* on 4 November 1886 in Turin. Later he led the two operas from which these brief excerpts are drawn. As the dates of these broadcasts make clear, Toscanini always programmed them together. The three broadcasts and the studio session are identical in their unaffected simplicity.

Cherubini, Luigi (1760–1842)

Unissued Repertory
String Quartet in E-flat Major: Scherzo (4 Apr. 1943)

Officially Issued Repertory
Ali Baba: Overture (3 Dec. 1949): RCA 60278 (broadcast of **3 Dec. 1949**)
Anacréon: Overture (22 Jan. 1938, 4 Feb. 1945, 9 Sept. 1945, 21 Mar. 1953):
　　RCA 60278 (broadcast of **21 Mar. 1953**)
Medea: Overture (18 Feb. 1950): RCA 60278 (broadcast of **18 Feb. 1950**)
Requiem in C Minor (18 Feb. 1950): RCA 60272 (broadcast of **18 Feb.**
　　1950)
Symphony in D Major (23 Mar. 1947, 8 Mar. 1952): RCA 60278 (**10 Mar.**
　　1952)

Although he never conducted a Cherubini opera, Toscanini had great respect for the composer. During the first half of the twentieth century, the overture to *Anacréon* was relatively popular and had been recorded on 78s by Ettore Panizza, Willem Mengelberg, Leo Blech, and (in a slightly truncated version) Herbert von Karajan. Among Toscanini's four broadcast performances (a fifth NBC account was not aired), the first is the most rhythmically flexible and sharply accented. It has a slightly wider range of tempos than do the later readings. But all make a fine case for a work that without careful handling can sound unduly rambling and loose limbed. The performance of the Scherzo from the E-flat Major String Quartet was given by a full compliment of strings. It calls for virtuosic dash, sparkle, and élan, which Toscanini provided.

　　The overture to *Medea* and the C Minor Requiem that made up the NBC broadcast (and RCA recording) of 18 February 1950 were Toscanini's only performances of these works in the United States. The Requiem offers a prime example of the conductor's interest in unduly neglected repertory. Toscanini made a strong case for this work and took special pains with it. Ralph Hunter, who prepared the chorus for the performance, showed me his vocal score with Toscanini's detailed indications about phrasing and dynamics. As Hunter related, Toscanini was not satisfied with simply making the indications in the score, but went on to provide a rationale for each. In its careful shaping, textural transparency, and stark drama, Toscanini's performance makes clear why the work was admired by Beethoven and Berlioz.

Toscanini's own admiration of Cherubini is suggested in his view (extreme, to be sure) that the composer had "instrumental effects 100 years ahead of Stravinsky['s]."[29] When he performed the Symphony in D with the BBC Symphony in London in 1937, it may well have been the first time the work had been heard in that city since its premiere there in 1815. He took special pains with it—for example, incorporating Cherubini's revisions, made after the score was published. Toscanini's two NBC broadcasts and subsequent recording are all similar, the first of the three being distinguishable from the others by its ever so slightly quicker tempos in outer movements.

Cimarosa, Domenico (1749–1801)

Officially Issued Repertory

Il matrimonio per raggiro: Overture (12 Nov. 1949)
Il matrimonio segreto: Overture (14 Nov. 1943): Both performances issued on
    RCA 60278 from the broadcast accounts.

Each of these performances marks the only time Toscanini led this music in the United States. Both are lively, straightforward accounts that benefit from judicious balances in which strings do not swamp the other instruments.

Copland, Aaron (1900–90)

Unofficially Issued Repertory

El salón México (14 Mar. 1942)

Harvey Sachs suggested that Toscanini played American composers such as Barber, Gershwin, and Copland more "out of a sense of obligation" than anything else and was not "at home in such repertory."[30] To some extent this is true, but this performance has an idiomatic swing that suggests otherwise. Indeed, hearing it makes one wonder why Toscanini did not perform more Copland, particularly a work like *Appalachian Spring*, which has a melodic and harmonic style very much in keeping with his taste.

Creston, Paul (1906–85)

Unissued Repertory

Choric Dance No. 1, Op. 17a (1 Nov. 1942)
Frontiers (25 Nov. 1945)

Here, more than with Copland's *El salón México*, is an illustration of Sachs's view that Toscanini felt obligated to play certain American works. The conductor almost certainly would have respected the professionalism of these scores, but one wonders if he saw anything of substance in them.

Debussy, Claude (1862–1918)

Unofficially Issued Repertory
Marche écossaise (3 Apr. 1940)
Danse, orch. Ravel (13 Apr. 1940)
La damoiselle élue (13 Apr. 1940)

Officially Issued
Images: "Ibéria" (5 Nov. 1938, 13 Apr. 1940, 14 Nov. 1943, 11 Feb. 1945, 2 Mar. 1948, 25 Mar. 1950, 14 Feb. 1953): RCA 60265 (**2 June 1950**)
La mer (8 Jan. 1938, 13 Apr. 1940, 11 Apr, 1943, 11 Feb. 1945, 2 Mar. 1947, 29 Nov. 1947, 27 Mar. 1948, 29 Oct, 1949, 14 Feb. 1953): RCA 60265 (**1 June 1950**)
Nocturnes: *Nuages*; *Fêtes* (13 Apr. 1940, 15 Mar. 1952); *Fêtes* (27 Mar. 1948): RCA 60265 (*Nuages* from broadcast of **15 Mar. 1952**; *Fêtes* from broadcast of **27 Mar. 1948**)
Prelude to the Afternoon of a Faun (20 June 1943, 11 Feb. 1945, 27 Mar. 1948, 17 Feb. 1951, 14 Feb. 1953): RCA 60265 (from broadcast of **14 Feb. 1953**)

In 1908, Toscanini conducted the Italian premiere of Debussy's *Pelléas et Mélisande*. He had come to the score four years earlier and said he found "everything" in it "essential." Shortly thereafter he wrote to a friend:

> I hardly knew the name of [a] composer who has won all your sympathy: the Frenchman Debussy with his *Pelléas and Mélisande*. . . . His art overturns everything that has been done until now. He doesn't have [Richard] Strauss's technique, but he is a great genius, more elegant and undoubtedly more daring. On first venturing upon him, you are completely disoriented, but once you have begun to converse a little more freely with his language—and that of his inspirer Maeterlinck—you end up being fascinated. Thinking of the theater of Maeterlinck's characters, I can confirm my opinion that Debussy's music is the fulfillment of that art. However, our public today [1904] is not yet mature to sense this, let alone accept it.[31]

Although Toscanini did not conduct *Pelléas* at NBC, this letter certainly makes plain his attitude toward the composer and his openness to what was clearly a strange and "disorienting" idiom. For one thing, contrary to the invective later directed at Toscanini, it affirms his delight in "modern" music. Then, too, it makes clear his knowledge of Maeterlinck. And obviously it declares his responsiveness to Debussy. The two met in 1910 when Toscanini was in Paris with the Metropolitan Opera; Debussy attended several of the company's performances.

Aside from *Pelléas* and the works he conducted at NBC, the only other Debussy score to enter Toscanini's repertory was *Le martyre de saint Sébastien*.

Central to his approach to the composer was an insistence on clarity. Inner voices had to sound, textures had to be clear; the notion that musical "impressionism" could be equated with veiled sonority and blurred lines carried no weight with the conductor.

Such an approach is evident in the three unofficially issued performances that were given only one broadcast presentation. The dance was titled *Tarantelle styrienne* and published as a solo work. The march was originally composed as a piano duet but later orchestrated by the composer. Toscanini's only performances at NBC of these short works are models of taste, clarity, and lightness. The march, in particular, is played with a rhythmic steadiness that underscores its unity as a theme-and-variations in miniature.

Toscanini had prepared *La damoiselle élue* on one previous occasion—during his last season with the New York Philharmonic. His interest in the work is significant. It was completed in 1888, when Toscanini was twenty-one and in the third year of his long career. If not one of the most concise and mature of Debussy's efforts, this cantata, based on a text by Dante Gabriel Rossetti, is certainly harmonically daring for its time—more so, in fact than the two extracts from Stravinsky's *Petrushka* that Toscanini performed with the New York Philharmonic and NBC Symphony. In this rather ephemeral work, Toscanini manages to suggest plateaus of contrast and to preserve continuity while conveying the music's evanescent character. He had an able collaborator in the soprano Jarmila Novotna.

With "Ibéria," the differences from one account to another are primarily centered on tempo. The 1945 and 1948 performances are the fastest, those of 1938, 1943, and 1953 being considerably slower. Between these extremes is the 1950 recording. And stamping all of them is a remarkably subtle rhythmic elasticity that gives the lie to the notion that Toscanini was a rigid literalist. Milton Katims, a violinist in the NBC orchestra and himself a conductor, summed this up well:

> I suggested [to Toscanini] that one of the guest conductor's playing [at NBC] of the "Perfumes of the Night" movement of Debussy's *Ibéria* was dull because he played precisely what was printed on the page. . . . Maestro insisted that that was what he did! I brought the score over to the piano and asked him to play the section. As he played, I pointed out the slight *stringendi* here, the *poco ritardando* he made there, his rubato in another spot, etc.—none of which was in the score; . . . He protested that it wasn't possible to be a machine.[32]

A similar flexibility was present in Toscanini's approach to *La mer*, which he played more frequently than any other score during his years in the United States. Here, however, variations among these performances are not limited to tempo. They involve, in part, changes in style that were unfolding during Toscanini's tenure at NBC, most notably the gradual disappearance of portamento as an expressive device. In the earliest of Toscanini's surviving performances of this work—a 1935 account (once available on an EMI CD), one from 1936 with the New York Philharmonic (issued on CD in a poor aircheck by Music and Arts), and the 1938 NBC performance—one encounters some smoothed-away edges and a more pervasive legato style than was to be heard in later NBC accounts. By the time Toscanini recorded *La mer* in 1941 with the Philadelphia Orchestra, his basic approach had become a bit more angular and sharply etched, the prevailing atmosphere of the recording probably tied as much to the greater tonal richness of that orchestra as to the conductor's evolving style.

The relatively dry acoustics of studio 8H may have contributed to Toscanini's obsession with clarity in *La mer*. Granted, he had always sought it, gaining approval from Debussy to amend the score with doublings and rebalancings so that everything would "sound." But the resonance-free ambience of 8H made even greater clarity possible, and with the 1943 broadcast, one encounters the music as if it had been X-rayed; things are all too clinical, almost coldly detailed. In its way, it is a brilliant performance, but one that, in spite of all the details it exposes, seems less expressive than others, in particular the NBC accounts of 1938 and 1953 and the studio recording of 1950.

Toscanini never performed *Sirènes*, the third of the three orchestral nocturnes by Debussy, possibly because, alone among them, it calls for a chorus. And he never recorded any in the studio, the two that were issued being drawn from broadcasts. That RCA chose the 1948 account of *Fêtes* for release is surprising. Perhaps it is the only one Toscanini approved. But it is the most intense of the three broadcasts and is less well recorded than the last one (available on videocassette). And neither has the subtlety of the 1940 reading, which is more supplely shaped.

There are those critics and musicians who have found Toscanini's way with *Prelude to the Afternoon of a Faun* unidiomatic. Even some of his staunchest admirers among the members of the NBC Symphony were critical of his approach to this score. As the principal cellist Frank Miller noted, "If one could say that he did anything poorly, it would be something like . . . *The Afternoon of a Faun*: he did this piece too straight, conducting it in three right from the start, and it didn't have the freedom we have come to expect in it."[33]

Yet in rehearsing the work, Toscanini would admonish the orchestra, "libero, libero" (freely, freely). And Miller's comments notwithstanding, Toscanini did play the work freely—not so freely as did others, perhaps, but still without rigidity. His concern for clarity, however, makes the rhythm seem less free than it otherwise might be were the overall execution less precise and clear. One is most aware of this in the 1951 performance, where Toscanini took pains in rehearsal to achieve his ends. Other performances, particularly that of 1953, where the more distant and resonant acoustics of Carnegie Hall are a major asset, have a slightly softer focus that brings Toscanini's subtle, carefully gauged rubato to the fore. Owing to some imprecise moments in that performance, the RCA release of it incorporates a few substitutions from the dress rehearsal.

Degeyter, Pierre (1848–1932)

Unofficially Issued Repertory
"The Internationale," arr. Toscanini (7 Nov. 1943)

As in his arrangement of "The Star-Spangled Banner," Toscanini's treatment of "The Internationale" lends it the dignity and stature befitting a national anthem.

Donizetti, Gaetano (1797–1848)

Officially Issued Repertory
Don Pasquale: Overture (20 June 1943, 13 Mar. 1948): RCA 60309 (**5 Oct. 1951**)

Aside from differences in acoustical ambience, these performances are sufficiently similar to permit undetectable substitutions from one to the other. The same might be said for a 1921 acoustic recording of the work Toscanini made with the La Scala Orchestra (RCA 60315) were its sound not so primitive.

Dukas, Paul (1865–1935)

Unofficially Issued Repertory
Ariane et Barbe-bleue: Suite (2 Mar. 1947)

Officially Issued Repertory
The Sorcerer's Apprentice (12 Feb. 1938, 20 Jan. 1943, 18 Mar. 1950): RCA 60322 (**19 Mar. 1950**)

Although Toscanini had led the American premiere of Dukas's opera *Ariane et Barbe-bleue* at New York's Metropolitan in 1911, he came to judge it a dull work. But he believed that passages were worth preserving, and he arranged this suite from it, his NBC performance being the only one he ever gave. What Toscanini admired in the music remains a mystery, but as a piece of musical history, the performance has some value.

The Sorcerer's Apprentice provides one instance where Toscanini's NBC performances indisputably surpass a New York Philharmonic recording he made. His 1929 version with that orchestra was unduly rushed, probably to permit the work to be contained on two sides of a single 78 disc; the NBC recording, in its slower tempo, was spread over three sides in its initial 78 rpm release. More important, it succeeds far better in conveying the music's wit and programmatic content, as do Toscanini's broadcast performances.

Dvořák, Antonín (1841–1904)

Unofficially Issued Repertory

Cello Concerto in B Minor, Op. 104 (28 Jan. 1945)
Scherzo capriccioso, Op. 66 (20 Apr. 1940, 28 Jan. 1945)

Officially Issued Repertory

Symphony No. 9 in E Minor, Op. 95, "From the New World" (5 Nov.
  1938, 13 Dec. 1941, 18 Mar. 1950, 31 Jan. 1953): RCA 60729
  (**2 Feb. 1953**)
Symphonic Variations, Op. 78 (4 Dec. 1948, 17 Nov. 1951): RCA 60336,
  videocassette only (telecast **4 Dec. 1948**)

Aside from the works he played at NBC, the only other Dvořák pieces in Toscanini's repertoire were the *Carnival* and *Othello* Overtures and the Slavonic Dance No. 6. The omissions are striking. One would think that the composer's Sixth and Seventh Symphonies, with their melodic richness and clearly defined structures, would have appealed to Toscanini. But, as noted previously, in 1905 he read through the score of the Seventh and found it wanting. Yet that D minor work has far more to recommend it than the D minor Symphony of Martucci, which Toscanini played in Italy and the United States. Taste, even among the most cultivated of musicians, sometimes defies explanation, unless, in this case, personal fondness for a composer and Italian patriotism are considered.

Owing possibly to union restrictions, commercial release of the 1948 broadcast of the *Symphonic Variations* has been confined to video editions, in which the sound is excellent and displays studio 8H at its best. The performance hardly differs from the one Toscanini directed three years later, though the earlier one is marginally tauter.

Toscanini's first two performances of the "New World" Symphony are studies in extremes. The earliest (and the only one to contain a first-movement repeat) is the most rhythmically elastic, with greater contrast between the first and second subjects in the first movement and a more expansive introduction to it. The 1950 and 1953 accounts are almost identical: free of mannerisms and marked by less rubato than in 1938, but still without the hard-driven rigidity of the overly intense 1941 performance. In the main, Toscanini projected the same textural transparency, formal unity, and dramatic tension in this score that he brought to those of Beethoven and Brahms, thereby emphasizing the way in which Dvořák echoes their classicism. Indeed, under Toscanini, the "New World" rightly emerges as a symphony as distinguished as any of those by Brahms.

The account of Dvořák's familiar cello concerto, if blemished by technical lapses from the soloist, Edmund Kurtz, is a prime example of how Toscanini made the familiar sound fresh. The expansive but rhythmically flexible opening ritornello and the shaping of all the orchestral portions (sometimes with retouched scoring) give passages a less folksy, more stately symphonic ethos. This creates a formal integrity, dramatic profile, and imperious grandeur not always associated with his work—traits that, again, suggest Dvořák's closeness to Brahms. The performance marks Toscanini's sole presentation of the piece in the United States.

The two performances of the *Scherzo capriccioso* stand as cogent evidence against the claim that Toscanini's interpretations were always the same. These readings are markedly different, the earlier one considerably broader, more richly inflected, and more liberal use of *stringendo*, and a more *Ländler*-like second subject.

Elgar, Sir Edward (1857–1934)

Unofficially Issued Repertory
Introduction and Allegro for Strings, Op. 47 (20 Apr. 1940)

Officially Issued Repertory
Enigma Variations (4 Feb. 1939, 18 Nov. 1945, 5 Nov. 1949, 17 Feb. 1951, 5 Jan. 1952): RCA 60287 (**10 Dec. 1951**)

Toscanini's earliest performance of the *Introduction and Allegro for Strings* was probably the one he gave in 1937 with the BBC Symphony. Using a full complement of strings in this NBC presentation, he produced a transparent sonority suggestive of a chamber orchestra. With its sharp contouring and tautly drawn lines, the performance is a model of clarity and unity, and it is surprising that Olin Downes, in reviewing the concert for the *New York Times*, said not a word about either the work itself or Toscanini's performance.

As Toscanini's Beethoven performances had been indicted in some (doubtlessly narrow-minded) quarters for being "too Italian," so, too, his Elgar was ridiculed in the press—after a 1935 BBC performance of the *Enigma Variations*—for being "un-English." Responding to such criticisms, the English conductor Sir Landon Ronald suggested that Elgar's "idiom was obviously no secret for Toscanini. Some of the best performances I have heard were from the composer himself, but Toscanini excelled because he has a genius for conducting Elgar has not."[34] Similar corrective responses came from such eminences as Sir Adrian Boult and Ernest Newman. Boult noted: "An artist of the caliber of Toscanini seems to have the power of grasping the essence of the style of any music he touches, and it has been a great experience to hear . . . the beauties of everything he has rehearsed . . . in what seems to be inevitably the right musical language."[35]And Newman observed: "When Toscanini conducted the 'Nimrod' of the Enigma Variations, some of us may have been conscious of a slight non-English accent in the music, but in spite of that the performance soared to a height and plumbed a depth I have never known it to approach since."[36] The question, then, is, if Toscanini's conception lacked national traits (as most performances usually do), what, then, best defines it? The answer is, more than anything else, its flair for the dramatic, its plateaus of contrast from one variation to another, and its shaping and building of climaxes. In short, it is a view that sees the work whole in the tradition of classical variation style. Central to that style, of course, is the harmonic backbone that forms the variations' central nervous system. Many critics, to be sure, who subscribed to the senseless notion that Toscanini "Italianized" everything he led, saw him as a conductor who responded to music in terms of its melodic line at the expense of its vertical harmonic structure. Nothing disproves such nonsense better than his approach to the *Enigma Variations*. Indeed, when rehearsing the work with the BBC Symphony, he took special care with its harmonic underpinnings: "Is only 'armony, but is lovely music," he told the orchestra, "and it must be alive."[37]

In all of Toscanini's surviving accounts, which, in addition to those already cited, include a 1935 BBC concert performance once available on an EMI CD, the basic approach seems the same, the dissimilarities from one performance to the next involving differences in sonority or in precision. His very last performance, however, suggests he was taking special care with some details and balances and with conveying the delicacy of the music's tender moments. The two Elgar works that Toscanini led at NBC comprise the only ones by the composer in his repertory.

Enesco, Georges (1881–1955)

Unofficially Issued Repertory
Romanian Rhapsody No. 1, Op. 11 (14 Dec. 1940, 13 Jan. 1946)

This pleasant potboiler was once moderately popular, and Toscanini's two performances of it have a welcome liveliness that negates none of the music's charm.

Falla, Manuel de (1876–1946)

Unofficially Issued Repertory
El amor brujo (28 Jan. 1939; Ritual Fire Dance and Dance of Terror only, 3 Sept. 1944)

Josephine Burzio's singing in the complete performance of 1939 sounds harsh and steely, traits one might ascribe to flaws in the somewhat strident recording produced by the NBC engineers. Some reviewers, however, criticized her overly brilliant tone, which suggests that the engineering may not have been at fault. One unidentified critic writing in *Musical America* (10 February 1939) found, on the other hand, her singing had "an animal intensity and power" used "to superb effect." Both the positive and negative views of Burzio might be applied as well to Toscanini's conception of the music. Richly colored almost to the point of garishness, at times fiercely pushed, it is a very intense, almost raw account of the score. The two excerpts from the later broadcast do nothing to dispel the impression left by the earlier performance.

Fernandez, Oscar Lorenzo (1897–1948)

Unissued Repertory
Reisado di pastore: Batuque (14 May 1940)

Fernandez was a distinguished Brazilian composer with a marked national style. The *batuque* is a Brazilian dance, and this one—the concluding movement of a suite—had gained considerable popularity in its day. Toscanini may have prepared it as an appropriate inclusion for his 1940 South American tour, where it was presented twice, once in São Paulo, once in Rio de Janiero. Lasting about four minutes, it makes a striking effect in its reiterated patterns and ostinato bass. In this regard it is redolent of Ravel's *Boléro*, albeit on a smaller scale. In this Washington, D.C., concert, which launched the South American tour, Toscanini played the work with verve and great rhythmic impetus.

Foroni, Jacopo (1825–58)

Unissued Repertory
Overture in C Minor (2 Sept. 1945)

During his short life, Foroni gained distinction as a composer of opera and of orchestral works. In 1849 he settled in Stockholm, where he had great success as a conductor. Toscanini played only two of Foroni's works, this C minor overture and another in A major. This was the only performance of Foroni that Toscanini gave in the United States. The work—well crafted, conventional, and not very interesting of itself—commands some attention as representative of nineteenth-century Italian orchestral music.

Franchetti, Alberto (1860–1942)

Unissued Repertory
Cristoforo Colombo: Act II: Nocturne (14 Dec. 1940)

Although he left orchestral and chamber works, Franchetti achieved his greatest success as a composer of opera. Toscanini conducted four of those operas, preparing *Cristoforo Colombo* more frequently than any of the others—eight times in all—but never in the United States. This brief, atmospheric, but relatively inconsequential excerpt is thus the only surviving document of a Toscanini performance of Franchetti's music.

Franck, César (1822–90)

Unofficially Issued Repertory

Les éolides (12 Nov. 1938, 27 Apr. 1940, 7 Feb. 1944, 5 Mar. 1949, 13 Dec. 1953)

Officially Issued Repertory

Psyché: Psyché and Eros (14 Jan. 1939, 5 Jan. 1952): RCA CD 60322 (**7 Jan. 1952**)

Rédemption: Symphonic Interlude (2 Mar. 1947, 15 Mar. 1952): RCA 60335, videocassette only (telecast of **15 Mar. 1952**)

Symphony in D Minor (14 Dec. 1940, 24 Mar. 1946): RCA CD 60320 (first movement from the **24 Mar. 1946** broadcast; remainder from the broadcast of **14 Dec. 1940**)

Toscanini's five performances of *Les éolides* at NBC as well as several that he gave with the New York Philharmonic bespeak his fondness for this symphonic poem depicting Aeolius and based on a work by Lecomte de Lisle. Each of the NBC performances reveals the conductor's command of balances, sensitivity to orchestral color, and ability to produce subtle dynamic shadings. But the account from 1938 stands out because of its slightly greater freedom. Its rubato, applied always in the best of taste, is never so free as to violate the basic pulse, but it adds a tempestuous undercurrent to the music that suits its character perfectly. What is more, Toscanini's phrasing in 1938 is marked by subtly arched dynamic gradations (absent from the other performances) that heighten the melodic profile. It is also worth noting that the 1938 performance discredits the notion that the NBC Symphony had not, at this early stage of its existence, become sensitized to Toscanini's demands (see chapter 2, note 2). Such subtle rhythmic shadings could be produced only by a highly responsive orchestra.

Toscanini's interest in the Symphonic Interlude from *Rédemption* attests to his nineteenth-century roots. During the earlier part of the twentieth century this excerpt had been fairly popular, gaining four 78 rpm recordings (this at a time when many of Mozart's major piano concertos were still unrecorded). The excellent sound on the video of the 1952 telecast does the performance justice. Like the one on the broadcast of 1947, the performance is beautifully shaped and exemplifies Toscanini's ability to build plateaus of tension and resolution. Neither performance of *Psyché and Eros* differs radically from the conductor's 1952 studio recording: all three provide excellent examples of his skill at sustaining a gentle sensuousness within a rhythmically secure framework that precludes sentimentality.

The first commercial release of Toscanini's account of the celebrated Franck symphony did not occur until twenty-six years after his death in a composite that Toscanini favored, made up of the first movement from the 1946 broadcast and the second and third movements from the 1940 one. It is quite likely that Toscanini rejected the earlier first movement because of a poorly executed solo. Otherwise, that performance, in its broader tempo and stricter rhythm, proves more intense, with a stronger climax than Toscanini was able to generate six years later. There, accelerations occassionally break the mood of this remarkably moody music. Both performances, however, convey the movement's eerie gloom and, in effect, comprise a reaction against those performances in which pulse, line, and structure were frequently ruptured in the name of "expression." In fact, it was such tasteless extremes that led Toscanini to write a scathing letter (never mailed) to Leopold Stokowski.[38]

Gershwin, George (1898–1937)

Unofficially Issued Repertory
Piano Concerto in F Major (2 Apr. 1944)
Rhapsody in Blue (1 Nov. 1942)

Officially Issued Repertory
An American in Paris (14 Nov. 1943, 18 Mar. 1945): RCA 60307 (**18 May 1945**)

One might not expect Toscanini to be responsive to Gershwin, and the opening ritornello of the concerto is a bit stiff rhythmically, lacking some of the swagger implicit in its Charleston-like motif. But with the entry of the soloist, Oscar Levant, Toscanini seems to relax, and the performance, as with that of his only NBC presentation of *Rhapsody in Blue*, proves surprisingly stylish from a conductor to whom jazz could not have been all that familiar.

The studio recording of *An American in Paris*, made exactly two months after Toscanini's second broadcast performance of the work, has justly been cited as an example of how fine studio 8H could sound under ideal conditions. In this case, those conditions were achieved by removing seats from the floor and placing the orchestra where the audience ordinarily sat. All three of Toscanini's surviving performances of this work (probably the only ones he led) evince his musicality and responsiveness to its jazz idiom, while suggesting an elegance not always encountered in ostensibly more idiomatic performances. And as William Youngren has pointed out in his annotations for the RCA CD, Toscanini's basic tempo, while sometimes called "too fast," is identical to that favored by the composer.

Gilbert, Henry F. (1868–1928)

Unissued Repertory
Comedy Overture on Negro Themes (7 Feb. 1943)

A student of Edward MacDowell, Gilbert gained widespread distinction for his ballet *The Dance in Place Congo*, which was performed in 1918 at the Metropolitan Opera. Toscanini was not the first major European conductor to turn to the *Comedy Overture*. In 1911, Max Fiedler performed it with the Boston Symphony. Toscanini's carefully prepared performance at NBC may seem a bit too straitlaced for music of such folksy style.

Gillis, Don (1912–78)

Unissued Repertory
Symphony No. 5½ (21 Sept. 1947)

Possibly out of appreciation for Gillis's work as a producer of the NBC Symphony broadcasts, Toscanini lavished exceptional care on this thoroughly professional but ultimately inconsequential ten-minute, four-movement exercise in musical humor. In the context of the maestro's comparative stiffness in directing Gilbert's *Comedy Overture*, this presentation of the Gillis symphony displays surprising whimsy and sparkle. Toscanini was clearly responding to the work's subtitle, "A Symphony for Fun."

Giordano, Umberto (1867–1948)

Unofficially Issued Repertory
Il Re: Dance of the Moor (10 Dec. 1949)
Siberia: Prelude to Act II (10 Dec. 1949)

Born the same year as Toscanini, Giordano had an especially successful career in Italy as an operatic composer. He is best known for *Andrea Chénier*. Toscanini directed five operas by Giordano, including *Siberia* and the world premiere of *Il Re*. These two instrumental excerpts, performed with precision and exceptional clarity, reveal Giordano as a superb orchestrator and master of mood.

Glinka, Mikhail (1804–57)

Officially Issued Repertory
Jota aragonesa (7 Nov. 1943, 3 Sept. 1944, 4 Nov. 1945, 28 Feb. 1948, 4 Mar. 1950): RCA 60308 (broadcast of **4 Mar. 1950**)
Kamarinskaya (21 Dec. 1940): RCA 60323 (broadcast of **21 Dec. 1940**)

Jota aragonesa most likely entered Toscanini's repertory in 1943 with his first NBC performance. Unfortunately, his remarkable responsiveness to this colorful score is not well conveyed in the rushed, at times ragged account of 1950, the one chosen for commercial release. Far more effective and better recorded are the three earliest NBC presentations, all executed with greater precision and less rigidity than that of 1950. Here is one of a few instances where it would seem that RCA, in seeking Toscanini's approval of a broadcast performance, presented him with the most recent of possible choices, following a not-always-accurate assumption that the last account offered the most up-to-date sound. Worse yet, such a policy may well have deprived Toscanini of hearing earlier and musically superior efforts. The performance of *Kamarinskaya* is suitably atmospheric and manifests the conductor's sensitivity to orchestral color.

Gluck, Christoph Willibald (1714–87)

Officially Issued Repertory

Iphigenia in Aulis: Overture (28 Jan. 1939, 18 Feb. 1941, 22 Nov. 1952): RCA 60280 (broadcast of **22 Nov. 1952**)

Orfeo ed Euridice: Act II (1 Apr. 1945, 22 Nov. 1952): RCA 60280 (broadcast of **22 Nov. 1952**)

Act II: Dance of the Blessed Spirits (no broadcast; recording session only): RCA 60280 (**4 Nov. 1946**)

The three performances of the overture to *Iphigenia in Aulis* employ the enriched orchestration and concert ending of Wagner's arrangement. All are remarkably similar and favor a slightly broader tempo than that adopted by most other conductors of the time, the one issued by RCA being the broadest of the three.

Toscanini's two broadcasts of the second act of *Orfeo ed Euridice* are interesting for a number of reasons. For one, of the 117 operas in the conductor's repertory, it is the oldest. Completed in 1762, it is one of but four from the eighteenth century that he directed, the others being Gluck's *Armide* and Mozart's *Don Giovanni* and *Magic Flute*. When he led productions at La Scala and the Metropolitan Opera, he discarded its overture and interpolated an aria, trio, and chorus from other Gluck works. The production was pilloried in Italy, with one critic calling it "Morpheus and Euridice." The reaction in New York to the Met's production, however, was quite different: the eminent Henry Krehbiel called Toscanini's treatment of the music "loving" and the production "the most interesting incident of the operatic season [1909–10]."[39]

The word "loving" seems especially significant in that it applies equally well to Toscanini's two broadcasts of the second act. Toscanini was so intense an artist, his recreative style so dramatic and powerful, that it can easily be forgotten that delicacy and tenderness also stamped his work. Such tenderness is apparent at the close of Act II, where the chorus comments on Orfeo's leading Euridice from Hades. Toscanini's sustained, lyrical tempo for this portion brings out the spirit of Elysium to which the chorus alludes and the loving ethos of Orfeo's sentiments. The 1945 performance of this chorus is broader than in 1952, suggesting an almost churchly reverence. The slightly faster pace of the later account preserves the requisite tenderness but adds a felicitous suggestion of sensuality absent in 1945.

With the Dance of the Furies, the situation is reversed, the earlier account being faster, almost to the point of becoming febrile. In 1952, Toscanini's greater breadth made the music seem less trivial and more terrifying. In both performances he augmented Gluck's orchestra (as he doubtless must have done at La Scala and the Metropolitan) with additional brass and (at one point) tam-tam. Thus, although he made a considerable effort to suggest what he believed was an appropriate eighteenth-century sonority in the music of Haydn and Mozart, he was all too ready to invoke different standards in the opera house if he felt the music's dramatic intent was better served by so doing.

Nan Merriman, who sang the role of Orfeo in both broadcasts, wrote about the pains Toscanini took in preparing the later one:

> We had our first piano rehearsal . . . a full nine months before. We began . . . by studying the score—the orchestral score. I [became] aware of every orchestral color behind the vocal part. . . . [Toscanini] described to me the quality of sound he wanted and told me why he wanted it so. He was anything but capricious—he had excellent reasons for every effort he asked his soloists and orchestra to make . . . [writing] out for me . . . annotations of the minutest sort: *"piano quasi parlando, con emozione, sempre più calmo. . . .* A blueprint, a treasure."[40]

Forty-three years earlier, Toscanini had written similar directions in Louise Homer's score when she was preparing the role for his Metropolitan Opera production.

The 1946 recording of the brief Dance of the Blessed Spirits was made as a filler for Toscanini's second recording of Mozart's "Haffner" Symphony, duplicating a practice favored in his first recording of that work in 1929 with the New York Philharmonic, where that excerpt also filled out the album. Neither offers anything markedly different from Toscanini's accounts of the complete act.

Goldmark, Karl (1830–1915)

Unofficially Issued Repertory
Symphony in E-flat Major, Op. 26, "Rustic Wedding": In the Garden; Serenade (3 Sept. 1944)

Evidently viewing this work more as a suite than as a symphony, Toscanini never programmed the entire score, choosing instead to play only excerpts from it, usually the two he presented on this single occasion at NBC. The performances are striking for their unaffected simplicity, clarity, and tenderness.

Gould, Morton (1913–96)

Unissued Repertory
A Lincoln Legend (1 Nov. 1942)

At the time Toscanini led this performance of *A Lincoln Legend*, Gould was working as an arranger for CBS. Speaking at a luncheon in 1985, the composer recalled that the CBS musicians would playfully twit one another with the jibe, "Hey, Toscanini's looking for you." As Gould related the story, Toscanini had heard *A Lincoln Legend* on the radio and decided to program it. He left a message for Gould at CBS asking the composer to call him. The message was relayed: "Hey, Toscanini wants to see you." Naturally thinking it was a joke, Gould initially ignored it, nearly losing a coast-to-coast broadcast in the process. Ultimately he was convinced of its legitimacy, and his conversation with Toscanini led to this performance. The work, masterfully orchestrated with touchingly evocative moments, incorporates Civil War allusions such as "The Battle Hymn of the Republic" and "The Old Gray Mare," the former often transmogrified into dissonant, almost tortured variations.

Graener, Paul (1872–1944)

Unofficially Issued Repertory
The Flute of Sans-Souci (5 Nov. 1938)

Graener composed in nearly all genres and achieved considerable success with his operas. The title of this work alludes to the castle of Frederick the Great, where the monarch created a court orchestra and composed for flute. This fifteen-minute suite for chamber orchestra recalls baroque idiom, even to the point of calling for a harpsichord in the third of its four movements. But it also suggests a folk-tune style that Graener often used in his music. Toscanini's performance has a relaxed verve and lightness and a broadly sustained slow movement.

Grieg, Edvard (1843–1907)

Unofficially Issued Repertory
Holberg Suite, Op. 40 (27 Apr. 1940)

This music rarely appears on concert programs today, yet has remained sufficiently popular to have gained a number of recordings in the CD catalog. Listening to some of those recordings sets Toscanini's performance off in a revealing light, underscoring its directness, freedom from affectation, and natural, singing gracefulness. In its stark simplicity, it shines as an extraordinarily sophisticated reading.

Griffes, Charles Tomlinson (1884–1920)

Unofficially Issued Repertory
The White Peacock (7 Feb. 1943)

Composed in 1915, this four-and-a-half-minute work is still heard, if less frequently than when Toscanini performed it. The first of the *Roman Sketches*, Op. 7, it was originally intended for piano. Had Debussy never written *Prelude to the Afternoon of a Faun*, it is quite possible that *The White Peacock* would never have appeared. Toscanini directed it with evocative color, but for all of the effort that probably went into the performance, the music sounds rather faceless.

Grofé, Ferde (1892–1972)

Officially Issued Repertory
Grand Canyon Suite (7 Feb. 1943, 2 Sept. 1945): RCA 60307 (**11 Sept. 1945**)

Toscanini's two broadcast performances of this work are essentially identical to his studio recording. The seriousness with which he approached it is suggested by William Carboni's recollection of one of the rehearsals:

> [Toscanini] kept asking Grofé if the tempo was right . . . ; after all, Grofé was the composer and the Old Man always felt the composer was much more important than the conductor. Every time he asked Grofé anything, he always called him "Maestro"; and Grofé was just in heaven. When it was all over, the Old Man called him up to the podium to ask him if everything was all right, and Grofé said yes and was so overcome as he backed away that he backed into the chairs and fell over them.[41]

Handel, George Frideric (1685–1759)

Unofficially Issued Repertory
Concerto Grosso in B Minor, Op. 6 No. 12 (18 Feb. 1938, 27 Nov. 1947)
Concerto Grosso in D Major, Op. 6 No. 5: Minuet (20 June 1943)

Both performances of the Op. 6 No. 12 are atypical for a major symphony orchestra director of the time in that Toscanini employed a relatively small ensemble and a harpsichord for the continuo part, which is clearly audible over the strings. Granted, the approach lacks many trappings of authentically styled presentations of baroque music: dotted rhythms are not overdotted, trills do not begin from the upper auxiliary note, and ornamentation in general is sparse. But in spirit and overall sonority, these readings, with their lean string tone and minimal vibrato, foreshadow period-instrument presentations and provide one of many examples of Toscanini's sensitivity to eighteenth-century style. Toscanini was not alone in playing this music with a small ensemble. Bruno Walter presented it with the NBC Symphony using a similarly reduced orchestra, but he favored piano for the continuo part. Toscanini's account of the Minuet from Op. 6 No. 5 is a model of courtly grace and disproves the notion that he was always rigid and tightfisted when conducting baroque or classical works.

Harris, Roy (1898–1979)

Unofficially Issued Repertory
Symphony No. 3 (16 Mar. 1940)

Completed in 1938, this symphony received its radio premiere in this performance. Despite being subsequently championed by Leonard Bernstein, the work lost much of its initial appeal by the end of the century. Yet, as is heard in this Toscanini account, it makes one wonder if a revival is not in order. The sustained intensity of its opening and the controlled jubilation of its close lend the music a power and dignity it does not always attain in the hands of lesser conductors. This is surely one of Toscanini's finest accounts of American music. It is not, however, a note-perfect reading: the timpanist misses two important entrances, one two bars after rehearsal number 43, the other one bar after 53 (Schirmer score).

Haydn, Franz Joseph (1732–1809)

Unofficially Issued Repertory
Symphony No. 31 in D Major, "Hornsignal" (27 Oct. 1938)
Symphony No. 92 in G Major, "Oxford" (19 Mar. 1944)
Symphony No. 104 in D Major, "London" (31 Oct. 1943)

Officially Issued Repertory
Sinfonia concertante in B-flat Major, Op. 84 (14 Oct. 1939, 6 Mar. 1948):
        RCA 60282 (broadcast of **6 Mar. 1948**)
Symphony No. 88 in G Major (19 Feb. 1938): RCA 60281 (**8 Mar. 1938**)
Symphony No. 94 in G Major, "Surprise" (20 June 1943, 24 Jan. 1953):
        RCA 60281 (**26 Jan. 1953**)
Symphony No. 98 in B-flat Major (22 Jan. 1938, 25 Mar. 1945, 19 Nov.
        1949): RCA 60281 (**25 May 1945**)
Symphony No. 99 in E-flat Major (1 Feb. 1941, 2 July 1944, 12 Mar. 1949):
        RCA 60282 (broadcast of **12 Mar. 1949**)
Symphony No. 101 in D Major, "Clock" (4 Apr. 1942): RCA 60282 (first
        movement **12 June 1947**, balance **6 Nov. 1946**)

Toscanini's interest in Symphony No. 31 is astonishing. At the time he programmed it, the work (like so many of Haydn's earlier symphonies) was ignored by virtually all major conductors, as is reflected by the lack of any recording of the score until after World War II. And Toscanini's attention to the music was not a matter of passing attraction. He had played it in 1934 with the New York Philharmonic and had planned a second NBC presentation for 8 November 1952, a plan that was scrapped to accommodate a performance of Beethoven's Eighth Symphony. Equally astonishing for its time is the style of Toscanini's presentation: a small orchestra that permits the four horns Haydn calls for to cut through the sonority, vibrantly enriching the color. Enhancing the spirit (if not the letter) of what we now call "authenticity" is a harpsichord, whose audibility attests to the small ensemble being used. The tempos for the first, third, and fourth movements are very lively, but never breathless; indeed, the tempo of the third movement exemplifies what many advocates of "authenticity" believe to be suitable for an eighteenth-century symphonic minuet.

The performance of Symphony No. 92 is less commanding. With exceptionally quick tempos for the first, third, and fourth movements, the overall conception has a slick glibness that often suggests Toscanini is skimming across the music's surface. This was Toscanini's only presentation of the work in the United States. He did, however, perform it at Oxford in 1937 with the BBC Symphony.

Toscanini's only NBC presentation of Symphony No. 104 (possibly the only time he ever performed the work) has some impressive moments, and he considered approving it for commercial release. After hearing a recording of the work made by a chamber orchestra under Edwin Fischer, however, he decided against it, finding Fischer's account superior. Robert C. Marsh has claimed that Fischer's "faster" tempo for the minuet convinced Toscanini of the inappropriateness of his own.[42] But the two conductors adopted virtually identical tempos for this movement, as well as for others. Where Fischer's performance scores over Toscanini's is in its greater nuance, its slightly more flexible pulse, and its resulting greater expressivity. This then, is an instance of the excessive intensity that infused many of Toscanini's wartime performances, but that was certainly not typical of his work in general. When he listened to this 1943 effort years later, he must have recognized its shortcomings: its rhythmic stiffness, its lack of inflection, and a prevailing tenseness.

When Toscanini led the first of his two NBC performances of the *Sinfonia concertante*, it marked his first American performance of the score and probably the first time he played it. In 1939 the work had not been recorded and was relatively unknown. Here, too, is another instance of Toscanini's interest in what was, for its day, unfamiliar repertory. Heard in the context of subsequent performances by other conductors, Toscanini's tempos sound unorthodox: broader than usual in the two initial movements, faster in the finale. In keeping with his usual treatment of Haydn, the orchestra is reduced. Of the two NBC performances, the later one (issued by RCA) is more precisely executed by the orchestra's first-desk soloists, but the earlier one gains from slightly greater rhythmic elasticity.

Speaking about Toscanini's only NBC broadcast of Symphony No. 88, the NBC violinist Josef Gingold noted:

> After the performance the Old Man came up beaming and said: "Did you hear the beautiful tempo *primi violini* took in the finale?" [People backstage] laughed at the idea of the violins taking a tempo, and he said: "*Si*, they took the tempo." Of course it was his tempo; but within a hair's breadth it could be a tiny bit on the fast side; and once it started, there was nothing he could do; so, smart man that he was, he took what he got—which happened to be perfect—and played along with it.[43]

Gingold's comments are interesting in the context of Toscanini's studio recording, made two months after the broadcast. In the later effort, the tempo for the finale is slightly accelerated relative to that for the broadcast. Both, however, have a wonderfully pointed rhythmic inflection that brings out the music's humor and the ways (as is typical of Haydn) in which the movement seems to have difficulty getting started. Indeed, here is a prime example of Toscanini's sensitivity to the wit that underlies the classical style. Equally impressive is his expansive treatment of the second movement. Sustained with uncommon breadth in the broadcast and even slightly more in the recording, it demonstrates Toscanini's refusal to trivialize Haydn's slow movements by playing them more briskly than the composer's specifications for tempo (in this case largo) suggest. As a result, the movement acquires a sustained intensity, its *fortissimo* eruptions have a welcome power, and the thirty-second-note figurations accompanying those eruptions gain exceptional clarity. Only in the first movement (with a repeated exposition in both performances) is Toscanini's conception unconvincing, his unorthodox speed lending the music a breathlessness that masks its inherent charm.

Surely one of Toscanini's most controversial (and possibly least satisfying) Haydn interpretations is embodied in his two NBC broadcasts and studio recording of the "Surprise" Symphony. The tempos for the first and third movements are outrageously fast, so much so in the latter that it sounds more like a one-to-the-bar scherzo than a three-to-the-bar minuet. That the orchestra managed to execute these movements clearly at Toscanini's tempo is impressive, but the perception remains that the conductor's overdrive robs the music of its contour. The 1943 broadcast is marginally less offensive in this regard, but insufficiently so to redeem it. That these movements can sustain an unusually fleet pace is clear from a superb performance that Guido Cantelli led at NBC (available on a Music and Arts CD). But his slightly greater expansiveness permits motifs to have greater focus and harmonic motion to acquire better definition.

Toscanini's approach, essentially identical in all three performances, is far more convincing in the second and fourth movements. He does not exaggerate the explosive chord in the second movement that has inspired the symphony's nickname, but he clarifies the many surprises in the finale, where each recurrence of the main theme generates an unexpected turn of melody, timbre, or dynamics. Nevertheless, from a conductor who was one of the major Haydn proponents of his time, Toscanini's performances of this work are major disappointments.

The maestro's interpretation of Symphony No. 98 is another matter. To judge from the available evidence, the work entered his repertory in 1937 in a performance with the Vienna Philharmonic. As with the *Sinfonia concertante*, he was then exploring relatively unknown music; no recording of the score was available, and when Toscanini made one in 1945, he was the first conductor of major international reputation to have done so.[44]

When preparing for the first of his three NBC broadcasts of the work, Toscanini may well have read (or recalled) Sir Donald Tovey's essay about it.[45] He was, understandably, an admirer of Tovey's writing. Both were concerned with music as music and focused on such matters as structure, coherence, balance, and unity. Then, too, Toscanini, in responding to a laudatory introduction to the BBC Symphony in 1935 from its director, Sir Adrian Boult, said, "I am only an honest musician." In a similar vein, Tovey wrote, "As a plain musician, I believe music to be music."[46] Toscanini may have been influenced by Tovey's suggestion that the slow movement of the work "might be called [Haydn's] Requiem for Mozart."[47] Haydn had been shaken by Mozart's death, which occurred during Haydn's stay in London when the Symphony No. 98 was written and where it had its premiere. As in the Symphony No. 88, Toscanini invested this slow movement, an Adagio, with an unorthodox breadth that to this day remains atypical of its usual rendering. (He did the same in the first movement's introduction, another Adagio.) And in marked contrast to his way with the "Surprise" Symphony, none of his tempos is exceptionally fast. They are, to be sure, slightly quicker in the first and third movements than those adopted by such noted Haydn conductors as Sir Thomas Beecham and George Szell. But Toscanini's seeming briskness is partly the result of the clarity he secures. Often, the more cleanly the music is articulated, the faster the tempo seems. In this instance, Toscanini's concern for clarity must have been tied to his regard for Haydn as an orchestrator. He particularly delighted in the combination of flutes and basses in the symphony's third movement.[48]

The 1938 and 1945 performances have a vibrant liveliness inflected with bracing accents and well-sprung rhythm. The 1938 account, the only one to include a first-movement repeat, is slightly freer than the others. The 1949 performance is strange—one of the few readings of anything from Toscanini that is best described as bland, lacking the accents and animation that stamp his other performances of the score. Certainly the RCA recording of 1945, if wanting some of the freedom of the 1938 broadcast, is thoroughly representative of the maestro's finest work.

Toscanini's three NBC broadcasts of the Symphony No. 99 (the last of which was issued by RCA) are his only surviving accounts of a work he performed with the New York Philharmonic and the Philadelphia Orchestra. All three are similar, if not identical, in their relatively fleet outer movements, rippling minuet, and beautifully sustained slow movement, and all omit a first-movement repeat. The earliest among them (B. H. Haggin's favorite), although more cleanly executed than the wartime account of 1944, offers, after the broadest introduction, the speediest first movement. In this respect, the last of the three broadcasts is less extreme and more traditional and was surely the wisest choice for commercial release. It is also worth noting that all stand in marked contrast to the only widely circulated recording of the time—one made by Sir Thomas Beecham. Save for the slow movement, Beecham's tempos (in the first of his two studio recordings of the piece) are so much slower than Toscanini's, they make the symphony sound like a totally different work.

Of the eight Haydn symphonies in Toscanini's repertory, No. 101 is the score with which his association is the longest. It was the first Haydn symphony he conducted, appearing on his initial concert with the La Scala orchestra on 26 April 1896, a little more than a month after his podium debut.[49] It also appeared on his first (1926) and last (1945) concerts with the New York Philharmonic. Moreover, it is the only Haydn symphony he recorded twice—the first time in 1929 with the New York Philharmonic—and the only Haydn symphony he ever included when touring (in 1930 for the Philharmonic's trip to Europe).

It is thus ironic and most surprising that Toscanini gave but a single broadcast account of the score at NBC, and that one in the spontaneously organized special series underwritten by the United States Department of the Treasury in 1941. Among his other surviving concert presentations, one with the Hague Residential orchestra from 1938 is far too inferior sonically to permit anything but superficial judgment; the other, from a 1945 pension concert with the New York Philharmonic, is a major document.

The two studio recordings that Toscanini made of this work (like his pair of recordings of Mozart's "Haffner" Symphony) have fostered one of the most common (and frequently misleading) generalizations about his allegedly changing style: specifically, that the first recording embodies an "earlier," more flexible and expansive Toscanini, the second one, a "later," fleeter, less elastic conductor.[50] Granted, there are key differences between the two performances. Aside from the omission in the earlier account of a first-movement repeat present in the later one, the most notable differences center upon the weightier tone of the Philharmonic and Toscanini's preference with that orchestra for a few rhetorical touches at cadential points that he later discarded. The 1942 broadcast and 1946–47 NBC recording also correct a textual error that Toscanini followed in 1929 in the trio of the Minuet.[51]But tempos in both studio recordings, contrary to generally held views, are virtually identical, a fact I once illustrated on a broadcast by splicing the first-movement exposition from 1929 to the first ending of the exposition in the later recording, thereby creating a repeat in which no discernible change in tempo is evident. Without such a direct comparison, what may cause the Philharmonic version to seem slower is its inferior sound, which lacks the clarity of the NBC recording. And the broadcast of 1942 is essentially a copy of that recording save for its omission of the first-movement repeat.

It is with the 1945 Philharmonic version (with the first-movement repeat included) that the main differences between that orchestra and the NBC Symphony can be heard. Purged of the few rhetorical emphases that Toscanini favored in 1929, the 1945 performance still retains greater attractiveness than either of his NBC accounts. Despite tempos that do not really vary from those Toscanini took at NBC, the Philharmonic boasts greater tonal allure and more nuanced execution, especially with regard to subtle dynamic gradations. Put simply, the Philharmonic, nine years after Toscanini's departure as its director, remained a superior ensemble. But taken of itself, the NBC recording is admirable and thoroughly representative of a conception that, over nearly three decades, exhibited almost no change.

Like his Mozart, Toscanini's Haydn was concerned with clarity and stylishness. The New York Philharmonic double bassist Martin Bernstein told me that he never played either a Mozart or a Haydn symphony under Toscanini simply because the conductor always reduced the number of basses when performing the music. Thus, the sonority was never too heavy. It was further defined by a relatively pure string tone employing little vibrato. With the winds and brass given a prominence they did not always acquire in the Haydn performances of Toscanini's peers, color and texture were especially well defined, as was motivic profile.

When Toscanini was active, Haydn was far less familiar to the public than he is today, and conductors such as Bruno Walter, Wilhelm Furtwängler, and Willem Mengelberg—all exponents of the Austro-German tradition—had fewer Haydn symphonies in their repertory than did Toscanini. Indeed, one wonders what attracted Toscanini to Haydn. Perhaps it was the music's burly, peasantlike character, its brusque dynamics, brash harmonic turns, stark contrasts, rustic minuets, and folksy rondo themes—traits that make so many of Haydn's symphonies "surprise" symphonies. They must have also appealed to Toscanini as traits that stamp Haydn as the artistic progenitor of Beethoven. But most of all, it may well have been the composer's humanity that delighted him. Citing a flute part in one of Haydn's symphonies, Toscanini noted, "It is in the low register, not perfect, but how human."[52] All the same, he most surely had to have been aware of the artistry behind the humanity. He once refused, for example, to perform a Haydn symphony he had planned for a concert, saying: "There is no time to prepare it properly. In Haydn, there is no hiding or covering anything."[53] And more often than not, Toscanini uncovered in the composer's music the wit, drama, daring, and originality that define its greatness.

Hérold, Louis-Joseph-Ferdinand (1791–1833)

Officially Issued Repertory
Zampa: Overture (4 Apr. 1943, 27 Aug. 1944, 2 Aug. 1952): RCA 60310
   (**5 Aug. 1952**)

Each of the broadcasts on which this work appeared comprised what were called "light classics," and each of Toscanini's performances—flamboyant and brash, yet tightly controlled—is virtually indistinguishable from the others.

Hoffstetter, Roman (1742–1815)

Unissued Repertory
Serenade in F Major (4 Apr. 1943, 27 Aug. 1944)

In 1964, the English musicologist Alan Tyson established that the Op. 3 quartets once attributed to Haydn had in fact been composed by Hoffstetter. But at the time Toscanini gave these two performances, Haydn was assumed to have been the composer. Both accounts have an expressive delicacy and intimacy that bespeak an often overlooked side of Toscanini's recreative personality.

Humperdinck, Engelbert (1854–1921)

Unissued Repertory
Königskinder: Prelude to Act III (17 Nov. 1946)

Officially Issued Repertory
Hansel and Gretel: Prelude (13 Jan. 1946, 2 Aug. 1952): RCA 60310 (**5 Aug. 1952**)

Toscanini had led *Königskinder* in the theater, and this performance—the only one he gave of this prelude in the United States—may well have been his backward glance at that production. The piece echoes Wagner's *Tristan* and Tchaikovsky's "Pathétique" Symphony and sounds like the kind of vapid background music favored in Hollywood films of the 1940s to suggest "classical" music. The writing for winds, however, is very effective and well handled by Toscanini.

Both concert performances of the *Hansel and Gretel* Prelude are essentially identical to the studio effort, produced three days after the 1952 broadcast. All are unorthodox in that they maintain an uncommonly broad basic tempo. The effect of this pacing is to bring various references to the opera into a unified entity having a greater continuity than was customary for the recorded performances by Toscanini's contemporaries, notably Willem Mengelberg and Sir Adrian Boult.

Kabalevsky, Dmitri (1904–87)

Unofficially Issued Repertory
Symphony No. 2 (25 Mar. 1945, 26 Feb. 1949)

Officially Issued Repertory
Colas Breugnon: Overture (11 Apr. 1943, 21 Jan. 1945, 7 Apr. 1946, 21 Sept. 1947, 4 Mar. 1950, 8 Mar. 1952): RCA 60310 (**8 Apr. 1946**)

Both performances of the symphony are vibrant, at times even flashy, but their style suits the music well. Toscanini's interest in this work may well have sprung from the American-Russian alliance in World War II, which prompted the conductor to turn to a number of Russian scores, possibly out of a sense of patriotic duty. The present loss of interest in this work is suggested by the paucity of modern recordings of it. Of the two Toscanini performances, the latter is the more communicative, in good measure because of its superior sound, having a very wide dynamic range and exceptional presence.

Although Toscanini's concept of the jovial *Colas Breugnon* Overture remained unchanged, differences among his performances exist and concern a slightly rushed tempo in the broadcast of 1950 and instances of imprecision in a few others. Most successful are the first and last broadcasts, both slightly more relaxed than the studio recording and more precisely executed than some of the other presentations.

Kalinnikov, Vassily (1866–1901)

Unissued Repertory
Symphony No. 1 in G Minor (7 Nov. 1943)

It is unfortunate that this work is rarely heard today. If not a masterpiece, it is nonetheless well crafted and features considerable melodic inventiveness. Toscanini's taut performance, the only one he ever gave of the score, brings out its long singing lines and suits the music perfectly.

Kennan, Kent (1913–)

Unissued Repertory
Night Soliloquy (7 Feb. 1943)

Like some of the other American works on the broadcast of 7 February 1943, Kennan's *Night Soliloquy*, a piece that lasts slightly less than four minutes, is thoroughly professional but rather characterless, often echoing the style of Debussy. The carefully shaped performance features some lovely playing of an extended passage for solo flute.

Kodály, Zoltán (1882–1967)

Unofficially Issued Repertory
Marosszék Dances (8 Feb. 1941)

Officially Issued Repertory
Háry János: Suite (29 Nov. 1947): RCA 60279 (broadcast of **29 Nov. 1947**)

Toscanini first performed the *Marosszék Dances* with the New York Philharmonic in 1930, an American premiere. His interest in them may have grown partly from his friendship with the composer. But he was also a sympathetic interpreter, the sharp contouring and rhythmic vitality of the performance being ideally suited to the music.

This performance of the suite from *Háry János* is the only one of the work that Toscanini led in the United States and possibly the only one he ever gave. In an interview broadcast in the United States in 1963, the composer was asked if Toscanini's performance of *Háry János* was as good as Kodály's own. "Better," he replied, because Toscanini, being a conductor, had more "patience" than a composer in gaining desired ends. Surprisingly, Kodály did not comment about some of Toscanini's unorthodox tempos for some sections—especially those that were slightly slower than the norm.

Two other Kodály works were in Toscanini's repertory: *Summer Evening*, a relatively brief piece that Kodály dedicated to Toscanini, and the *Psalmus Hungaricus*, which Toscanini first led with the La Scala Orchestra in 1926 and again with the New York Philharmonic in 1929. Kodály said in the 1963 interview that Toscanini had wished to perform it at NBC as well but had been unable to find a satisfactory tenor.

Liadov, Anatoly (1855–1914)

Officially Issued Repertory
Kikimora (7 Nov. 1943, 13 Jan. 1946, 11 Dec. 1948, 26 July 1952): RCA 60323 (**29 July 1952**)

What probably attracted Toscanini to this relatively lightweight piece is its colorful and skillful orchestration. All four broadcasts and the studio recording are distinguished by the color, detail, and clarity of the playing.

Liszt, Franz (1811–86)

Unofficially Issued Repertory
Orpheus (26 Nov. 1938)
From the Cradle to the Grave (8 Feb. 1941)
Hungarian Rhapsody No. 2 (4 Apr. 1943)

Toscanini played none of these works during his decade with the New York Philharmonic. Quite likely, the performance of each of the two tone poems is unique in the conductor's career. He did lead Liszt's most famous and popular orchestral work, *Les préludes*, in Italy, but not in the United States. Both of these less familiar tone poems exemplify the contemplative Lizst, and Toscanini played them with a relaxed clarity that testifies to his ability to sustain a long, unbroken line. In contrast, he made the far less interesting Hungarian Rhapsody a rousing affair, while avoiding the freewheeling bombast with which it was sometimes invested.

Loeffler, Charles Martin (1861–1935)

Unissued Repertory
Memories of My Childhood (7 Jan. 1939, 1 Nov. 1942)

Alsatian by birth, American by choice, Loeffler grew up in Russia, hence the subtitle of this work, *Life in a Russian Village*. But if Russian through inspiration and through use of some thematic material, the music, with its frequently evocative tone and contrasted moods, is more suggestive of Ives's *Holidays*. These two performances are most likely the only ones Toscanini gave of the piece, which won a $1000 prize in 1924 at the Chicago North Shore Festival. The earlier presentation of this thirteen-minute work is the more interesting reading, not because of its slightly greater breadth, but owing, rather, to its greater flexibility and clarity.

Mancinelli, Luigi (1848–1921)

Unofficially Issued Repertory
Venetian Scenes: Flight of the Lovers (25 June 1944, 13 Jan. 1946, 13 Mar. 1948)

Whatever reasons Toscanini may have had for programming this work, its inclusion on his broadcasts adds nothing of consequence to what we know either of

Italian orchestral music or of Toscanini. But the flawed performance of 1946—which required the conductor to stop the orchestra after a few measures and begin the work anew—suggests that Toscanini, notwithstanding his exceptional control of an ensemble, was not immune to mishaps.

Massenet, Jules (1842–1912)

Unofficially Issued Repertory
Scènes alsaciennes (18 July 1943)

Although he recorded the "Fête bohème" from Massenet's *Scènes pittoresques* with the La Scala Orchestra in 1921, this 1943 performance is the only orchestral work by Massenet that Toscanini conducted in its entirety in the United States. One does not ordinarily associate the conductor with this repertory, but the reading, if occasionally hard driven in some of the faster sections, is also beautifully balanced and colorful in others. In its unveiling of a little-known side of the conductor, this is a significant performance.

Martucci, Giuseppe (1856–1909)

Unofficially Issued Repertory
La canzone dei ricordi (29 Feb. 1941)
Notturno; *Novelletta* (13 Oct. 1938, 13 Mar. 1948, *Novelletta* only)
Piano Concerto No. 1 in B-flat Minor, Op. 66 (20 Jan. 1946, 17 Jan. 1953)
Symphony No. 1 in D Minor, Op. 75 (26 Jan. 1938)
Symphony No. 2 in F Major, Op. 81 (30 Mar. 1940)
Tarantella (13 Feb. 1938, 8 Feb. 1941)

An issue often raised about Toscanini's programming was his inclusion of inferior music such as this. Yet one can understand the rationale that led him to turn to it. Martucci, in addition to composing, had been active as a conductor and had introduced significant German repertory from Beethoven to Wagner in Italy. Indeed, it is quite likely that he acquainted Toscanini with some of Beethoven's symphonies. Harvey Sachs summed up the conductor's attitude succinctly: "Toscanini held Martucci in the highest regard as a man and artist."[54] Thus, not only did Toscanini feel indebted to Martucci as a kind of older role model, he also respected the composer as a consummate professional, a master of the orchestra (both as conductor and composer), and a craftsman in full command of his material.

The problem, however, is that the material is mainly barren, lacking imagination, character, and inventiveness. The shorter works—*Tarantella*, *Novelletta*, and *Nocturne*—have, to be sure, considerable charm. But the symphonies, for all their craftsmanship, comprise more technique than substance, and the piano concerto, more than anything else, sounds like a parody of the romantic concerto style at its weakest. Of the two performances, the later one, with Horszowski as soloist, offers a more colorful and subtle account of the solo part. Both symphonies are superbly played. The *Canzone*, for all the lovely singing of Bruna Castagna, seems utterly wanting in dimension. One cannot help but wonder if Toscanini did not recognize these shortcomings, but simply refused to let them neutralize his admiration for Martucci. Whatever the deficiencies of this music, hearing it illuminates a portion of what remains generally unknown terrain.

Mendelssohn, Felix (1809–47)

Unofficially Issued Repertory
Die schöne Melusine Overture, Op. 32 (1 Nov. 1947, 11 Dec. 1948)
Hebrides Overture, Op. 26 (4 Nov. 1945)
String Quintet No. 2 in B-flat Major, Op. 87: third movement (1 Nov. 1947)
Symphony No. 3 in A Minor, Op. 56, "Scottish" (5 Apr. 1941)
Violin Concerto in E Minor, Op. 64 (9 Apr. 1944)

Officially Issued Repertory
A Midsummer Night's Dream, Opp. 21 and 61
    Overture only (24 Jan. 1942, 10 Feb. 1951)
    Overture with Incidental Music: Intermezzo, Nocturne, Scherzo, "You Spotted Snakes," "Wedding March," Finale (1 Nov. 1947): RCA 60283 (**4 Nov. 1947**; "You Spotted Snakes" recorded but rejected for release by Toscanini)
    Scherzo only: RCA 60284 (**6 Nov. 1946**)
String Octet in E-flat Major, Op. 20 (30 Mar. 1947): RCA 60283 (broadcast of **30 Mar. 1947**)
    Scherzo only, arr. for winds by Mendelssohn (18 Mar. 1945): RCA 60284 (**1 June 1945**)
Symphony No. 4 in A Major, Op. 90, "Italian" (5 Feb. 1938, 14 Mar. 1942, 12 Mar. 1949, 28 Feb. 1954): RCA 60284 (broadcast of **28 Feb. 1954**, but with portions of the rehearsals of **26 and 27 Feb.**)
Symphony No. 5 in D Major, Op. 107, "Reformation" (19 Nov. 1938, 8 Nov. 1942, 9 Sept. 1945, 30 Mar. 1947, 13 Dec. 1953): RCA 60284 (broadcast of **13 Dec. 1953**)

The unofficially issued items comprise an important document from Toscanini's NBC years, their lack of wide availability having denied the conductor's work a dimension it should have. Neither of the overtures was played by Toscanini during his decade with the New York Philharmonic. The two readings of *Melusine* (the later one being a shade more flexible) feature a less weighty sonority and slightly faster tempos than are favored by most conductors, yet both performances have a blend of tension and almost gossamer lightness, the

NBC winds providing rich coloring. The *Hebrides* Overture offers a cogent example of Toscanini's freedom, but exercised in the best of taste, framed by a rhythmic pulse that, while subtly varied, is always well defined and colored by an exceptional transparency of texture. As a result, the music emerges with all of its atmosphere preserved, its formal coherence intact.

One may wonder why Toscanini would program a work from a relatively unfamiliar Mendelssohn quintet. Aside from the then common practice of including chamber works on orchestral programs, the obvious answer is that he liked it. And as attested by the performance, he was totally responsive to its delicate, songful simplicity. Those who view Toscanini mainly in terms of the lion who roared at rehearsals and who in concert produced sonically and emotionally shattering climaxes should hear this performance to discover a different side of his commanding artistic temperament: the capacity to convey a gentle, unaffected tenderness.

The same might also be said of his only NBC performance of the "Scottish" Symphony, its slow movement, in particular, exhibiting a sustained, flowing lyricism. And in a work that some conductors of the period often pulled apart rhythmically, Toscanini's performance serves as a reminder of the classical unity that lies at the heart of this music. Typical in this regard is the way he honors Mendelssohn's assai animato indication in the first movement's exposition without causing (as many other conductors do at this point) an awkward rupture of the basic pulse.

The performance of the Violin Concerto renewed a collaboration with Jascha Heifetz begun in Toscanini's years with the New York Philharmonic and continued in 1940 when the two recorded (but did not perform in public) the Beethoven Concerto. What they produced in the Mendelssohn remains controversial. B. H. Haggin, for example, found Heifetz's phrasing "mannered and sentimentally distorted," traits I (and others) fail to hear.[55] To be sure, tempos in the outer movements are uncommonly quick, with Heifetz (as noted in chapter 2) launching into the finale at far greater speed than he had favored in rehearsal. But regardless of how one views the performance, it remains interesting as a response to the traditions of the time, Toscanini and Heifetz stripping away the cloying sweetness that characterized many other presentations of the period. Mendelssohn, after all, did mark the first movement Allegro molto. Admittedly, though, he may not have envisioned it as quite so streamlined.

Neither of Toscanini's studio recordings of the *Midsummer Night's Dream* music does him complete justice. In the case of an earlier version with the Philadelphia Orchestra, poor sound veils the performance. But even there, as in the 1947 remake, the playing is sometimes tenser and more rigid than in the broader accounts of the 1947 broadcast. This is especially noticeable in the Wedding March, which in that broadcast has an unorthodox breadth that lends it an appropriate dignity and solemnity absent from the studio versions. It is possible that the studio version of 1947 is faster than that of the broadcast in order to permit its being contained on one 78 rpm side. This would also explain why an important da capo was omitted in that studio version. (In the Philadelphia recording, the tempo for the Wedding March was also faster than in the 1947 broadcast, but the da capo omitted from the 1947 recording was observed. Because the Philadelphia recordings were never issued in their original 78 rpm format, it is impossible to be certain about how the time limitations of a single side may have affected his tempo. But the CD transfer of the performance suggests that the Wedding March was spread over two sides.)

The Scherzo in the broadcast account comes closer to the virtuosic magic of Toscanini's 1929 recording with the New York Philharmonic. In all the broadcast accounts of the overture, a fairyland lightness is conveyed by an uncommonly fleet tempo that is nevertheless subjected to pointed modifications and is never so swift as to preclude clean articulation. It is mainly in these modifications that the broadcast accounts differ from the 1947 studio version. The Philadelphia recording of the finale is preceded by a brief Melodrama that echoes the Wedding March. The 1947 broadcast and subsequent recording preface the finale with the initial bars of the overture; both are included as individual pieces in the published score.

The commercial releases of the octet and the "Reformation" Symphony are drawn from broadcasts, that of the former comprising Toscanini's only American performance of the work, that of the latter one of the miracles of his old age, having an expansive control and intensity unmatched in any of his previous presentations of the score. One of the criticisms made of Toscanini's repertory was the attention he paid to this symphony at the expense of Mendelssohn's "musically superior" "Scottish" Symphony, which the conductor performed only once at NBC. What is overlooked in such a view is that Toscanini's unorthodox approach to the "Reformation" Symphony—characterized by a fierce opening movement, a graceful, lilting second movement, and a uniquely expansive finale in which the perorational "Ein feste Burg" is stunningly dramatic and grand—transformed a potentially second-rate score into a potent masterpiece. The octet is played with verve and buoyancy, but for all the clarity Toscanini produced, some transparency is lost in the arrangement for string orchestra supported with double basses, which, of course, are not called for in Mendelssohn's original. The recording of the Scherzo from the octet in Mendelssohn's arrangement with winds is astonishing for its lightness and the virtuosic execution of the orchestra.

Toscanini's performances of the "Italian" Symphony are more traditional than those he gave of the "Reformation." Unfortunately, only the 1938 broadcast includes the important first-movement repeat, and that account is the only one in the group that seems flaccid and uncommitted. It is almost as if Toscanini were thinking of the next day's benefit concert featuring the Ninth Symphony.

In his other broadcasts, Toscanini favored a first movement made to sound more rapid than it actually was by a clarity of detail that lent the music a well-focused motivic profile. And in the finale, Toscanini emphasized its tarantella-like character by having the timpani double a significant rhythmic pattern that runs through the movement. The RCA reissue on CD of the 1954 broadcast is the first to acknowledge the use of the dress-rehearsal material, most notably in the first movement, which in the broadcast had greater rhythmic freedom. Both approaches have validity, but Toscanini evidently preferred the tauter line he achieved in rehearsal.

Meyerbeer, Giacomo (1791–1864)

Unofficially Issued Repertory
Dinorah: Overture (12 Jan. 1938)
L'étoile du nord: Overture (prepared for the broadcast of 3 Nov. 1951 but not performed)

From a historical point of view, these are two of the most interesting performances of Toscanini's NBC years. The overture to *L'étoile du nord* was given a complete uninterrupted run-through at a dress rehearsal but never broadcast, a loss for radio audiences since it had virtually vanished from the repertory. At the time Toscanini performed them, both works were unfamiliar, and they have remained so despite the expansion of our musical horizons engendered by the long-playing record. Toscanini, however, was steeped in the grand-opera tradition and had directed productions of four Meyerbeer operas—*Dinorah*, *L'Africaine*, *Les Huguenots*, and *Le prophète*. Most obvious in his performance of these two overtures is the conviction he brought to the music and his total identification with its flamboyant and, at times, vapid material. This is especially true of *L'étoile*, which reiterates rather mundane ideas in a loosely knit work of eight minutes. Played with less verve, animation, and rhythmic contouring, the music might sound pompous and pretentious, but Toscanini, without making it seem like a masterpiece, gives it dignity and attractiveness.

The thirteen-and-a-half-minute overture to *Dinorah* (the Italian title of *Le pardon de Ploërmel*) is, despite some inconsequential moments, more interesting—its ideas more imaginative, its scoring (calling for an offstage chorus) more unusual. The music makes no new harmonic or melodic gestures and often sounds like a mixture of Weber, Berlioz, and Offenbach, through which a bit of Beethoven occasionally seeps. And if brashly theatrical at times, it is nonetheless attractive. Toscanini played it with great verve and commitment, drawing sharp contrasts between its quiet and explosive moments and, most of all, holding together what could easily become an embarrassingly disjointed piece. In these Meyerbeer performances, we may get some notion of how Toscanini conducted French grand opera in the theater.

Mignone, Francisco (1897–1986)

Unissued Repertory
Fantasies brasileiras (14 Nov. 1943)
Four Brazilian Sketches (2 Apr. 1944)
A Brazilian, Mignone had gained considerable respect as a composer, one of his operas having been directed by no less a judge and conductor than Richard Strauss. Both of these works, if sometimes post-Wagnerian in harmonic style, remain within the diatonic idiom. Both exemplify professional craftsmanship and polish, but neither displays much personality.

Mozart, Leopold (1719–87)

Officially Issued Repertory
Toy Symphony (15 Feb. 1941): RCA 60308 (broadcast of **15 Feb. 1941**)

At the time of this performance, the work was attributed to Haydn. Often too closely microphoned, the reading is hurried, rather rigid, and charmless.

Mozart, Wolfgang Amadeus (1756–91)

Unofficially Issued Repertory
Piano Concerto No. 27 in B-flat Major, K. 595 (5 Dec. 1943)
Sinfonia concertante in E-flat Major, K. 364 (15 Feb. 1941)
Symphony No. 29 in A Major, K. 201 (3 Sep. 1944)
Symphony No. 38 in D Major, K. 504, "Prague" (14 Feb. 1938)

Officially Issued Repertory
Bassoon Concerto in B-flat Major, K. 191 (8 Nov. 1947): RCA 60286
    (**18 Nov. 1947**)
Divertimento in B-flat Major, K. 287 (3 Nov. 1946, 8 Nov. 1947): RCA
    60286 (**18 Nov. 1947**)
Overtures:
    Don Giovanni (27 Jan. 1946): RCA 60309 (broadcast of **27 Jan. 1946**)
    The Magic Flute (8 Jan. 1938, 1 Feb. 1941, 31 Oct. 1943, 3 Nov. 1946,
        8 Nov. 1947, 26 Nov. 1949): RCA 60310 (broadcast of **26 Nov. 1949**)
    The Marriage of Figaro (5 Dec. 1943, 8 Nov. 1947): RCA 60286
        (broadcast of **8 Nov. 1947**)
Symphonies:
    No. 35 in D Major, K. 385, "Haffner" (7 Jan. 1939, 5 Dec. 1943,
        3 Nov. 1946): RCA 60286 (**4 Nov. 1946**)
    No. 39 in E-flat Major, K. 543 (6 Mar. 1948): RCA 60285 (broadcast of
        6 Mar. 1948)
    No. 40 in G Minor, K. 550 (25 Dec. 1937, 27 Jan. 1946, 4 Dec. 1948,

11 Mar. 1950, 21 Mar. 1953): RCA 60285 (**7 Mar. 1938, 27 Feb. 1939**); RCA 60271 (**12 Mar. 1950**)

No. 41 in C Major, K. 551, "Jupiter" (20 Apr. 1940, 4 Feb. 1945): RCA 60285 (**22 June 1945** and **11 Mar. 1946**)

The notion that Toscanini was an ineffective Mozart interpreter springs partly from the scant attention he paid the composer in the theater—four performances of *Don Giovanni* (all in South America in 1906), a few of *The Magic Flute*, and none of any of Mozart's other operas. But the notion may also come, at least in part, from a startling admission the conductor made to B. H. Haggin: "I will tell you frankly," Toscanini stated, "I find Mozart boring. Not G-Minor [K. 550]: that is great tragedy, and not concerti, but other music. It is always beautiful—but is always the same."[56]

No doubt this boredom is reflected in some of Toscanini's Mozart. Indeed, his only NBC account of the "Prague" Symphony, with its swift, uninflected outer movements, sounds a bit glib. And some of the studio recordings of Mozart have similar shortcomings. Still, Toscanini often displayed a grasp of Mozart's style that foreshadowed many of the traits found in today's authentically styled, period-instrument presentations of the composer's music. For one thing, as with Haydn, he always played Mozart with a reduced orchestra. This approach was typified in a concert he directed with members of the New York Philharmonic in 1934—not in Carnegie Hall, but in the more intimate Town Hall, where, in addition to performing Wagner's *Siegfried Idyll* in its original scoring, he had led a performance of Mozart's Symphony No. 29 with a chamber orchestra.

A similarly sized ensemble is employed in all of these presentations, with a resulting textural clarity and heightening of color that were probably startling in their day and a far cry from the more bass-heavy, sometimes more thickly textured Mozart performances of such ostensible stylists as Sir Thomas Beecham and Bruno Walter. To be sure, contemporary voices were raised against many of Toscanini's tempos, which were often judged too fast for Mozart, especially in slow movements, where, unlike some other conductors, he never transformed an andante into an adagio. Similarly, his bracing pace for minuets was the antithesis of Beecham's leaden crawls. The issue, of course, is not whether or not one likes or dislikes Toscanini's approach, but that modern practices that have evolved from scholarly investigations have some antecedents in his view of Mozart.

Sometimes that view is compelling, as in the Piano Concerto, K. 595. According to the soloist in the NBC performance, Mieczyslaw Horszowski, this was Toscanini's favorite Mozart concerto. The affinity shows, with orchestral portions, in addition to their pointed transparency, having a gentle lyric delicacy well suited to the music. It is interesting, too, that Toscanini believed that the work's Larghetto—contrary to the 4/4 time specified in editions of the period—was an alla breve movement. Ultimately this belief was corroborated when the pianist Rudolf Serkin found a manuscript that confirmed it, which led to modern editions specifying the appropriate meter.

Aside from untidy playing in the first movement of the Symphony No. 29, the performance is, for its time at least, a revelation. One has only to compare it to other commercial recordings of the work then available—one made by Serge Koussevitzky, the other by Beecham—to recognize how Toscanini's approach, in its lightness, transparency, and unaffected simplicity, comes far closer to modern scholarship's view of Mozart than the waywardly heavy-handed style of Beecham or the livelier but thickly textured reading of Koussevitzky. Similarly, the *Sinfonia concertante*—lean, transparent, and urgent—seems the model harbinger of modern Mozart playing, especially with the minimal vibrato used by the two soloists, Mischa Mischakoff and Carlton Cooley, and the NBC strings. None of these performances, to be sure, with their unaccented grace notes, for example, boasts features scholarship now deems fitting. Nonetheless, each, in various ways, suggests Toscanini's instincts for historical rectitude.

All of the commercially issued performances of the opera overtures are drawn from broadcasts, and all feature a light sonority and well-defined textures. But the one of *The Magic Flute* (like every one of Toscanini's surviving accounts of the piece) has a nervous, breathless scurry that neutralizes some of the music's charm and playfulness. It might be argued, of course, that this is a two-beats-to-the-bar allegro, and Toscanini's seemingly untraditional speed is simply honoring Mozart's specifications. However one views his approach, it is best served by his BBC recording of 1938. Among the NBC broadcasts, the most interesting (if not satisfying) account is that of 1941, which features the most broadly sustained introduction and a very fast main section having a few rebalancings that Toscanini never duplicated.

It was not until RCA's complete *Toscanini Collection* that the overture to *The Marriage of Figaro* (always credited in previous releases to the 1947 broadcast) was actually issued in that 1947 version. Earlier incarnations, while attributed to 1947, used the broadcast of 1943, a slower reading that has merit, but one that Toscanini did not, presumably, approve for release. The thoroughly decent *Don Giovanni* overture sounds a bit cool, suggesting a certain antipathy for the opera.

Of the other recordings, that of the Symphony No. 39—a broadcast account of Toscanini's only performance of the work with an American orchestra—can be heard to far better advantage in RCA's CD edition than in the painfully shrill LP transfers of earlier years. But superior sound only partially rescues an occasionally brash reading that, for all its clarity and verve, misses some of the music's lyricism and grace.

The three other symphonies of which Toscanini left recordings were given, at one time or another, more sympathetic concert recordings. Most interesting is his changing view of the "Haffner," which varied not only from one performance to another but sometimes from dress rehearsal to subsequent broadcast, the quick pace for the first movement in the 1946 rehearsal being replaced by a considerably slower one before an audience.

The conductor's two recordings of the work (with the New York Philharmonic in 1929 and the NBC Symphony in 1946) exemplify extremes. The earlier version, contrary to prevailing views, is not always "more relaxed" than the later one, whose outer movements are pushed forward with a blazing virtuosic intensity unmatched in any of Toscanini's subsequent surviving performances. The inner movements, in contrast, are more expansive in the earlier account, the Minuet almost to the point of being ponderous. With the passage of time, the extremes of this Philharmonic version, with its awkward ritardandos at the beginning of the first movement, were gradually effaced in favor of more conventional pacing and less rhythmic freedom. But inconsistencies of tempo remained, the 1943 and 1946 broadcasts being generally broader and slightly more flexible than the 1946 recording. Indeed, in the 1943 broadcast, Toscanini avoided the awkward ritards imposed in the 1929 recording by playing the passage where they occurred in tempo. But that tempo was suddenly accelerated at measure 35. In short, while avoiding an earlier rupturing of pulse, he generated another, if less clumsy one. And throughout the first movement in the 1943 rendition these shifts in tempo were maintained: a ritardando made at the onset of the development and a repetition of the accelerando at measure 35 imposed on the corresponding section of the recapitulation. Only in a live 1935 BBC performance (issued on a BBC CD) and the 1939 NBC broadcast do remnants of the awkward 1929 ritards and expansiveness remain. What all the performances share, however, is an aptly scaled-down sonority and textural transparency. A word about the 1946 studio recording: it is unfortunately the Toscanini performance from which his view of the "Haffner" has probably become best known. Toscanini was not completely happy with it and approved it reluctantly. It is the most rigid of all his surviving performances and suffers from the sonic liability of NBC's studio 3A—a smaller, acoustically drier version of studio 8H. In both studio recordings Toscanini observed the second movement's exposition repeat, which he omitted in all his NBC broadcasts.

The traits that suggest period-instrument style in Toscanini's "Haffner" stamp his other Mozart performances as well, especially his two studio recordings and five NBC broadcasts of the Symphony No. 40. Toscanini held the score in sufficiently high regard to include it on his first NBC concert. Of his two studio recordings, the earlier one, with its slightly greater precision and sharper inflection, is the more dramatic. All of Toscanini's surviving performances, however, lack the greater refinement of Sir Thomas Beecham's approach and the broadly paced, bass-heavy style of Bruno Walter. Toscanini's view provides a grim, restless G Minor, one typical of *Sturm und Drang* but tempered by clarity and rhythmic elasticity. Noteworthy in particular is the way in which he invariably broadened the tempo for the finale's second subject. Significantly, too, he always projected the Andante with a genuine "walking" gait, thereby avoiding sentimentality. Of all his surviving NBC performances, the most satisfying, perhaps, is his last, from 1953. It is preserved in the best sound and offers the most meticulous balances, a marginally slower Minuet, and exceptional precision. As a result, it best conveys what was, for its time, Toscanini's radical view of this work, one that is still obvious in his two studio efforts. In all of his performances, Mozart's revised orchestration (with clarinets) is used. And except where time limitations of a broadcast interfered, a first-movement repeat (as in both studio efforts) was observed.

Toscanini's three surviving NBC performances of the "Jupiter" Symphony offer studies in contrast. Indeed, here is an instance where the often inaccurate generalization about "earlier" and "later" Toscanini style does apply. The performance on the 1940 broadcast is everything the 1945 broadcast and subsequent studio recording are not: free from excessive haste, texturally transparent, and remarkably flexible in rhythm. In the 1940 broadcast, the first movement, for example, begins far more broadly (and grandly) than in the later efforts, yet by the time the end of the exposition is reached, the tempo has accelerated (with exceptional smoothness) to the point where it matches the pace favored throughout in 1945. To be sure, traits that stamp the later efforts are in this earliest one as well, notably an unsentimentalized Andante and an undistended Minuet. But in 1940, the richly polyphonic finale was given just enough breadth to prevent its sounding like the scrambled mess it sometimes does in the studio recording. Dangerous as superlatives often are, it might well be argued that this 1940 "Jupiter" is Toscanini's most expressive Mozart performance. As was typical of his era, Toscanini observed none of the score's four major repeats in its outer movements.

The maestro's recording of the Divertimento, K. 287, like his two broadcast performances, assigns Mozart's solo violin to an entire string section (save for the cadenza) and omits the second Minuet. The 1946 broadcast, probably Toscanini's first performance of the work, was (as noted in chapter 2) given to show Koussevitzky the appropriately stylish way of performing the piece. Even if, unlike his peer, Toscanini recognized that a cadenza was meant to follow a 6/4 chord, one could hardly consider his omission of a movement and augmentation of a solo part "stylish" in the most literal sense of the term. Nevertheless, in its own peculiar way, the conception is trim, unhurried, and beautifully shaped while remaining utterly free of mannerisms. The 1946 broadcast is at times marginally broader than the subsequent broadcast and recording, but the differences are not significant.

Little need be said of the two studio recordings of the Bassoon Concerto, which duplicates the interpretive quirks of the broadcast that preceded it (see the entry for 8 November 1947 in chapter 2).

Mussorgsky, Modest (1839–81)

Unofficially Issued Repertory

Boris Godunov: Act III: Introduction and Polonaise (11 Apr. 1943)
Khovanshchina: Prelude to Act I (12 Mar. 1944, 13 Dec. 1953)

Officially Issued Repertory

Pictures at an Exhibition (orch. Ravel) (29 Jan. 1938, 20 Apr. 1940, 14 Feb.
     1948, 24 Jan. 1953): RCA 60287 (**26 Jan. 1953**)

Toscanini directed *Boris Godunov* at La Scala and conducted its American premiere at the Metropolitan Opera. These two brief excerpts from the work are,
unfortunately, all that survive of his conception, and they are superbly played.
Khovanshchina, in contrast, was never directed by Toscanini in the theater. What
probably attracted him to its prelude is the music's suggestion of dawn, well
communicated in both performances; the later one, with its superior sound,
seems more colorful.

Toscanini considered the Ravel adaptation of *Pictures at an Exhibition* one of
the two greatest treatises on orchestration, the other being the one written by
Berlioz. And he surely must have reveled in the challenges it posed with respect
to producing appropriate color and balances. As always, he was scholarly in his
approach, going back to the original piano version and discovering that Ravel
had used a corrupt text in making his orchestration. Thus, where necessary,
Toscanini revised Ravel. Harris Goldsmith, in his annotations for the RCA CD
of Toscanini's recording, was the first to point this out, noting, in particular,
how Toscanini corrected the final cadence of the Goldenberg-Schmuyle section
by "restoring the composer's C, D-flat, B-flat, B-flat."

Each of Toscanini's broadcast accounts of the work, in addition to their
richness of color and detail, is marked by his flair for drama and his awareness of
the need to draw contrasts from one section to the next. And his studio recording is not only thoroughly representative of the conception exemplified in his
broadcasts, but also sonically extraordinary. It was in fact, used often in its day for
audio demonstrations.

Nicolai, Otto (1810–49)

Unissued Repertory

The Merry Wives of Windsor: Overture (18 July 1943)

After a sustained and beautifully shaped introduction, the performance becomes
rigid and graceless.

Olivieri, Alessio

Unissued Repertory

"Garibaldi's War Hymn" (9 Sept. 1943)

Those who delight in finding fault with Toscanini might well cite this performance to best represent him as an alleged "Italian bandmaster." Executed as it is here, with several da capos, the piece grows progressively wearisome despite the considerable energy and conviction that Toscanini brought to it. What should not be forgotten, however, are the wartime excesses of patriotism that led to trivia like this being played.

Paganini, Nicolò (1782–1840)

Officially Issued Repertory

Moto perpetuo, Op. 11 (29 Jan. 1938, 16 Mar. 1940): RCA 60308 (**17 Apr. 1939**)

Although ordinarily virtuosity should never be an end in itself, the technical prowess of the NBC Symphony's first violins in executing in unison this display piece almost makes one think otherwise. The studio recording of 1939 is essentially identical to the two broadcast accounts, but the vastly superior sound achieved by the NBC engineers for the 1940 broadcast conveys far better the tonal luster of the orchestra's strings.

Ponchielli, Amilcare (1834–86)

Officially Issued Repertory

La Gioconda: Dance of the Hours (4 Apr. 1943, 26 July 1952): RCA 60308 (**29 July 1952**)

The two broadcast performances of this lightweight fare hardly differ from each other or from Toscanini's 1952 recording.

Prokofiev, Sergei (1891–1953)

Officially Issued Repertory

Symphony No. 1 in D Major, Op. 25, "Classical" (21 Oct. 1939, 25 June 1944, 13 Jan. 1946, 15 Nov. 1947, 25 Mar. 1950, 10 Nov. 1951): RCA 60323 (**15 Oct. 1951**)

This is the only work by Prokofiev that Toscanini led. (A performance with the NBC Symphony of the composer's *Russian* Overture, Op. 72, was planned in 1938 but never materialized.) The conductor's fondness for the "Classical" Symphony is obviously suggested by his six NBC presentations of it—more than he

gave to any symphony by Haydn or Mozart, and more than he accorded the
Second, Fourth, Fifth, Seventh, or Eighth Symphony of Beethoven. But fondness must not have been the only issue: the work's brevity made it an ideal concert opener, much in the manner of an overture.

As was true of the majority of works in his repertory, Toscanini's view of
the "Classical" Symphony was constantly changing, the earliest NBC account
being the fastest and leanest. Over the years, the tempo became less extreme, but
the unusually slow pace favored for the second movement in the conductor's
1951 studio recording remains atypical of his other performances, and the élan
he achieved in the broadcasts of 1939 and 1944 is not quite matched in that studio version.

Puccini, Giacomo (1858–1924)

Unissued Repertory

Manon Lescaut: Act II: Minuet (2 July 1944)

Officially Issued Repertory

La bohème (Acts I and II: 3 Feb. 1946; Acts III and IV: 10 Feb. 1946): RCA
    60288 (broadcasts of **3** and **10 Feb. 1946**, with some corrections
    from rehearsals)
Manon Lescaut: Act III: Intermezzo (2 July 1944, 10 Dec. 1949): RCA 60309
    (broadcast of **2 July 1944**)

Toscanini led seven Puccini operas in the theater—*La fanciulla del West, Madama
Butterfly, Tosca, Turandot, Le villi*, and the two represented in the RCA recordings cited above. The NBC broadcasts of *La bohème* could not have been better
timed, the first of them occurring almost fifty years to the day after Toscanini
had led the premiere of the opera in Turin. It would be wrong to assume that
this NBC performance is a replica of that premiere. For one thing, Toscanini's
views were always changing. Moreover, the demands of a staged performance—
particularly of a work that is unfamiliar—will affect such basic issues as tempo,
phrasing, balance, and the like.

Heard in the context of the familiarity bred in a half century's existence, this
concert performance is best characterized by its freedom from sentimentality, its
dramatic power, and its exceptional care with the role of the orchestra. One
has only to listen to the close of Act II to encounter more theatrical ambience
than may be experienced in some staged presentations. In general, Toscanini
assembled a strong cast. Jan Peerce, the Rodolfo of the performance, noted its
effect on the conductor himself: "[t]ears were coming down [Toscanini's] face;
it wasn't put on: nobody saw it, just us. We singers . . . could see the man and
what the music meant to him." Peerce added, "[T]o satisfy Toscanini we had to
undo a lot of things we learned from others."[57] He also pointed out that the

faulty orchestral entry at the opera's close was probably caused by Toscanini's beating a measure where he said he would not.

This performance of the minuet from *Manon Lescaut* preceded one of this opera's Act III intermezzo given on the same broadcast, which RCA released. It exemplifies Toscanini's gift for achieving subtle nuances of rhythm and dynamics.

The lack of affectation and freedom from sentimentality that stamp Toscanini's *Bohème* are also evident in the intermezzo from *Manon Lescaut*, which is more fluid in the broadcast of 1944 than in the considerably broader account of 1949. The earlier version was thus the wiser choice for RCA's *Toscanini Collection*. Note, however, that the performance included there is inaccurately identified as being from 1949. Correct dating was given in the limited-edition booklet accompanying RCA's eighty-two-CD *Toscanini Collection*.

Ravel, Maurice (1875–1937)

Unofficially Issued Repertory
Boléro (21 Jan. 1939)
La valse (27 Apr. 1940, 14 May 1940, 21 Nov. 1943)

Officially Issued Repertory
Daphnis et Chloé: Suite No. 2 (26 Nov. 1938, 19 Nov. 1949): RCA 60322
   (**21 Nov. 1949**)

Toscanini performed *Boléro* more frequently with the New York Philharmonic than with the NBC Symphony and included the work in the Philharmonic's 1930 tour of Europe. During that tour, after a performance in Paris attended by Ravel, the composer refused to stand and take a bow after *Boléro* was played, ostensibly because of his displeasure with Toscanini's tempo, which, he told a friend, was "twice too fast."[58] We cannot know how fast that Parisian performance may have been, but it is almost certain that Ravel's "twice too fast" is gross hyperbole. For one thing, the composer's 1931 recording of the work is only marginally slower than Toscanini's NBC broadcast account, itself no swifter than that of many other conductors. But Toscanini surely would never have approved its release, marred as it is by a few instances of untidy execution.

It was after Ernest Ansermet's NBC performance of *La valse* that Toscanini said, "When he plays *La Valse* is different from my *La Valse*, but is good."[59] I have not heard that Ansermet performance, but his commercially released recordings of the work offer a gentler, more slyly atmospheric conception than do any of Toscanini's three NBC accounts, all of which are similar and suggest a waltz that evolves from a sardonic coolness into a grotesque, ironic transmogrification of tradition. The earliest of these three performances features an ever so slightly greater flexibility.

Some of the musicians who played the second *Daphnis et Chloé* suite under Toscanini told me that he was not at ease with this music and had difficulty beating some of its complex rhythms. This caused his unusually expressive and precise right hand to go "digging for the beat" instead of indicating it. Nevertheless, as the double bassist David Walter has noted, "the exact execution Toscanini insisted on from each woodwind at the beginning achieved something different from the usual impressionist effect of the passage played without exactness." Walter goes on to make a particularly interesting observation about the conductor:

> I would say what was most outstanding in Toscanini's work was his organization of time and rhythm and dynamics into form; and this made him . . . most effective in music with clearly delineated rhythmic and formal structure, as against music that made its effect with color. In other words, he was a classicist rather than an impressionist. And so he did well with Ravel's *Boléro*; and if he had played [more] modern music, I think he would have done well with Bartók's Concerto for Orchestra and Stravinsky's neo-classical works.[60]

In the main, one might say that Toscanini's execution of *Daphnis et Chloé* both in concert and in his studio recording reflects a certain discomfort with the idiom. All the same, the performance generates moments of great energy and clarity. And whatever his discomfort with the music, he included it in the NBC Symphony's 1950 tour, perhaps to display the virtuosity of the orchestra. Of his three surviving performances, the 1938 broadcast account is the most atmospheric.

Respighi, Ottorino (1879–1936)

Officially Issued Repertory
The Fountains of Rome (14 Feb. 1939, 23 Mar. 1947, 17 Feb. 1951, 22 Dec. 1951): RCA 60262 (**17 Dec. 1951**)
The Pines of Rome (19 Mar. 1944, 22 Mar. 1952, 14 Mar. 1953): RCA 60262 (**17 Mar. 1953**)
Roman Festivals (30 Mar. 1940, 10 Dec. 1949): RCA 60262 (**12 Dec. 1949**)

That Toscanini programmed these engaging scores rather frequently while ignoring many works of greater consequence from the same period probably contributed to his being judged inimical to modern music. As this point is taken up in a few other instances in this volume, it will suffice to say here that he invested these glittering showpieces with a dignity, power, and drama that other conductors rarely matched.

Unfortunately, Toscanini's NBC recordings of these works do not tell the whole story about what he could achieve with them, partly because the technology of the time could not capture the extraordinary dynamic range he wished to project. Moreover, in his Philadelphia Orchestra recording of *Roman Festivals* and a live New York Philharmonic account from 1945 of *Pines*, one encounters a flexibility and tonal richness absent from the studio product. In the main, one might say that Toscanini had a special feeling for this music, rooted in part, perhaps, in his friendship with Respighi. But more important, he suggested an elegance and nobility in these scores rarely encountered in other performances.

Rieti, Vittorio (1898–1994)

Unissued Repertory
Symphony No. 4, "Tripartita" (25 Nov. 1945)

Completed in 1944, this work received its radio premiere in Toscanini's presentation. In many respects, this three-movement, seventeen-minute score owes much to Stravinsky, particularly his Symphony in C. The lightness of spirit, the jagged rhythms, and the clear orchestral texture bespeak Stravinskian neoclassicism, and Toscanini's performance conveys these traits sympathetically. But what can loosely be called "personality" is often absent from this highly competent but two-dimensional echo of a great master.

Roger-Ducasse, Jean-Jules (1873–1954)

Unofficially Issued Repertory
Sarabande (7 Apr. 1946)

The title is misleading in that this is not a dance but a symphonic poem calling for an offstage chorus. All of the elements of French impressionism are here save one—originality. Toscanini had planned his first American performance of this piece in 1914 for a concert that was ultimately canceled. He was attracted to its style and had prepared it three times with the New York Philharmonic. One can admire the care he lavished on the score, but this effort fails to make the music interesting enough to sustain anything but passing attention.

Rossini, Gioachino (1792–1868)

Unofficially Issued Repertory
Sonata No. 3 for Strings (15 Nov. 1952)

Officially Issued Repertory
Overtures:
    The Barber of Seville (21 Nov. 1943, 21 Mar. 1954): RCA 60289
        (28 June 1945)

La Cenerentola (22 Oct. 1938): RCA 60289 (**8 June 1945**)

La gazza ladra (12 Apr. 1941, 25 June 1944): RCA 60289 (**28 June 1945**)

L'Italiana in Algeri (although on programs for the NBC orchestra's 1950 tour, this overture was never broadcast): RCA 60289 (**14 Apr. 1950**)

Semiramide (5 Feb. 1938, 13 Mar. 1948, 17 Nov. 1951): RCA 60289 (**28 Sept. 1951**)

The Siege of Corinth (no NBC performance other than the studio recording): RCA 60289 (**14 June 1945**)

Il Signor Bruschino (5 Apr. 1941, 8 Nov. 1942, 11 Nov. 1945): RCA 60289 (**8 June 1945**)

La scala di seta (29 Jan. 1938, 5 Mar. 1949): No studio recording with the NBC Symphony.

William Tell (28 Jan. 1939, 16 Mar. 1940, 9 Sept. 1943, 15 Mar. 1952, 17 Jan. 1953): RCA 60310 (**1** and **29 Mar. 1939**); RCA 60289 (**19 Jan. 1953**)

William Tell: Passo a sei (19 Nov. 1938, 4 Apr. 1943, 5 Jan. 1953): RCA 60309 (**8 June 1945**)

In some quarters, it became almost a cliché of Toscanini criticism (erroneous, to be sure) to say that he was an ideal interpreter of Rossini but not of Beethoven. There is a double irony in this. For one thing, the conductor directed only two Rossini operas in the theater—The Barber of Seville and William Tell. Then, too, even the composer's overtures were not so central to his repertory as were the symphonies of Beethoven or Brahms or Debussy's La mer. Over and beyond this, however, his NBC studio recordings of Rossini overtures—recordings that prompted praise from those who denigrated his Beethoven—do not, in the main, represent his finest accounts of those works.

Certainly the three overtures he recorded with the New York Philharmonic—The Barber of Seville in 1929, L'Italiana in Algeri and Semiramide in 1936 —are better played and, despite the sonic limitations of older engineering, more tonally alluring than his NBC Symphony Rossini recordings of later vintage. But so, too, are his NBC broadcast performances vis-à-vis studio counterparts. Most notable in this regard are La Cenerentola and La gazza ladra, both of which display greater inflection, clarity, and breadth in concert than in recordings.

Inflection is a key to Toscanini's Rossini. Typical of this aspect of his approach to the composer is his treatment of the ascending scales in the overture to La scala di seta. It is interesting to compare his style to that of Herbert von Karajan, whose tempo for the music is virtually identical to Toscanini's. But Karajan plays the ascending scales very straight, with almost no nuance in dynamics. Toscanini, in contrast, imposes a crescendo that parallels the ascending scale, giving it an animation that Karajan's account lacks. One hears this clarity in his only studio recording of the work (with the BBC Symphony in 1938) and even better in the 1949 NBC broadcast, where the articulation of the solo oboe is much cleaner than in the NBC broadcast of 1938.

Toscanini took Rossini quite seriously. Several members of the NBC Symphony have told me that he proved especially demanding in rehearsals for these overtures, implying that this was not easy music. Interestingly, too, when it was suggested to him that the overture to *William Tell* was "cheap," Toscanini responded, "You try to compose something as good."[61] That overture is, of course, a work with which Toscanini became strongly associated. Surprisingly, though, he prepared it but once during his decade with the New York Philharmonic. Not until he made the first of his two NBC recordings and gave the piece five broadcast performances did the connection become firm. And the second of those two recordings shines as his finest studio effort on behalf of Rossini. Though the two are similar, they have a few marked differences in tempo, the storm section being slower in 1939, the finale slower in 1953. And among the broadcast presentations, one hears changing notions about tempo, phrasing, and dynamics. Here, then, is another example of how Toscanini was constantly altering his interpretive viewpoint. But he always invested the finale with a dignity and power absent from the more lightly inflected readings of most other conductors.

Part of the problem with Toscanini's NBC recordings of Rossini (the 1953 *William Tell* Overture excepted) is that even for their time they are often substandard sonically, veiling detail he took pains to secure and blurring the overall clarity of the finely focused textures he favored. The broadcast accounts of *Semiramide* and *Il Signor Bruschino*, in particular, have greater color and presence than the studio versions do. The RCA CD edition makes the most of them, but to hear what Toscanini could achieve in this repertory, one must, in the main, turn to the broadcasts. The same might be said for the charming but inconsequential Passo a sei from *William Tell*.

The Rossini string sonatas became relatively well known only after Toscanini's death. At the time of his broadcast performance of this one (the only time he directed it) they were still novelties (see the entry for 15 November 1952 in chapter 2). He played this product of Rossini's youth with an unaffected simplicity that suits its style well.

Roussel, Albert (1869–1937)

Unofficially Issued Repertory
The Spider's Feast (19 Feb. 1938, 7 Apr. 1946)

This suite, arranged by the composer from a ballet score of 1912, is another example of competent but relatively characterless impressionism. The contrast between these two Toscanini performances is at times extreme, the earlier and more effective one having a shape, gossamer delicacy, and rhythmic elasticity that makes the slightly faster, more rigid, and less graceful later one sound perfunctory in comparison.

Rubinstein, Anton (1829–94)

Unissued Repertory

Valse caprice, orch. Mueller-Berghaus (21 Dec. 1940)

The Mueller-Berghaus orchestration is garish to the point of sounding vulgar, and Toscanini's fierce performance neutralizes whatever charm this minor *morceau* may have. On other occasions, the conductor did display sympathy for fluff like this (see the entry in this chapter for Vieuxtemps).

Saint-Saëns, Camille (1835–1921)

Officially Issued Repertory

Danse macabre, Op. 40 (8 Jan. 1938, 25 Mar. 1950): RCA 60322 (**1 June 1950**)

Symphony No. 3 in C Minor, Op. 78 (15 Nov. 1952): RCA 60320 (broadcast of **15 Nov. 1952** and dress rehearsal of **14 Nov. 1952**)

During Toscanini's decade with the New York Philharmonic, the Saint-Saëns Third Symphony had been a staple of his repertory, but were it not for his lone NBC presentation, we would have nothing to document his unusual and compelling approach to the score. When first issued on LP, the 1952 broadcast became a hi-fi demonstration disc. More importantly, it helped to revive interest in a work that had begun to slip from public favor but is surely the finest of the composer's symphonies. Toscanini's account is like no other I have heard: slower in the outer movements, more majestic, and showing concern for rhythmic firmness, structural unity, and motivic profile. As was true of the conductor's performances of Mendelssohn's "Reformation" Symphony, his approach to the Saint-Saëns Third bestows a power and dignity on a work that can otherwise seem pretentious, bombastic, and even banal. The breadth and grandeur of the finale's close, for example, suggests a nobility lacking in most other performances, which seem frenetic, even hysterical, by comparison. Aside from a slight (and easily correctable) treble emphasis, RCA's CD transfer, which restored this long-out-of-print performance to circulation, is first rate.

Although Toscanini gave only one performance of *Danse macabre* with the New York Philharmonic and two broadcast accounts at NBC, he included it on both of the latter's tours, possibly because he felt it showed off the orchestra. As in the composer's Third Symphony, he avoided the potential melodrama of this tone poem, concentrating instead on clarity, rhythmic steadiness, and coherence. The studio recording from 8H shows how acceptable (if not ideal) the hall could sound.

Scarlatti, Domenico (1685–1757)

Unofficially Issued Repertory
The Good Humored Ladies, arr. Tommasini (5 Feb. 1938, 24 Mar. 1946)

This work was arranged by Tommasini as a ballet score based on music by Scarlatti and prepared for Diaghilev in 1917. The orchestration is stylish and includes a harpsichord. Both of these performances have a relaxed balletic grace. The later one features a slightly more precise ensemble, but the earlier one benefits from a repeat that was eliminated in the 1946 broadcast.

Schubert, Franz (1797–1828)

Unofficially Issued Repertory
Symphony No. 2 in B-flat Major, D. 125 (12 Nov. 1938, 23 Mar. 1940, 26 Mar. 1944)
Grand Duo in C Major, D. 812, orch. Joachim (15 Feb. 1941)

Officially Issued Repertory
Symphony No. 5 in B-flat Major, D. 485 (14 Mar. 1953): RCA 60291 (**17 Mar. 1953**)
Symphony No. 8 in B Minor, D. 759, "Unfinished" (14 Oct. 1939, 24 Jan. 1942, 5 Mar. 1949, 11 Mar. 1950): RCA 60290 (**12 Mar.** and **2 June 1950**)
Symphony No. 9 in C Major, D. 944 (1 Jan. 1939, 11 Nov. 1945, 23 Feb. 1947, 7 Feb. 1953): RCA 60291 (**25 Feb. 1947**); RCA 60290 (**9 Feb. 1953**)

That Toscanini should program the Schubert Second Symphony at all, let alone three times, is surprising. For one thing, it is likely that the work entered his repertory only with the first of the NBC performances; early Schubert symphonies were rarely encountered on orchestral programs, and it was not until the advent of the long-playing record that all of the composer's symphonies were recorded.

As is true of Toscanini's Mozart and Haydn, the style of these presentations is ideal, with a relatively small body of strings permitting winds and brass to cut through with piquant color. Tempos are bracing in the first and third movements, and the variations that comprise the second movement are linked by a steady pulse that binds sections together. Most striking, though, is the finale, rendered with a relaxed, *gemütlich* charm that is ordinarily not associated with Toscanini's approach to the Viennese classics. This charm comes in part from his unhurried tempo; but it is also rooted in the conductor's exceptional care in observing Schubert's legato phrasing, a care that gives the movement's main theme a graceful, singing line rarely encountered in other performances. Among these three accounts, the earliest is played with the greatest precision, but Toscanini's overall conception of the work remained unchanged from one performance to another.

At the time Toscanini programmed Joseph Joachim's orchestration of the Grand Duo, this four-hand work was erroneously believed to be the sketch of a lost "Gastein" Symphony that Schubert never orchestrated. But this in no way detracts from Toscanini's carefully shaped, grandly conceived reading, a prize of his NBC years that gives the music all the stature of the composer's "Great" C Major Symphony, D. 944.

Toscanini's only NBC broadcast of the Fifth Symphony most likely marks the first time he performed it, his only subsequent account being that of the recording session three days later. Both are essentially identical and are characterized by fast tempos, light sonorities, and well-focused woodwinds (the work is scored without brass or timpani). At the time of these performances, Toscanini's way with this youthful score was unorthodox in its prevailing litheness, with far more animation than in the considerably slower and widely admired version recorded by Sir Thomas Beecham, probably the preferred set of the 78 rpm era. But as with Toscanini's Mozart, his reading of this symphony now seems a harbinger of period-instrument style. Where it differs from such style is in its greater precision and modern (but reduced-vibrato) string tone. Still, for its time, Toscanini's approach—tauter than the more expansive and flexible style of Beecham and less weighty than the sonority favored by Koussevitzky in the only other recording of the period to gain wide circulation—was unconventional.

Also unconventional in many ways were Toscanini's renditions of the "Unfinished" and Ninth Symphonies. His 1950 studio recording of the former, fine as it is (especially in the RCA CD transfer with its superior sound), does not do him complete justice. For one thing, available evidence suggests that he preferred the first movement with its exposition repeated, only one of his NBC broadcasts having omitted it. But with the studio recording having been made in the 78 rpm format (the last of the conductor's recordings to be so issued), the extra disc the desired repeat would require would have made the set uncompetitive in terms of price. Also, part of the recording was made after the orchestra's continental tour, on which the work was performed five times, and suggests a slightly jaded conception (if only when judged against the broadcast accounts, which are marginally less rigid, sometimes broader in tempo, and more pointedly inflected). It is especially interesting to hear the second movement in the 1939 and 1949 broadcasts. Here are prime examples of Toscanini's rhythmic freedom, applied with his usual good taste. Alterations of the basic pulse are made not only with the greatest smoothness but with the apparent recognition that rubato (literally, "robbed time") requires that things stolen from one measure be repaid in another. And quieter sections of the movement have instances of ethereal delicacy. Not to be ignored either is the simple, unaffected directness with which the first movement's celebrated (and sometimes sentimentalized) second subject is stated. As Toscanini conceived this symphony, it was richly expressive—fierce, grim, and tender—while remaining firmly rooted in classical tradition.

So, too, with Toscanini's conception of the Ninth Symphony, which, when judged against all the recordings of the period made by other conductors, was strikingly unorthodox. Toscanini left three recordings of the work: the two discussed here and a 1941 account with the Philadelphia Orchestra that was not released until a quarter of a century after being produced. Surviving, too, in addition to all of the maestro's NBC broadcasts of the work is a sonically dim concert performance with the New York Philharmonic from 1936. These recordings cover nearly three decades, and despite basic differences among them, they share enough similarities to suggest that certain aspects of Toscanini's view of the work varied minimally.

The Ninth Symphony was a Toscanini specialty and appeared on his very first orchestral program in 1896. Indeed, considering his fondness for the score, it is surprising that he programmed it for only four broadcasts at NBC and did not include it in the orchestra's 1950 tour. What makes Toscanini's view of the music so unusual, at least for its time, are its pacing and rhythmic rectitude. Insofar as pace is concerned, the most notable of Toscanini's deviations lies in his recognition that *andante* means "walking." Thus, neither the first movement's introduction nor the entire second movement is unduly protracted. In fact, in the latter, Toscanini takes Schubert's *con moto* qualification quite literally, transforming what is often an attempt to create a slow movement where none exists into a crisp two-to-the-bar march, but one modified by a number of subtly gauged modifications of pulse that prevent rigidity. To this day, his tempo for the second movement remains unusual and controversial.

Almost as unorthodox is Toscanini's way with the opening movement. In addition to his "walking" through the introduction, his adherence to Schubert's *non troppo* qualifications of the main Allegro provides the music with uncommon breadth and stature and allows a smooth transition from the opening Andante. Furthermore, modifications of the basic pulse are minimal, so that the second subject and closing measures are played in tempo. As a result, the movement is never fragmented, the return in the coda of its opening theme is well integrated, and its final measure is perceived as an echo of primary motivic material.

Such an approach is a far cry from the admired recordings of Wilhelm Furtwängler and Bruno Walter. Interesting, too, is one of the earliest electrical recordings of the work, made in 1928 by Sir Hamilton Harty. Harty's tempo for the movement's coda is about half the pace he favors for its main Allegro. The

effect is to set the coda off from the rest of the movement, in the process destroy-
ing its structural relevance. Similarly, under Harty, Walter, Furtwängler, and
Mengelberg, the second movement is, in varying degrees, rather incoherent,
consisting of a series of disconnected (though often very expressive) episodes
rather than a unified whole.

Aside from an uncommonly quick third movement, the remainder of Toscanini's conception of the score is not that unusual. And his studio recordings of
this work, for which he had special affection, do him justice. The recording
from 1947 suffers from an inferior CD transfer, and the 1953 broadcast and
recording are less than perfect in the articulation of the triplets in the finale.
Still, the 1953 recording is sonically good and in most details similar to the 1941
Philadelphia version. One striking difference, however, is a marked allargando
for the dissonant eruptive chords in the finale's coda in 1941, chords that are
played in tempo in all of Toscanini's later performances. It is this distinction
between the 1941 recording and subsequent ones that has provided one of many
examples used by critics to argue for an "earlier" and "later" Toscanini style.
However, as discussions elsewhere in this book suggest, such a view may be an
oversimplification, the rhythmic distensions of 1941 being less marked in Toscanini's 1936 and 1938 performances. In the 1947 broadcast and recording,
Toscanini placed particularly heavy stress on the accents in the first movement's
introduction, a practice that was not observed in his other performances. It is
unfortunate that the RCA CD transfer of the 1947 recording is not better. In
better remastering, it might shine as one of Toscanini's finest NBC efforts.

To this day, Toscanini's view of the Schubert Ninth remains controversial:
heroic but at times insufficiently lyrical for some tastes, its unity, clarity, and
cumulative power are nonetheless compelling. In every one of his surviving
performances, Toscanini ignored all of Schubert's six da capos save the first one
in the third movement, which he always observed.

Schumann, Robert (1810–56)

Unofficially Issued Repertory
Symphony No. 2 in C Major, Op. 61 (29 Mar. 1941, 17 Mar. 1946)

Officially Issued Repertory
Manfred, Op. 115: Overture (19 Nov. 1938, 10 Nov. 1946, 3 Jan. 1953):
     RCA 60292 (**11 Nov. 1946**)
Symphony No. 3 in E-flat Major, Op. 97, "Rhenish" (29 Jan. 1938, 16 Mar.
     1940, 18 Mar. 1945, 12 Nov. 1949): RCA 60292 (broadcast of
     12 Nov. 1949)

Toscanini conducted relatively little Schumann. He never performed the First
Symphony or the *Overture, Scherzo, and Finale*, and it seems that he prepared the

Fourth Symphony only once—in 1931 (in Mahler's orchestration) with the New York Philharmonic. The Second Symphony was performed more often, but Toscanini turned most frequently to the two works that he approved for release—the *Manfred* Overture and "Rhenish" Symphony—the only other Schumann composition to enter the conductor's repertory being a single presentation of the Cello Concerto with Alfred Wallenstein and the New York Philharmonic in 1933.

Toscanini's relatively narrow focus on Schumann is surprising in light of the sympathy he displayed for those works he did perform. The *Manfred* Overture provides a prime example of his refusal to distend rhythm excessively and sectionalize the music. Focusing on clarity and integrity, he rebalanced some of the parts. His studio recording, if not quite as sonically realistic as the reproduction of the broadcasts of 1946 and 1953, represents a conception that varied hardly at all and is typified by continuity and a freedom from sentimentality.

With the exception of a poorly balanced 1940 broadcast of the "Rhenish" Symphony, all of Toscanini's NBC accounts of this score are impressive. Here is a conception usually ignored by those critics who allege that the conductor always favored streamlined, uncommonly fast tempos. In the outer movements, Toscanini's pacing is generally more expansive than that adopted by other conductors and—with a few tasteful revisions in orchestration, mostly involving redistribution of voices—stamped with a transparency and color absent from other conductors' performances. Particularly interesting is a timbral contrast he draws in the first movement by having the horns play with mutes. In annotations for Toscanini's RCA recording of the work, Harris Goldsmith suggests this was done to simulate an effect Schumann called for by specifying that valved and natural horns alternate. As natural horns were an anomaly in this pre–period instrument era, Toscanini's recourse to mutes seems an imaginative alternative.

The original LP release of the 1949 broadcast of the "Rhenish" was a sonic disaster, blemished by a bass deficiency and high-frequency emphasis that lacerated the ears. Although the 1992 RCA CD rectifies this ghastly distortion, it does not have the presence and richness of the best NBC reference discs. But RCA's 1999 remastering offers a major improvement in this regard (see Appendix 8).

In the main, the release of the 1949 "Rhenish" was a wise choice. Granted, it lacks some of the breadth of the 1945 account and the expressive phrasing of the 1938 performance. But it conveys, as they do, the music's nobility, lyricism, and joy, while preserving its motivic profile and structural integrity, traits that stamp the score as perhaps Schumann's most successful attempt at echoing the classicism of Beethoven. In short, this is a work of which Toscanini proved an especially sympathetic interpreter.

There are a number of reasons Toscanini's two accounts of the Second Symphony are among the most interesting of his surviving performances. For one, they preserve his conception of a important nineteenth-century score. Over and beyond that, though, is Toscanini's view of the work, which in many respects is so strikingly unorthodox, it forces one to hear the music in a totally new—and often compellingly revealing—light. Most intriguing are Toscanini's unusual revisions of Schumann's orchestration, revisions that clarify the aesthetic not only of the music but of the conductor as well.

Like so many of his contemporaries (and contrary to common belief), Toscanini did not see a score as inviolate, and in a number of his performances, from Beethoven to Debussy, we find retouchings in orchestration. But none is more striking than those he instituted at the close of the first and fourth movements of this work. In the first movement's coda, Toscanini rewrites the trumpet part, playing the instrument's descending fourth (measures 371–74) as an ascending fifth (C–G) and echoing a configuration occurring earlier in the movement. Clearly this is not a revision made merely to produce a more attractive sound. Rather, it grows from an apparent belief that the ascending fifth, which is central to the movement's structure and recurs in other movements as well, demands reiteration at this point, as a kind of leitmotif. One may question this belief, but the impulse prompting it is obviously based on a carefully gauged artistic judgment, not aimless whim or the desire to enrich color. The same holds true for Toscanini's revision of the finale's close, where in measures 519 ff. Schumann has the trumpet rest. Toscanini, however, adds a part for the instrument, which imitates the ascending woodwind lines in measures 518 ff., thereby filling out an otherwise uncomfortably thin texture and emphasizing further the ascending fifth central to the work's motivic structure. Then, four bars before the final chords (measure 585), Toscanini transposes the trumpet up a fifth (C to G), again emphasizing the interval so central to the music. In this instance, however, the effect is too piercing, almost vulgar in fact. Toscanini must have come to realize this, for he expunged this upward transposition from his performance of 1946, which retains all of his other revisions.

Oddly, in a 30 March 1941 review, the *New York Times* notes only that "Toscanini has touched up the instrumentation in the finale." The starkly exposed revision in the first movement's coda is ignored, and neither the aforementioned countermelodies nor the added transposition in the finale's coda is mentioned. With the long-playing record having made a work like the Schumann Second far more familiar than it was in 1941, no critic could ignore the obvious and radical alterations Toscanini introduced.

Other aspects of his conception also deserve comment: the relatively fast tempos for the initial two movements; the expansive pace of the finale, sustained with greater control and rhythmic security in the earlier of the two performances; and a slow movement that moves somewhat faster than Schumann's indication of adagio suggests, but that integrates the movement's fugal digression with less awkwardness than when the movement moves more slowly.

Although the 1946 performance is often impressive, it lacks the intensity, commitment, control, and subtle flexibility of the earlier one. It has become a cliché to say Toscanini made one hear the familiar as if it were new. But this is precisely what his performances of the Schumann Second—with their bracing tempos, organic unity, and majestic, noble finale—do. In short, these are among the glories of Toscanini's years at NBC.

Shostakovich, Dmitri (1906–75)

Officially Issued Repertory
Symphony No. 1 in F Minor, Op. 10 (14 Jan. 1939, 12 Mar. 1944): RCA
    60323 (broadcast of **12 Mar. 1944**)
Symphony No. 7 in C Major, Op. 60, "Leningrad" (19 July 1942): RCA
    60293 (broadcast of **19 July 1942**)

The background for Toscanini's only NBC performance of the "Leningrad" Symphony—an American premiere—is given in chapter 2 (see the entry for 19 July 1942). However one judges the performance, the concentration the seventy-five-year-old Toscanini was able to muster in memorizing in less than two weeks a new, lengthy, and difficult score he had never previously seen remains extraordinary. After performing it once more the following fall with the New York Philharmonic, Toscanini never returned to this piece, which Bartók, of course, mocked in his Concerto for Orchestra and which Toscanini ultimately felt was "junk."

Toscanini initially performed the First Symphony in 1931 with the New York Philharmonic when the work was but six years old. In addition to his two NBC presentations, he led it in 1937 with the BBC Symphony. After the 1944 NBC broadcast (used in the RCA recording) he never again directed the score. Both NBC broadcasts are remarkably similar, the earlier one benefiting from a touch more humor than the later, marginally swifter account.

Sibelius, Jean (1865–1957)

Unofficially Issued Repertory
Lemminkäinen Suite, Op. 22: "Lemminkäinen's Return" (7 Dec. 1940)
Symphony No. 4 in A Minor, Op. 63 (27 Apr. 1940)

Officially Issued Repertory
En Saga, Op. 9 (18 Feb. 1939, 7 Dec. 1940, 15 Mar. 1952): RCA 60335,
    videocassette only (telecast of **15 Mar. 1952**)
Finlandia, Op. 26 (18 Feb. 1939, 7 Dec. 1940, 26 July 1952): RCA 60294
    (**5 Aug. 1952**)
Pohjola's Daughter, Op. 49 (7 Dec. 1940): RCA 60294 (broadcast of **7 Dec. 1940**)

Lemminkäinen Suite, Op. 22: "The Swan of Tuonela" (18 Feb. 1939, 7 Dec.
      1940, 27 Aug. 1944): RCA 60294 (broadcast of **27 Aug. 1944**)
Symphony No. 2 in D Major, Op. 43 (15 Jan. 1938, 18 Feb. 1939, 7 Dec.
      1940): RCA 60294 (broadcast of **7 Dec. 1940**)

The reading of "Lemminkäinen's Return" takes the typical Sibelius reiteration
of rapidly articulated note patterns—music, in other words, that can, in lesser
hands, sound like sonic doodling or busywork—and invests it with strength,
tension, and cumulative impact. Even more impressive is Toscanini's only NBC
performance of the Fourth Symphony, which he prepared but once in his decade with the New York Philharmonic. It is perhaps a truism to say that simplicity in creative or re-reative art is the most difficult of achievements, but the
idea is no less germane for that. And in a score that can easily be undermined by
interpretive excesses, Toscanini hews to a direct, unaffected statement conveying the pervasive dolefulness of this extraordinary work in all its sweep. Nothing sounds forced or affected, every detail is in place, and at the conclusion of the
performance, no doubt remains that the Fourth Symphony is a twentieth-century masterpiece, as much a harbinger of the modern malaise as anything in
Mahler. RCA's failure to release Toscanini-approved test pressings of this performance has kept one of his major achievements from a broad audience.

      The release on videocassette of the 1952 broadcast of *En Saga* added a work
to Toscanini's "official" discography, although (as with nearly all the video releases) it is unlikely that he approved the performance for release. But as it was
probably never proposed to him for release, it is just as likely that he did not
reject it. In any event, heard in the context of his two other NBC accounts and
a 1936 New York Philharmonic performance (issued in 1998 as part of a fund-
raising set for that orchestra), it does, contrary to the norm, provide one example of the way Toscanini's tempos occasionally accelerated with his advancing
years, the 1949 and 1952 versions being tauter and faster than the Philharmonic
account. Between those extremes lies the 1939 broadcast: less intense than those
of later years, but with greater urgency than in 1936.

      As previously noted, RCA's frequent practice when considering a Tosca-
nini broadcast performance for commercial issue was (as in the case of the Sibelius Second) to opt for the most recent version, probably under the assumption
that it offered the best sound. Toscanini, to be sure, approved the 1940 broadcast of the Second Symphony for release, but one wonders if RCA offered him
the possibility of judging it against his two earlier broadcasts. None is quite like
the others, especially with respect to tempo. Most striking in this regard is the
finale, which, in the 1939 version, has a breadth and atmosphere absent from the
fleeter accounts of 1938 and 1940. Also fascinating is a June 1938 performance
with the BBC Symphony once available from EMI on CD. Here, of course, the
warmer, more resonant acoustic of London's Queen's Hall provided a totally
different coloration from the drier, closer, harsher ambience of studio 8H, the

Toscanini during a 5 August 1952 NBC Symphony rehearsal in Carnegie Hall of Sibelius's *Finlandia*. Note the conductor's unusual attire, which reflects the lack of air conditioning in the hall. *Walfredo Toscanini*

NBC trumpets, in particular, having a more piercing sonority than their BBC counterparts. Then, too, the tempo for the third-movement Trio is broader (and arguably less idiomatic) in the 1939 and 1940 performances than in the earlier BBC performance and 1938 broadcast. Here, then, is still another example of Toscanini rethinking his view of a given work. Unlike so many scores of which his conception changed, this one did not sustain his interest: the 1940 broadcast marked the last time he performed it.

As with the Second Symphony, RCA chose the most recent of Toscanini's broadcasts of "The Swan of Tuonela" for release. In this case, however, the differences among the three performances are minimal, each exemplifying a freedom from lushness and sentimentality, thereby heightening the music's brooding gloom without permitting it to cloy. After his last NBC broadcast of the work, Toscanini directed the piece one more time, in his last appearance with the New York Philharmonic, a pension-fund concert of 13 January 1945. As captured in unofficial releases of the performance, the conductor's basic understanding of the work remains unchanged, but possibly owing to the Carnegie Hall acoustics, the overall tone is fuller and the prevailing ambience warmer, lending the music an aura of mystery absent from the NBC accounts.

The three broadcasts of *Finlandia* are similar: assertive, brassy in tone, and sharply chiseled, with the marked contrasts between the music's contemplative and explosive passages made all the more pointed by a consistent pulse. So, too, with the 1952 recording, which captures uncommonly rich detail in an unnaturally close perspective. The 1940 broadcast of *Pohjola's Daughter*, issued by RCA and probably the only performance of the work Toscanini conducted in the United States, is remarkable for its clarity of texture.

Siegmeister, Elie (1909–91)

Unissued Repertory
Western Suite (25 Nov. 1945)

This performance was a radio premiere and is another example of Toscanini's conducting of minor fluff with total commitment. Brilliantly orchestrated, the work draws upon familiar tunes—most notably "Bury Me Not on the Lone Prairie"—sometimes counterpointed to each other and sometimes fragmented. What is more interesting about the performance, aside from its virtuosic clarity, is Toscanini's apparent feeling for the idiom. One might think that his musical roots sprang not from a Parma conservatory but from a Texas ranch. Musicianship and a sense of style, of course, permit the transcending of national boundaries.

Sinigaglia, Leone (1868–1944)

Unissued Repertory

Piedmont Suite: Over the Fields and Woods; Rustic Dance (21 Apr. 1941)
Le baruffe chiozzotte: Overture (23 Feb. 1947)

Toscanini conducted Sinigaglia's *Piedmont Dances* in 1905 before an audience in Turin that objected to its use of Italian tunes. Five years later, when Sinigaglia dedicated the *Piedmont* Suite to him, Toscanini noted, "Yes, it [the suite] is new, but we're still dealing with those rhapsodies fabricated out of popular Piedmontese themes. . . . The Suite is dedicated to me—help."[62] Toscanini never played this music with the New York Philharmonic, and his programming of two excerpts from it at NBC may have sprung more from an obligation to an old acquaintance than from a liking for music that is surely inconsequential.

The overture (to Goldoni's play of the same name) received its premiere at La Scala in 1907 under Toscanini's direction. Though hardly innovative, it nonetheless has charm and wit that Toscanini's performance conveys.

Smetana, Bedrich (1824–84)

Officially Issued Repertory

The Bartered Bride: Overture (26 Jan. 1938, 17 Nov. 1946): RCA 60310
    (broadcast of **17 Nov. 1946**)
The Moldau (26 Feb. 1938, 13 Dec. 1941, 26 Mar. 1944, 9 Sept. 1945,
    21 Sept. 1947, 15 Mar. 1950, 14 Mar. 1953): RCA 60279 (**19 Mar. 1950**)

Of the two performances of the *Bartered Bride* overture, the earlier one is somewhat lighter and less harsh, and it is unfortunate that the later one was chosen for commercial release. The 1950 studio recording of *The Moldau* mirrors all of the broadcast performances save for one detail: an abrupt tempo transition into the "wedding" sequence, which is made more smoothly in all of the broadcast accounts. Otherwise, the studio effort—comprising another example of how good 8H could sound—typifies Toscanini's interpretation of this score in its richness, detail, color, cantabile lines, and grand climax.

Smith, John Stafford (attrib.) (c. 1750–1836)

Officially Issued Repertory

"The Star-Spangled Banner" (6 Dec. 1941, 4 Apr. 1942, 19 July 1942,
    9 Sept. 1943, 1 Sept. 1945, 2 Sept. 1945): RCA 60307 (**19 Mar. 1942**)

As the dates suggest, it was the ethos of World War II that prompted Toscanini's performances of the national anthem. That patriotic impulse also prompted his tossing it into the stewpot of anthems used by Verdi in his *Hymn of the Nations*. All of the performances listed here are for orchestra only, the last of the three broadcasts incorporating Toscanini's brief canonic overlay in the middle section. All of his performances feature a stately, unaffected tempo that lends the music a fitting dignity. It is regrettable that the studio recording preceded Toscanini's tasteful canonic addition.

Sousa, John Philip (1854–1932)

Unissued Repertory
"Semper Fidelis" (27 Aug. 1944)

Officially Issued Repertory
"El Capitan" (27 Aug. 1944): RCA 60307 (**18 May 1945**)
"The Stars and Stripes Forever" (4 Apr. 1943, 25 May 1944): RCA 60307
    (**18 May 1945**)

Toscanini's performance of "Semper Fidelis" (a minor piece in the context of his entire repertory) is, in its small way, extraordinary. He obviously took the piece with the same seriousness that he brought to Beethoven, and as a result, it is conveyed with a jubilant yet relaxed humor unmatched in any other performance I have ever heard. The source of his humor lies in his attention to rhythmic profile and to the triplet motif that runs through the music. And in the trio section, a carefully gauged crescendo suggests a passing parade, transforming the music into a miniature tone poem.

   All of these in-concert performances of the two other marches feature a more flexible rhythm and greater inflection than that of their comparatively rigid studio counterparts. On the NBC Symphony's 1950 tour, "The Stars and Stripes Forever" was a standard encore in Northern cities (in Southern ones it was "Dixie").

Strauss, Johann, Jr. (1825–99)

Unissued Repertory
Voices of Spring (15 Feb. 1941, 13 Jan. 1946)

Officially Issued Repertory
On the Beautiful Blue Danube (6 Dec. 1941): RCA 60308 (**11 Dec. 1941** and
    19 Mar. 1942)
Tritsch-Tratsch Polka (2 Feb. 1941): RCA 60308 (**5 June 1941**)

It is most likely that Johann Strauss's music did not enter Toscanini's repertory until 1941. Oddly enough, the lone Strauss work that Toscanini prepared for broadcast more than once—*Voices of Spring*—is also the only one among the three he played that he did not record.

On tour with the NBC Symphony in 1950. From left to right: the maestro's son,
Walter; NBC's Al Walker (partly concealed); Toscanini; and David Sarnoff.
BMG Classics

Another of the clichés of criticism leveled against the conductor is the
notion that his response to this repertory was utterly unidiomatic in its stern
gracelessness. There is certainly some truth to this, especially if one judges Toscanini's Strauss solely on the basis of his studio efforts. But the broadcast performances tell a different story. Indeed, the single broadcast performance of *The
Blue Danube*—in its *gemütlich* lilt, subtle modifications of tempo, and freedom
from haste—is everything the glib studio product is not. Moreover, the CD
transfer of the original 78 rpm recording of the piece in RCA's generally
admirable *Toscanini Collection* is an incompetent restoration. The broadcasts of
Voices of Spring are also more flexible and graceful than the Strauss recordings
Toscanini produced in the studio.

Letterhead for the 1950 NBC Symphony tour. *Edwin Bachmann*

Strauss, Richard (1864–1949)

Unofficially Issued Repertory

Ein Heldenleben, Op. 40 (1 Feb. 1941)

Officially Issued Repertory

Death and Transfiguration, Op. 24 (1 Jan. 1938, 17 Nov. 1946, 8 Mar. 1952): RCA 60295 (**10 Mar. 1952**, with portions from broadcast of **8 Mar. 1952**)

Don Juan, Op. 20 (14 Oct. 1939, 14 May 1940, 14 Feb. 1948, 25 Mar. 1950, 28 Feb. 1954): RCA 60296 (**10 Jan. 1951**)

Don Quixote, Op. 35 (22 Oct. 1938, 11 Dec. 1948, 22 Nov. 1953): RCA 60295 (broadcast of **22 Nov. 1953**, with considerable material drawn from preceding dress rehearsal)

Salome: Dance of the Seven Veils (14 Jan. 1939): RCA 60296 (broadcast of **14 Jan. 1939**)

Till Eulenspiegel's Merry Pranks, Op. 28 (16 Mar. 1940, 17 Mar. 1946, 5 Mar. 1949, 1 Nov. 1952): RCA 60296 (**4 Nov. 1952**)

Tastes, even in so sophisticated and knowledgeable a musician as Toscanini, are sometimes eccentric and difficult to comprehend. Although the conductor was a great admirer of Strauss the musician (he had contempt for Strauss the man), he paid far more attention to some works than others, programming, for example, *Death and Transfiguration* more frequently than some of Strauss's other tone poems; *Heldenleben* is a prime case in point, having been prepared by Toscanini only twice during his years with the New York Philharmonic and once at NBC. One wonders if his relative lack of interest was partly tied to the work's having been dedicated to and frequently performed by Willem Mengelberg, Toscanini's predecessor at the Philharmonic and a conductor whose interpretive style was anathema to Toscanini. Mengelberg made a justly admired recording of the work with the Philharmonic in 1928, and it is interesting to hear how Toscanini's performance differs from it: somewhat less weighty in overall sonority, with fewer rhetorical emphases, it comprises a less melodramatic reading, one that underplays some of the music's raucous clatter but nonetheless conveys its sharp contrast of mood and the rich color of Strauss's orchestration. And the performance is made all the more compelling by the exceptionally clear, well-balanced sound of NBC's acetates, whose presence and impact are astonishing for the technology of 1941.

Toscanini's attraction to *Death and Transfiguration* (considered by many the weakest of Strauss's major tone poems) may well have been rooted in its peculiar difficulties of balance, which posed the kind of problems he delighted in trying to solve. "This is very difficult," he would admonish the NBC musicians at the beginning of rehearsals of the work. Those rehearsals were among his most demanding and made an unusually strong impact on the musicians. Indeed, some of them considered the rehearsal for the conductor's last broadcast of the piece "a high point of their lives."[63] The NBC recording of the work, produced two days after the last broadcast performance and (although not so credited) incorporating portions of that broadcast, is thoroughly representative of Toscanini's approach to the score: texturally transparent, intense, yet free of the mawkishness that can sometimes weaken the music's effect. And it surpasses the conductor's earlier recording of the work with the Philadelphia orchestra, especially in its greater clarification of detail. In short, this is another instance of Toscanini's making what some feel is not quite a top-drawer score sound better than it actually is. The 1952 broadcast and recording provide examples of Toscanini's pacing having become slightly broader with the passage of time.

As with *Death and Transfiguration*, RCA has not provided completely accurate provenance for the recording of *Don Quixote*, which is drawn not only from the 22 November 1953 broadcast but also from considerable rehearsal material for that broadcast. Such a pastiche was necessitated by several technical slips in the concert account. At the time, Toscanini had just made a belated return to NBC for this first appearance of his last season, a commitment that he may well have regretted undertaking.

Amazingly, though, the RCA release does not sound like a pastiche. In many respects, it has an integration and sense of character absent from the often superb 1938 broadcast with the cellist Emanuel Feuermann, the only Toscanini performance of the work at NBC not to feature the first-desk cellist, Frank Miller. (In all the NBC presentations the viola solo was played by Carlton Cooley.) Aside from its prevailing freedom from bombast and its typical attention to detail, Toscanini's handling of this music is stamped by its suggestion of charac-

ter (Quixote's and Panza's), maintained without obscuring the classical theme-
and-variation structure on which the work is built. In every way this commercially issued reading illustrates the conductor's command of the piece. Still, it *is*
a pastiche, which may explain why the broadcast performance of 1948 seems
marginally finer in its integration.

Also representative of Toscanini is his 1951 recording of *Don Juan*. Atypically, it was not made at a time when the work had been prepared for public performance. This was a difficult period for the conductor, a strained knee having
required him to cancel several concerts between November 1950 and January
1951. Consequently, the control, clarity, and integrity of the recorded performance remain all the more remarkable, lending the recording virtues that
make it thoroughly competitive with the broadcast accounts. The earliest of
the broadcasts offers a bit more flexibility and intensity, and the last of them
(from Toscanini's final season) is astonishing for its rich inflection. Were it not
for some badly exposed flaws in the ensemble, that performance might rank as
the most compelling of his NBC accounts. All share a basic tempo that is slightly
broader than that usually favored by such distinguished interpreters of the score
as Fritz Busch, Fritz Reiner, George Szell, and the composer himself.

A similar uncommon breadth stamps Toscanini's 1952 recording of *Till
Eulenspiegel*, but in this case it is not typical of all of his surviving performances
of the work. Purely on sonic grounds, RCA's recording may be the most
impressive of any Toscanini left; it is surely one of his best in its presence, dynamic range, and accuracy of timbre. But the brilliant clarity somehow deprives
the score of some of its inherent wit. In part, this may be because the concertmaster, Mischa Mischakoff, in the broadcasts of 1946 and 1949, conveys more
humor in his solos than did the very able Daniel Guilet in the 1952 recording.
But the slightly swifter tempos of those broadcasts permit the music's impish,
raucous humor to emerge more fully than in the broadcast and recording of
1952. In short, fine as that recording is, it should not be taken as Toscanini's only
view of the score.

Toscanini was to conduct the Italian premiere of Strauss's *Salome*, and the
conflict that arose between the composer and conductor over this has been
amply documented by Harvey Sachs.[64] Ultimately, Strauss led the Italian premiere on 22 December 1906 in Turin, Toscanini conducting another performance five days later at La Scala. He never conducted a Strauss opera again.
Strauss, a fine conductor himself, said of Toscanini after hearing him conduct,
"You feel that there is only one thing for you to do; take your baton, break it in
pieces, and never conduct again."[65]

During his years in America, Toscanini presented the Dance of the Seven
Veils twice, once in 1935 with the New York Philharmonic and on the NBC
broadcast here noted. The Philharmonic performance was released in 1998 in a
ten-CD set issued to benefit that orchestra. It is a slightly slower account than

that of the NBC broadcast. But the vastly superior sound of the latter (uncommonly good for its vintage) discloses far more of the color of Strauss's masterful orchestration and conveys more of the controlled eroticism that typifies Toscanini's performance.

Stravinsky, Igor (1882–1971)

Officially Issued Repertory
Petrushka: Tableaux I and IV (21 Jan. 1940): RCA 60323 (broadcast of
    21 Dec. 1940)

Toscanini's relationship to Stravinsky commands some interest. The conductor was to lead the first La Scala production of the composer's *Chant du rossignol* in 1926 but withdrew because of exhaustion. In his autobiography Stravinsky acknowledges Toscanini's "meticulous" preparation and "deep knowledge" of the score, as well as his exceptional degree of "self-effacement."[66]Aside from the flirtation with *Le chant du rossignol*, the only other Stravinsky scores that Toscanini led were "Fireworks," the "infernal Dance" from *Firebird*, and the first and fourth tableaux of *Petrushka*.

Forty-three years after the NBC performance of those tableaux, it was commercially released for the first time in a Franklin Mint LP edition and subsequently reissued on CD by RCA. It is remarkably idiomatic, similar in phrasing, tempo, and detail to the composer's own recording, save that the earlier orchestration of 1911 is used. And the full, bright sound of the NBC reference discs used for these releases bespeaks a recording technology well ahead of its time and suggests why Toscanini never objected to studio 8H.

Strong, George Templeton (1856–1948)

Unissued Performance
Die Nacht (21 Oct. 1939)

The title of this work by an American composer reflects his studies in Germany, where he came under the influence of Lizst. Strong had been an outspoken critic of what he felt was the neglect shown in the United States of its native composers. Perhaps this is what led Toscanini to Strong's work. This symphonic suite, if highly competent, sounds characterless today.

Suppé, Franz von (1819–95)

Officially Issued Repertory
Poet and Peasant: Overture (18 July 1943): RCA 60308 (broadcast of **18 July
    1943**)

Toscanini in rehearsal in studio 8H, c. 1945. *Walfredo Toscanini*

Toscanini's only performance with an American orchestra of a von Suppé score (and the only work by the composer that he ever directed) was the one he gave of this overture at NBC. Despite the typical Toscanini thrust that stamps some portions of the performance, other portions are marked by a relaxed ease generated by rubato and portamento. In short, this is a fine interpretation of a minor but charming score.

Tchaikovsky, Peter Ilyich (1840–93)

Unofficially Issued Repertory
Eugene Onegin: Waltz (27 Aug. 1944)
The Tempest: Symphonic Fantasy after Shakespeare, Op. 18 (12 Mar. 1944)
Voyevoda, Op. 3: Overture (19 Apr. 1941)

Officially Issued Repertory
Piano Concerto No. 1 in B-flat Minor, Op. 23 (19 Apr. 1941, 25 Apr. 1943): RCA 60319 (**6** and **14 May 1941**): RCA 60321 (broadcast of **25 Apr. 1943**)
Manfred Symphony, Op. 58 (21 Dec. 1940, 21 Jan. 1945, 10 Nov. 1946, 28 Feb. 1948, 3 Dec. 1949, 10 Jan. 1953): RCA 60298 (**5 Dec. 1949**)

The Nutcracker Suite, Op. 71a (6 Apr. 1940, 25 Apr. 1943, 25 June 1944,
17 Nov. 1951): RCA 60297 (**19 Nov. 1951**)
Romeo and Juliet: Fantasy Overture (15 Oct. 1938, 6 Apr. 1940, 7 Apr. 1946,
12 Nov. 1949, 21 Mar. 1953): RCA 60298 (**8 Apr. 1946**)
Symphony No. 6 in B Minor, Op. 74, "Pathétique" (29 Oct. 1938, 6 Apr.
1940, 19 Apr. 1941, 15 Nov. 1947, 4 Mar. 1950, 21 Mar. 1954):
RCA 60297 (**24 Nov. 1947**)

Tchaikovsky was not a composer for whom Toscanini felt a strong affinity. He
led only one of his operas, the Italian premiere at La Scala of *Eugene Onegin*—a
production that was received coolly and had only three performances. Aside
from this opera and the works presented at NBC, the only other Tchaikovsky
piece in Toscanini's repertory was the Andante cantabile from the String Quartet, Op. 11. Thus, two staples of the symphonic repertory, the Fourth and Fifth
Symphonies, were ignored by the conductor, the latter in his view being
"banal."[67]

Given Toscanini's relative lack of interest in Tchaikovsky, it is surprising
that he performed the obscure *Voyevoda* Overture (a prelude to Tchaikovsky's
first opera, not to be confused with his Op. 78 symphonic poem of the same
name) and *Tempest* Symphonic Fantasy. Toscanini may have been attracted to
the way in which the latter piece foreshadows the composer's *Manfred* Symphony, a score the conductor admired and played often. Both overtures were
given vibrant, dramatic readings, but the waltz from *Eugen Onegin* is rigid and
somewhat graceless.

Most of Toscanini's interest in Tchaikovsky's developed relatively late in his
career. For example, the two broadcast accounts and studio recording with
Horowitz are probably his only presentation of the celebrated piano concerto.
All are similar in their virtuosic, straightforward approach, but the 1943 account,
which was not released commercially until the LP era, is most interesting, mainly
because it features greater flexibility and inflection.

In the conversation with B. H. Haggin in which Toscanini dismissed the
Fifth Symphony as "banal," he also noted that Tchaikovsky's *Manfred* Symphony contained "not one banal note." This view did not prevent him, however, from excising a few scattered measures from the first movement and 118
measures from the finale—about a quarter of its total length. In his annotations
for Toscanini's RCA recording of the work, Harris Goldsmith summarized this
huge excision: " a slow section that remarkably foreshadows late Sibelius, some
engaging variants on the 'orgy' music, and a fugato based on the movement's
opening material." Most remarkable about Toscanini's cut in this movement is
the way in which it tightens an otherwise loose structure. Still, it is, to say the
least, extreme and, perhaps, the most striking of many examples of how the
maestro did *not* play music "exactly as written." Furthermore, Toscanini made
a few revisions in orchestration: substitution of an organ for harmonium at the

work's close and addition of horn and double bass in the third movement (all in a work that Toscanini deemed Tchaikovsky's finest).

Given his admiration for this score, it is fitting that Toscanini's 1949 recording of the *Manfred* Symphony does justice to his interpretive view. Produced in Carnegie Hall, it shines sonically as one of his finest studio efforts. Musically, it blends continuity and passion with lightness and grace, the third movement having a caressing delicacy. One might argue that his first NBC broadcast of *Manfred* offers a slightly more fiery finale and a more brilliantly and lightly executed second movement. But these are minor differences in a conception that changed little over the years. Even in his last broadcast performance, despite some loss of control and flagging of intensity, the basic projection diverged hardly at all from its predecessors.

The same does not hold true for *The Nutcracker Suite*, a work that appeared in 1896—only four years after its completion—on Toscanini's first symphonic concert. The most appealing of Toscanini's surviving performances is his first NBC broadcast account. Here the concluding Waltz of the Flowers has a lilt and relaxation that he never duplicated. It is also free of the gratuitous closing chords imposed on later presentations. Absent from this earliest account, too, are the unstylish tamperings with the harp cadenza that infect his later readings. Moreover, with each successive performance (and in the 1951 studio product) the overall approach became slightly less balletic, and less charming.

It was not until 1934 (with the New York Philharmonic) that the *Romeo and Juliet* Fantasy Overture entered Toscanini's repertory. Although not all of his NBC accounts are equally successful, they share a freedom from the kind of excess that can easily make this piece sound sentimental and bombastic. The love music, for instance, is never distended, so that its incipient lushness does not become vulgar; furthermore, its recurrence in minor tonality is made to sound all the more expressive as a result of being played in tempo. And the section depicting the Montague-Capulet feud has a tense dialectic of controlled fury.

In general, Toscanini's conception of this work remained unchanged from one performance to the next, the main differences among them resulting from a varying proficiency of execution. In this regard, the 1946 studio recording, with its few imprecisions and sonic limitations, does not match the finest broadcast performances, notably those of 1938, 1940, and 1953, the last of these offering a blend of virtuosity and exceptionally fine reproduction. Toscanini, to be sure, objected to some of the problems in the 1946 recording and insisted that a portion of the timpani part be overdubbed on a 78 rpm master. At least that recording can now be heard in RCA's CD edition to better advantage than in any of its previous incarnations.

Of all Toscanini's Tchaikovsky performances, the most unorthodox is that of the "Pathétique" Symphony. He first performed the work in 1898, when, of course, it was still "modern," but not until forty years later did he return to it in the first of his NBC broadcast presentations. Toscanini claimed he came back to the score because he had come to the realization that it was "honest" music. Doubtless this was a truthful statement. Still, one wonders what promoted the sudden change of heart after four decades of neglect. It is possible that Toscanini was drawn to the work from having read Sir Donald Tovey's essay about it, which was published in 1935 in volume 2 of his *Essays in Musical Analysis*. Toscanini, of course, admired Tovey's writing, which reflected an analytical approach similar to Toscanini's own. And in writing of the "Pathétique," Tovey called it "the most dramatic of all [Tchaikovsky's] works."[68]

Whatever prompted Toscanini's renewed interest, the symphony remained a core work in his repertory at NBC and was included on the orchestra's 1950 tour. The NBC violinist Joseph Gingold has provided some pointed comments about Toscanini's unorthodox view of the work:

> He came to the rehearsal [in 1938] with the preconceived idea that the orchestra was set in its way of playing the symphony, and he was right. We came to . . . the D-major melody [in the first movement], which traditionally we had all played with a *ritardando* on the first three notes. He stopped: "*Signori, perché?* Why? Is written so, eh? *Ancora.*" We started again; and again we made the *ritardando*: it was so ingrained in us we couldn't help it. And he threw a fit. "*Si, tradizione!* The first *asino* the first jackass did it that way and everyone follow him." Then he pointed to the score: "*This is my tradizione!* So play like this."[69]

Yes, the score was his tradition, except (as in the case of *Manfred*) when he chose to alter it. But in the "Pathétique" he honored it. More than anything else, his performances stripped away cobwebs of sentimentality, imbuing the music with a dramatic continuity, tautness of structure, and freedom from excess that set his approach apart from those of such other distinguished conductors as Koussevitzky and Stokowski, both of whom freely imposed tempo modifications on the work. But it should be noted that Toscanini was not alone in revolting against such excesses imposed in the name of expression, as a 1930 recording made by Oskar Fried illustrates. Interestingly, too, in 1938, when portamento still shaped much of the NBC Symphony's string playing, Toscanini permitted none in the opening movement's D major theme.

Among all of Toscanini's NBC broadcasts of the "Pathétique," the first and the last are the least successful. Though cleansed of bad habits, the 1938 performance is sometimes too nervous and impetuous. Conversely, the 1954 account (Toscanini's penultimate public appearance) reflects the anxiety he must have felt about his impending retirement. As some musicians in the orchestra noted, "He was all there in the rehearsal, but not in the performance."[70] Of his two studio recordings, the NBC version of 1947 is superior both sonically and musically. The Philadelphia Orchestra recording of 1942 may be more attractive tonally, but the performance is not as organic and seems at times to ramble, per-

haps as a result of awkward pauses imposed in producing individual four-minute
segments on 78 rpm discs.

The 1947 recording would, in fact, be a fine representation of Toscanini at
his best were it not that the RCA CD edition is substandard technically. The
1947 broadcast from studio 8H comprises virtually an identical interpretation
preserved in better sound. Along with the 1940 and 1950 broadcasts, it shines as
one of Toscanini's finest surviving efforts with the music. Distinguished, too, is
the 1941 benefit performance. In most respects it is similar to the other commanding accounts. All feature a first-movement development having tremen-
dous energy tempered by exceptional control that in no way compromises
Tchaikovsky's specification of *feroce*. If anything, the tight rein is arguably more
effective in projecting the savage ethos implicit in the word's literal meaning—
"ferocious."

All of the broadcasts except the last featured a third movement of tremen-
dous sweep and cumulative impact played marginally slower in 1947 and thereafter than in previous accounts. In each instance, its effect was so great, it sparked
a mesmerized audience into applause. And, of course, there was Toscanini's
attention to detail, balance, and dynamics. With regard to this last aspect, let it
be recalled that Tchaikovsky called for an unprecedented gamut of volume.
This motivated the Philadelphia Orchestra's Sol Schoenbach to stuff his bassoon with cotton, handkerchiefs, and socks to convey the *ppppp* immediately
before the first-movement development when playing the work under Toscanini. He knew that the maestro did not favor the practice adopted by other
conductors, who, in order to achieve the specified dynamic, substituted a bass
clarinet for Tchaikovsky's bassoon.[71] In the 1940 broadcast Toscanini did employ
the bass clarinet in the passage, but this was an exception to a generally intran-
sigent stance. Perhaps such intransigence was impractical. In the case of the
"Pathétique," however, it transformed what was often sentimentalized and vul-
garized into a conception that was animated not only by passion but by an intellect that renounced excess.

Thomas, Ambroise (1811–96)

Officially Issued Repertory
Mignon: Overture (14 Mar. 1942, 26 July 1952): RCA 60310 (**19 Mar.
1942**) and 60322 (**29 July 1952**)

Toscanini directed only two of Thomas's operas in the theater, *Mignon* and
Hamlet, the overture to the former being the only work by the composer that he
led in the concert hall. Both broadcasts of that overture were followed by studio recordings, all four performances being essentially identical and carefully
shaped. As the later recording offers the better sound, it is the preferred version.

Tommasini, Vincenzo (1878–1950)

Unofficially Issued Repertory
Carnival of Venice (15 Jan. 1938, 29 Mar. 1941, 13 Mar. 1948)

Toscanini had collaborated with Tommasini on the posthumous completion of Boito's opera *Nerone*. Their fruitful association doubtless contributed to the conductor's programming of some of Tommasini's lighter scores such as this. Subtitled *Variations in the Style of Paganini*, the work is superbly orchestrated, occasionally charming, and of no consequence. All of Toscanini's three NBC performances make the most of it and provide further examples of how he usually lavished as much care on lesser works such as this as he did on Beethoven's, Wagner's, or Verdi's.

Vaughan Williams, Ralph (1872–1958)

Unofficially Issued Repertory
Fantasia on a Theme by Thomas Tallis (15 Oct. 1938, 18 Nov. 1945)

Toscanini never performed this work with the New York Philharmonic, his first presentation of it probably being given in May 1938 with the BBC Symphony. This is music well suited to the conductor's style. Its rich string sonorities are projected with pointed tonal shadings that bring out the color implicit in Vaughan Williams's masterful scoring and complement the music's eerie modal harmonies. Both performances exemplify Toscanini's sensitivity to the expressive power of timbre. The slightly less opulent sound of the earlier version is most likely a result of its being less sumptuously recorded; it is also a slightly broader, more intense reading. But both performances preserve a conception that adds dimension to Toscanini's NBC years.

Verdi, Giuseppe (1813–1901)

Unofficially Issued Repertory
Aida: Overture (30 Mar. 1940)
Don Carlos: "O don fatale" (25 July 1943)
La forza del destino: "Pace, pace, mio dio" (25 July 1943)
String Quartet in E Minor: third and fourth movements (27 Jan. 1946)

Officially Issued Repertory
Preludes and overtures:
> *La forza del destino*: Overture (31 Jan. 1943, 27 Jan. 1946, 8 Nov. 1952):
>> RCA 60310 (**28 June 1945**), 60309 (**10 Nov. 1952**)
> *Luisa Miller*: Overture (25 July 1943): RCA 60309 (broadcast of **25 July 1943**)

La traviata: Prelude to Act I (no concert broadcast): RCA 60309
(**10 Mar. 1941**)
Prelude to Act III (31 Jan. 1943): RCA 60309 (**10 Mar. 1941**)
I vespri siciliani: Overture (24 Jan. 1942): RCA 60309 (broadcast of
24 Jan. 1942)
Vocal works:
Aida: complete opera in two broadcasts (26 Mar. 1949, 2 Apr. 1949):
RCA 60300 (broadcasts of **26 Mar.** and **2 Apr. 1949**)
Un ballo in maschera: complete opera in two broadcasts (17 Jan. 1954,
24 Jan. 1954): RCA 60301 (broadcasts of **17 Jan. 1954** and **24 Jan.
1954**)
Falstaff: complete opera in two broadcasts (1 Apr. 1950, 8 Apr. 1950):
RCA 60251 (broadcasts of **1 Apr.** and **4 Aug. 1950**)
Hymn of the Nations (3 Jan. 1943, 25 May 1944): RCA 60299 (**8** and **20
Dec. 1943**; soundtrack of Office of War Information film)
I Lombardi: Act III Trio (31 January 1943): RCA 60276 (broadcast of
31 Jan. 1943)
Luisa Miller: "Quando le sere" (25 July 1943): RCA 60299 (broadcast of
25 July 1943)
Nabucco: "Va, pensiero" (31 Jan. 1943): RCA 60299 (broadcast of
31 Jan. 1943)
Otello: complete opera in two broadcasts (6 Dec. 1947 and 13 Dec.
1947): RCA 60302 (broadcasts of **6** and **13 Dec. 1947**)
Requiem: (4 Mar. 1938, shortwave only, 23 Nov. 1940, 27 Jan. 1951):
RCA 60299 (broadcast of **27 Jan. 1951**, with considerable material
drawn from rehearsals)
Rigoletto: Act III (25 July 1943, 25 May 1944): RCA 60276 (broadcast of
25 May 1944)
Te Deum: (23 Nov. 1940, 2 Dec. 1945, 14 Mar. 1954): RCA 60299
(broadcast of **14 Mar. 1954**)
La traviata: complete opera in two broadcasts (1 Dec. 1946 and 8 Dec.
1946): RCA 60303 (broadcasts of **1** and **8 Dec. 1946**)

Note: The published recordings of the Requiem, Aida, Ballo, Falstaff, and Otello incorporate, in varying degrees, rehearsal material or corrections recorded in specially held sessions. Some of these are acknowledged in RCA's annotations; some are not.

Of all the composers in Toscanini's repertory, Verdi was probably closest to him. The conductor's third appointment as music director of La Scala (1920–29) may have produced the most organic Verdi productions of the century. During that appointment the composer's operas formed the core of Toscanini's work. He directed a dozen in all, more than those of any other composer he led in the theater. The extraordinary integrity of Toscanini's Verdi at La Scala was noted by the young Herbert von Karajan, who wrote after witnessing Toscanini's production of *Falstaff* in 1929:

From the first . . . I was completely disconcerted by the perfection which had been achieved. . . . For the first time I grasped what "direction" meant. To be sure, Toscanini had employed a stage director; but basically the essential conception came from him. The agreement between the music and the stage performance was something totally inconceivable for us: instead of people senselessly standing around, here everything had its place and its purpose.[72]

The key word in Karajan's comment is "agreement." We know, for example, that Toscanini took great pains with all the details of production, even to the point of objecting to the shoes worn by the cast of *Falstaff* for being anachronistic. But, most significantly, such care suggests that the overall pacing and musical approach of Toscanini's productions may have differed from his concert performances of Verdi's opera at NBC. Even some surviving NBC evidence suggests that those productions were not necessarily typical of a specific interpretive view; the dress rehearsals for *La traviata* and *Falstaff*, for example, were paced differently from their broadcast presentations. Then, too, the 1943 broadcast of the third act of *Rigoletto* is often broader and more rhythmically inflected than the 1944 concert performance released by RCA. Similarly, the 1943 broadcast account of the aria "Eri tu" (from *Ballo*) features far more rubato than in the 1954 broadcasts of the complete opera released by RCA. In part this may be rooted in the different styles of the two singers, Frank Valentino in 1943 and Robert Merrill in 1954. Still, it would seem that with operatic works, as well as symphonic ones, Toscanini was constantly revising his views.

But over and beyond this issue should be the obvious one that the exigencies of staging must affect the musical pacing of an opera. Consequently, some of the faster tempos in Toscanini's broadcast performances may well have been at variance with what he did in the theater. It is interesting, for example, to compare a recording of his staged 1937 Salzburg production of *Falstaff* to the 1950 NBC broadcasts released by RCA. Similarities not withstanding, the earlier version has greater breadth, wit, and (understandably) theatrical ambience. In short, although all of the conductor's broadcasts of operas are valuable documents of his view of Verdi, they should not necessarily be taken as *completely* representative of how he may have performed the composer in the opera house.

Of the three nonoperatic vocal works by Verdi in Toscanini's NBC repertory, *Hymn of the Nations* is the least consequential. By any standards, it is a potboiler, and were it not for the patriotic fervor generated by World War II, it is unlikely that he would have performed it. And what he did perform appended to Verdi's original the national anthems of Russia and the United States. Moreover, he made a significant alteration of the text, changing "Italia, patria mia" (Italy, my country) to "Italia, patria mia tradita" (Italy, my betrayed country). During the anti-Communist hysteria of the 1950s, the Soviet "Internationale" was excised from prints of the film. The Library of Congress videocassette

Toscanini conducting Verdi's *Hymn of the Nations* in studio 8H, December 1943
(and facing page). *Walfredo Toscanini*

restores it, as does the RCA CD, which draws on the original sound track. Whatever the limitations of the work itself, Toscanini invested it with a dignity and musicality that avoided potential bombast and excess.

   With the Te Deum and Requiem, of course, musicality and dignity were never in question. Toscanini led the Italian premiere of the Te Deum in 1898. Shortly before that performance he met with Verdi to discuss the interpretation. At the meeting Toscanini hoped the composer would go to the piano to illustrate his view of certain problematic passages. Instead, Verdi directed Toscanini to the keyboard and asked him to begin playing the work. The conductor did so, making a small rallentando at one point. "Bravo," said Verdi, to which Toscanini responded: "Maestro, if you knew how much this has been bothering me. . . . Why didn't you write the *rallentando*?" "Had I written it," Verdi replied, "a bad musician would have exaggerated it; but if one is a good musician, one feels and plays it just as you have done."[73]All of Toscanini's surviving NBC per-

formances of the work are similar and share the nobility, solemnity, and rhythmic subtlety that quite likely stamped the 1898 premiere.

　　Toscanini may have been the most commanding exponent of his time of
the Requiem. He led the work on twenty-nine occasions, the first of them at La
Scala on 27 January 1902 to mark the first anniversary of Verdi's death. Forty-
nine years later to the day, he directed his last performance of the score in an
NBC broadcast, which—modified by several patches of rehearsal material used
to correct flaws in the performance—was the one issued by RCA. Most listeners have gained familiarity with Toscanini's view of the work from this version.
It shares many features with his other surviving performances (those given at
NBC, one with the BBC in London from 1938, and a 1950 La Scala account).
All have a fire, a soaring lyricism, and a muted delicacy that shape an exceptionally dramatic conception of a score sometimes tagged "Verdi's greatest
opera."

Toscanini during the December 1943 *Hymn of the Nations* performance.
Walfredo Toscanini

Yet in many respects the commercially released reading—for all its many virtues and the improved clarity and impact of RCA's CD transfer—does not do Verdi complete justice. For one thing, the solo singing is not always what it should be. Then, too, Toscanini's control is slightly less firm than in some of his previous efforts. It should be remembered that the recorded performance marked his return to NBC after a weak knee had forced him to cancel all his earlier broadcasts of that season. It is possible that he was not fully up to the demands of the work. And, as noted in chapter 2 (see the entry for the broadcast of 27 January 1951), frantic last-minute scrambling was necessary to bring together a chorus that Toscanini deemed sufficiently large. But what most sets the performance apart from some of Toscanini's earlier efforts is its greater thrust and rigidity. Often the music lacks the rubato that stamps some of his earlier accounts. Toscanini's original instincts were to reject the performance. It was only when RCA officials presented him with alternative rehearsal material that could be patched with the acceptable portions that he agreed to its release. One wonders, too, if the company provided an opportunity for him to audition his similar but more disciplined 1948 performance, which was not aired, or his often more interesting 1940 broadcast of the work, where, despite a few technical slips that the maestro might not have tolerated, the overall conception is more subtly modulated. This said, the 1951 version, despite its shortcomings, stands as a major achievement and one of Toscanini's most important and memorable recordings.

Of the remaining vocal works released by RCA, the chorus "Va, pensiero" from *Nabucco* is in some ways the most revealing. Drawn from Toscanini's only NBC broadcast of the piece, it proves especially interesting for his choice of tempo—one that permits the music to flow, yet conveys its mixture of longing, pastoral gentleness, and prayerful simplicity, emotions implicit in its text and conveyed with an apt lyricism. One wonders, too, how many other conductors manage to produce the dynamic inflections and gradations that distinguish this performance.

Of the three overtures issued by RCA, only that to *La forza del destino* is not taken from a broadcast. The 1952 studio account is superior to Toscanini's earlier NBC recording of 1945: flexible, fiery, and stamped with a tastefulness that prevents vulgarity, an effect Verdi himself had complained about when criticizing a conductor who brought the brass in too loudly, transmogrifying its religious theme into what the composer felt was a "warlike fanfare."[74]

The overtures to *Luisa Miller* and *I vespri siciliani* are Toscanini's only surviving performances of each and are characterized by taut lines and firm rhythm. Ironically, the preludes to Acts I and III of *La traviata*, which are preserved in two of Toscanini's most admired recordings (made in 1929 with the New York Philharmonic), were all but ignored on the broadcasts, only the Act III prelude being programmed and it but once. Both, however, were recorded in 1941 with the NBC Symphony. Surprisingly, the prelude to Act I is marginally slower than its Philharmonic predecessor.

As noted in chapter 2, the performance of the overture to *Aida* (the only one Toscanini ever directed) was a world premiere of an unpublished work. Verdi wisely rejected this exercise in a Wagner-styled symphonic overture in favor of the familiar brief prelude. It is interesting to hear the exercise, however, if only to discover how even a genius can miss the artistic bull's-eye in a piece that often sounds rambling, despite Toscanini's tightly organized account.

The two quartet movements are a bit of a curiosity, but they have an exceptional vitality and verve in Toscanini's presentation with a string orchestra. The operas from which the two brief vocal excerpts are drawn were both part of Toscanini's repertory in the theater, *La forza* having been the most frequently performed among them. Each gives a tantalizing suggestion of the sweep and intensity of his productions.

Responding in 1933 to a questionnaire sent to famous musicians by the *Berliner Börsen Zeitung*, Toscanini remarked: "In Verdi's operas, I value not only

the melodic richness but the effectiveness and sure musical dramatic power."[75]
Given the conductor's identification with the composer, it is probably safe to say
that one of posterity's greatest losses is the lack of recordings of Toscanini's productions of Verdi at La Scala and the Metropolitan Opera. Still, what NBC preserved and RCA has issued, if not necessarily representative of his staged performances or of his best work, is often compelling. Given limitations such as
occasionally weak casting, they are uneven. But when everything more or less
fell into place, as in the complete *Otello*, a performance of towering merit
resulted.

Vieuxtemps, Henri (1820–81)

Unissued Performance
Ballade and Polonaise (14 Dec. 1940)
This is music of minor merit at best, but it is nonetheless fascinating to hear
how sympathetically Toscanini plays it, with sixteen violins in unison performing with precision, lilt, and tastefully applied portamento that reveal surprising
sympathy for the salon style.

Vivaldi, Antonio (1678–1741)

Unofficially Issued Repertory
Concerto Grosso in D Minor, Op. 3 No. 11 (25 Dec. 1937, 14 Mar. 1954)
Violin Concerto in B-flat Major, P. 405 (22 Nov. 1947)

The earlier performance of the D minor concerto is a bit more vibrant, sharply
etched, and intense, even though the tempos in both are almost identical. For
their time, both were reasonably stylish accounts, at least from the leader of a
major symphony orchestra, but the edition Toscanini used in both is clearly the
work of a modern editor, the closing chords, for example, having no place in the
Urtext. And surprisingly—in contrast to Toscanini's performances of similarity
styled works by Bach and Handel—neither performance employs a harpsichord.

The violin concerto is an unimaginative work, very much inferior to Vivaldi's best efforts, and nothing in the performance—with small orchestra and a
harpsichord—makes its barrenness of invention any more attractive.

Wagner, Richard (1813–83)

Unofficially Issued Repertory
The Flying Dutchman: Overture (19 Feb. 1938, 25 Feb. 1939, 31 Mar. 1946)
Parsifal: excerpts, arr. Toscanini (23 Mar. 1940)
Rienzi: Overture (3 Dec. 1938)

Tannhäuser: Prelude to Act III, original version (25 Feb. 1939, 6 Jan. 1946, 29 Dec. 1953)
Act II: "Dich, teure Halle" (22 Feb. 1941)

Officially Issued Repertory

Nonoperatic works:
A Faust Overture (5 Mar. 1938, 29 Mar. 1941, 27 Oct. 1946): RCA 60305 (**11 Nov. 1946**)
Siegfried Idyll: (12 Feb. 1938, 6 Jan. 1946, 26 July 1952, 7 Mar. 1953): RCA 60296 (**11 Mar. 1946**) and RCA 60264 (**29 July 1953**)
Operatic works with voice:
Götterdämmerung: Dawn, Siegfried-Brünnhilde duet, and Siegfried's Rhine Journey (22 Feb. 1941): RCA 60304 (broadcast of **22 Feb. 1941**)
Brünnhilde's Immolation (22 Feb. 1941): RCA 60304 (**24 Feb. 1941**)
Die Walküre: Act I, Scene 3 (22 Feb. 1941, 6 Apr. 1947): RCA 60264 (broadcast of **22 Feb. 1941**)
Orchestral music from operas:
Götterdämmerung: Dawn and Siegfried's Rhine Journey: concert version by Toscanini (5 Mar. 1938, 25 Feb. 1939, 25 May 1944, 6 Jan. 1946, 24 Nov. 1946, 20 Mar. 1948, 26 Feb. 1949, 17 Dec. 1949, 24 Nov. 1951, 4 Apr. 1954): RCA 60296 (**17 Mar. and 14 May 1941**) and RCA 60306 (**22 Dec. 1949**)
Siegfried's Death and Funeral Music: concert version by Toscanini (3 Dec. 1938, 22 Feb. 1941, 17 Dec. 1949, 29 Dec. 1951, 7 Mar. 1953): RCA 60304 (**14 May 1941**) and RCA 60306 (**3 Jan. 1952**)
Lohengrin: Prelude to Act I: (5 Mar. 1938, 22 Feb. 1941, 29 Dec. 1951, 4 Apr. 1954): RCA 60306 (**17 Mar. and 6 May 1941**) and RCA 60305 (**22 Oct. 1951**)
Prelude to Act III: concert ending by Humperdinck (5 Mar. 1938, 20 Mar. 1948, 7 Mar. 1953): RCA 60305 (**22 Oct. 1951**)
Die Meistersinger von Nürnberg: Prelude to Act I (22 Jan. 1938, 7 Jan. 1939, 21 Oct. 1939, 14 Mar. 1942, 4 Feb. 1945, 6 Jan. 1946, 18 Mar. 1950, 7 Feb. 1953, 4 Apr. 1954): RCA 60305 (**11 Mar. 1946**)
Prelude to Act III: concert ending by Humperdinck (19 Nov. 1938, 28 Nov. 1943, 24 Nov. 1951): RCA 60305 (**26 Nov. 1951**)
Parsifal: Prelude and Good Friday Spell (5 Mar. 1939, 12 Apr. 1941, 4 Apr. 1942, 9 Apr. 1944, 6 Apr. 1947, 17 Dec. 1949); Good Friday Spell only (12 Nov. 1938, 21 Oct. 1939, 6 Dec. 1941); Prelude only (5 Mar. 1938): RCA 60305 (**22 Dec. 1949**)
Siegfried: Forest Murmurs (3 Dec. 1938, 30 Nov. 1942, 27 Aug. 1944, 20 Mar. 1948, 29 Dec. 1951, 4 Apr. 1954): RCA 60304 (**29 Oct. 1951**)
Tannhäuser: Overture (Dresden version) (5 Mar. 1938, 25 May 1944, 4 Dec. 1948): RCA videocassette 60330 (**4 Dec. 1948**)

Overture and Bacchanale (28 Nov. 1943, 20 Mar. 1948, 8 Nov. 1952, 4 Apr. 1954): RCA 60306 (broadcast of **8 Nov. 1952**)
Tristan and Isolde: Prelude and Liebestod (5 Mar. 1938, 25 Feb. 1939, 22 Feb. 1941); Prelude only (28 Nov. 1943, 29 Dec. 1951, 7 Mar. 1953): RCA 60306 (Liebestod only, **19 Mar. 1942**) and RCA 60264 (**7 Jan. 1952**)
Die Walküre: Ride of the Valkyries (5 Mar. 1938, 25 Feb. 1939, 28 Nov. 1943, 20 Mar. 1948, 17 Dec. 1949, 29 Dec. 1951, 7 Mar. 1953): RCA 60306 (**11 Mar. 1946**) and RCA 60264 (**3 Jan. 1952**)

In his response to the *Berliner Börsen Zeitung* questionnaire mentioned earlier, Toscanini equated Wagner with Verdi: "Among operas, I value those of Verdi and Wagner above all"; he went on to observe that both were the "representatives of Italian and German national music."[76] Toscanini refused to state a preference for a specific Wagner opera, but he did imply a strong affection for *Parsifal*. The roots of his attraction to Wagner have been clarified by Toscanini himself. He heard the composer's music for the first time as an eleven-year-old when the overture to *Tannhäuser* was performed in Parma. Six years later he was a cellist in the orchestra for a production of *Lohengrin*, which he claimed "overwhelmed" him.[77] And throughout his life, Wagner remained at the core of his repertory. Toscanini inaugurated his initial season at La Scala in 1898 with the first uncut production in Italy of *Die Meistersinger*. He had nine Wagner operas in all in his repertory, though he shunned *Das Rheingold* and thus never led a complete *Ring* cycle. Throughout his career in the concert hall, all-Wagner programs were frequent, eleven being given during his seventeen years at NBC.

Listening to Toscanini's three NBC performances of the overture to the *Flying Dutchman* reveals not only the inherent strengths of each reading, but also the differences among them, which again contradict the generalization that his tempos (especially in German works) became faster and faster as he aged. The swiftest of these readings is the 1939 performance. But pace does not tell the whole story: the 1946 account lacks the strong profile of the earlier two, mainly as a result of its slightly less assertive accents and less marked inflection. Each of the three readings, however, offers an appropriately stormy ethos, with the NBC brass cutting through the overall sonority to produce a richly expressive color.

Toscanini's single NBC performance of the overture to *Rienzi* is another matter altogether. Indeed, it is surprising that he programmed so infrequently a work for which he clearly had great affinity, this NBC account being his only presentation in the United States. Possibly because of his knowledge of the opera, this reading of its overture is strikingly different from what one ordinarily hears in the concert hall: more broadly paced, with a prevailing loftiness and restraint that take this familiar work out of the rough-and-tumble "Lone Ranger" category into which less sensitive performances often place it.

Toscanini's preference for the original version of the prelude to Act III of *Tannhäuser* (see the entry for 25 February 1939 in chapter 2) in all three of these NBC presentations made sense. Although this earlier version—as Wagner obviously came to realize—is too long for the opera house, it is ideal for the concert hall. Again refuting commonly made claims, the fastest of these three performances is the earliest, the slowest, that of 1946. Despite the differences in tempo, all three affirm Toscanini's ability to sustain long lines while avoiding slackness and to build carefully gauged climaxes. Owing to its superior sound, the performance of 1953 is preserved with a tonal opulence absent from its two predecessors. The joyous account of "Dich, teure Halle" (sung by Helen Traubel) makes one wish that Toscanini had recorded the entire opera when he directed it at Bayreuth in 1930.[78]

Although Toscanini's recordings of Wagner are among his most representative studio efforts, a few fail to do him justice. Most notable in this regard is the RCA edition of the prelude to *Die Meistersinger*. Because Toscanini programmed the work with exceptional frequency, it is worth examining all of his surviving performances of it, not only to illustrate how his approach varied from one account to the next, but also to offer still another of several examples that dispel the notion that the conductor tended over the years to speed up tempos. Although timings are rarely an accurate gauge of quality of style, they prove instructive in the following dozen uncut Toscanini performances.

1936: New York Philharmonic, 9:22
1937: Vienna Philharmonic, 9:09
1938: NBC Broadcast, 9:00
1939 (7 Jan.): NBC Broadcast, 9:00
1939 (21 Oct.): NBC Broadcast, 9:30
1942: NBC Broadcast, 8:38
1946: NBC Broadcast, 8:58
1946: Recording, 8:57
1946: La Scala Orchestra, 9:25
1950: NBC Broadcast, 8:59
1953: NBC Broadcast, 9:13
1954: NBC Broadcast, 9:04

No pattern, either of increased haste or of expansiveness, is discernible here. That fastest reading comes relatively early; the next fastest is the studio recording. The timing for the broadcast account of two months before that suggests that tempos for these two performances are essentially identical. Here, however, sound plays a crucial role; the considerably greater clarity and definition of the 1946 broadcast exposes Toscanini's care in delineating Wagner's rich polyphony, a richness masked in RCA's inferior recording.

On purely musical grounds, the 1936 performance is magnificent: grand, full bodied, flexible. The first NBC broadcast matches it in grandeur and suppleness, but the cramped sound of studio 8H drains heft from the orchestra. In varying ways the broadcasts of October 1939, 1942, and 1950 sound either cavalier, bland, or mechanical. The 1954 broadcast, the last performance Toscanini led before an audience, is stronger than one might expect, given the tension of that last concert. In terms of weight, the 1953 broadcast comes closest to the New York Philharmonic account, but it lacks some of that earlier version's shape and control. In short, we see here how Toscanini rethought his conception of a work he performed frequently.

But there were always instances where his Wagner varied little, if at all. A prime case is provided by the prelude to Act III of *Die Meistersinger*. And the similarities among his performances are not confined to pacing. Indeed, the 1943 broadcast account from studio 8H is virtually indistinguishable from the 1951 Carnegie Hall recording in matters of balance, timbre, and overall sonority. In other words, this is one instance in which a studio recording is thoroughly representative of Toscanini's work before an audience.

The same does not hold true for his 1946 recording of *A Faust Overture*. In the context of his three NBC broadcast performances and 1935 BBC concert account (once available on an EMI CD), the recording sounds unyielding and rigid. Incidentally, the 1941 broadcast marks the first time Toscanini performed the work from an uncorrupt score in which an erroneous E-natural at measure 58 was correctly printed as E-flat.

That the pattern with *A Faust Overture* was not a prevailing trait is illustrated by the many performances of Dawn and Siegfried's Rhine Journey from *Götter-dämmerung*. Here, again is a remarkable example of inconsistency, even among the conductor's three studio efforts, those from 1936 with the New York Philharmonic and from 1949 with the NBC Symphony being a minute longer than the 1941 NBC recording. And the broadcast performances feature an even greater variety of pace and lack of a prevailing pattern, the slowest of all of Toscanini's surviving performances being the broadcast of 26 February 1949. (The performance on Toscanini's last concert is marginally even slower but, owing to the occasion, cannot be considered typical of anything save the stress of the moment.)

As this is one of the works to which Toscanini turned most frequently, his varying approaches to it are especially significant and are considered more fully in the next chapter. But it should be noted here that they involved more than merely tempo, the application of rubato also varying from one account to the next. Significant, too, is Toscanini's arrangement of this music. Unlike Humperdinck's, for example, which many other conductors favored, the maestro's retains Wagner's original orchestration and offers more of the opera. This makes for smoother transitions from one section to the next and creates a more satisfying concert piece.

Toscanini's three studio versions of the *Siegfried Idyll* (two at NBC and a 1936 New York Philharmonic account) have evidently been ignored by those

who insist that his tempos were invariably more rapid in later years, each succeeding recording being slightly more expansive than its predecessor. All are
beautiful. Those made with the NBC Symphony have a more intimate sonority than that of the New York Philharmonic. Indeed, this more intimate ambience is closer to Wagner's original chamber-orchestra version. None of his
broadcast performances adds significantly to what the recordings tell us of his
conception: all three, in slightly varying ways, preserve the gentle, delicate, even
caressing style that stamped his response to this score.

The prelude to Act I of *Lohengrin* also exists in three studio recordings. As
with those of the Rhine Journey, the earliest (New York Philharmonic, 1936)
and latest (NBC, 1951) are broader than the 1941 recording. But the most
expansive of Toscanini's NBC accounts was given on the broadcast of 1941. At
nine minutes, it is sixteen seconds longer than the 1936 recording. At the other
extreme is the 1951 broadcast, which at slightly less than eight minutes is the
fastest of all and surely atypical. And although the 1936 and 1951 recordings are
certainly representative, neither quite matches the sustained ethereal aura projected on the 1941 broadcast.

Two studio recordings (the earlier one from 1936 with the New York Philharmonic) and three broadcasts of the prelude to Act III of *Lohengrin* differ little, save for affirming that the Philharmonic (despite the limitations of 1936
recording technique) was slightly more virtuosic and tonally alluring than the
NBC Symphony. But all share a precision that Saul Goodman, the timpanist in
that 1936 recording, defined in a conversation with me as Toscanini's ability to
make the choirs of the orchestra "fuse into one instrument."

Unlike many conductors who performed a concert version of Siegfried's
Funeral Music from *Götterdämmerung*, Toscanini favored including a depiction
of Siegfried's death. The logic is impeccable: a funeral, after all, is impossible
without a corpse. Toscanini's shifting interpretive view is centered upon pace,
the greatest contrast among surviving versions being between the 1941 NBC recording and the later one of 1952, which is slightly more than a minute longer.
The greater breadth creates a compelling intensity, but the less expansive readings also prove convincing, mainly because of Toscanini's demand for rhythmic
precision. The NBC double bassist David Walter took special note of this,
pointing out the care the conductor took with the rhythmic complexities of
the timpani part.[79] Still, the 1952 recording, in its grand dignity, unflagging
control, and sustained somberness stands as one of the extraordinary achievement of his old age.

Some critics have wondered why Toscanini turned with relative frequency
to such comparative potboilers as Forest Murmurs from *Siegfried* and the Ride of
the Valkyries from *Die Walküre*.[80] In the case of the former, it would seem the
music's evocation of nature through a rich, colorful orchestration requiring particular care with balance offered the kind of technical challenge that Toscanini

welcomed. All surviving versions attest to his success in meeting this challenge, the studio recording being thoroughly representative.

This is not the case with the Ride of the Valkyries. Each of Toscanini's seven NBC broadcast performances featured it as the concluding work on all-Wagner programs. Evidently Toscanini viewed this tempestuous affair as a rousing closer, yet his performances varied in tempo and overall character, some faster and thunderous, others broader and more sharply inflected, a contrast relected in the divergent characters of the conductor's two studio recordings.

As noted in chapter 2, the excerpts from *Parsifal* arranged by Toscanini are ineffective in purely orchestral form, and for all of the care lavished on the performance, its overall effect proves wearisome.

With detailed records of timings kept for individual performances at Bayreuth, it is intriguing to learn that Toscanini's *Parsifal* was the slowest to take place there—a full forty-five minutes longer than the 1882 premiere of the opera directed by Wagner's disciple, Hermann Levi. This breadth is certainly reflected in his concert performances of the prelude and Good Friday Spell, where, despite a prevailing expansiveness, Toscanini, as Denis Matthews has noted, "never lost the sense of a continuous line."[81] The conductor's only studio recording of the music, though certainly broad, is not the slowest of his surviving performances, its duration being almost a minute less than his 1935 concert performance with the BBC Symphony. Still, it shares with all the others clarity of melodic line, steadiness of pulse, and sharp focus of texture. The NBC violinist Joseph Gingold, who later became concertmaster of the Cleveland Orchestra under George Szell, spoke of how Toscanini approached his music:

> And the marvelous way he could conduct slow tempos—the control. He is the only conductor I know who conducted the *Parsifal* Prelude in four instead of the customary eight; he didn't give the silent downbeat most conductors give to insure unanimity at the very beginning. He said, "Is no cadenza per me. I start to beat when we start to play." And he did, and the violins came in together. Also, he beat it all in four, and with his superb stick control, it was always together.[82]

According to Bruno Walter, Mahler said of Toscanini's performance of *Tristan and Isolde*, "He conducts it in a manner entirely different from ours, but magnificently in its way."[83] And the bass Alexander Kipnis equated Toscanini's *Tristan* with Wilhelm Furtwängler's, suggesting that both conducted it in a "lyrical" style that departed from traditional German performance.[84] In one of his most perceptive moments, B. H. Haggin characterized how Toscanini's concert performances of the prelude and Liebestod changed over the years, becoming gradually more expansive and culminating in the NBC broadcast of 1951 and the studio recording a month later in January 1952. There are attractive aspects of both the faster and slower performances, but most interesting, as Haggin himself notes, is that these changes "are not only fascinating in themselves," but moving in what they tell us about Toscanini, indicating how each work he played frequently "was not . . . [a] routine act but a fresh application of attention and energy."[85]

One might add to Haggin's and Kipnis's views that Toscanini's concert performances of *Tristan* excerpts, whether faster or slower, convey two key aspects of the music: its sensuality and melodic richness. *Tristan* is such a harmonically innovative work that its continuous flow of melody is sometimes forgotten. But not in a Toscanini performance.

The two versions of the overture to *Tannhäuser* did not enter Toscanini's official discography until many years after his death, the original Dresden edition appearing only on the videocassette of the 4 December 1948 telecast. It is virtually identical to an NBC broadcast of a decade earlier, but is preserved in considerably better sound. The 1952 Overture and Bacchanale, a good performance of itself, has neither the shape nor the commitment of the 20 March 1948 broadcast, the first of Toscanini's concerts to be televised and one preserved in excellent sound on an RCA videocassette. Indeed, some may find the ambience of studio 8H in that performance more attractive than the less well focused acoustic of Carnegie Hall in the 1952 performance. In contrast to many of Toscanini's other readings of Wagner, those of the *Tannhäuser* opener remained essentially unchanged over the years: orthodox in tempo, at some points a shade slower than the pace taken by such an eminent Wagnerian as Furtwängler, and colored by prominent brass.

The existence of approved commercial releases of Toscanini conducting vocal excerpts from Wagner operas is owed to the broadcast of 22 February 1941. Two performances from the event—Act I, Scene 3, of *Die Walküre* and Dawn, the Brünnhilde-Siegfried duet, and Siegfried's Rhine Journey from *Götterdämmerung*—were issued by RCA, the latest CD edition featuring exceptionally fine sound for the vintage. Two days after the broadcast, Toscanini and Helen Traubel recorded the Immolation Scene from that opera, a performance that, although mainly a duplicate of their collaboration on the broadcast, sounds slightly less expressive, possibly as a result of less imposing sound.

At the time of these performances, Traubel and Lauritz Melchior were two of the Metropolitan Opera's celebrated Wagnerians, and all three performances are among the prizes of the Toscanini discography. The tempo for Siegfried's Rhine Journey in this context is sometimes identical to that of Toscanini's studio recording of a few months later, his speediest surviving account of the music. At other times, however, it is considerably slower. In short, this extended version before a Carnegie Hall audience shows us a more flexible, almost improvisational conductor.

Save for the casting, the 1947 broadcast of *Die Walküre* (with Rose Bampton and Set Svanholm) hardly differs from the commercially issued broadcast account of 1941. It should be noted, though, that one of the most revealing of unofficial Toscanini recordings cited in Appendix 8 is a two-CD Myto set offering orchestral and vocal rehearsals for that 1947 broadcast and an uninterrupted dress rehearsal of the entire scene that, in the context of the other preparations, proves especially meaningful. The sound throughout, evidently drawn from clean copies of NBC reference discs, is surprisingly vivid.

How should Toscanini's Wagner be assessed? Just as the conductor's Beethoven was sometimes pilloried for being too Italian, so his Wagner was judged insufficiently German. One might argue, however, that he out-Germaned the Germans at their own game, the slow tempos favored by many German conductors being even slower with Toscanini. Even the ostensible snail's pace of Hans Knappertsbusch's *Parsifal* at Bayreuth resulted in a total timing of twenty-five minutes less than Toscanini's performance. But a danger persists in judging the forward momentum of a performance exclusively on pacing, particularly in terms of timings. Despite their breadth, Toscanini's tempos in Wagner sound fluid and forward moving not only because of their prevailing firmness of pulse, but also because of the clarity of their articulation. As any musician knows, the cleaner the articulation, the faster the tempo can seem.

Perhaps the best way to characterize Toscanini's Wagner is to say that it offers a prime illustration of his constantly fluctuating viewpoint. Doubtless some of his Wagner departed from the Austro-German approach of Mahler or Walter. But its intensity, clarity, conviction, and attention to Wagner's specifications exposes key aspects of the composer's personality.[86] And the variety in these NBC performances serves as a constant reminder of the unceasing "self-dissatisfaction" that drove Toscanini almost compulsively to seek previously unrecognized sense in music with which he was long familiar and which he dearly loved.

Waldteufel, Emile (1837–1915)

Officially Issued Repertory
The Skaters Waltz (26 June 1944): RCA 60308 (**28 June 1945**)

It was not until he came to NBC that Toscanini ventured into the pops repertory, playing works such as this for the first time. It is interesting to compare his broadcast performance with the studio effort of one year later. Although their timings are within a few seconds of each other, the broadcast account, with its more liberal use of portamento and greater inflection of the recurring main theme, sounds more relaxed and graceful. If nothing else, this suggests how misleading timings of themselves can sometimes be in gauging the character of a performance.

Weber, Carl Maria von (1786-1826)

Officially Issued Repertory

Overtures:

Euryanthe (12 Feb. 1938, 3 Nov. 1951): RCA 60292 (**29 Oct. 1951**)

Der Freischütz (5 Jan. 1952): RCA 60310 (**25 May 1945**) and 60292
(**5 Aug. 1952**)

Oberon (19 Mar. 1944, 2 Aug. 1952, 28 Feb. 1954): RCA 60292
(**5 Aug. 1952**)

Invitation to the Dance, arr. Berlioz (19 Feb. 1938, 12 Mar. 1949, 13 Dec.
1953): RCA 60308 (**28 Sept. 1951**)

In addition to the Weber works that Toscanini conducted at NBC, he also led the Jubilee and Ruler of the Spirits Overtures and some operatic excerpts in the concert hall. In the theater he conducted Der Freischütz and Euryanthe. And had the Anschluss not made his return in Salzburg in 1938 unthinkable, he might have led a Freischütz there that summer, as it was the opera he was asked to direct.

The maestro's surprisingly few NBC performances of the overture to Der Freischütz bespeak a remarkable feeling for it. (Aside from the single broadcast performance, another was given at a benefit concert in 1945.) Both of his NBC recordings and the broadcast (as well as a surviving air check of a 1936 New York Philharmonic broadcast) suggest that his view of the work changed little over the years. In general, his slightly unorthodox tempo for the main section was broader than was common, which lent it an air of mystery. Of the two studio recordings, the earlier one stands alone among the preserved performances in its slightly quicker tempo, a distinction possibly created by the need to contain the work on a single 78 rpm disc, the later recording having been done, of course, on tape.

In the case of the overture to Oberon, the 1954 broadcast echoes the two previous ones and the 1952 recording except in one key aspect—tempo. In this, his last performance of the work, Toscanini favored what was for him an uncommonly expansive pace, one far closer to orthodoxy than the almost breathless speed of his other surviving accounts. This raises a key issue: was this, like some of his other NBC performances, a reversion to an earlier view, or was it the product of a tired conductor? It certainly does not evince a loss of control that one might associate with old age, the playing being precise and incisive. And with the slower tempo, the two key ritardandos that Toscanini always imposed (one in the development and one in the coda) fit more comfortably in the overall structure. All of the other performances are remarkably similar. Despite the fact that their tempo seems outrageously fast, clear articulation is not compromised. The care Toscanini took in preparing the work has been described in detail by the NBC violinist Samuel Antek.[87]

Of the three broadcasts of Berlioz's orchestration of *Invitation to the Dance*, only that of 1938 matches the more *relaxed grace* of Toscanini's 1938 recording with the BBC Symphony. The later broadcasts, like the 1951 recording, have less rhythmic elasticity, each digression from the main theme being played less freely, with stricter adherence to the tempo established in the first statement of that theme.

Wolf-Ferrari, Ermanno (1876–1948)

Unissued Performance

Le donne curiose: Overture (18 Nov. 1945, 19 Nov. 1947)

Officially Issued Repertory

The Secret of Suzanne: Overture (20 Jan. 1946): No NBC recording.

Toscanini's only NBC broadcast of the overture to *The Secret of Suzanne* offers no apparent departures from the performance he recorded for Victor in 1921 with the La Scala Orchestra (RCA 60315). But the vastly superior sound of the 1946 broadcast exposes far more about the conception in terms of orchestral color, balance, and weight.

Toscanini also directed *Le donne curiose*, though only at New York's Metropolitan Opera. The overture is a delightfully charming score played with grace and wit in both of these superbly reproduced performances.

4

RECONSTRUCTING TOSCANINI

During the last quarter of the twentieth century, deconstruction became a dominant force in academic life, with a resulting impact on critical thinking that extended beyond the university. In an especially cogent article, Michiko Kakutani defined the movement as "a method of textual analysis that has been applied to literature, history, even law and that focuses on language's 'unreliability'." Such a tenet, she demonstrates, permits traditional readings of history to be "overturned," creating "an ahistorical world" that "denies the two pillars of human civilization: memory and truth."[1]

As the twentieth century drew to a close, such ahistorical reasoning was applied to judging Toscanini. Criticisms were hurled at the maestro to the effect that his stand against Hitler and agreement (in 1936) to conduct—without fee— the newly formed Palestine Symphony were gestures made merely to appeal to New York's Jewish population. His outspoken (and life-threatening) criticism of Mussolini has not prevented revisionist thinkers from branding the conductor a Fascist. From such ludicrous views, it is but a short step to equally absurd notions about the maestro's art and his seventeen-year association with NBC. Too young to have a memory of the NBC Symphony, some writers, by ignoring verifiable truth, have alleged that those broadcasts pandered to commercialism and that Toscanini was an anti–intellectual obsessed with speed, whose reputation was derived from a cult of older critics blind to his many shortcomings. These critics, it has been claimed, like the NBC network itself, promoted the conductor with unprecedented hype. All such claims comprise, at best, misleading half-truths and, at worst, outright falsehoods.

As an adjunct to such reasoning, nonmusicians have argued that a recreative artist like Toscanini is far less important than the creative artist. This is, in some ways, true. But for those who cannot read a score and hear its content in their mind's ear, unperformed music is no more intelligible from the printed page than is a painting to a blind person. In short, unperformed music is, for most people, nonexistent.

Professional musicians do more than simply bring music to life. They function, in many respects, as critics, projecting interpretive views. As we can learn a good deal about literature or the visual arts by reading criticism, so, too, can we glean many insights by studying the performances of the most accomplished interpreters of music. This is certainly true for Toscanini. Critical examination of his NBC performances—both the successful and the unsuccessful ones—provides not only a fascinating walk into history but also a revelation of how the act of re-creation in the arts parallels the struggle for perfection that drives the output of any serious writer, painter, or composer.

Nothing exemplifies this better than Toscanini's performances of works that recurred frequently on his programs. Here is reflected the artist's struggle to get it right. Most of all, these performances clearly refute a number of other misconceptions, specious allegations, and assessments made in the vacuum of ignorance that became part of the late-twentieth-century backlash against the conductor in particular and the NBC project in general.

The difficulty of accurately evaluating of Toscanini's achievements has been well defined by Harvey Sachs:

> It is obvious that the whole problem of Toscanini criticism at this date [1979] . . . and certainly in the future is and will continue to be insidiously bound up with his recordings. Unfortunately those recordings do not and cannot represent him adequately. . . . Toscanini did not begin to record regularly until he was past seventy; and nearly all of the currently available recordings of his core repertory were made when he was in his eighties. . . . The point is they do not give us any real perspective on his work.[2]

Sachs's view still pertains, but less firmly so, partly because all the recordings Toscanini made for RCA (and a handful he made in 1926 for Brunswick) were reissued in 1992 on compact disc. Never before had all of them been available at the same time. Save for a small number of recordings produced in the late 1930s for HMV, RCA's eighty-two CDs encompass his entire official discography. Thus it is now possible to compare his multiple (often remarkably different) recordings of a work central to his repertory.[3] Then, too, RCA's release on videocassette and laser disc of the conductor's ten NBC telecasts further profiles his work (see Appendix 7).

But most telling are the NBC Symphony broadcasts, which provide compelling refutations of certain generalizations that have become less supportable than they were when Sachs was writing and access to most of the broadcasts was impossible. Consider Sachs's claim (not without merit, to be sure) that the Toscanini recordings do not give any reliable perspective on his work. As one example he cites three surviving accounts of Beethoven's Missa Solemnis: a poorly recorded 1935 air check of a New York Philharmonic broadcast, the

1940 NBC broadcast, and the 1953 RCA recording. As Sachs notes, each successive performance is faster than its predecessor, the earliest being among the "slowest" one could hear, the 1940 version being a minute faster, and that of the 1953 being nine minutes faster still, with the earliest version offering the greatest rhythmic flexibility. In short, from the available evidence, it would seem that since all these performances took place in Carnegie Hall (so that acoustics were not a factor in determining tempo changes), Toscanini evinced a clear pattern of growing refinement and simplification, a pattern mirrored in some (but certainly not all) of the works for which he left multiple studio recordings.

But most significantly, this pattern, as many examples in chapter 3 should suggest, is even less prevalent in the NBC broadcasts. This has several implications, one of which is that it may be misleading to compare a concert performance to a studio recording. Indeed, comparison of other Toscanini concert performances to a studio recording of the same work made at about the same time demonstrate that the latter are usually faster and less rhythmically free than their live counterpart. This distinction is especially apparent in the 1952 finale of the Beethoven Ninth, the opening movement of the 1946 Mozart "Haffner" Symphony, the 1944–45 Piano Concerto No. 1 of Beethoven, the 1947 Wedding March from Mendelssohn's *Midsummer Night's Dream*, and the 1939 Beethoven *Leonore* Overture No. 1, to cite but some examples.

Still, this pattern does not always pertain either. The 1940 and 1951 broadcasts of the Verdi Requiem provide a perfect case in point to support Sachs's argument, the earlier one being slower and more rhythmically inflected. Then, too, examples exist where a concert performance differs hardly, if at all, from a chronologically close studio account, outstanding instances being the 1946 *Meistersinger* Prelude, the 1952 Weber *Oberon* Overture, the 1947 Tchaikovsky "Pathétique" Symphony, and the 1953 Schubert's Ninth Symphony.

The main point here about Toscanini's evolving performance style is that it defies generalization and easy categorization. Sachs himself is aware of this, pointing out examples to be gleaned solely from studio recordings in which the later Toscanini proves more expansive than the earlier one. As he notes, Toscanini's "way of performing given pieces of music changed radically over the years because he was a highly reflective and self-critical artist who was rarely convinced that he had done his job decently, let alone well."[4]

The key issue, then, remains whether there was an evolving pattern generated by this self-criticism. If one goes by the 1940 and 1951 accounts of the Verdi Requiem or Toscanini's 1933 New York Philharmonic Beethoven Fifth and more familiar 1952 RCA recording, to cite but two examples, the inferences Sachs drew from the three performances of the Missa Solemnis still stand. In fact, evidence supporting them is surely what must have led B. H. Haggin and Robert C. Marsh (even before Sachs was writing) to analyze the conductor's style in terms of its earlier "expansive" approach and subsequent "simpler" directness.[5] And in developing this concept, first presented by Haggin, Marsh has suggested that Toscanini's way with Italian music remained relatively fixed, whereas his treatment of the German repertory initially embraced a more Teutonic "traditional" view that gradually gave way to a streamlined, cantabile *bel canto* style.[6] Granted, Marsh admits this is a generalization to which exceptions may exist. Furthermore, at the time he was writing (1954), he could not have had access to the wealth of live material that has surfaced since then and leaves his analysis open to doubt.

Were one to accept the Haggin-Marsh dichotomy of two Toscanini styles, it would be particularly fascinating to speculate about the quality of, say, the maestro's 1913 performance of the Beethoven Ninth Symphony with the Metropolitan Opera Orchestra. If one embraced the notion of a refinement and simplicity developing over the years, one might then infer that this 1913 Ninth Symphony was grand and expansive, with a marked use of rubato. But the more one listens to the earliest evidence—studio recordings dating from 1920 to 1936, New York Philharmonic air checks from Toscanini's last years with that orchestra, and unreleased recordings of a variety of works made with the La Scala Orchestra in the late 1920s (as well as all of the conductor's NBC broadcasts)—the shakier such an inference becomes. The 1913 Beethoven Ninth and the 1952 studio recording, while probably differing in a number of details, might well have been closer than originally imagined. Consider, for example, Richard Aldrich's review of the 1913 performance in the *New York Times*:

> In all the nuances of the performance, the melodic line was not interrupted, nor in all the plastic shaping of the phrase was the symmetry of the larger proportion of the whole lost sight of. It was rhythmically of extraordinary vitality. . . . There were subtle and significant modulations of tempo, but never of a distorting sort.[7]

These words could apply equally well to Toscanini's recording of the work made thirty-nine years later. This suggests that Toscanini's development as an artist defies the simple dichotomy of earlier and later styles. Although the spate of Toscanini material that has appeared since 1980 makes this especially clear, it could in fact be seen earlier. As suggested in the previous chapter, most critics have found the conductor's first recordings of Haydn's "Clock" Symphony and Mozart's "Haffner" Symphony (both with the New York Philharmonic in 1929) and of Beethoven's Fourth Symphony (with the BBC Symphony in 1939) to be more genial, relaxed, and gracious than his later ones with the NBC Symphony. In the case of the Beethoven, this does not hold true, the earlier version being generally tenser, less flexible, and less subtly inflected. In the case of the Haydn, the two versions are almost identical. In the case of the Mozart, tempos in 1929 are sometimes (if not always) more driven, the prevailing ethos sometimes fiercer.

When one goes beyond the recordings, further interesting suggestions emerge. Consider, for example, two surviving air checks from Toscanini's last years with the New York Philharmonic: a 1935 performance with Vladimir Horowitz of the Brahms D-Minor Piano Concerto and a 1936 performance of Beethoven's *Coriolan* Overture. Both are febrile, rigid, and overwrought, creating a breathlessness often claimed to be more typical of Toscanini's later years at NBC. Because no other Toscanini performance of the concerto survives, we cannot surmise if the 1935 account is representative of his view. But the Philharmonic *Coriolan* most decidedly is not, having none of the rhythmic inflection and breadth of some later NBC efforts.

Revealing, too, are three performances of the Brahms Fourth Symphony: a 1935 New York Philharmonic account and two NBC broadcasts of the work, one from 1939, the other from 1948. The 1935 version is similar to the admirable 1951 NBC recording. The 1939 NBC broadcast, from an era thought to be more typical of Toscanini's "earlier" style, is fast, unyielding, at times even brutal. But the 1948 broadcast is altogether different: the most expansive of the conductor's NBC readings, it has a rhythmic give-and-take absent from all his other NBC accounts. Unique among them as well is the sustained breadth of the finale that heightens the cumulative effect of its reiterated bass. In other words, it exhibits every characteristic attributed to Toscanini's "earlier" period.

A similar situation obtains for the maestro's 1935 New York Philharmonic broadcast of the Brahms Third Symphony, which lacks the shape, control, and grandeur of his finest NBC presentations, notably those of 1938, 1942, and February 1948. And when one goes back even further to some La Scala Orchestra recordings from the late 1920s, the Haggin-Marsh hypothesis seems even weaker. Never released commercially, these recordings (available for auditioning along with all the NBC Symphony broadcasts at the New York Public Library for the Performing Arts) display traits allegedly more typical of Toscanini's work at NBC than of his years with the New York Philharmonic: lean sonority, minimal rhythmic inflection, and tempos sometimes faster than the norm. Such traits make one wonder if the many distinctions that can be made between Toscanini's two approved recordings of the Beethoven Seventh Symphony (with the New York Philharmonic in 1936 and with NBC in 1951) display anything beyond the later one's inferiority. Unfortunately, it is the one from which Toscanini's conception of the music became more familiar in the post–78 rpm era.

Doubtless those who may have known both and were unfamiliar with the NBC broadcasts might well have assumed the existence of a prevailing earlier and later Toscanini style. But the 1951 performance, lacking the precision and rhythmic inflection of the 1936 recording and marked by a first movement pushed harder than in any other surviving Toscanini account, suggests mainly the decline in control and the compromise of standards that can accompany advancing years.[8]

Listening to playback at RCA's Camden, N.J., studio, 1942. *RCA*

This is not to say that Toscanini's last years at NBC were always inferior to earlier ones. Granted, his grip loosened somewhat with the passing of time, as is evinced in the second movement of the 1953 broadcast of Tchaikovsky's *Manfred* Symphony. But there are instances during the final three seasons when the conductor surpassed earlier achievements, notably in such scores as Mozart's Symphony No. 40, Mendelssohn's "Reformation" Symphony, Brahms's *Tragic Overture*, and Siegfried's Death and Funeral Music from Wagner's *Götterdämmerung*, to cite but a few performances that defy the generalized pattern.

In the quest for such a pattern, what is easily overlooked is that Toscanini was, above all else, human, and consequently had good and bad days as would any professional in any field. Thus he produced magnificent and inferior performances, as well as many that fell between these extremes. Evidence suggests that this pertains to his work with many orchestras, not only the one created by NBC.

Such variable quality notwithstanding, a thread of recurring and definable traits runs through Toscanini's NBC performances and binds them together, stamping them as the product of an extraordinarily individual, communicative, and vibrant musician. Some of these recognizable traits have been cited often enough to make their repetition seem almost a cliché. Toscanini's flair for drama, his raising of the standards of orchestral execution, his insistence on continuity and cohesion, his care with dynamics and balances, and his ability to project exceptional transparency, *cantabile* lines, and overwhelming climaxes have been hailed again and again.

Over and beyond such obvious attributes, however, are others—ignored entirely or noted infrequently or inaccurately—that define the Toscanini style in general and in particular his work at NBC. Paramount among them are the conductor's tempos. "The correct tempo! Oh how difficult," the maestro once said.[9] Probably no other facet of his style has been so egregiously misjudged, the pervasive notion being that his choice of pace was invariably faster than what one usually encountered. It is indisputable that some of Toscanini's tempos were exceptionally, even at times outrageously, fast. It is doubtful that any conductor ever played the third movement of Haydn's "Surprise" Symphony or Mendelssohn's overture to *A Midsummer Night's Dream* more quickly than Toscanini did. In the case of the Haydn, the tempo, as noted previously, seems absurd, the movement converted into a breathless one-to-the-bar race that destroys its character as a minuet. With the Mendelssohn overture, however, the tempo works not only because the music—marked allegro di molto—can be articulated cleanly at Toscanini's pace, but also because his tempo conveys the fairyland atmosphere of the play.

But this is only one aspect of Toscanini's approach to pace. Equally characteristic are his many choices of tempo that are considerably slower than what one might expect, as is shown both in the broadcasts and in his commercially released recordings. No other conductor has left readings of the slow movement of Haydn's Symphony No. 88 or of the finale of Mendelssohn's "Reformation" Symphony in which the music is played with the sustained breadth Toscanini favored. And there are many other examples from RCA discs of this uncommon expansiveness, such as the overture to Weber's *Freischütz*, the finale of the Beethoven Fifth (1939 recording), the opening movements of the Brahms Third and Schumann "Rhenish" Symphonies, and the finale of the Brahms Second. And though the performances have not had wide circulation, a similar breadth exists in the finales of the Second Symphonies of Schubert, Schumann, and Borodin; Wagner's overture to *Rienzi*; and portions of Brahms's *German Requiem*.

The key point is that Toscanini's tempos, rather than being unusually fast, were simply unorthodox in that they did not conform to typical parameters. In this regard he was no different from other conductors of the time, especially Wilhelm Furtwängler, who is often thought to be Toscanini's interpretive opposite. Contrary to general notions, Furtwängler's tempos were not always slow. Sometimes he favored pacing that was faster than Toscanini's even in music where one might not expect it, such as the slow movement of the Haydn Symphony No. 88 and the finales of the Brahms First and Beethoven "Pastoral" and Ninth Symphonies. Faster than Toscanini's, too, are the first movements of George Szell's and Serge Koussevitzky's justly admired recordings of Mendelssohn's "Italian" Symphony. Toscanini's tempo for that movement may seem fast because of the exceptionally clean articulation he secures, which gives the music's motivic profile a sharpness of focus that neither Szell nor Koussevitzky duplicates. In fact, when Koussevitzky's two studio recordings are juxtaposed to Toscanini's NBC readings, the music's profile in the Koussevitzky readings sounds flat—Koussevitzky seems to be merely skimming the surface of the work.

It is probably safe to say that Toscanini never accepted a conventional tempo solely because it had become traditional. He did not hold tradition sacrosanct, as evidenced by the careful consideration he brought to his choice of pace. Granted, that choice was not always convincing. Nor was it the product of an Italian who responded differently from the way a German might have. Some of Toscanini's faster tempos, alleged to reflect "too Italian" an outlook, were virtually identical to those favored by Austro-Germans in German music. As surviving recordings indicate, Franz Schalk, Felix Weingartner, and Erich Kleiber played the first movement of Beethoven's "Pastoral" Symphony every bit as fast as did Toscanini, and at times even faster.

Like many conductors, Toscanini changed his mind about tempo. Studying the NBC Symphony broadcasts discloses that Toscanini's pacing, rather than accelerating over the years, was the product of his rethinking interpretive problems. The most obvious case in point is provided by his surviving performances of the Brahms Third Symphony. No two are paced quite the same, and the slowest among them are the last ones. Again, this characterizes the work of many conductors of the period. As more and more live performances by such eminences as Furtwängler, Sir Thomas Beecham, Bruno Walter, and Otto Klemperer, among others, appear on CD, it is increasingly clear that a studio recording of a given work does not necessarily represent a fixed conception, only an interpretive view of the moment.

Related to Toscanini's often unorthodox tempos is his unusual use of rubato, alluded to by Jacques Barzun in the foreword to this volume. This may well be the most frequently ignored aspect of the maestro's conducting, which has been pilloried for being metronomic and unyielding. Undoubtedly examples of such rigidity exist, but they are the exception rather than the rule. Far more often than not, Toscanini typified his time in recognizing the need to modify pulse in order to generate shape and enrich expression. Many musicians who played under Toscanini have told me how remarkably "free" his rhythm could be, adding that this freedom was governed by such "good taste" that its presence was not readily perceived. As Milton Katims, a violist in the NBC Symphony (as well as a distinguished chamber-music performer and conductor) put it, Toscanini employed "a rubato so subtle that the listener was almost never aware of it."[10]

Providing an indirect revelation of this subtlety is a concert Toscanini did not direct: the conductorless program given by the NBC Symphony in the fall of 1954 to raise support for its continuance. Many of the Toscanini trademarks survived in this concert: cohesion, transparency, freedom from mannerisms, and tempos that pressed forward. Yet, as noted in chpter 2, each performance suffered to varying degrees from rhythmic rigor mortis. Conspicuously absent was the modulated pulse that stamps nearly all of Toscanini's work. Without it, his performances would be not so much enlivened as embalmed. One has only to listen, for example, to the slow movement of the Beethoven First Symphony in either of the conductor's two studio recordings (BBC, 1937; NBC, 1951) to discover a barely discernible inflection of pulse, one beat lengthened a fraction, another so shortened. As a result the music never sounds square or rigid; it moves forward, not because the tempo is fast, but because the rhythm is fluid.

But what sets Toscanini's application of rubato apart from the way it was used by some of his peers is in that elusive area of good taste. To be more specific, a Mengelberg, Walter, or Furtwängler might distend pulse to the point where the line was broken, pulse ruptured, and structure compromised. Whereas they seemed to follow to the letter the kind of freedom espoused by Wagner in his famous treatise on conducting, Toscanini followed it more in spirit, never permitting such freedom to interfere with coherence and unity.[11]

This said, Toscanini's rhythmic freedom could, on occasion, be surprisingly conspicuous. In the 1939 NBC broadcast of the Beethoven First Symphony, for instance, there is a startling distension of the tempo in the exposition of the second movement, a distension he did not impose in a 1936 New York Philharmonic performance or in any of his other surviving accounts. In fact there are some instances in which Toscanini's rhythmic displacements are so extreme, they seem more emblematic of Mengelberg or Walter: the unspecified glaring ritardando in nearly all of Toscanini's performances of Beethoven's *Coriolan* Overture, the jarring first-movement tempo shifts in his 1929 recording of Mozart's "Haffner" Symphony, unusual broadening in Weber's *Oberon* Overture, and the stretching of pulse in the first-movement developments of Beethoven's "Eroica" and Brahms's First Symphonies. Sometimes, as in the case of the "Haffner," one encounters a gradual disappearance of this rhythmic freedom with each subsequent performance of the work. But with other scores, it might vanish only to recur in a subsequent reading.

A characteristic of this freedom and a trait that lends many of Toscanini's performances their tension and drive is anticipation of the downbeat—a feature not shared by most other conductors of the period, the one musician of Toscanini's era who favored it being pianist Artur Schnabel. Ironically, because each was sometimes antipathetic toward the other's strong views, they never performed together. Yet both shared a grasp of classical style and a strong affinity for Beethoven. And in their willingness to anticipate the beat, they displayed a rhythmic security that permitted freedom—the taking of chances, as it were—but in a fashion that preserved rather than violated basic pulse and formal balance.

If a good deal of the Toscanini style defies easy categorizing, particularly with respect to his tempos, his work at NBC does contain some patterns that invite generalization. Most obvious among them, perhaps, is that as he grew older, his rhythm became less flexible. This is not to say that his performances grew increasingly fleet. metronomic, or slack. But his rubato became less obvious. And in some instances where Toscanini had once favored a very subtle rubato (as in 1939 for the second subject of the first movement of Beethoven's Second Symphony), the passage was later played strictly in tempo. It may be this change in style that has promoted the inaccurate notion that Toscanini's tempos accelerated and his performances became less subtle as he grew older. Nuance and subtlety, more often than not, remained, but more careful listening was required to discern them.

Also disappearing from Toscanini's later performances was the occasional use of portamento encountered in the NBC broadcasts during their first three seasons. For the first third of the twentieth century, portamento was a common expressive device, particularly in string playing, and it can be heard frequently in the recordings made by such ensembles as the Busch, Flonzaley, and Pro Arte Quartets. It was also common, if somewhat less so, in orchestral performances, as is attested by many recordings of the period. To judge from Toscanini's studio recordings with the New York Philharmonic and the BBC Symphony (all produced before 1940), he had no objection to its sparing application, but he did not favor it as a major expressive device. Thus its use was not prohibited during the early years of the NBC Symphony, so long as it was applied tastefully. But the conductor seems to have developed a growing preference for its omission, as exemplified by his NBC accounts of Mozart's Symphony No. 40.

That Toscanini did not immediately purge portamento from his NBC performances underscores his willingness to give an orchestra its head in certain matters. This is most apparent in his concern for sonority. Many conductors, for example, produced a characteristic orchestral tone that became a kind of trademark for their interpretive style. The example that perhaps springs first to mind is the "Philadelphia sound" created by Leopold Stokowski: a creamy, colorful, yet blended lushness in which free bowings produced a seamless flow of string tone.

Nothing in Toscanini's surviving work at NBC or elsewhere suggests such opulence. Granted, his recordings with the New York Philharmonic, the BBC Symphony, and the Philadelphia Orchestra exhibit a sonority that (in varying degrees) is fuller and more tonally alluring than the comparatively thinner, coarser tone of the NBC Symphony. Interestingly, too, Toscanini's Philadelphia Orchestra recordings suggest that while he modified Stokowski's bowings, he did not alter the orchestra's characteristic sound.

In other words, Toscanini, unlike some of his peers, was not concerned with sound for sound's sake. It is hard to imagine, for instance, that he would (as Koussevitzky did on one occasion) have the recapitulation of the main theme of the finale of Beethoven's "Eroica" Symphony stated by seven horns. Toscanini might alter a bowing to modify timbre or redistribute voices to enhance clarity, but such changes were founded on a structural or expressive point that transcended sound for its own sake.

Of course, one of the key questions in trying to define the sonority Toscanini favored at NBC is to what extent the overly dry acoustics of studio 8H affected his concept of a desirable sound. It is clear, for example that the clipped, brusque chords that one might assume the ambience of 8H engendered also existed in Toscanini performances given in more resonant environs. Such staccato chording was complemented by a relatively pure string tone colored by a narrow, comparatively constricted vibrato. This permitted the winds and brass their due, generating a textural clarity and richness of detail often absent from the work of other conductors. Contributing also to a characteristic Toscanini sound was the tight timpani timbre produced by his frequently favoring the use of hard sticks by the timpanist Karl Glassman. Of course, such a generalization could be subject to various modifications, depending on the repertory at hand. (Curiously, Toscanini would sometimes allow the trumpeter Harry Glantz a self-indulgent vibrato that seems anomalous in the overall texture).

The important point is that the dryness of 8H promoted the kind of sound Toscanini sought. This is not to say, however, that he favored the wooden deadness of some of his earliest NBC recordings. But the 8H acoustic reinforced the

Toscanini during a filming in studio 8H in 1944. *BMG Classics*

secco quality he sometimes demanded and fostered the clarity he inevitably required. In fact, some of the musicians in the orchestra have suggested to me that the 8H acoustics engendered a vicious circle, the sound of the hall exaggerating Toscanini's conception of sonority and making the orchestra sound at times like a caricature of itself. This is why, some argue, the NBC Symphony broadcasts from Carnegie Hall (both before and after 1950 and as early as 1938) are similar to those from studio 8H in their close, flat perspective and dry, crisp ambience. They also lack the weight suggested in the more distantly microphoned AM broadcasts of Toscanini's New York Philharmonic concerts from Carnegie Hall.

The lighter weight of the NBC Symphony may be partly the product of 8H, but it stems from other factors as well. Many orchestras created for radio seem to have been bass shy. In some cases this may have been simply the result of having fewer double basses than was customary. But it may have also been tied to reduction of bass tone imposed in broadcast transmissions to avoid overload and the distortion it might produce. Then, too, the bass deficiency of the NBC Symphony may be owing in part to Toscanini's possibly having suffered a hearing loss. Several reliable sources have claimed that well into his eighties

Toscanini during a broadcast in studio 8H, c. 1949. *BMG Classics*

Toscanini could still hear the triangle clearly. But it seems likely that in his later years some auditory failing must have occurred, not only because of the inevitable effects of aging, but also as a result of the onslaught of decibels sustained over years on the podium. This was partially confirmed by the NBC bassist Michael Krasnopolsky, who told me that in his later years Toscanini would ask the basses to play more softly, claiming their tone was too full to permit him to hear the upper registers clearly.

It is possible that the lightness of the NBC Symphony's sound contributed to the notion that Toscanini was more concerned with melody than with harmony. Granted, some of his performances are not shaped by the emphasis of harmonic movement that stamped Furtwängler's work. But in music where harmonic support was structurally central—the finales of Brahms's *Haydn Variations* and Fourth Symphony, for example—he always brought out the reiterated bass line.

The sound of a Toscanini orchestra, as most listeners came to know it, was the sound of the NBC Symphony. Toscanini had insisted, of course, that the ensemble meet world-class standards. In many respects it did. Its strings were on a par with those of any orchestra, but the quality of the winds and the brass was variable—partly because of occasional changes in personnel. Some of the individual players were as good as one could want, but, in general the winds and the brass did not quite match their counterparts in Toscanini's New York Philharmonic.

To this day the notion persists that Toscanini was a literalist, following the score to the letter, "exactly as written." As any thorough musician knows, such literalness is impossible. The passages cited in chapter 3 noting Toscanini's revisions of an *Urtext* (and there are many others less obvious) in order to make things sound give the lie to any notions of literalism. What might be said, though, is that Toscanini was a literalist in the most general kind of way—that is, he tried to get to the essentials of a score as well as they could be inferred. He would not hesitate to alter the text of a score if it might help clarify an important line or a significant aspect of structure.

Typical in this regard is an incident cited by Samuel Antek: after admonishing an NBC musician for not playing *piano* and hearing the man's protest that his part was marked *forte*, Toscanini responded "What? Forte? Forte? . . . What means forte? . . . Is a thousand fortes—all kinds of fortes. Sometimes a forte is a pia-a-a-no, piano is a forte."[12] In other words, *forte* was *forte*, except when Toscanini chose to interpret otherwise. In doing so, of course, he acted precisely as any nonliteralist conductor of his day did. Also implicit in his response is the notion of context. Just as sixty-five degrees Fahrenheit may be warm or cool, depending on whether it is December or July, so, too, dynamic indications such as *forte* or *piano* are invariably relative to the passages in which they appear. Demonstrated in the repeated performances of a given work on Toscanini's NBC

Toscanini checking a detail in a score during a Carnegie Hall rehearsal.
BMG Classics

broadcasts is the way in which he was rethinking his far-from-literal, as-written interpretation not only in such an obvious matter as tempo, but also in balance, voice leading, phrasing, and dynamics.

Related to Toscanini's flexible antiliteralism was his basic pragmatism. It has often been said that unlike Leopold Stokowski, he had no interest in the recording process and its technicalities, viewing the studio as simply a place in which to give another performance. In part, this is surely true. Nevertheless he was willing to accommodate the exigencies that recording and broadcasting sometimes imposed. It is possible, for example, that the unusually fast tempo of the first movement of the Beethoven Eighth Symphony in his 1939 recording was dictated by the need to contain the movement on two 78 rpm sides while retaining an exposition repeat. Conversely, when a change of program on a 1952 broadcast that included that symphony created the possibility of the broadcast's running beyond its allotted hour, Toscanini dropped the repeat. He was equally pragmatic with Mozart's Symphony No. 40, omitting its first-movement repeat

Toscanini with his son, Walter, in the basement of the Villa Pauline, c. 1950, listening to playbacks of an NBC broadcast. Note that the maestro is conducting, which suggests he was pleased with the performance. *Walfredo Toscanini*

(included in both of his recordings of the work) when time restrictions so dictated. Similarly, in his 1947 recording of the Mendelssohn Wedding March, Toscanini omitted a da capo in order to permit the piece to be contained on one 78 rpm side. Despite such pragmatism, other instances exemplify an intransigence that would not admit compromise, most notably regarding the first-movement repeat in the Brahms Third Symphony. Here, it would seem, Toscanini recognized that omission of this repeat would compromise the music's formal balance and aesthetic integrity.

The inconsistency implicit in both this intransigence and this flexible pragmatism is evident in other aspects of Toscanini's performances. Consider, for example, the opening measures of the finale of Beethoven's Seventh Symphony—sometimes played in tempo, sometimes not, their pulse expanded to suggest an introduction to the movement. By contrast, the maestro always meticulously observed Beethoven's sforzando marking at measures 131, 139, 141, and 142 of the same movement. Yet he could be inconsistent in interpreting the accents in the introduction to the first movement of the Schubert Ninth Symphony and in the introduction to the finale of the Brahms First. The point is that one could never be sure with Toscanini. His mind remained so active, his quest for discovering new sense so thorough, and his self-dissatisfaction so intense that to make a prediction of how a Toscanini performance of one of his repertory staples might differ from its predecessors was usually impossible.

There were, of course, key works in his repertory about which he seemed far less certain than about others, in which one encounters the greatest variety in his interpretive approach. Brahms's music provides the most striking case in point, but almost as varied are his readings of Wagner, Mozart, and, in some instances, Beethoven.

Given such inconsistencies, one wonders why Toscanini's performances have prompted so many misleading generalizations. Perhaps the answer lies in certain traits that did remain constant. Toscanini might vary tempo, phrasing, balance, voice leading, or rubato from one performance to the next. Some of his performances might seem overwrought and excessively rushed, some on occasion even indifferent. But always, regardless of prevailing virtues or flaws, they displayed a concern for continuity, textural clarity, cantabile lines, and dramatic impact. This last trait may well have had its source in Toscanini's years spent in the theater and in a dialectic of, on the one hand, intense emotional commitment and, on the other, tight intellectual and technical rein. It is these recurring traits (admirable in themselves, but accompanied by other virtues in the most memorable of Toscanini's performances) that may have led to the notion that Toscanini was the same from one performance to the next. It is easy, for instance, to hear in his first two NBC presentations of Tchaikovsky's "Pathétique" Symphony how his view departed from the sentimental, distended readings that often were given at the time. But the second of the two performances is superior, better controlled and less inappropriately nervous. Unless carefully compared, however, the two may seem identical.

And here lies another factor that has been overlooked in Toscanini criticism, particularly in the writing of journalists of his time who were among his staunchest advocates and who as a result sometimes failed to distinguish between inspired and flawed performances, hearing virtues in the latter that did not exist. Especially culpable in this regard was Olin Downes. In a review of 7 November 1943, he called Toscanini's only NBC performance of Haydn's Symphony No. 104 "flawless," ignoring the reading's hard-driven lack of nuance and inflection. He did not mention the vulgar transposition of the trumpet line in the 1941 performance of Schumann's Second Symphony and totally disregarded the occasionally loose ensemble and febrile pacing that mar the 1948 telecast of the Beethoven Ninth. In a review of 4 April 1948 he not only hailed this performance as impressive, but also cited it for its "lyricism and breadth." With that telecast now available on videocassette, one can discover how the words "breadth" and "lyricism," while apropos, no doubt, for some Toscanini accounts of the Ninth, simply do not apply to the 1948 performance.

An ill-judged appraisal of a different kind is Lawrence Gilman's *Toscanini and Great Music*, published to coincide with the formation of the NBC Symphony. Gilman had been a music critic for the *New York Herald Tribune* and, during Toscanini's New York Philharmonic years, the author of the orchestra's program notes. He was also an occasional intermission speaker on its Sunday afternoon broadcasts. Familiar with Toscanini's work and, like Downes, a staunch admirer of it, he was capable of sensitive, cultivated criticism. But when he came to Toscanini, that cultivation gave way to hagiographic vagueness. A prime case in point is this comment about the conductor's treatment of the first-movement development of Beethoven's "Eroica" Symphony. There, according to Gilman, "Beethoven seems to hurl his rage and defiance and despair against a heedless sky . . . conveyed to us [by Toscanini] with a Mediterranean clarity and a Gothic unsentimental power."[13] What is Mediterranean clarity? How does it differ from Baltic or Caspian clarity? Such vague writing permeates much of the book and is fodder for those who like to attack (with some justification) an alleged Toscanini cult. With the phonograph and radio having enabled a musical awareness impossible for the nonperformer to have attained during the first half of the twentieth century, such superficial meandering would, one might assume, have difficulty passing for legitimate criticism had it been written twenty-five years later.

Or would it? The hero worship that Toscanini engendered may well have been responsible for more recent hostility toward him, hostility that, in its own way, also falls short of anything that can be judged enlightened or informative. *Understanding Toscanini*, by Joseph Horowitz (1986), provides the most cogent case in point. With an insidiously misleading vocabulary, a disregard for the historian's responsibility to check all available sources, and a seemingly a priori biased view that sets out to find any evidence—regardless of how accurate or typical it may be—to indict Toscanini, NBC, and the alleged commercialization and popularization of classical music, Horowitz produced a book that is often deceiving and at times irresponsible. To prove Toscanini's tempos were always outrageously fast, Horowitz cites the conductor's supposed fascination with speed and how he would implore his chauffeur to drive faster and faster. To indict Toscanini's NBC Symphony recordings as typical of an "all-purpose formula," developed by the conductor to fit divergent styles, the author cites a mere handful of them. And sometimes, as with the prelude to Act I of *Lohengrin* (about which more will be said later), he uses Toscanini's least typical performance of the work to illustrate an alleged weakness in the conception.

Under ordinary circumstances, a book marred by such glaring faults would hardly be worth mentioning. But like so much that has been written about Toscanini—favorable and unfavorable—it generalizes and misleads by ignoring considerable evidence. Worse yet, it seems to have catalyzed further anti-Toscanini writing of the most superficial and ill-judged sort. Especially appalling in this regard are comments by Norman Lebrecht in *The Maestro Myth*. Aware, perhaps, of Horowitz's oblique suggestion that Toscanini's rejection of Hitler was a way of appealing to New York's heavily Jewish population, Lebrecht equates the conductor with that dictator, dismisses his anti-Fascist stance as "nonideological," and claims that his "courage" in the face of such dictators "lacked moral conviction."[14]

Horowitz and Lebrecht, and other writers like them, almost seem to believe that the larger the innuendo and inaccuracy, the greater its chance for credibility. Aside from its basic dishonesty, such writing can mislead those too uninformed to recognize its departure from truth. It thus generates further criticism that either echoes such insidious negativism or extends it to utter senselessness. Consider, for example, these reviews of two reissues of recordings of the Brahms B-flat Major Piano Concerto—one featuring Vladimir Horowitz and Toscanini, the other Emil Gilels and Fritz Reiner. Both reviews appeared in the September–October 1991 issue of *American Record Guide* and were written by the same author. He calls the Horowitz-Toscanini account an example of "a near helpless soloist held captive within the metronomic clutches of a godfather imprisoned by two basic concepts: first, that the best music was written by Verdi and Rossini, and second that other music should have been." Aside from ignoring Toscanini's prevailing tastes—particularly his love of Beethoven and Wagner—the review might be taken as an expression of dissatisfaction with the interpretive approach, an obvious prerogative of any critic. But that critic finds in the Gilels-Reiner version "a testimony to the titanic conducting of Reiner" and "the youthful vigor of Gilels." What is absurd here (beyond the ludicrous style) is that the two performances are remarkably similar in their virtuosity, rhythmic solidity, trim orchestral sonority, and overall pacing and spirit, and to damn one while extolling the other is nonsense.

Of themselves such absurd reviews are hardly worth attention, but they are symptomatic of an anti-Toscanini cult rooted in ignorance and lacking musical sophistication. The release of videocassettes of Toscanini's telecasts led one critic, for example, to compare him to Leonard Bernstein, noting that Toscanini, unlike Bernstein, did not know how to conduct for television. But a conductor does not conduct for television: he conducts for the orchestra, and to do otherwise would be to shirk his responsibility and pander to the audience.

None of this is said with the intent of offering untempered praise as a corrective of such myopic criticism. Like every great conductor, Toscanini gave bad performances, many of which he acknowledged. And he never gave a definitive performance of anything for the simple reason that any work of art defies a single correct definitive interpretation. At the same time, he certainly was never guilty of the sins attributed to him in recent years by critics who, to judge from their comments, have no awareness of what the score of a work in question specifies.

A typical case in point is Joseph Horowitz's allegation that Toscanini made the opening chords of the Beethoven Seventh Symphony sound like "guillotine chops," whereas, according to Horowitz, Furtwängler (a favorite of the critic) "with his notoriously 'indecisive' downbeats makes them well up from the depth." Beethoven gave two specific indications about how those chords should be played—*forte* and staccato—and that is how Toscanini played them. One well may prefer the less clipped style of Furtwängler, but in analytical criticism of the kind Horowitz is ostensibly trying to present, Toscanini's attention to Beethoven's specifications demands acknowledgment. Failure to do so is dishonest and misleads those who cannot read a score and thus recognize how Toscanini honored it.

Equally misleading is Horowitz's comparison of the two conductors' approach to Wagner's prelude to Act I of *Lohengrin*. He writes that Toscanini's reading is "distinctly mobile," Furtwängler's "much slower"—a fact speciously supported by citing for their respective performances timings of 7:35 (Toscanini) and 9:50 (Furtwängler). But the latter performance is in fact ten seconds faster than the 9:50 specified on the record label, an inaccuracy Horowitz failed to spot. Worse, he chose the most atypical of Toscanini's eight surviving performances of the work (a 1951 broadcast account then in limited circulation), one that is a full minute faster than two of his three studio recordings of the piece and faster still than the 9:01 of his 1941 NBC broadcast. If not a prime example of a deconstructionist's manipulation of truth to fit a preconceived notion, such criticism is at the very least an egregious instance of subjective selectivity that distorts reality by omitting key facts. Horowitz argues that Furtwängler grasps a German tradition that Toscanini's "Italianate" style, with its "all-purpose intensity," fails to convey. Yet the author (in addition to ignoring relevant Toscanini performances) never considers that Bruno Walter and Artur Bodanzky—conductors with clear Austro-German orientation—left recordings of the *Lohengrin* Prelude to Act I that come far closer to Toscanini's than to Furtwängler's, both barely exceeding eight minutes. The main flaw in Horowitz's methodology is that it ignores a good deal of available evidence that does not fit his view. Moreover, in promoting Furtwängler at Toscanini's expense, Horowitz is guilty of the very sort of cultish hero worship for his man that he condemns in those who idolized Toscanini. Such blind idolatry, of course, fails to take into account the merit that often exists in divergent readings of a masterpiece.

No less reprehensible and myopic is Horowitz's description of Toscanini on television. The italics are mine:

From the front [Toscanini's] eyes were ceaselessly, hypnotically *perturbed*. As they passed left and right under Toscanini's *flaring* brow, *no glint of pleasure* broke their *worried* spell. Serving Wagner, they said, was *precarious* work; at any moment something might go wrong. During episodes of high excitement, Toscanini's churning right arm *whipped* his baton in *strenuous* half circles. . . . His left hand vibrated *convulsively*. . . . The total impression—of the hypnotic *unhappy* face, . . . the *relentlessly churning* arm—was of *insatiable* feeling, *traumatic intensity, obsessive power*.[15]

As criticism this is irresponsible. Many experienced musicians believed Toscanini had a remarkably controlled yet expressive demeanor on the podium directed solely toward practical purposes. The conductor Frank Brieff, an NBC Symphony violist, called Toscanini's baton technique "elegant." Horowitz has every right to disagree, but his use of subjective modifiers such as "traumatic," "obsessive," and "insatiable" tells us nothing about pertinent podium practice in general or Toscanini in particular. All that emerges is the author's seemingly obsessive dislike for the conductor.

Yet despite such blindness to historical, visual, and musical fact on the part of some critics, Toscanini has been better served at the close of the twentieth century than at any time since his death simply because he is better represented to the public than at any time during his life. Over and beyond RCA's eighty-two-CD edition and ten videos of his NBC telecasts, all of his recordings with the BBC Symphony and some with that orchestra that have never before been released have gained CD transfers. And with the advent of the compact disc, a number of small companies have been issuing Toscanini's broadcast and concert performances on independent European labels (see Appendix 8).

The appearance of such material has made it possible, for example, to compare the maestro's 1951 telecast and studio recording of the Brahms First Symphony and to hear how each (though but a few days apart) differs from the

Toscanini sight-reading at the piano, c. 1943.
Walfredo Toscanini

other. Then, too, one can compare his 1941 studio account of the work to the later one as well as to those of 1937 and 1940 given before an audience. Critics listening to all five accounts, regardless of whether or not they like the conductor's approach, would be deaf if they failed to recognize the number of ways in which each version varies from the other. And the same holds true for a number of other works performed frequently by Toscanini at NBC, a fact that utterly confutes Joseph Horowitz's notion of an "all-purpose formula" that produced a codifiable Toscanini style.

In lacking this uniformity, Toscanini was no different from many other conductors of his time. But his peers, most likely, were denied the luxury accorded Toscanini of being able to rehear their performances as often as they chose—to provide, in effect, a response to them. As noted in the previous chapter, Toscanini asked to audition all of his broadcasts of the Brahms Third Symphony before recording it in 1952, a practice he must have pursued with regard to other works before returning to them. This is in no way surprising from what may have been the most self-critical of conductors.

Toscanini rarely lavished praise on the NBC musicians, and he told Guido Cantelli never to say "bravo" to the orchestra.[16] To the uninformed this might suggest that Toscanini was cold and uncaring. But his view sprang from his attitude toward himself. Refusing to pat himself on the back, he expected the musicians with whom he worked to be subject to similar standards. When he listened in 1951 to a tape recording of his 1944 broadcast of Act IV of *Rigoletto*, he said, "I don't know if I would be able to conduct that as well today." According to the sound engineer Sandro Cicogna, who had been working with him, "It was the closest I ever heard him come to praising himself or anything he had done."[17]

It has been said in some quarters that Toscanini was not an intellectual, but this is debatable and depends in part upon how one conceives the term. In the narrowest sense, perhaps, he was not. What intellectual, after all, would watch wrestling on television, as Toscanini often did? In a broader sense, however, he was as intellectual (though perhaps not as stuffy or pretentious) as the most stereotypically rigorous academician. It has been demonstrated in both the Sachs and Marek biographies that he possessed a broad knowledge of painting and literature and that he knew a good deal of Shakespeare by heart (and in English). But over and beyond his broad interest in and knowledge of arts other than his own, his approach to music was that of an intellectual—analytical and aesthetic. His admonitions to an orchestra might sound excitable, with such commands as "play with blood." And his performances undoubtedly bespeak an intense emotional involvement. But primary in his focus on any work was his keen analytical dissection of it. Nothing illustrates this better than a story related by John W. Freeman, who, in addition to being a professional critic for many years, knew the Toscanini family:

> Seriousness mattered most to him. For that reason I was surprised by the Maestro's willingness to look over a student piece I had composed. I offered it to him the way you might send a greeting card, thinking he would give it no more than a civil glance. Instead he scrutinized the score for what seemed like hours in an agony of concentration, then put it down and went to the piano, where he discussed every point from memory. He found a few kind words ("not bad") for some of the phrases and transitions, but his face clouded when he came to the end, where first and second themes were played simultaneously. There was a bar where the harmonization of the two themes could not be made to coincide. "It sounds modern," he said, "but it doesn't sound good. Not because of the dissonance but because it makes no sense. You put it this way to be clever. It would be more clever to invent something new, something right for this place.[18]

Toscanini listening to a playback of a recording with NBC's principal second violinist, Edwin Bachmann. *Edwin Bachmann*

"It makes no sense." Most revealing about Toscanini's response is its foundation in aesthetic scrutiny. His rejection of Freeman's close came not from a subjective dislike, but from its seeming falseness, its artificiality—its failure, in Toscanini's judgment, to become, through artistic manipulation, just and true. And this aesthetic scrutiny, possibly more than any other single trait, embodies an intellectual and the quintessential Toscanini. It explains why he would question traditional performance practices, why he might go to extreme lengths to seek out a manuscript simply to justify a single dynamic indication, and why he could correctly infer omissions in an edition of Mozart's Piano Concerto, K. 595. He might respond to music "with blood," but he was above all else a sophisticated, probingly thoughtful musician. As much as anything, Toscanini's NBC Symphony broadcasts, in the way they unveil his constantly changing conception of a given work, document the cerebral nature of his artistic temperament.

Those who like to take potshots at Toscanini have condemned his limited repertory. Granted, his programs were in some respects repetitious, but no more so than those of many other conductors. They were admittedly somewhat more eccentric, sometimes beginning with a lengthy major score and concluding with a shorter work or a minor one by a less-than-first-rate composer. Still, taken in total, Toscanini's NBC programs were interesting and varied. He has been pilloried, to be sure, for being inimical to modern music and for his seeming conservatism. Overlooked in such criticism is Toscanini's place in history. Because of the unprecedented length of his career, he was often considered a contemporary of Stokowski (born in 1882), Klemperer (born in 1885), and Furtwängler (born in 1886). But Toscanini, who was born in 1867, was closer to the generations of Nikisch (born in 1855) and Mahler (born in 1860). In the earlier part of Toscanini's career, Wagner was viewed as a radical modern, and Brahms, Tchaikovsky, and Verdi were still composing. Then, too, Puccini, Debussy, Ravel, and Richard Strauss were all still creating important scores at a time when Toscanini had gained international renown. With every one of these composer having produced works that were central to Toscanini's repertory, it seems fair to say that, rather than being unsympathetic to modern music, he was immersed in some of the newest, most respected, and often most strikingly innovative music of his time, a fact underscored by the great number of premieres he led.

Important to consider as well is the breadth of his repertory in terms of the styles it encompassed. How many conductors of Toscanini's era proved equally comfortable with major masterpieces (both old and contemporary) from the Austro-German, French, Italian, and Russian schools? How many were sympathetic to such diverse scores as Haydn's "Clock" and Franck's D Minor, Dvořák's "New World," and Tchaikovsky's *Manfred* Symphonies; Strauss's *Don Juan* and Debussy's *La mer;* Gluck's *Orfeo ed Euridice* and Boito's *Mefistofole;* Beethoven's *Fidelio* and Puccini's *La bohème*? Or consider, as well, that many eminent interpreters of the Austro-German repertory, notably Bruno Walter and Furtwängler, never played—as Toscanini did at NBC—such significant works as Beethoven's *Consecration of the House* Overture or Brahms's Second Serenade. And remember that Toscanini led the Cherubini C Minor Requiem, often written about as a major masterpiece, at a time when it was rarely performed. Then there was the interest he helped to stimulate in Berlioz in an era when the composer's reputation was held in far less esteem than it is today. Of course repetitions occurred on his NBC programs. This is to be expected of any performer having, as Toscanini did, passionate preferences and who, it should not be forgotten, did not become a full-time symphonic conductor until well into the second half of his career.

For future generations a key issue may be how much of the unreleased Toscanini–NBC material, given its intrinsic worth, will be made widely available. With the general public's relatively cool response to historical performances, it seems unlikely that commercial issues from major record companies of in-concert performances Toscanini or his heirs have approved for release will appear. The fees imposed by the musicians' union make such releases potentially unprofitable. More than likely, small independent companies will continue, as they have been doing, to fill the void in this area. The problem with their efforts, however, is that they release material indiscriminately, seemingly interested only in capitalizing on Toscanini's name with performances that are either musically or sonically inferior. More feasible would be family-approved releases drawn from primary sources of broadcast performances of scores for which Toscanini left no commercially released recording. The more such material appears, the harder it will be to make the kind of specious judgments and vague or inaccurate generalizations fobbed off by some writers as serious criticism.

Toscanini's NBC years stand as a monument to part of the best in the human spirit—the struggle to create order from chaos, perfection from imperfection. Whatever their shortcomings, they comprise a record of total commitment in which an artist gave wholly, often perhaps compulsively, of himself in order to achieve his idealized realization of beauty in a broad range of music that shines as one of the glories of Western civilization.

Appendix 1

NONBROADCAST TOSCANINI
NBC SYMPHONY ORCHESTRA CONCERTS

6 Feb. 1938: New York City, Benefit for the Italian Welfare League
Beethoven: Symphony No. 1
The Beethoven Ninth Symphony, which concluded this concert, was broadcast.

13 Dec. 1938: Newark, New Jersey
Weber: *Oberon*: Overture
Wagner: *Siegfried*: Forest Murmurs
Brahms: *Variations on a Theme by Haydn*
Tchaikovsky: Symphony No. 6, "Pathétique"
Wagner: *Die Meistersinger*: Prelude

27 Dec. 1938: Baltimore, Maryland
Repeat of the program given on 13 December.

10 Jan. 1939: Boston, Massachusetts
Scarlatti-Tommasini: *The Good Humored Ladies*
Ravel: *Daphnis et Chloé*: Suite No. 2
Brahms: Symphony No. 3
Wagner: *Siegfried*: Forest Murmurs
    Götterdämmerung: Siegfried's Funeral

31 Jan. 1939: Chicago, Illinois
Rossini: *The Barber of Seville*: Overture
    La Cenerentola: Overture
Brahms: *Variations on a Theme by Haydn*
Wagner: *Siegfried*: Forest Murmurs
Beethoven: Symphony No. 3, "Eroica"
Weber-Berlioz: *Invitation to the Dance*
Wagner: *Die Meistersinger von Nürnberg*: Prelude

1 Feb. 1939: Pittsburgh, Pennsylvania
Weber-Berlioz: *Invitation to the Dance*
Wagner: *Siegfried*: Forest Murmurs
Brahms: *Variations on a Theme by Haydn*

Beethoven: Symphony No. 3, "Eroica"
Wagner: *Die Meistersinger von Nürnberg*: Prelude

7 Feb. 1939: Providence, Rhode Island
Repeat of program of 1 February 1939.

14 Mar. 1939: Washington, D. C.
Respighi: *The Fountains of Rome*
Wagner: *Götterdämmerung*: Dawn and Siegfried's Rhine Journey
    Tannhäuser: Overture (Dresden version)
Beethoven: Symphony No. 7

21 Feb. 1940: Newark, New Jersey
Beethoven: *Leonore* Overture No. 2
Rossini: *William Tell*: Passo a sei; Soldier's Dance
Beethoven: Symphony No. 7
Wagner: *Parsifal*: Prelude and Good Friday Spell
Strauss: *Till Eulenspiegel's Merry Pranks*

24 Mar. 1943: New York City, benefit for National Foundation for Infantile Paralysis
Brahms: Symphony No. 1
Beethoven: Symphony No. 1
The balance of this program, made up of three works by Wagner, was broadcast.
See entry for this date in chapter 2.

25 Apr. 1943: New York City, war bond concert
    Tchaikovsky: Symphony No. 6, "Pathétique"
The balance of this all-Tchaikovsky program, consisting of *The Nutcracker Suite* and the First Piano Concerto, with Horowitz, was broadcast. See the entry for this date in chapter 2.

18 Apr. 1944: New York City
It is not clear how much, if any, of this huge concert was broadcast. See the entry for this date in chapter 2.

31 Oct. 1944: New York City
Rossini: *The Barber of Seville*: Overture
Verdi: *Nabucco*: "Va, pensiero"
    Rigoletto: Quartet (Ribla, Merriman, Peerce, Valentino)
    I vespri siciliani: Overture
    La traviata: Prelude to Act III
    Un ballo in maschera: "Eri tu" (Valentino)
Ponchielli: *La Gioconda*: Dance of the Hours

19 Feb. 1945: New York City, benefit for National Foundation Infantile Paralysis
Weber: *Der Freischütz*: Overture
Brahms: Piano Concerto No. 2 (Horowitz)
Ravel: *La valse*
Mussorgsky-Ravel: *Pictures at an Exhibition*
Originally scheduled as the first two works on this concert were Mendelssohn's *Ruy Blas* Overture and Beethoven's Piano Concerto No. 5 in E-flat Major, "Emperor."

25 Sept. 1945: New York City, benefit for the Italian Welfare League
Beethoven: *Egmont*: Overture
  Leonore Overture No. 2
  Symphony No. 9 (Andreotti, Merriman, Peerce, Alvary)

Sept. 1947: Ridgefield, Connecticut, benefit for Ridgefield Library and Historical Association
Rossini: *L'Italiana in Algeri*: Overture
Beethoven: Symphony No. 1
Mendelssohn: *A Midsummer Night's Dream*: Nocturne; Scherzo
Wagner: *Siegfried Idyll*
J. Strauss: *Voices of Spring*
  Tritsch-Tratsch Polka
Sousa: "The Stars and Stripes Forever"

26 Apr. 1948: New York City, benefit for New York Infirmary Building Fund
Verdi: Te Deum
  Requiem (Nelli, Merriman, McGrath, Scott)

20 Apr. 1949: New York City, benefit for City College of New York
Beethoven: *The Creatures of Prometheus*: Overture
  Symphony No. 3, "Eroica"
Wagner: *Tannhäuser*: Overture and Bacchanale
  Die Walküre: Act I, Scene 3 (Bampton, Svanholm); Ride of the Valkyries

7 Oct. 1949: Ridgefield, Connecticut
Mendelssohn: Symphony No. 4, "Italian"
Debussy: *Prelude to the Afternoon of a Faun*
Saint-Saëns: *Danse macabre*
Wagner: *Siegfried*: Forest Murmurs
Waldteufel: *The Skaters Waltz*

22 Dec. 1951: New York City, benefit for Italian flood victims
Cherubini: *Anacréon*: Overture
Beethoven: Symphony No. 1
This concert concluded with Respighi's *Fountains of Rome* and Brahms's Fourth Symphony, both of which were broadcast.

29 Mar. 1952: New York City, benefit for the Building Fund of the New York Infirmary
Beethoven: Symphony No. 1
The Beethoven Symphony No. 9, which concluded this concert, was broadcast.

Appendix 2

THE NBC SYMPHONY ORCHESTRA TOURS

South America, 1940

13 June 1940: Rio de Janeiro
Rossini: *La Cenerentola*: Overture
Beethoven: Symphony No. 3, "Eroica"
Mignone: *Congada*
Smetana: *The Moldau*
Berlioz: *Roméo et Juliette*: Queen Mab Scherzo
Wagner: *Parsifal*: Good Friday Spell
    Die Meistersinger von Nürnberg: Prelude to Act I; Prelude to Act III

14 June 1940: Rio de Janeiro
Schubert: Symphony No. 9
Paganini: *Moto perpetuo*
Brahms: *Variations on a Theme by Haydn*
Ravel: *La valse*
Gomes: *Il guarany*: Overture

15 June 1940: São Paolo
Rossini: *The Barber of Seville*: Overture
Beethoven: Symphony No. 7
Mignone: *Congada*
Weber-Berlioz: *Invitation to the Dance*
Mendelssohn: *A Midsummer Night's Dream*: Scherzo
R. Strauss: *Death and Transfiguration*

19 June 1940: Buenos Aires
Mozart: *The Magic Flute*: Overture
Brahms: Symphony No. 1
Franck: *Les éolides*
Respighi: *The Fountains of Rome*
Wagner: *Parsifal*: Good Friday Spell
    Die Meistersinger von Nürnberg: Prelude

20 June 1940: Buenos Aires
Rossini: *The Barber of Seville*: Overture
Beethoven: Symphony No. 7
Aquirre: Two Dances
Paganini: *Moto perpetuo*
Brahms: *Variations on a Theme by Haydn*
R. Strauss: *Till Eulenspiegel's Merry Pranks*

23 June 1940: Buenos Aires
Mozart: Symphony No. 40
Beethoven: *Leonore* Overture No. 3
Wagner: *Siegfried Idyll*
    Tristan und Isolde: Prelude and Liebestod
    Siegfried: Forest Murmurs
    Tannhäuser: Overture (Dresden version)

25 June 1940: Buenos Aires
Schubert: Symphony No. 9
Debussy: "Ibéria"
Wagner: *Lohengrin*: Prelude to Act I; Prelude to Act III
R. Strauss: *Death and Transfiguration*

27 June 1940: Buenos Aires
Weber: *Oberon*: Overture
Brahms: Symphony No. 2
Barber: *Adagio for Strings*
Saint-Saëns: *Danse macabre*
Tchaikovsky: *Romeo and Juliet*: Fantasy Overture
Ravel: *La valse*

29 June 1940: Buenos Aires
Cherubini: *Anacréon*: Overture
Beethoven: Symphony No. 6, "Pastoral"
Alberto Williams: Symphony No. 7
Smetana: *The Moldau*
Wagner: *Tristan und Isolde*: Prelude and Liebestod
    Die Walküre: Ride of the Valkyries

1 July 1940: Buenos Aires
Rossini: *La Cenerentola*: Overture
Beethoven: Symphony No. 5
Mendelssohn: *A Midsummer Night's Dream*: Nocturne; Scherzo
Weber-Berlioz: *Invitation to the Dance*
Mussorgsky-Ravel: *Pictures at an Exhibition*
Wagner: *Die Meistersinger von Nürnberg*: Prelude

3 July 1940: Montevideo

Rossini: *The Barber of Seville*: Overture
Beethoven: Symphony No. 7
Mendelssohn: *A Midsummer Night's Dream*: Nocturne; Scherzo
Weber-Berlioz: *Invitation to the Dance*
Paganini: *Moto perpetuo*
Smetana: *The Moldau*
Debussy: *La mer*

4 July 1940: Montevideo

Beethoven: *Egmont*: Overture
Brahms: Symphony No. 2
Respighi: *The Fountains of Rome*
Wagner: *Tristan und Isolde*: Prelude and Liebestod
　　　Die Meistersinger von Nürnberg: Prelude

8 July 1940: São Paulo

Beethoven: *Egmont*: Overture
Brahms: Symphony No. 2
Fernandez: *Reisado do pastoreio*: Batuque
Berlioz: *Roméo et Juliette*: Queen Mab Scherzo
Rossini: *William Tell*: Passo a sei; Soldiers' Dance
Wagner: *Tristan und Isolde*: Prelude and Liebestod
　　　Tannhäuser: Overture (Dresden version)
Gomes: *Il guarany*: Overture

9 July 1940: Rio de Janeiro

Beethoven: *Egmont*: Overture
Brahms: Symphony No. 1
Fernandez: *Reisado do pastoreio*: Batuque
Respighi: *The Fountains of Rome*
Wagner: *Siegfried*: Forest Murmurs
Debussy: *La mer*

10 July 1940: Rio de Janeiro

Cherubini: *Anacréon*: Overture
Beethoven: Symphony No. 5
Mendelssohn: *A Midsummer Night's Dream*: Nocturne; Scherzo
Weber-Berlioz: *Invitation to the Dance*
Wagner: *Die Meistersinger von Nürnberg*: Prelude
Portions of this concert were broadcast by shortwave to the United States.

The 1950 Transcontinental United States Tour

14 Apr. 1950: New York City
Rossini: *L'Italiana in Algeri*: Overture
Beethoven: Symphony No. 3, "Eroica"
Strauss: *Don Juan*
Debussy: *La mer*

17 Apr. 1950: Baltimore, Maryland
Repeat of the program for 14 April.

19 Apr. 1950: Richmond, Virginia
Kabalevsky: *Colas Breugnon*: Overture
Tchaikovsky: Symphony No. 6, "Pathétique"
Brahms: *Variations on a Theme by Haydn*
Ravel: *Daphnis et Chloé*: Suite No. 2
Emmet: "Dixie" (encore)

22 Apr. 1950: Atlanta, Georgia
Rossini: *La scala di seta*: Overture
Brahms: Symphony No. 1
Schubert: Symphony No. 8
Saint-Saëns: *Danse macabre*
Dukas: *The Sorcerer's Apprentice*
Emmet: "Dixie" (encore, played twice)

25 Apr. 1950: New Orleans, Louisiana
Beethoven: *Egmont*: Overture
Brahms: Symphony No. 4
Debussy: "Ibéria"
Glinka: *Jota aragonesa*
Wagner: *Siegfried*: Forest Murmurs
    Die Meistersinger von Nürnberg: Prelude

27 Apr. 1950: Houston, Texas
Rossini: *La Cenerentola*: Overture
Beethoven: Symphony No. 3
Smetana: *The Moldau*
Wagner: *Parsifal*: Good Friday Spell
Tchaikovsky: *Romeo and Juliet*: Fantasy Overture

29 Apr. 1950: Austin, Texas
Wagner: *Die Meistersinger von Nürnberg*: Prelude
Dvořák: Symphony No. 9
Schubert: Symphony No. 8
Saint-Saëns: *Danse macabre*
Rossini: *William Tell*: Overture

1 May 1950: Dallas, Texas

Kabalevsky: *Colas Breugnon*: Overture
Tchaikovsky: Symphony No. 6, "Pathétique"
Brahms: *Variations on a Theme by Haydn*
Mendelssohn: *A Midsummer Night's Dream*: Scherzo
Ravel: *Daphnis et Chloé*: Suite No. 2

3 May 1950: Pasadena, California

Beethoven: *Egmont*: Overture
Brahms: Symphony No. 4
Debussy: "Ibéria"
Glinka: *Jota aragonesa*
Wagner: *Siegfried*: Forest Murmurs
      Die Meistersinger von Nürnberg: Prelude
Sousa: "The Stars and Stripes Forever" (encore)

5 May 1950: Pasadena, California

Rossini: *La Cenerentola*: Overture
Beethoven: Symphony No. 3, "Eroica"
Smetana: *The Moldau*
Wagner: *Parsifal*: Good Friday Spell
Tchaikovsky: *Romeo and Juliet*: Fantasy Overture

7 May 1950: San Francisco, California

Rossini: *L'Italiana in Algeri*: Overture
Beethoven: Symphony No. 3, "Eroica"
Strauss: *Don Juan*
Debussy: *La mer*
Wagner: *Siegfried*: Forest Murmurs (encore)

9 May 1950: Portland, Oregon

Kabalevsky: *Colas Breugnon*: Overture
Tchaikovsky: Symphony No. 6, "Pathétique"
Brahms: *Variations on a Theme by Haydn*
Mendelssohn: *A Midsummer Night's Dream*: Scherzo
Ravel: *Daphnis et Chloé*: Suite No. 2
Wagner: *Siegfried*: Forest Murmurs (encore)

10 May 1950: Seattle, Washington

Rossini: *La Cenerentola*: Overture
Beethoven: Symphony No. 3, "Eroica"
Smetana: *The Moldau*
Wagner: *Parsifal*: Good Friday Spell
Tchaikovsky: *Romeo and Juliet*: Fantasy Overture
Kabalevsky: *Colas Breugnon*: Overture (encore)

15 May 1950: St. Louis, Missouri
Rossini: *La scala di seta*: Overture
Beethoven: Symphony No. 3, "Eroica"
Strauss: *Don Juan*
Debussy: *La mer*

17 May 1950: Chicago, Illinois
Rossini: *L'Italiana in Algeri*: Overture
Brahms: Symphony No. 1
Strauss: *Don Juan*
Debussy: *La mer*

19 May 1950: Detroit, Michigan
Rossini: *La Cenerentola*: Overture
Beethoven: Symphony No. 3
Smetana: *The Moldau*
Wagner: *Parsifal*: Good Friday Spell
Tchaikovsky: *Romeo and Juliet*: Fantasy Overture

21 May 1950: Cleveland, Ohio
Beethoven: *Egmont*: Overture
Brahms: Symphony No. 4
Schubert: Symphony No. 8, "Unfinished"
Saint-Saëns: *Danse macabre*
Rossini: *William Tell*: Overture

23 May 1950: Pittsburgh, Pennsylvania
Kabalevsky: *Colas Breugnon*: Overture
Tchaikovsky: Symphony No. 6, "Pathétique"
Brahms: *Variations on a Theme by Haydn*
Mendelssohn: *A Midsummer Night's Dream*: Scherzo
Ravel: *Daphnis et Chloé*: Suite No. 2

25 May 1950: Washington, D. C.
Rossini: *La scala di seta*: Overture
Brahms: Symphony No. 4
Schubert: Symphony No. 8, "Unfinished"
Saint-Saëns: *Danse macabre*

23 May 1950: Pittsburgh, Pennsylvania
Kabalevsky: *Colas Breugnon*: Overture
Tchaikovsky: Symphony No. 6, "Pathétique"
Brahms: *Variations on a Theme by Haydn*
Mendelssohn: *A Midsummer Night's Dream*: Scherzo
Ravel: *Daphnis et Chloé*: Suite No. 2

25 May 1950: Washington, D.C.
Rossini: *La scala di seta*: Overture
Brahms: Symphony No. 4
Schubert: Symphony No. 8, "Unfinished"
Saint-Saëns: *Danse macabre*
Dukas: *The Sorcerer's Apprentice*
The Brahms Fourth replaced the originally scheduled Brahms First, a substitution possibly rooted in the fact that Toscanini and the NBC Symphony had performed the latter in the nation's capital a decade earlier on their previous appearance in that city.

27 May 1950: Philadelphia, Pennsylvania
Rossini: *La scala di seta*: Overture
Brahms: Symphony No. 1
Schubert: Symphony No. 8, "Unfinished"
Debussy: *La mer*
Sousa: "The Stars and Stripes Forever" (encore)
Emmet: "Dixie" (encore)
Originally programmed for this final concert of the tour were Beethoven's *Egmont* Overture, the Brahms Fourth Symphony, Debussy's "Ibéria," Glinka's *Jota aragonesa*, and the Forest Murmurs from Wagner's *Siegfried* and the prelude to his *Meistersinger von Nürnberg*.

Appendix 3

WORKS PERFORMED BY TOSCANINI AT NBC ABSENT FROM HIS NEW YORK PHILHARMONIC PROGRAMS

Atterberg: Symphony No. 6
Barber: *Adagio for Strings*
    Essay No. 1 for Orchestra
Bazzini: *Saul*: Overture
Beethoven: Piano Concerto No. 1
    Piano Concerto No. 3
    Fantasia in C Minor for Piano, Chorus, and Orchestra, "Choral Fantasy"
    Consecration of the House Overture
    Fidelio
    String Quartet in C Major, Op. 59 No. 3: Finale
    String Quartet in B-flat Major, Op. 130: Cavatina
    Septet for Woodwinds, Horn, and Strings in E-flat Major
Bellini: *Norma*: Introduction and Druids' Chorus
Berlioz: *The Damnation of Faust*: Scene 7; Dance of the Sylphs
    Les francs-juges: Overture
Bizet: *L'Arlésienne*: Suites 1 and 2
    Carmen: Suite
Boccherini: String Quartet in D Major, Op. 6 No. 1
    String Quintet in E Major, Op. 13 No. 5: Minuet
Boito: *Mefistofele*: Prologue
Bolzoni: *Medieval Castle*: Serenade
    Minuet in B
Brahms: *Gesang der Parzen* for Chorus and Orchestra
Brahms (orch. Rubbra): *Variations and Fugue on a Theme by Handel*
Castelnuovo-Tedesco: *A Fairy Tale* Overture
    The Taming of the Shrew Overture
Catalani: *Loreley*: Dance of the Water Nymphs
    La Wally: Prelude to Act IV
Cherubini: *Ali Baba*: Overture
    Requiem in C Minor
    String Quartet in E-flat Major: Scherzo
    Symphony in D Major

Cimarosa: *Il matrimonio per raggiro*: Overture
    Il matrimonio segreto: Overture
Copland: *El salón México*
Creston: *Choric Dance No. 2*
    Frontiers
Debussy: *Marche écossaise*
    Danse
Degeyter: "The Internationale"
Donizetti: *Don Pasquale*: Overture
Dukas: *Ariane et Barbe-bleu*: Suite
Dvořák: Cello Concerto in B Minor
    Scherzo capriccioso
Elgar: *Introduction and Allegro for Strings*
Emmett: "Dixie" (arr. Frank Black)
Fernandez: *Reisado do pastoreio*: Batuque
Foroni: Overture in C Minor
Franchetti: *Cristofo Colombo*: Nocturne
Glinka: *Jota aragonesa*
Gluck: *Orfeo ed Euridice*: Act II
Gomes: *Il guarany*: Overture
Gould: *A Lincoln Legend*
Grieg: *Holberg Suite*
Griffes: *The White Peacock*
Grofé: *Grand Canyon Suite*
Handel: Concerto Grosso No. 5: Minuet
Harris: Symphony No. 3
Haydn: *Sinfonia concertante*, Op. 84
    Symphony No. 92
    Symphony No. 94
    Symphony No. 104
Hérold: *Zampa*: Overture
Hoffstetter (attrib. Haydn): Serenade
Humperdinck: *Hansel and Gretel*: Prelude
    Königskinder: Prelude
Kabalevsky: *Colas Breugnon*: Overture
    Symphony No. 2
Kalinnikov: Symphony No. 1
Kodály: *Háry János*: Suite
Liadov: *Kikimora*
Lizst: *From the Cradle to the Grave*
    Hungarian Rhapsody No. 2
    Orpheus
Loeffler: *Memories of My Childhood*
Mancinelli: *Venetian Scenes*: Flight of the Lovers
Martucci: Piano Concerto in B-flat Minor

Massenet: *Scènes alsaciennes*
Mendelssohn: *Hebrides* Overture
    String Octet in E-flat Major
    String Quintet No. 2 in B-flat Major: Adagio and Lento
    Symphony No. 3
    Die schöne Melusine Overture
Meyerbeer: *Dinorah*: Overture
Mignone: *Congada*
    Fantasia brasileira
    Four Brazilian Churches
Mozart: Bassoon Concerto, K. 191
    Divertimeno, K. 287
    Don Giovanni: Overture
    The Marriage of Figaro: Overture
    Sinfonia concertante, K. 364
    Symphony No. 39
Mussorgsky: *Boris Godunov*: Act III: Introduction and Polonaise
    Khovanshchina: Prelude
Nicolai: *The Merry Wives of Windsor*: Overture
Olivieri: "Garibaldi's War Hymn"
Ponchielli: *La Gioconda*: Dance of the Hours
Puccini: *La bohème*
    Manon Lescaut: Act I, Minuet; Act III, Prelude
Ravel: *La valse*
Rieti: Symphony No. 4, "Tripartita"
Rossini: *La Cenerentola*: Overture
    La gazza ladra: Overture
    The Siege of Corinth: Overture
    Sonata No. 3 for Strings
    William Tell: Passo a sei; Soldiers' Dance
Rubinstein: (orch. Mueller-Berghaus): *Valse caprice*
Schubert: Symphony No. 2
    Symphony No. 5
    Grand Duo (orch. Joachim)
Sibelius: *Pohjola's Daughter*
    Symphony No. 2
Siegmeister: *Western Suite*
Smith (attrib.): "The Star-Spangled Banner" (It is possible that Toscanini
    performed this work with the New York Philharmonic during the
    orchestra's tour of Europe in 1930.)
Sinigaglia: *Piedmont Suite*: Over the Woods; Rustic Dance
Sousa: "El Capitan"
    "Semper Fidelis"
    "The Stars and Stripes Forever"

Strauss, J.: *On the Beautiful Blue Danube*
    Tritsch-Tratsch Polka
    Voices of Spring
Strong: *Die Nacht*
Suppé: *Poet and Peasant*: Overture
Tchaikovsky: Piano Concerto No. 1
    Eugene Onegin: Waltz
    The Nutcracker Suite
    Symphony No. 6
    Voyevoda: Overture
Vaughan Williams: *Fantasia on a Theme by Thomas Tallis*
Verdi: *Aida*
    Un ballo in maschera
    Don Carlos: "O don fatale"
    Falstaff
    La forza del destino: Overture
    Hymn of the Nations
    I Lombardi: Act III Trio
    Luisa Miller: Overture
    Nabucco: "Va, pensiero"
    Otello
    Rigoletto: Act III
    La traviata
Vieuxtemps: Ballade and Polonaise
Vivaldi: Violin Concerto, P. 405
Wagner: *Rienzi*: Overture
    Tannhäuser: "Dich, teure Halle"
Waldteufel: *The Skaters Waltz*
Wolf-Ferrari: *Le donne curiose*: Overture

Appendix 4

WORKS PERFORMED BY TOSCANINI WITH THE NEW YORK PHILHARMONIC ABSENT FROM HIS NBC SYMPHONY ORCHESTRA PROGRAMS

Bach: Brandenburg Concerto No. 6
    Cantata 209: "Non sa che sia dolore"
    Christmas Oratorio: Prelude to Part 2
    Concerto for Violin in A Minor
    Concerto for Two Violins in D Minor
    Mass in B Minor: Kyrie
    Prelude, Chorale, and Fugue (orch. Albert)
    Chorale preludes (orch. Respighi):"Nun komm der Heiden Heiland";
        "Meine Seele erhebt den Herren"; "Wachet auf"
    Toccata and Fugue in D Minor (orch. Wood)
J. C. Bach: Sinfonia, Op. 18 No. 1
    Sinfonia, Op. 18 No. 3
Beethoven: Piano Concerto No. 5
    Triple Concerto
    King Stephan: Overture
"Believe Me If All Those Endearing Young Charms"
Berlioz: *Benvenuto Cellini*: Overture
Borodin: *Prince Igor*: Polovtsian Dances
Brahms: *Gesang aus Fingal* for Women's Chorus, Op. 17
    Serenade No. 1
Bruckner: Symphony No. 4
    Symphony No. 7
Busch: *Variations on a Theme by Mozart*
Castelnuovo-Tedesco: Cello Concerto
    The Prophets
    Variations for Violin
Chasins: *Flirtations in a Chinese Garden*
Cherubini: *Faniska*: Overture
Debussy: *Le martyre de saint Sébastien*: La cour des lys
De Sabata: *Gethsemane*
    Juventus
Franck (orch. Pierné): *Prelude, Chorale, and Fugue*
Goossens: Sinfonietta

Handel: *Susanna*: Overture
Hanson: Symphony No. 2
Honegger: *Pastorale d'été*
    Pacific 231
D'Indy: *Istar Variations*
Kodály: *Psalmus Hungaricus*
    Summer Evening
Kozeluch: String Quartet No. 2: Andante and Allegro
Monteverdi: *Sonata sopra Sancta Maria*
Mossoloff: *Iron Foundry*
Mozart: Piano Concerto, K. 466
    Piano Concerto, K. 467
    Masonic Funeral Music (orchestral portions only)
    A Musical Joke
    Symphony No. 1
    Symphony No. 28
Paër: *Il sargino*: Overture
Pizzetti: *Concerto dell'estate*
    Introduction to the Agamemnon of Aeschylus
    La pisanella: Suite
    Rondo veneziano
Raff: Symphony No. 3
Respighi: *Ballata delle gnomidi*
Rimsky-Korsakov: *The Snow Maiden*: Suite
Roussel: Symphony No. 4
Saint-Saëns: Cello Concerto
Sammartini: Symphony No. 3
Schelling: *Impressions from an Artist's Life*
Schubert (orch. Brahms): "Ellen's Second Song," Op. 52
    Wanderer Fantasy (arr. Liszt)
Schumann: Cello Concerto
    Symphony No. 4 (orch. Mahler)
Stravinsky: *Fireworks*
Tommasini: *Prelude, Fanfare, and Fugue*
    Serenata: Chiari di luna
    Tuscan Landscape
Viotti: Violin Concerto in A Minor
Vivaldi: Violin Concerto in A Major, P. 12
    Violin Concerto in B-flat Major, P. 405
    The Four Seasons: Winter
    Concerto for Four Pianos (arr. Bach)
Wagenaar: Symphony No. 2
Weber: *Ruler of the Spirits*: Overture
Welprik: *Dances and Songs of the Ghetto*
Wetzler: *The Basque Venus: Symphonic Dance in Basque Style*

Appendix 5

NBC SYMPHONY ORCHESTRA PERSONNEL

Violin
Antek, Samuel[2]
Bachmann, Edwin[2] (principal
 second violin)
Baker, Israel
Barenblatt, Lucien[1]
Birkenholz, Arcadie[1]
Bloom, Tobias[2]
Bolignini, Remo[2]
Ciompi, Giorgio
Clifton, Henry[1]
Compinsky, Manuel[1]
Feldhan, Benjamin
Ferrara, Luigi[1]
Frank, Philip[1]
Galimir, Felix
Galindo, Rafael[1]
Gasselin, Jacques[1]
Gegner, William[1]
Gingold, Josef[1]
Glickman, Harry
Golodner, Maurice[1]
Goodrich, Frank[2]
Gorner, Josef
Graeler, Louis
Guilet, Daniel[2] (concertmaster,
 1952–54)
Gurowitsch, Frank
Hollander, Max

Katz, Theodore
Kissel, Samuel
Koutzen, Boris
Kundell, Bernard
Kurtz, Arved
Larner, Jacques
Lookofsky, Harry
Lubie, Williard
Lustgarten, Alfred
Mischakoff, Mischa[1] (concertmaster,
 1937–52)
Moss, Marshall
Nosco, Henry
Pitkowsky, Paul
Pratz, Albert
Rabinowitz, Samuel
Risman, Julius
Robbins, Bernard
Rushkin, Jascha
Sarser, David
Sasso, Angelo[1]
Sharrow, Saul[2]
Shulman, Sylvan[1]
Shumsky, Oscar
Siegl, Henry
Silverman, Ralph[1]
Smit, Kolman[2]
Sopkin, Stefan[2]
Spielberg, Herman[2]

[1]Charter member of the NBC Symphony
[2]Member of the orchestra for all of its seventeen seasons

Spinelli, Sal
Steinhardt, Laurence
Suskind, Seymour[2]
Vitetta, Marius
Weinberg, Herman[1]
Winter, Paul[1]

Viola

Borodkin, Herbert
Brieff, Frank
Carboni, William
Colletta, Harold
Cooley, Carlton[2] (co-principal,
  1937–42; principal, 1942–54)
Dawson, David
Epstein, David
Fleitman, Leon[1]
Fuchs, Herbert
Gordon, Nathan
Granick, Arthur[2]
Helfand, Maurice[2]
Hersh, Ralph
Katims, Milton
Kievman, Louis[1]
Kreiner, Edward[1]
Lifschey, Elias[1]
Metz, Reuben[1]
Moldovan, Nicolas
Patchook, Sol[1]
Posner, Selig
Primrose, William[1] (co-principal,
  1937–42)
Serly, Tibor[1]
Tuchinsky, Jacques[1]
Vardi, Emanuel

Cello

Benditzsky, Naoum
Bernstein, Jacob
Edison, Abraham[1]
Gara, Emmerich
Gusikoff, Isadore
Heifetz, Benar
Koutzen, George
Kurtz, Edmund
La Marchina, Robert

Lustgarten, Edgar[1]
Mazzucchi, Oswaldo[1] (principal,
  1937–39)
Miller, Frank (principal, 1939–54)
Prinz, Milton[1]
Rose, Leonard
Rostal, Leo
Saleski, Gdal[1]
Schwarzmann, Jascha[1]
Shapiro, Harvey[1]
Shulman, Alan[2]
Silberstein, Ernst[1]
Sophos, Anthony
Stern, Carl[1]
Ziegler, Carl

Bass

Botti, Walter
Brennand, James
Fiore, Gerald
Giobbe, Luigi
Greenberg, Henry[1]
Kestenbaum, Milton
Koukly, George[1]
Krasnopolsky, Michael
Levitan, Samuel[2]
Mancini, John
Oliver, David[1]
Pitchersky, Meyer[1]
Pfeiffer, Max
Shachner, Harold
Sklar, Philip[2] (principal)
Smith, Harold
Sollner, Frank
Torke, George[1]
Van de Graaf, John[1]
Walter, David
Zimmerman, Oscar

Flute

Coppola, Carmine (principal after
  Wummer)
de Vries, Hendrik[1]
Gaskins, Ben[1]
Gershunoff, Aaron
Heim, F. William

[Flute]
Koukoukis, Nicholas
Lora, Arthur
Morris, Robert
Moskovitz, Harry
Renzi, Paul, Jr.
Wummer, John[1] (principal,
    1937–42)

Oboe
Bloom, Robert[1] (principal,
    1937–45)
Corne, René
Halpern, Sidney[1]
Kelly, Chauncy
Penza, Saverio
Prior, Ferdinand
Renzi, Paolo (principal, 1945–54)
Shulman, Harry

English horn
Ghignatti, Filippo[2] (principal)

Clarinet
Duques, Augustin[1] (first principal)
Freeman, Harold
Gallodoro, Alfred
Green, Louis[1]
Grisez, Georges[1]
Klein, Louis
McGinnis, Robert
Pepper, John
Shapiro, Wallace
Weber, David
Williams, Alexander (principal
    after Duques)

Bassoon
Carmen, Elias (principal after
    Sharrow)
Kirchner, Morris
Kohon, Benjamin
Letellier, Louis
Masucci, Sabatino
Polisi, William[2] (first principal)
Reines, Abraham[2]

Sharrow, Leonard[2] (principal after
    Polisi)
Zegler, Manuel

French horn
Berv, Arthur (principal after
    Stagliano)
Berv, Harry
Berv, Jack
Brown, William
Cerino, Arturo[2]
Clement, Harold
Corrado, Alfredo
Dultgen, Fred[1]
Hilmer, Henry[1]
Moore, Richard
Miranda, Tony
Rescigno, Joseph[2]
Stagliano, Frank[2] (first principal)

Trumpet
Baker, Bernard[1] (principal, 1937–40)
Crisara, Raymond
Falcone, Frank
Glickstein, David
Glantz, Harry (principal, 1940–54)
Klass, Sol[1]
Pennino, Humbert[1]
Venezial, Frank

Trombone
Clark, John
DiBiase, Neal (principal after Ruta)
Epstein, Jack[1]
Lewis, Sam
Ostrander, Allen
Pearlstein, Abraham
Ruta, Armand[1] (first principal)
Simons, Gardell (principal after
    Ruta)
Warms, Gerhard
Wolfstont, Melvin

Tuba
Bell, William[1] (principal)
Jenkel, Herbert

Torchinsky, Abraham

Timpani
Glassman, Karl[2] (principal)

Percussion
Albright, Fred
Edison, Harry[2]
Grupp, David[1]
Grupp, Martin
Gusikoff, David[1]
Stitman, Harry[1]
Wolf, Jacob

Harp
Newell, Laura[1]
Vito, Edward[2]

Piano and Celeste
Balsam, Artur
Brenner, Vladimir[1]
Kahn, Joseph[2]
Wild, Earl

Contractors
Sheild, LeRoy
Spitalny, H. Leopold[1]

Appendix 6

PRESERVATION OF THE NBC SYMPHONY ORCHESTRA BROADCASTS

The finest and most complete source for the NBC Symphony Orchestra broadcasts are the recordings made by the network's engineers during the concerts. Often called "reference" discs, these are sixteen- and seventeen-inch acetates recorded at 33⅓ revolutions per minute with a groove width used for commercial 78 rpm discs of the pre-LP era. Owing to their greater diameter and slower speed, these reference discs could contain up to twenty minutes per side, about five times the capacity of a conventional twelve-inch 78 rpm record. Moreover, they were sonically superior, with quieter surfaces, wider frequency response, and greater dynamic range.

The production of such discs was not confined to the NBC Symphony broadcasts. It was the network's practice to record all its programs, in some cases for airing at a later date or for distribution to network-affiliated stations. That is why many broadcasts of the period were introduced with the announcement, "The following program is transcribed." For Toscanini, NBC took special pains, sometimes producing as many as ten sets of discs for a single concert. Some were intended for NBC's library, others for Toscanini, and still others (where applicable) for a sponsor.

Among other existing sources are those produced for airing outside the United States. Some, with announcements in Spanish and Portuguese, were made for broadcast in Mexico and South America. Sometimes these discs were recorded with a microphone placement radically different from the one used by NBC, which occasionally resulted in badly skewed balance. A case in point is the Spanish-language recording of the 1942 broadcast of the Brahms Second Symphony and *Tragic* Overture (the former issued on CD in Music and Arts set 995), where balances are so distorted strings are often smothered by the brass.

Beginning in 1944 and continuing for five years, Armed Forces Radio incorporated excerpts from Toscanini's NBC broadcast in its V-disc project. V-discs were twelve-inch 78s pressed on vinyl and distributed to American servicemen based in the United States and abroad. Some were dubbed from reference recordings; others were taken down in California from a cross-continental transmission over telephone lines. In either case, they were usually substandard in comparison to other sources. Once valued for performances that could not otherwise be heard, they have become historical relics, the excerpts and shorter works they contained having appeared either in superior Toscanini performances or in more complete and better sounding editions. Owing to union regulations, the Toscanini V-discs were not for sale, and the masters for them were destroyed after the project ended. A complete list of Toscanini V-discs is printed in Marsh, *Toscanini and the Art of Conducting* (pp. 147–49).

After the end of World War II, the BBC began to record the NBC Symphony broadcasts for airing in England. Though somewhat noisier than the NBC acetates, the BBC discs are sonically excellent, with an equalization that gave greater emphasis to lower frequencies and, as a result, somewhat fuller sonority.

When reel-to-reel tape recording became available, NBC employed the new technology in recording the broadcasts but continued to produce reference discs, perhaps owing to a suspicion that the tapes' shelf life might be short. The transfer of the broadcasts to Carnegie Hall at the beginning of the 1951–52 season yielded (despite NBC's close microphone placement, which suggested the dryness of studio 8H) a sonic improvement complemented by the superiority of reel-to-reel technology. As a result, some of the tapes produced during this period have a clarity, color, presence, and impact that give perhaps the best idea of the sonority Toscanini favored during his NBC years.

In 1962, radio station WRVR in New York City, in cooperation with Toscanini's son, Walter, began what proved a short-lived series intended to survey all of the maestro's commercially released recordings and NBC Symphony broadcasts. The latter were presented exactly as they were aired, save for the excision of the original announcements, which were replaced with appropriate new ones written and delivered by John C. De Witt. The portion devoted to the broadcasts was titled *The Complete Recordings of Arturo Toscanini: The NBC Era.* In the approximately six months of the series' existence, the first two seasons of broadcasts were presented. To judge from De Witt's comments, it was Walter Toscanini's original intent to continue the project, the 1939 Beethoven cycle having been announced as the concerts that would be featured in the rebroadcast of the orchestra's third season. But in the fall of 1962, the series was abruptly canceled. I wrote to Walter Toscanini, voicing disappointment over the cancellation. In a courteous, lengthy letter he replied, saying that the great investment in money and time that the project required made its continuance impossible.

This may well have been true, but another significant factor may have influenced his decision: it is quite possible that the series catalyzed more sales of reel-to-reel recorders than did any other program on the air. Obviously, the value of the Toscanini family archive, which at the time was up for sale, would be substantially reduced were a great number of copies of all the broadcasts to gain circulation. Still, as a source for the first two years of Toscanini's NBC concerts, the WRVR project is significant. Often, if not always, it drew upon the NBC acetates. Then, too, it served what may have been its prime intent: stimulating a waning interest in the maestro. Moreover, those broadcasts have served as sources for many unofficial releases from independent CD producers.

One other source of Toscanini's NBC broadcasts deserves mention: recordings produced from air checks by Mirko Paneyko, who had gained considerable prominence as a designer of custom-built audio installations and was an admirer of Toscanini. Beginning as early as 1941 and continuing through 1950, he recorded transcription-sized discs directly off the air. His initial efforts were technically mediocre, but later ones often had a fullness and naturalness that were occasionally weightier and more musical than the transcriptions produced by NBC. Indeed, according to Anthony Paterno, Toscanini was so impressed when he visited Paneyko and heard his discs, he asked, "Why can't NBC do that?" Whether it was the recordings themselves or the superior equipment on which they were reproduced that prompted this response is unclear. Paneyko ultimately gave up designing audio installations in an attempt to market high-fidelity television. Unfortunately, he was a half century ahead of his time. The market was not ready for his innovations, and he ultimately went bankrupt and had to sell his recordings.

If nothing else, the variety of the sources for Toscanini's NBC broadcasts bespeaks the extraordinary fascination he exerted. But it is the week-to-week professional competence of NBC's own efforts that remains the most thorough record of the maestro's achievements. They shine as the most comprehensive and formidable documentation afforded any conductor active during the seventeen years that NBC retained Toscanini and his orchestra.

Appendix 7

THE TOSCANINI VIDEOS

The release on videocassettes and laser discs of the ten NBC Symphony broadcasts that the network elected to televise stands as a major achievement in sonic and visual restoration. Drawing upon deteriorated kinescopes of the telecasts, RCA enhanced the fading contrast of the picture and replaced the excruciatingly distorted sound on the film with that of the excellent NBC reference discs and tapes. Heard through a high-quality audio system, the fidelity is, for its time, state of the art.

Perhaps the most remarkable feature of these videos is the way they vivify Toscanini's extraordinary simplicity, clarity, and grace on the podium. Not all the performances in the series exemplify his best work, but what can be seen is a master conductor, working for the orchestra, not for the audience. Every gesture, every look has point and purpose, the eyes almost hypnotic, the baton seemingly balletic in its expressive but always clear indication of the beat.

The lone reservation one might have about these resurrections is RCA's decision to excise all of the original commentary in favor of newly written brief introductions delivered—with consummate professionalism, to be sure—by Martin Bookspan. From a commercial point of view, this alteration may have been pragmatic, many viewers surely finding the original announcements increasingly tedious on repeated playing. But their excision falsifies—or at least veils—history, obliterating the style of the original presentations. These were, after all, significant landmarks in the evolution of television. Some of the telecasts had distinctive features, which are noted in the following overview. Broadcast dates are in boldface type.

20 Mar. 1948 (RCA 60333)
Wagner: *Lohengrin*: Prelude to Act I
 Tannhäuser: Overture and Bacchanale
 Siegfried: Forest Murmurs
 Götterdämmerung: Dawn and Siegfried's Rhine Journey
 Die Walküre: Ride of the Valkyries
If the camera work for this initial telecast seems awkward at times, one must

consider the special circumstances that affected the video image. For one thing, a televised concert was a novelty, and no standards for production existed. Then, too, all of the camera work during the broadcast was, in effect, improvisational. Aware of Toscanini's unpredictable temperament and his dislike of any intrusion during rehearsals, NBC opted to avoid preparing for the telecast by bringing cameras into studio 8H before the actual airing. Thus, key decisions about the production were reached on the spot. In the light of what must have often been guesswork, the results are surprisingly good.

3 Apr. 1948 (RCA 60332)

Beethoven: Symphony No. 9

In this concert, Toscanini's only performance of the Ninth Symphony to take place in studio 8H, NBC's camera work was more sophisticated. Two visual aspects of the program are noteworthy. One, which Harvey Sachs points out, is in the orchestral double fugue that follows the alla marcia in the finale. Here Toscanini, purely by exercising control with his beat and his glance, realigns an ensemble that has fallen into slight disarray. The other example is at the conclusion of the performance. As the audience bursts into applause, Toscanini, refusing to bow, turns to the orchestra and signals it to rise; he then retreats backstage to bring forth Robert Shaw, who prepared the chorus. Only when Shaw is there to share the applause with him does Toscanini acknowledge it.

13 Nov. 1948 (RCA 60334)

Brahms: Double Concerto
  Liebeslieder Waltzes
  Hungarian Dance No. 1

Of all the telecasts, this one is, at least in one respect, the most revealing. Possibly owing to the relative intimacy of conducting but a small chorus and two pianos in the *Liebeslieder Waltzes*, Toscanini displayed a range of facial expression that is astonishing both for its breadth and for its indication of an emotional involvement that he almost always concealed in front of a full orchestra. A deteriorated kinescope has caused the loss of a portion of the video in the Double Concerto.

4 Dec. 1948 (RCA 60336)

Mozart: Symphony No. 40
Dvořák: *Symphonic Variations*
Wagner: *Tannhäuser:* Overture (Dresden version)

Either inadequate lighting or underexposed film has affected the video quality of this release, so that things often look darker than they should. Nevertheless, many of the camera angles are well chosen to show Toscanini and the orchestra simultaneously, so that he is seen in an appropriate context. At one point near the end of the overture to *Tannhäuser* there is a briefly repeated segment of the cellists Frank Miller and Benar Heifetz glancing knowingly at each other. This repetition was necessitated by the deterioration of a small piece of film that could not be used in this restoration.

26 Mar. and 2 Apr. 1949 (RCA 60331)

Verdi: *Aida*

In some ways, *seeing* this unstaged production detracts from the performance, preventing any illusion of the theater one might conjure up solely from listening. One interesting extramusical feature revealed in this video is the sight of a member of the audience putting his hands over his ears; perhaps the strident *fortissimo* acoustics of studio 8H were painful.

3 Nov. 1951 (RCA 60337)

Weber: *Euryanthe*: Overture
Brahms: Symphony No. 1

For this, the first Toscanini telecast from Carnegie Hall, the camera work was often awkward. Aside from shooting at peculiar angles, it also focused pointlessly and excessively on the orchestra at the expense of Toscanini. But when on camera, his podium technique is fully revealed.

29 Dec. 1951 (RCA 60338)

Wagner: *Lohengrin*: Prelude
    Siegfried: Forest Murmurs
    Tristan und Isolde: Prelude and Liebestod
    Götterdämmerung: Siegfried's Death and Funeral Music
    Die Walküre: Ride of the Valkyries

Here is one of the more satisfying videos, not only because of the high level of the performances, but also because Toscanini can be seen to fine advantage. This should be required viewing for every student of conducting: the clarity of Toscanini's beat and the way in which he subdivides it, when necessary, are models of how a great conductor directs for the benefit of the orchestra and the music, not the audience.

15 Mar. 1952 (RCA 60335)

Franck: *Rédemption*: Symphonic Interlude
Sibelius: *En Saga*
Debussy: Nocturnes: *Nuages*; *Fêtes*
Rossini: *William Tell*: Overture

Of the four Carnegie Hall telecasts, this one features the poorest camera work: Toscanini is shown more often than not only from the shoulders up, making it impossible to see what he is doing with the baton.

22 Mar. 1952 (RCA 60339)

Beethoven: Symphony No. 5
Respighi: *The Pines of Rome*

In this video, RCA corrected an exposed ensemble flaw in the Beethoven but wisely avoided dubbing in a first-movement exposition repeat, which, for this performance, Toscanini did not observe. Seeing Toscanini in this telecast of the Fifth Symphony reveals how, in the finale, he was adversely affected by the heat generated from the lights required. Given his eighty-five years, it is all the more remarkable that he managed as well as he did. One visual detail should not be overlooked: for the brief cadenza in the first movement of the Beethoven, Toscanini does not beat time, giving the oboist free rein. Fledgling conductors should take note: soloists require no direction. In the main, the camera work for this telecast is far superior to that of the preceding week.

One other (non-RCA) Toscanini video deserves comment: the film Toscanini agreed to make for the Office of War Information in December 1943. Superbly restored by the Library of Congress on videocassette (LCMV-001), its historical and musical value is great. It has all the flaws one would expect from wartime propaganda. But it offers revealing pictures of a seemingly youthful seventy-six-year-old Toscanini conducting Verdi's overture to *La forza del destino* and *Hymn of the Nations*, in which Jan Peerce shines. The "Internationale," excised from later prints of the film because of the strongly anti-Communist sentiment prevalent in the United States at the time, has been restored.

It should be pointed out, too, that for anyone interested in the Toscanini videos, Harvey Sachs's essay "Watching Toscanini" is indispensable. (See Sachs, *Reflections on Toscanini*, 148 ff.) Its jargon-free lucidity and cogent insights are a welcome corrective to some of the nonsense written about Toscanini on television.

Appendix 8

DISCOGRAPHY

This discography covers all of Toscanini's officially released recordings: those made with the NBC Symphony and with other orchestras as well. It also cites the major unofficial compact disc releases of performances from NBC broadcasts. Owing to distinctive features of each of these categories, their content is summarized and specified in individual sections.

The RCA *Toscanini Collection*

This collection of eighty-two CDs, begun in 1990 and completed in 1992, marked the first time that all of Toscanini's RCA recordings gained simultaneous availability. It includes all his approved performances with the NBC Symphony (seventy-four discs), the acoustic (and sonically antediluvian) ones made in 1920–21 with the La Scala Orchestra (one disc), and the few from the 1930s and early 1940s with, respectively, the New York Philharmonic (three discs) and the Philadelphia Orchestra (four discs).

In the main, these CDs comprise the best representation Toscanini has ever received from RCA, not only because of the completeness of the collection but also as a result of its superior technical quality. Sonic distortion such as synthetic stereo, detail-blurring electronic reverberation, and extreme high-frequency emphasis, imposed on some of the conductor's recordings in earlier extended-play editions, has been avoided. In most instances RCA held to its promise that this collection would be based upon the earliest, most sonically reliable sources for each recording, without any imposition of "improvements" that might disfigure the sound Toscanini approved. Certainly many performances can be heard to better advantage in these CDs than in any previous incarnation. Particularly impressive are transfers of the New York Philharmonic recordings and some of the earlier NBC items, especially the 1941 Brahms First and the 1941 studio accounts of excerpts from Wagner's *Götterdämmerung*.

But despite its prevailing excellence, the collection is not quite as good as it should have been. All the Philadelphia Orchestra recordings, for example, were transferred from the poorly prepared tapes used for a 1976 LP edition. The Haydn Symphony No. 98, the 1946 Tchaikovsky "Pathétique" Symphony, and the 1947 Schubert Ninth Symphony are too noisy, and the last also suffers from insufficient presence. Then, too, a few transfers border on the amateurish, the most notable instances being the crackly noise in *The Beautiful Blue Danube*, and a bad edit in the 1953 *Egmont* Overture that causes an absurd rhythmic lurch that Toscanini never imposed. Nor is the 1939 *Egmont* Overture as good as it could have been: despite a claim to the contrary in the accompanying annotations, RCA used the inferior Victor in-concert recording of the performance instead of the sonically superior NBC acetate (which can be heard in two unofficial editions). And the Brahms *Academic Festival* Overture is as painfully shrill in this CD transfer as it was in an earlier LP edition.

In 1998 RCA embarked on a major remastering project for a number of items in the collection. These are included in the listings and may be distinguished from their earlier CD counterparts by their longer (ten-digit) catalog number. In the few instances where these remasterings prove superior to their earlier CD counterparts, the improvement is specified. Also specified are all of the relatively few non–NBC items in the collection. Where no orchestra is identified, the NBC Symphony is the ensemble. Note, too, that the 1926 New York Philharmonic items, having been recorded for Brunswick, make up the only examples among Toscanini's recordings made in the United States that were not originally done for RCA Victor.

Bach: Suite No. 3 in D Major for Orchestra, BWV 1068: Air
    8 Apr. 1946, Carnegie Hall: RCA 60308

Barber: *Adagio for Strings*
    19 Mar. 1942, Carnegie Hall: RCA 60307

Beethoven: Violin Concerto in D Major, with Jascha Heifetz
    11 Mar. 1940, studio 8H: RCA 60261

Beethoven: Piano Concerto No. 1, with Ania Dorfmann
    9 Aug. 1945, Carnegie Hall: RCA 60268

Beethoven: Piano Concerto No. 3, with Artur Rubinstein
    29 Oct. 1944, NBC broadcast, studio 8H: RCA 60261

Beethoven: Piano Concerto No. 4, with Rudolf Serkin
    26 Nov. 1944, NBC broadcast, studio 8H: RCA 60268

Beethoven: *Consecration of the House* Overture
    16 Dec. 1947, studio 8H: RCA 60267

Beethoven: *Coriolan* Overture
    1 June 1945, studio 8H: RCA 60267

Beethoven: *The Creatures of Prometheus*: Overture
    18 Dec. 1944, studio 8H: RCA 60267

Beethoven: *Egmont*: Overture
  18 Nov. 1939, NBC broadcast, studio 8H: RCA 60268
  19 January 1953, Carnegie Hall: RCA 602270 and 74321-55835
This new transfer corrects the faulty tape edit in the earlier edition.

Beethoven: *Fidelio*
  10 and 17 Dec. 1944, broadcasts, studio 8H (with substitution of
    Leonore's "Abscheulicher!" from recording session of 14 June 1945
    Carnegie Hall), RCA 60273
This substitution has also been issued separately as RCA 60280.

Beethoven: *Leonore* Overture No. 2
  25 Nov. 1939, NBC broadcast, studio 8H: RCA 60267

Beethoven: *Leonore* Overture No. 3
  4 Nov. 1939, broadcast, studio 8H: RCA 60255
  1 June 1945, studio 8H: RCA 60267
  17 Dec. 1944, studio 8H: included in complete *Fidelio*, RCA 60273

Beethoven: Missa Solemnis
  30 and 31 Mar., 2 Apr. 1953, Carnegie Hall: RCA 60272 and 74321-
    55837

Beethoven: String Quartet in F Major, Op. 135: second and third
    movements
  18 Mar. 1938, studio 8H: RCA 60267

Beethoven: Septet for Woodwinds, Horn, and Strings in E-flat Major
  26 Nov. 1951, Carnegie Hall: RCA 60270

Beethoven: Symphony No. 1
  21 Dec. 1951, Carnegie Hall: RCA 60252 and 74321-55835
  30 Mar. 1921, finale only, La Scala Orchestra, Camden, N.J., RCA
    60315

Beethoven: Symphony No. 2
  7 Nov. 1949 and 5 Oct. 1951, Carnegie Hall: RCA 60253 and 74321-
    55835

Beethoven: Symphony No. 3
  28 Oct. 1939, NBC broadcast, studio 8H: RCA 60269
  28 Nov. and 5 Dec. 1949, Carnegie Hall: RCA 60252
  6 Dec. 1953, NBC broadcast, Carnegie Hall: RCA 60271 and 74321-
    5583
The new transfer features greater presence and more natural string tone, but its
insert annotations erroneously identify the performance as that of 28 November
and 5 December 1949.

Beethoven: Symphony No. 4
  3 Feb. 1951, NBC broadcast, Carnegie Hall: RCA 60254 and 74321-
    55835

Beethoven: Symphony No. 5
>   27 Feb. and 1 and 29 Mar. 1939, studio 8H: RCA 60270
>   22 Mar. 1952, NBC broadcast, Carnegie Hall: RCA 60255 and 74321-55835

This new transfer, in its greater definition and presence, is vastly superior.
>   24 Dec. 1920, finale only, La Scala Orchestra, Camden, N.J.: RCA 60315

Beethoven: Symphony No. 6
>   12 Jan. 1952, NBC broadcast, and 14 Jan. 1952 (both Carnegie Hall): RCA 60255 and 74321-55836

Beethoven: Symphony No. 7
>   9 Nov. 1951 and NBC broadcast of 10 Nov. 1951: RCA 60253 and 74321-55836
>   9 and 10 Apr. 1936, New York Philharmonic, Carnegie Hall: RCA 60316

Beethoven: Symphony No. 8
>   17 Apr. 1939, studio 8H: RCA 60269
>   10 Nov. 1952, Carnegie Hall: RCA 60255 and 74321-55836

Beethoven: Symphony No. 9
>   31 Mar. and 1 Apr. 1952, Carnegie Hall: RCA 60256 and74321-55836

Berlioz: *The Damnation of Faust*: Rákóczy March
>   2 Sept. 1945, NBC broadcast, studio 8H: RCA 60322
>   24 Dec. 1920, La Scala Orchestra, Camden, N.J.: RCA 60315

Berlioz: *Harold in Italy*
>   28 Nov. 1953, rehearsal, and 29 Nov. 1953, NBC broadcast, Carnegie Hall: RCA 60275

Berlioz: *Roman Carnival* Overture
>   10 Jan. 1953, Carnegie Hall: RCA 60322 and 74321-66924

Berlioz: *Roméo et Juliette*
>   9 and 16 Feb. 1947, NBC broadcasts, studio 8H: RCA 60274

This substitutes the Queen Mab Scherzo from the NBC Carnegie Hall broadcast of 10 November 1951 for the 1947 performance. The 1951 performance is also on RCA 60322 and 74321-66924.
>   17 Feb. 1947, Carnegie Hall: Romeo Alone; Festivities at the Capulets; Love Scene: RCA 60274
>   9 Feb. 1942: Queen Mab Scherzo, Philadelphia Orchestra, Academy of Music: RCA 60314

Bizet: *L'Arlésienne*: Suite
>   19 Sept. 1943, NBC broadcast, studio 8H: RCA 60274
>   11 Mar. 1921, Farandole only, La Scala Orchestra, Camden, N.J.: RCA 60315

Bizet: *Carmen*: Suite (arr. Toscanini)
  5 Aug. 1952, Carnegie Hall: RCA 60274 and 74321-66924

Bizet: *Carmen*: Act IV, Aragonaise
  31 Mar. 1921, La Scala Orchestra, Camden, N.J.: RCA 60315

Boito: *Mefistofele*: Prologue
  14 Mar. 1954, NBC broadcast, Carnegie Hall: RCA 60276

Brahms: *Academic Festival* Overture
  6 Nov. 1948, NBC broadcast, studio 8H: RCA 60257

Brahms: Piano Concerto No. 2, with Vladimir Horowitz
  9 May 1941, Carnegie Hall: RCA 60319

Brahms: Double Concerto, with Mischa Mischakoff, violin, and Frank
    Miller, cello
  6 Nov. 1948, NBC broadcast, studio 8H: RCA 60259

Brahms: *Gesang der Parzen* for Chorus and Orchestra
  27 Nov. 1948, NBC broadcast, studio 8H: RCA 60260

Brahms: Hungarian Dances Nos. 1, 17, 20, and 21
  17 Feb. 1953, Carnegie Hall: RCA 60257 and 75321-59484

Brahms: *Liebeslieder Waltzes*
  13 Nov. 1948, NBC broadcast, studio 8H: RCA 60260

Brahms: Serenade No. 2
  27 Dec. 1942, NBC broadcast, studio 8H: RCA 60277

Brahms: Symphony No. 1
  10 Mar., 14 May, and 11 Dec. 1941, Carnegie Hall: RCA 60277
  6 Nov. 1951, Carnegie Hall: RCA 60257 and 74321-55838

Brahms: Symphony No. 2
  11 Feb. 1952, Carnegie Hall: RCA 60258 and 74321-55838

Brahms: Symphony No. 3
  4 Nov. 1952, Carnegie Hall: RCA 60259 and 74321-55838
The later transfer is superior.

Brahms: Symphony No. 4
  3 Dec. 1951, Carnegie Hall: RCA 60260 and 74321-55838

Brahms: *Variations on a Theme by Haydn*
  2 Feb. 1952, Carnegie Hall: RCA 60258 and 74321-59484
  10 Apr. 1936, New York Philharmonic, Carnegie Hall: RCA 60317

Catalani: *Loreley*: Dance of the Water Nymphs
  5 Aug. 1952, Carnegie Hall: RCA 60309 and 74321-72374

Catalani: *La Wally*: Prelude to Act IV
  5 Aug. 1952, Carnegie Hall: RCA 60309 and 74321-72374

Cherubini: *Ali Baba*: Overture
  3 Dec. 1949, NBC broadcast, studio 8H: RCA 60278

Cherubini: *Anacréon*: Overture
21 Mar. 1953, NBC broadcast, Carnegie Hall: RCA 60278
Cherubini: *Médéa*: Overture
18 Feb. 1950, NBC broadcast, studio 8H: RCA 60278
Cherubini: Requiem in C Minor
18 Feb. 1950, NBC broadcast, studio 8H: RCA 60272 and 74321-72373
Cherubini: Symphony in D Major
10 Mar. 1952, Carnegie Hall: RCA 60278 and 74321-59481
Cimarosa: *Il matrimonio per raggiro*: Overture
12 Nov. 1949, NBC broadcast, studio 8H: RCA 60278
Cimaroso: *Il matrimonia segreto*: Overture
14 Nov. 1943, NBC broadcast, studio 8H: RCA 60278
Debussy: "Ibéria"
2 June 1950, studio 8H: RCA 60265 and 74321-66924
18 Nov. 1941, Philadelphia Orchestra, Academy of Music, RCA 60311
Debussy: *La mer*
1 June 1950, studio 8H: RCA 60265 and 74321-66924
8 and 9 Feb. 1942, Philadelphia Orchestra, Academy of Music, RCA 60311
Debussy: Nocturnes: *Fêtes*; *Nuages*
27 Mar. 1948, NBC broadcast, studio 8H; 15 Mar. 1952, NBC broadcast, Carnegie Hall: RCA 60265; *Nuages* only, 74321-66924
Debussy: *Prelude to the Afternoon of a Faun*
13 Feb. 1953 rehearsal and 14 Feb. 1953 NBC broadcast, Carnegie Hall: RCA 60265 and 74321-66924
Donizetti: *Don Pasquale*: Overture
5 Oct. 1951, Carnegie Hall: RCA 60309 and 74321-72374
29 and 30 Mar. 1921, La Scala Orchestra, Camden, N.J.: RCA 60315
Dukas: *The Sorcerer's Apprentice*
19 Mar. 1950, Carnegie Hall: RCA 60322 and 74321-66924
18 Mar. 1929, New York Philharmonic, Carnegie Hall: RCA 60317
Dvořák: Symphony No. 9
2 Feb. 1953, Carnegie Hall: RCA 60279 and 74321-59481
The later transfer is superior.
Elgar: *Enigma Variations*
10 Dec. 1951, Carnegie Hall: RCA 60287
Franck: *Psyché*: Psyché and Eros
7 Jan. 1952, Carnegie Hall: RCA 60322 and 74321-66924
Franck: Symphony in D Minor
14 Dec. 1940 and 24 Mar. 1946, NBC broadcasts, studio 8H: RCA 60320

Gershwin: *An American in Paris*
    18 May 1945, studio 8H: RCA 60307

Glinka: *Jota aragonesa*
    4 Mar. 1950, NBC broadcast, studio 8H: RCA 60308

Glinka: *Kamarinskaya*
    21 Dec. 1940, NBC broadcast, studio 8H: RCA 60323

Gluck: *Iphigenia in Aulis*: Overture
    22 Nov. 1952, NBC broadcast, Carnegie Hall: RCA 60280

Gluck: *Orfeo ed Euridice*: Act II
    22 Nov. 1952, NBC broadcast, Carnegie Hall: RCA 60280

Gluck: *Orfeo ed Euridice*: Dance of the Blessed Spirits
    4 Nov. 1946, studio 3A, RCA 60280
    5 Apr. 1929, New York Philharmonic, Carnegie Hall: RCA 60318

Grofé: *Grand Canyon Suite*
    11 Sept. 1945, Carnegie Hall: RCA 60307

Haydn: *Sinfonia concertante*, Op. 84
    6 Mar. 1948, NBC broadcast, studio 8H: RCA 60282

Haydn: Symphony No. 88
    8 Mar. 1938, studio 8H: RCA 60281

Haydn: Symphony No. 94
    26 Jan. 1952, Carnegie Hall: RCA 60281 and 74321-59481

Haydn: Symphony No. 98
    25 May 1945, studio 8H: RCA 60281

Haydn: Symphony No. 99
    12 Mar. 1949, NBC broadcast, studio 8H: RCA 60282

Haydn: Symphony No. 101
    6 Nov. 1946 and 12 June 1947, studio 8H: RCA 60282
    29 and 30 Mar. 1929, New York Philharmonic, Carnegie Hall: RCA
        60316

Hérold: *Zampa*: Overture
    5 Aug. 1952, Carnegie Hall: RCA 60310

Humperdinck: *Hansel and Gretel*: Prelude
    5 Aug. 1952, Carnegie Hall: RCA 60310

Kabalevsky: *Colas Breugnon*: Overture
    8 Apr. 1946, Carnegie Hall: RCA 60310

Kodály: *Háry János*: Suite
    29 Nov. 1947, NBC broadcast, studio 8H: RCA 60279

Liadov: *Kikimora*
    29 July 1952, Carnegie Hall: RCA 60323

Massenet: *Scènes pittoresques*: "Fête bohème"
    31 Mar. 1921, La Scala Orchestra, Camden, N.J., RCA 60315

Mendelssohn: *A Midsummer Night's Dream*: Overture, Intermezzo, Nocturne, Scherzo, Wedding March, and Finale
4 Nov. 1947, Carnegie Hall: RCA 60283

Mendelssohn: *A Midsummer Night's Dream*: Overture, Intermezzo, Nocturne, "You Spotted Snakes," Wedding March, Scherzo, Melodrama, and Finale
11 and 12 Jan. 1942, Philadelphia Orchestra, Academy of Music, RCA 60314

Mendelssohn: *A Midsummer Night's Dream*: Nocturne
4 Feb. 1926, New York Philharmonic, Carnegie Hall: RCA 60317

Mendelssohn: *A Midsummer Night's Dream*: Scherzo only
6 Nov. 1946, studio 3A, RCA 60284; 4 Feb. 1926, New York Philharmonic, Carnegie Hall: RCA 60317; 30 Mar. 1929, New York Philharmonic, Carnegie Hall: RCA 60316; 9 Mar. 1921, La Scala Orchestra, Camden, N.J., RCA 60315

Mendelssohn: *A Midsummer Night's Dream*: Wedding March
11 Mar. 1921, La Scala Orchestra, Camden, N.J., RCA 60315

Mendelssohn: String Octet in E-flat Major
30 Mar. 1947, NBC broadcast, studio 8H: RCA 60283

Mendelssohn: String Octet in E-flat Major: Scherzo, arr. Mendelssohn
1 June 1945, studio 8H: RCA 60284

Mendelssohn: Symphony No. 4
26 and 27 Feb. 1954, rehearsals, and 28 Feb. 1954, NBC broadcast, Carnegie Hall: RCA 60284 and 74321-59480

Mendelssohn: Symphony No. 5
13 Dec. 1953, NBC broadcast, Carnegie Hall: RCA 60284 and 74321-59480

Mozart, L.: *Toy* Symphony
15 Feb. 1941, NBC broadcast, studio 8H: RCA 60308

Mozart, W. A.: Bassoon Concerto, K. 191, with Leonard Sharrow
18 Nov. 1947, studio 8H: RCA 60286

Mozart, W. A.: Divertimento, K. 287
18 Nov. 1947, studio 8H: RCA 60286

Mozart, W. A.: *Don Giovanni*: Overture
27 Jan. 1946, NBC broadcast, studio 8H: RCA 60309

Mozart, W. A.: *The Magic Flute*: Overture
26 Nov. 1949, NBC broadcast, studio 8H: RCA 60310

Mozart, W. A.: *The Marriage of Figaro*: Overture
8 Nov. 1947, NBC broadcast, studio 8H: RCA 60286

Mozart, W. A.: Symphony No. 35
4 Nov. 1946, studio 3A, RCA 60286

30 Mar. and 4 and 5 Apr. 1929, New York Philharmonic, Carnegie
Hall: RCA 60317

Mozart, W. A.: Symphony No. 39
6 Mar. 1948, NBC broadcast, studio 8H: RCA 60285
18 and 21 Dec. 1920, third and fourth movements, La Scala Orchestra,
Camden, New Jersey RCA 60315

Mozart, W. A.: Symphony No. 40
7 Mar. 1938 and 27 Feb. 1939, studio 8H: RCA 60285
12 Mar. 1950, studio 8H: RCA 60271 and 74321-59481

Mozart, W. A.: Symphony No. 41
22 June 1945 and 11 Mar. 1946, Carnegie Hall: RCA 60285

Mussorgsky: *Pictures at an Exhibition* (orch. Ravel)
26 Jan. 1953 Carnegie Hall: RCA 60287 and 74321-59484

Paganini: *Moto perpetuo*
17 Apr. 1939, studio 8H: RCA 60308

Pizzetti: *La Pisanelle*: Suite: Prelude to Act I
21 Dec. 1920, La Scala Orchestra, Camden, N.J., RCA 60315

Ponchielli: *La Gioconda*: Dance of the Hours
29 July 1952, Carnegie Hall: RCA 60308 and 74321-72374

Prokofiev: Symphony No. 1, "Classical"
11 Oct. 1951, Carnegie Hall: RCA 60323

Puccini: *La bohème*
3 and 10 Feb. 1946, NBC broadcasts, studio 8H: RCA 60288

Puccini: *Manon Lescaut*: Act III: Intermezzo
2 July 1944, NBC broadcast, studio 8H: RCA 60309

Ravel: *Daphnis et Chloé*: Suite No. 2
21 Nov. 1949, Carnegie Hall: RCA 60322 and 74321-66924

Respighi: *The Fountains of Rome*
17 Dec. 1951, Carnegie Hall: RCA 60262 and 74321-72374

Respighi: *The Pines of Rome*
17 Mar. 1953, Carnegie Hall: RCA 60262 and 74321-72374

Respighi: *Roman Festivals*
12 Dec. 1949, Carnegie Hall: RCA 60262 and 74321-72374
19 Nov. 1941, Philadelphia Orchestra, Academy of Music, RCA 60311

Respighi (after Galilei): *Ancient Airs and Dances*: Suite No. 1
18 Dec. 1920, La Scala Orchestra, Camden, N.J., RCA 60315

Rossini: *The Barber of Seville*: Overture
28 Jan. 1945, Carnegie Hall: RCA 60289
21 Nov. 1929, New York Philharmonic, Carnegie Hall: RCA 60318

Rossini: *La Cenerentola*: Overture
28 June 1945 Carnegie Hall: RCA 60289

Rossini: *La gazza ladra*: Overture
   28 June 1945, Carnegie Hall: RCA 60289
Rossini: *L'Italiana in Algeri*: Overture
   14 Apr. 1950, Carnegie Hall: RCA 60289 and 74321-72374
   10 Apr. 1936, New York Philharmonic, Carnegie Hall: RCA 60318
Rossini: *Semiramide*: Overture
   28 Sept. 1951, Carnegie Hall: RCA 60289 and 74321-72374
   10 Apr. 1936, New York Philharmonic, Carnegie Hall: RCA 60318
Rossini: *The Siege of Corinth*: Overture
   14 June 1945, Carnegie Hall: RCA 60289
Rossini: *Il Signor Bruschino*: Overture
   8 June 1945, Carnegie Hall: RCA 60289
Rossini: *William Tell*: Overture
   1 and 29 Mar. 1939, studio 8H: RCA 60310
   19 Jan. 1953, Carnegie Hall: RCA 60289 and 74321-72374
Rossini: *William Tell*: Passo a sei
   8 June 1945, Carnegie Hall: RCA 60309
Saint-Saëns: *Danse macabre*
   1 June 1950, studio 8H: RCA 60322 and 74321-66924
Saint-Saëns: Symphony No. 3
   14 Nov. 1952, rehearsal, and 15 Nov. 1952, NBC broadcast, Carnegie
      Hall: RCA 60320
Schubert: Symphony No. 5
   17 Mar. 1953, Carnegie Hall: RCA 60291 and 74321-59480
Schubert: Symphony No. 8
   12 Mar. and 2 June 1950, studio 8H: RCA 60290 and 74321-59480
Schubert: Symphony No. 9
   25 Feb. 1947, Carnegie Hall: RCA 60291
   9 Feb. 1953, Carnegie Hall: RCA 60290 and 74321-59480
The later transfer of the 1953 recording is markedly superior.
   16 Nov. 1941, Philadelphia Orchestra, Academy of Music, RCA 60313
Schumann: *Manfred*: Overture
   11 Nov. 1946, Carnegie Hall: RCA 60292
Schumann: Symphony No. 3
   12 Nov. 1949, NBC broadcast, studio 8H: RCA 60292 and 74321-
      59481
The later transfer is superior.
Shostakovich: Symphony No. 1
   12 Mar. 1944, NBC broadcast, studio 8H: RCA 60323
Shostakovich: Symphony No. 7
   19 July 1942, NBC broadcast, studio 8H: RCA 60293

Sibelius: *Finlandia*
  5 Aug. 1952, Carnegie Hall: RCA 60294 and 74321-59584

Sibelius: *Pojhola's Daughter*
  7 Dec. 1940, NBC broadcast, studio 8H: RCA 60294

Sibelius: "The Swan of Tuonela"
  27 Aug. 1944, NBC broadcast, studio 8H: RCA 60294

Sibelius: Symphony No. 2
  7 Dec. 1940, NBC broadcast, studio 8H: RCA 60294

Smetana: *The Bartered Bride*: Overture
  17 Nov. 1946, NBC broadcast, studio 8H: RCA 60310

Smetana: *The Moldau*
  19 Mar. 1950, studio 8H: RCA 60279 and 74321-59484

Smith (attrib.): "The Star-Spangled Banner"
  19 Mar. 1942, Carnegie Hall: RCA 60307

Sousa: "El Capitan"
  18 May 1945, studio 8H: RCA 60307

Sousa: "The Stars and Stripes Forever"
  18 May 1945, studio 8H: RCA 60307

Strauss, J.: *On the Beautiful Blue Danube*
  11 Dec. 1941 and 19 Mar. 1942, Carnegie Hall: RCA 60308

Strauss, J.: *Tritsch-Tratsch Polka*
  6 May 1941, Carnegie Hall: RCA 60308

Strauss, R.: *Death and Transfiguration*
  10 Mar. 1952, with portions of NBC broadcast of 8 Mar. 1952,
    Carnegie Hall: RCA 60295 and 74321-559484
  11 Jan. 1942, Philadelphia Orchestra, Academy of Music, RCA 60312

Strauss, R.: *Don Juan*
  10 Jan. 1951, Carnegie Hall: RCA 60296

Strauss, R.: *Don Quixote*
  22 Nov. 1953, NBC broadcast, with portions from rehearsal of 21 Nov.
    1953, Carnegie Hall: RCA 60295

Strauss, R.: *Salome*: Dance of the Seven Veils
  14 Jan. 1939, NBC broadcast, studio 8H: RCA 60296

Strauss, R.: *Till Eulenspiegel's Merry Pranks*
  4 Nov. 1952, Carnegie Hall: RCA 60296 and 74321-59484

Stravinsky: *Petrushka*: Tableaux 1 and 4
  21 Dec. 1940, NBC broadcast, studio 8H: RCA 60323

Suppé: *Poet and Peasant*: Overture
  18 July 1943, NBC broadcast, studio 8H: RCA 60308

Tchaikovsky: Piano Concerto No. 1, with Vladimir Horowitz
  6 and 14 May 1941, Carnegie Hall: RCA 60319
  25 Apr. 1943, NBC broadcast, Carnegie Hall: RCA 60321
Tchaikovsky: *Manfred* Symphony
  5 Dec. 1949, Carnegie Hall: RCA 60298
Tchaikovsky: *The Nutcracker Suite*
  19 Nov. 1951, Carnegie Hall: RCA 60297 and 74321-59484
Tchaikovsky: Symphony No. 6
  24 Nov. 1947, Carnegie Hall: RCA 60297
  8 Feb. 1942, Philadelphia Orchestra, Academy of Music, RCA 60312
Thomas: *Mignon*: Overture
  19 Mar. 1942, Carnegie Hall: RCA 60310
  29 July 1952, Carnegie Hall: RCA 60322 and 74321-66924
Verdi: *Aida*
  26 Mar. and 2 Apr. 1949, NBC broadcasts, studio 8H: RCA 60300
Verdi: *Un ballo in maschera*
  17 and 24 Jan. 1954, NBC broadcasts, Carnegie Hall: RCA 60301
Verdi: *Falstaff*
  1 and 8 Apr. 1950, NBC broadcasts, studio 8H: RCA 60251 and
    74321-723722
The newer transfer has greater presence and impact.
Verdi: *La forza del destino*: Overture
  28 June 1945, Carnegie Hall: RCA 60310
  10 Nov. 1952, Carnegie Hall: RCA 60309 and 74321-72374
Verdi: *Hymn of the Nations*
  8 and 20 Dec. 1943, studio 8H: RCA 60299
Verdi: *I Lombardi*: Act III: Trio
  31 Jan. 1943, NBC broadcast, studio 8H: RCA 60276
Verdi: *Luisa Miller*: Overture
  25 July 1943, NBC broadcast, studio 8H: RCA 60309
Verdi: *Luisa Miller*: "Quando le sere"
  25 July 1943, NBC broadcast, studio 8H: RCA 60299
Verdi: *Nabucco*: "Va, pensiero"
  31 Jan. 1943, NBC broadcast, studio 8H: RCA 60299
Verdi: *Otello*
  6 and 13 Dec. 1947, NBC broadcasts, studio 8H: RCA 60302
Verdi: *Otello*: Act III: Dances
  13 Mar. 1948, NBC broadcast, studio 8H: RCA 60309
Verdi: Requiem
  27 Jan. 1951, NBC broadcast, Carnegie Hall, with many patches of
    various rehearsals: RCA 60299 and 74321-72373

Verdi: *Rigoletto*: Act III (labeled Act IV by RCA, following a now-
discredited practice)
25 May 1944, NBC broadcast, Madison Square Garden: RCA 60276

Verdi: Te Deum
14 Mar. 1954, NBC broadcast, Carnegie Hall: RCA 60299 and 74321-
72373

Verdi: *La traviata*
1 and 8 Dec. 1946, NBC broadcasts, studio 8H: RCA 60303

Verdi: *La traviata*: Prelude to Act I
10 Mar. 1941, Carnegie Hall: RCA 60309
18 Mar. 1929, New York Philharmonic, Carnegie Hall: RCA 60318

Verdi: *La traviata*: Prelude to Act III
10 Mar. 1941, Carnegie Hall: RCA 60309
29 Mar. 1929, New York Philharmonic, RCA 60318

Verdi: *I vespri siciliani*: Overture
24 Jan. 1942, NBC broadcast, studio 8H: RCA 60309

Wagner: *A Faust Overture*
11 Nov. 1946, Carnegie Hall: RCA 60305

Wagner: *Die Meistersinger von Nürnberg*: Prelude to Act I
11 Mar. 1946, Carnegie Hall: RCA 60305

Wagner: *Die Meistersinger von Nürnberg*: Prelude to Act III
26 Nov. 1951 Carnegie Hall: RCA 60305 and 74321-59482

Wagner: *Die Walküre*: Act I, Scene 3
22 Feb. 1941, NBC broadcast, Carnegie Hall: RCA 60264

Wagner: *Die Walküre*: Ride of the Valkyries
11 Mar. 1946, Carnegie Hall: RCA 60306
3 Jan. 1952, Carnegie Hall: RCA 60264 and 74321-59482

Wagner: *Götterdämmerung*: Dawn and Siegfried's Rhine Journey (arr.
Toscanini)
17 Mar. and 14 May, 1941, Carnegie Hall: RCA 60296
22 Dec. 1949, Carnegie Hall: RCA 60306
8 Feb. 1936, New York Philharmonic, Carnegie Hall: RCA 60318

Wagner: *Götterdämmerung*: Dawn, Siegfried-Brünhilde duet, and Siegfried's
Rhine Journey
22 Feb. 1941, NBC broadcast, Carnegie Hall: RCA 60304

Wagner: *Götterdämmerung*: Siegfried's Death and Funeral Music
14 May 1941, Carnegie Hall: RCA 60304
3 Jan. 1952, Carnegie Hall: RCA 60306 and 74321-59482

Wagner: *Götterdämmerung*: Brünhilde's Immolation
24 Feb. 1941, Carnegie Hall: RCA 60304

Wagner: *Lohengrin*: Prelude to Act I
    17 Mar. and 6 May 1941, Carnegie Hall: RCA 60306
    22 October 1951, Carnegie Hall: RCA 60305
    9 Apr. 1936, New York Philharmonic, Carnegie Hall: RCA 60318

Wagner: *Lohengrin*: Prelude to Act III
    22 Oct. 1951, Carnegie Hall: RCA 60305
    9 Apr. 1936, New York Philharmonic, Carnegie Hall: RCA 60318

Wagner: *Parsifal*: Prelude to Act I
    22 Dec. 1949, Carnegie Hall: RCA 60305

Wagner: *Parsifal*: Good Friday Spell
    22 Dec. 1949, Carnegie Hall: RCA 60305

Wagner: *Siegfried*: Forest Murmurs
    29 Oct. 1951, Carnegie Hall: RCA 60305

Wagner: *Siegfried Idyll*
    11 Mar. 1946, Carnegie Hall: RCA 60296
    29 July 1952, Carnegie Hall: RCA 60264
    8 Feb. 1936, New York Philharmonic, Carnegie Hall: RCA 60317

Wagner: *Tannhäuser*: Overture and Bacchanale
    8 Nov. 1952, NBC broadcast, Carnegie Hall: RCA 60306

Wagner: *Tristan und Isolde*: Prelude and Liebestod
    7 Jan. 1952, Carnegie Hall: RCA 60264 and 74321-59482

Wagner: *Tristan und Isolde*: Liebestod
    19 Mar. 1942, Carnegie Hall: RCA 60306

Waldteufel: *The Skaters Waltz*
    28 June 1945, Carnegie Hall: RCA 60308

Weber: *Der Freischütz*: Overture
    25 May 1945, studio 8H: RCA 60310
    3 Jan. 1952, Carnegie Hall: RCA 60292

Weber: *Euryanthe*: Overture
    29 Oct. 1951, Carnegie Hall: RCA 60292
    Weber: *Invitation to the Dance* (orch. Berlioz)
    28 Sept. 1951,Carnegie Hall: RCA 60308

Weber: *Oberon*: Overture
    5 Aug. 1952, Carnegie Hall: RCA 60292

Wolf-Ferrari: *The Secret of Suzanne*: Overture
    10 Mar. 1921, La Scala Orchestra, Camden, N.J., RCA 60315

Officially Authorized Non-NBC or -RCA Releases

These fall into two groups. The first comprises studio recordings Toscanini made with the BBC Symphony between 1937 and 1939 that he approved for release. Together with the items in RCA's *Toscanini Collection*, they encompass all of the studio recordings he sanctioned for issue. The second consists of concert performances with the BBC Symphony and Philharmonia Orchestra of London that were sanctioned for release (without his approval) by the Toscanini estate after the conductor's death.

The BBC Studio Recordings

Beethoven: *Leonore* Overture No. 1, Queen's Hall, 1 June 1939
    Symphony No. 1, Queen's Hall, 25 Oct. 1937
    Symphony No. 4, Queen's Hall, 1 June 1939
    Symphony No. 6, Queen's Hall, 21 and 22 Oct. 1937

Brahms: *Tragic* Overture, Queen's Hall, 19 Oct. 1937

Mozart: *The Magic Flute:* Overture, Queen's Hall, 6 June 1938

Rossini: *La scala di seta*: Overture, Queen's Hall, 6 June 1938

Weber (orch. Berlioz): *Invitation to the Dance*, Queen's Hall 6 June 1938

Originally issued on 78 rpm discs, these recordings have had a number of extended-play releases. The finest LP edition (EMI Seraphim IC 6156) included a previously unreleased (rejected for issue by Toscanini) BBC Symphony studio recording made on 6 June 1939 in Queen's Hall of the overture to Beethoven's *Creatures of Prometheus* and a newly released Queen's Hall concert performance from 14 June 1935 with the BBC Symphony of the Beethoven Seventh. Neither of these nonapproved items has been issued on compact disc. As of May 2000, only the Brahms *Tragic* Overture among the approved BBC studio recordings has been officially released in that format (EMI 69783). The only CD edition of the others is an unauthorized two-disc Biddulph set (WHO 008–009) with adequate transfers, which are sonically inferior to those of the 1986 EMI LPs.

The BBC Concert Recordings

Beginning in 1987, EMI, Testament, and BBC Music released—with the authorization of the Toscanini estate—a number of concert performances that the conductor gave in London between 1935 and 1952. Like those cited above, they serve as revealing glosses on his work at NBC and are thus relevant to it. For one thing, they offer further evidence that his view of scores central to his repertory was never fixed. Moreover, as with his New York Philharmonic and Philadelphia Orchestra recordings, they provide the opportunity to hear him with ensembles that, in varying ways, were weightier and tonally more suave than the NBC Symphony. As the following list suggests, all of the Brahms performances with the Philharmonia Orchestra are from the cycle of the composer's works that Toscanini led in 1952. Although that cycle has been issued on CD in unauthorized editions, the three-disc Testament set is the finest sonically.

Beethoven: Missa Solemnis
  BBC Symphony, with Zinka Milanov, Kerstin Thorborg, Koloman von
    Pataky, and Nicola Moscona. Queen's Hall, 28 May 1939: BBC
    Music 4016-2
Beethoven: Symphony No. 7
  BBC Symphony, Queen's Hall, 12 June 1935: BBC Music 4016-2.
This performance took place two days earlier than the one of the Seventh Sym-
phony released in 1986 on LP by EMI.
Brahms: Symphony No. 1
  Philharmonia Orchestra, Royal Festival Hall, 29 Sept. 1952: Testament
    SB 3167
Brahms: Symphony No. 2
  BBC Symphony, Queen's Hall, 10 June 1938: Testament SBT 1015
  Philharmonia Orchestra, Royal Festival Hall, 29 Sept. 1952: Testament
    SB 3167
Brahms: Symphony No. 3
  Philharmonia Orchestra, Royal Festival Hall, 2 Oct. 1952: Testament
    SBT 3167
Brahms: Symphony No. 4
  BBC Symphony, Queen's Hall, 3 and 5 June 1935: EMI 69783.
  Philharmonia Orchestra, Royal Festival Hall, 2 Oct. 1952: Testament
    SBT 3167
Brahms: Tragic Overture
  Philharmonia Orchestra, Royal Festival Hall, 29 Sept. 1952: Testament
    SBT 3167
Brahms: *Variations on a Theme by Haydn*
  Philharmonia Orchestra, Royal Festival Hall, 2 Oct. 1952: Testament
    SBT 3167
Cherubini: *Anacréon*: Overture
  BBC Symphony, Queen's Hall, 3 June 1935: BBC Music 4016-2
Debussy: *La mer*
  BBC Symphony. Queen's Hall, 12 June 1935: EMI (two editions)
    60344, 69784
Elgar: *Enigma Variations*
  BBC Symphony, Queen's Hall, 5 June 1935: EMI 69784
Mendelssohn: *A Midsummer Night's Dream*: Nocturne; Scherzo
  BBC Symphony, Queen's Hall, 14 June 1935: Testament SBT 1015
Mozart, W. A.: Symphony No. 35
  BBC Symphony, Queen's Hall, 14 June 1935: BBC Music 4016-2.
Rossini: *Semiramide*: Overture
  BBC Symphony, Queen's Hall, 12 June 1935: Testament SBT 1015

Sibelius: Symphony No. 2
    BBC Symphony, Queen's Hall, 10 June 1938: EMI 63307

Wagner: *A Faust Overture*
    BBC Symphony, Queen's Hall, 12 June 1935: EMI 63044

Wagner: *Götterdammerung*: Siegfried's Death and Funeral Music
    BBC Symphony, Queen's Hall, 5 June 19835: EMI 63044

Wagner: *Parsifal*: Prelude and Good Friday Spell
    BBC Symphony, Queen's Hall, 5 June 1935: EMI 63044

The initial transfer of this release omitted three and a half minutes of the performance, an error corrected in a subsequent transfer issued with the same catalog number.

Unreleased NBC Symphony Recordings Rejected by Toscanini

Beethoven: Symphony No. 2: 18 Dec. 1944
    Symphony No. 7: 27 Oct. 1947
    Leonore Overture No. 3: 19 Dec. 1944

Berlioz: *The Damnation of Faust*: Rákóczy March: 14 May 1941
    Roméo et Juliette: Queen Mab Scherzo: 12 May 1947

Debussy: *La mer*: 9 Mar. 1944, 2 Dec. 1947
    Prelude to the Afternoon of a Faun: 17 Feb. 1953

Mendelssohn: *A Midsummer Night's Dream*: "You Spotted Snakes": 4 Nov. 1947

Wagner: *Tristan und Isolde*: Prelude: 19 Mar. 1942, 12 May 1947.

The 1942 recording has been unofficially released in a two-CD Pearl set (GEMS 2044).

The Unofficial Recordings

The first major batch of previously unpublished Toscanini material (mostly NBC broadcasts) was issued by the Texas-based Toscanini Society in 1969. Founded ostensibly as a nonprofit organization, it promised the release of nearly 100 LPs, a little more than half of which materialized. Sold only through the mail and variable in quality, these discs disappeared from the market when the Toscanini Society was threatened with a lawsuit for copyright infringement and forced out of business. Virtually all of the significant NBC Symphony items in the society's catalog subsequently appeared on CD in sonically superior sources. But of lasting value are the five issues of the society's magazine, *The Maestro*, many of them featuring valuable critical or bibliographic articles with information not easily gleaned elsewhere.

Shortly before the advent of CDs in 1982, another Toscanini Society was formed in England. Its small number of releases (all NBC broadcasts) were at best amateurish: labels of individual LPs were blank, every disc was mispitched (usually a half tone or more flat), and nearly all came from sonically poor sources.

Two factors have contributed to the spate of unofficial Toscanini releases that began in the last decade of the twentieth century: the advent of the compact disc and the expiration in Europe of the copyright on NBC broadcasts. Digital technology has enabled rapid and inexpensive production of CDs, and the "public domain" status of the broadcasts has permitted small independent entrepreneurs, some of them based in the United States, to jump into the market. Sometimes they evade copyright restrictions by claiming a release derives from "sources discovered" overseas. So long as the ouput of such companies remains small and the distribution of their releases remains relatively limited, they feel (with justification) secure from legal action.

However, when a company undertakes a major Toscanini project that encompasses many CDs of NBC broadcasts distributed to a worldwide mass market (as in the case of Naxos records), copyright restrictions have been invoked to prevent the sale of those releases in the United States. This is unfortunate. To be sure, not all aspects of the Naxos project are praiseworthy: its annotations are skimpy and superficial, a few of its releases are mispitched or inaccurately documented, and some give a false impression of a broadcast by deleting huge chunks of an announcer's commentary in a fashion that creates a new continuity and thus a skewed sense of what was actually aired.

Nonetheless, the Naxos project is the finest unofficial series of Toscanini's NBC broadcasts to have ever appeared. Most of its releases come from sonically superior sources (often clean copies of NBC reference discs). It also offers a few instances of multitiple broadcasts of a given work, thus providing valuable documentation of Toscanini's changing views. And despite restrictions on sale of the releases in the United States, they can be ordered by mail from large stores (such as Tower Records) in England and Canada.

The listing that follows is limited to unofficial releases of NBC Symphony broadcasts and, in the main, to companies whose CDs are sold either in major record stores or through mail order from the issuing company itself. Excluded are very small independent labels that have had restricted distribution and, in many cases, ceased operation. Usually the material they offered can be heard to better advantage in other editions. In the few instances where such releases encompass otherwise unissued performances, they are cited with a caveat about their distribution. Note, however, that even the most widely distributed of these unofficial releases are less readily obtainable than official ones. An asterisk (*) indicates a cited disc contains a complete concert; two asterisks (**) denote that it also includes all broadcast announcements.

Atterberg: Symphony No. 6
    21 Nov. 1943, studio 8H: dell'Arte 9019

Bach: Brandenburg Concerto No. 2
    29 Oct. 1938, studio 8H: Naxos 8.110825*

Bach: Suite No. 3 in D Major for Orchestra, BWV 1068
    22 Nov. 1947, studio 8H: Naxos 8.110835**

Beethoven: Choral Fantasy, with Ania Dorfmann, piano, and the
        Westminster Choir
    2 Dec. 1939, Carnegie Hall: Naxos 8.110824*; Relief CR: 1893*;
        Music and Arts 259
The Naxos disc is technically deficient and will not track, even on the finest
equipment.

Beethoven: Concerto No. 1 for Piano and Orchestra, with Ania Dorfmann
    12 Nov. 1944, studio 8H: Naxos 8.110826*

Beethoven: Concerto No. 3 for Piano and Orchestra, with Myra Hess
    24 Dec. 1946, studio 8H: Naxos 8.110804*

Beethoven: *Consecration of the House* Overture
    16 Mar. 1947, studio 8H: Music and Arts CD 264

Beethoven: *Coriolan* Overture
    11 Nov. 1939, studio 8H: Naxos 8.110823*
    24 Dec. 1946, studio 8H: Naxos 8.110804*
    6 Dec. 1953, Carnegie Hall: Music and Arts ATRA 3007

Beethoven: *The Creatures of Prometheus*: Adagio and Allegretto
    25 Nov. 1939, studio 8H: Naxos 8.110813*

Beethoven: *Egmont*: Overture
    18 Nov. 1939, studio 8H: Naxos 8.110814*; Relief CR 1885*
Both editions derive from sources superior to the one used by RCA in its *Toscanini Collection*.
    12 Nov. 1944, studio 8H: Naxos 8.11026*

Beethoven: *Fidelio*: Overture
    28 Oct. 1939, studio 8H: Naxos 110802-3**; Relief CR 1861

Beethoven: *Leonore* Overture No. 1
    25 Nov. 1939, studio 8H: Naxos 8.110813*; Relief CR 1891
The Naxos source is superior.

Beethoven: *Leonore* Overture No.2
    25 Nov. 1939, studio 8H: Naxos 8.110813*; Relief CR 1891

Beethoven: *Leonore* Overture No. 3
    4 Nov. 1939, studio 8H: Naxos 8.110815-16**
This transfer is superior to the one in RCA's *Toscanini Collection*.

Beethoven: Missa Solemnis, with Zinka Milanov, Bruna Castagna, Jussi
    Björling, Alexander Kipnis, and the Westminster Choir
    28 Dec. 1940, Carnegie Hall: Music and Arts 259*
Beethoven: String Quartet in F Major, Op. 135: Lento and Vivace
    1 Jan. 1938, studio 8H: Music and Arts 264
    25 Nov. 1939, studio 8H: Naxos 8.110813*
    12 Nov. 1944, studio 8H: Naxos 8.110826*
Beethoven: Septet for Woodwinds, Horn, and Strings in E-flat Major
    18 Nov. 1939, studio 8H: Naxos 8.1100814*; Relief CR 1885
Beethoven: Symphony No. 1
    28 Oct. 1939, studio 8H: Naxos 8.110802-3**; Relief CR 1861
Beethoven: Symphony No. 2
    4 Nov. 1939, studio 8H: Naxos 8.110815-16**; Relief CR 1861
Beethoven: Symphony No. 3, "Eroica"
    3 Dec. 1938, studio 8H: Music and Arts 264
    28 Oct. 1939, studio 8H: Music and Arts ATRA 684; Naxos 8.110802-
    3**; Relief CR 1891.
This performance is included in RCA's *Toscanini Collection*, where the sound is
superior to that of the Music and Arts and Relief CDs; but the Naxos transfer
offers the most musical ambience of all.
    1 Sept. 1945, studio 8H: Music and Arts 264
Beethoven: Symphony No, 4
    4 Nov. 1939, studio 8H: Naxos 8.110815-16**; Relief CR 1861
Beethoven Symphony No. 5
    11 Nov. 1939, studio 8H: Naxos 8.110823*; Relief CR 1871
    8 May 1945, studio 8H: Music and Arts 753
Beethoven: Symphony No. 6, "Pastoral"
    8 Jan. 1938, studio 8H: Dante Lys 401 (limited distribution)
    11 Nov. 1939, studio 8H: Naxos 8.110823*; Relief CR 1892
Beethoven: Symphony No. 7
    18 Nov. 1939, studio 8H: Naxos 8. 110184*; Relief CR 1885
The Naxos source is superior.
Beethoven: Symphony No.8
    25 Jan. 1939, studio 8H: Naxos 8.110813*; Relief CR 1892
The Naxos source is superior.
Beethoven: Symphony No, 9
    6 Feb. 1938, Carnegie Hall, with Vina Bovy, Kerstin Thorborg, Jan
        Peerce, Ezio Pinza, and the Schola Cantorum; Dante Lys 408
        (limited availability); Music andArts ATRA 3007
    2 Dec. 1939, Carnegie Hall, with Jarmila Novotna, Kerstin Thorborg,
        Jan Peerce, Nicola Moscona, and the Westminster Choir; Naxos
        8.110824*; Relief CR 1893*
Because of tracking problems with the Naxos CD, the Relief edition is preferable.

Berlioz: *The Damnation of Faust*
    Scene 3, Rákóczy March: 5 Apr. 1941, studio 8H: Music and Arts
        ATRA 614
    Scene 7: 16 Feb. 1947, studio 8H: Music and Arts 898

Berlioz: *Harold in Italy*, with William Primrose, viola
    21 Jan. 1939, studio 8H: Music and Arts 614

Berlioz: *Les francs-juges*: Overture
    5 Apr. 1941, studio 8H: Music and Arts 614

Berlioz: *Roméo et Juliette*: Love Scene
    5 Apr. 1941, studio 8H: Music and Arts 614

Bizet: *The Fair Maid of Perth*: Suite
    19 Sept. 1943, studio 8H: Music and Arts 898

Borodin: Symphony No. 2
    26 Feb. 1938, studio 8H: Relief CR 1887

Brahms: Concerto No. 2 for Piano and Orchestra, with Vladimir Horowitz
    6 May 1940, Carnegie Hall: Naxos 8.110805-6*
    23 Oct. 1948, studio 8H: APR 6001; Music and Arts 1007

Brahms: *A German Requiem* (sung in English), with Vivian della Chiesa,
        Herbert Janssen, and the Westminster Choir
    24 Jan. 1943, studio 8H: Memories 4164* (limited distribution); Naxos
        8.110839
The Memories edition is superior.

Brahms: Serenade No. 1
    First movement: 6 May 1940, Carnegie Hall: Naxos 8.110805-6*; 17
        Jan. 1943, studio 8H: dell'Arte 9022
    Fourth movement: 11 Nov. 1948, studio 8H: dell'Arte 9022

Brahms: Symphony No. 1
    25 Dec. 1937, studio 8H: Myto 89009*
    6 May 1940 Carnegie Hall: Naxos 8.110805-6*; Music and Arts 833
    17 Jan. 1943, studio 8H: Music and Arts 995

Brahms: Symphony No. 2
    3 Jan. 1943, studio 8H: Music and Arts 995

Brahms: Symphony No. 3
    8 Feb. 1941, studio 8H: Naxos 8.110827*
    20 Dec. 1942, studio 8H: Music and Arts 995
    31 Mar. 1946, studio 8H: Music and Arts 1007

Brahms: Symphony No. 4
    10 Jan. 1943, studio 8H: Music and Arts 995

Brahms: *Variations and Fugue on a Theme by Handel* (orch. Rubbra)
    7 Jan. 1939, studio 8H: dell'Arte 9020

Debussy (orch. Ravel): *Danse*
  13 Apr. 1940, studio 8H: Dante Lys 335-336* (limited distribution);
      Naxos 8.110811-2*

Debussy: "Ibéria"
  13 Apr. 1940, studio 8H: Dante Lys 335-336* (limited distribution);
      Naxos 8.110811-2*
  11 Feb. 1945, studio 8H: Dante Lys 335-336* (limited distribution)
  2 Feb. 1953, Carnegie Hall: Nuova Era 013.6328 (limited distribution)

Debussy: *La damoiselle élue*, with Jarmila Novotna and Hertha Glatz
  13 Apr. 1940, studio 8H: Dante Lys 335-336* (limited distribution);
      Naxos 8.110811-2*

Debussy: *La mer*
  13 Apr. 1940, studio 8H: Dante Lys 335-336* (limited distribution);
      Naxos 8.110811-2*
Both releases lack the opening two measures.
  11 Feb. 1945, studio 8H: Dante Lys 335-336* (limited distribution)
  14 Feb. 1953, Carnegie Hall: Nuova Era 013.6328 (limited distribution)

Debussy: *Marche écossaise*
  13 Apr. 1940, studio 8H: Dante Lys 335-336* (limited distribution);
      Naxos 8.110811-2*; dell'Arte 9021

Debussy: Nocturnes: *Nuages*; *Fêtes*
  13 Apr. 1940, studio 8H: Naxos 8.110811-2*

Debussy: *Prelude to the Afternoon of a Faun*
  11 Feb. 1945, studio 8H: Dante Lys 335-336* (limited distribution)
The Naxos set featuring the broadcast of 13 April 1940 also includes extensive
rehearsals of the two nocturnes and *Marche écossaise*.

Degeyter: "The Internationale" (arr. Toscanini)
  7 Nov. 1943, studio 8H: Relief CR 1886*

Dvořák: Concerto for Cello and Orchestra, with Edmund Kurtz
  28 Jan. 1945, studio 8H: Naxos 8.110819*

Dvořák: *Scherzo capriccioso*
  20 Apr. 1940, studio 8H: Grammofono 78544 (limited distribution)
      28 Jan. 1945, studio 8H: Naxos 8.110819*
This CD contains an eighteen-minute rehearsal of the *Scherzo capriccioso*, which,
though not so specifed, is for the NBC broadcast of 20 April 1940.

Dvořák: Symphony No. 9
  31 Jan. 1953, Carnegie Hall: Nuova Era 013.6311 (limited distribution)

Elgar: *Enigma Variations*
  17 Feb. 1951, Carnegie Hall: Relief CR 1888

Elgar: *Introduction and Allegro for Strings*
  20 Apr. 1940, studio 8H: Relief CR 1888

Falla: *El amor brujo:* Josephine Burzio
    28 Jan. 1939, studio 8H: Memories 4163 (limited distribution)

Franck: *Les éolides*
    12 Nov. 1938, studio 8H: Music and Arts 898

Franck: *Psyché et Eros:* Pschyé
    5 Jan. 1952, Carnegie Hall: Music and Arts 898

Franck: *Rédemption*
    15 Mar. 1952, Carnegie Hall: Music and Arts 898

This performance is also available on the RCA video of NBC telecast of this concert.

Franck: Symphony in D Minor
    14 Dec. 1940, studio 8H: Music and Arts 898
    24 Mar. 1946, studio 8H: dell'Arte 9021

The version of this symphony that Toscanini approved, included in RCA's complete collection, is an amalgam of these performances, incorporating the first movement from 1946, the balance from 1940.

Glinka: *Jota aragonesa*
    7 Nov. 1943, studio 8H: Relief 1886*

Gluck (arr. Wagner): *Iphigenia in Aulis:* Overture
    8 Feb. 1941, studio 8H: Naxos 8.110827*

Graener: *The Flute of Sans-Souci*
    5 Nov. 1938, studio 8H: dell'Arte 9024

Handel: Concerto Grosso No. 12
    22 Nov. 1947, studio 8H: Naxos 8.110835**

Harris: Symphony No. 3
    16 Mar. 1940, studio 8H: dell'Arte 9020

Haydn: Symphony No. 31
    29 Oct. 1938, studio 8H: Naxos 8.110825*; Relief CR 1842

Haydn: Symphony No. 98
    22 Jan. 1938, studio 8H: Relief CR 1842; Dante-Lys 401 (limited
        distribution)

Haydn: Symphony No. 99
    1 Feb. 1941, studio 8H: Naxos 8.110820*

Hoffstetter (attrib. Haydn): Serenade
    27 Aug. 1944, studio 8H: Relief GR 1842

Kabalevsky: *Colas Breugnon:* Overture
    11 Apr. 1943, studio 8H: dell'Arte 9020

Kalinnikov: Symphony No.1
    7 Nov. 1943, studio 8H: Relief CR 1886*

Kodály: *Marosszék Dances*
    8 Feb. 1941, studio 8H: Naxos 8.110827*

Liadov: *Kikimora*
    7 Nov. 1943, studio 8H: Relief GR 1886*
Liszt: *From the Cradle to the Grave*
    8 Feb. 1941, studio 8H: Naxos 8.110827*
Liszt: Hungarian Rhapsody No. 2
    4 Apr. 1943, studio 8H: dell'Arte 9024
Liszt: *Orpheus*
    26 Nov. 1938, studio 8H: Naxos 8.110818*; dell'Arte 9024
Martucci: *Danza-Tarantella*
    8 Feb. 1941, studio 8H: Naxos 8.110827*
Martucci: *La canzone dei ricordi:* Bruna Castagna
    29 Mar. 1941, studio 8H: Naxos 8.110836*
Martucci: Symphony No. 1
    26 Nov. 1938, studio 8H: Naxos 8.110818*
Massenet: *Scènes alsaciennes*
    18 July 1943, studio 8H: Music and Arts 898
Mendelssohn: *A Misdummer Night's Dream*: Overture; Incidental Music
    1 Nov. 1947, studio 8H: Music and Arts ATRA 268
Mendelssohn: Violin Concerto, with Jascha Heifetz
    9 Apr. 1944, studio 8H: Naxos 8.110816*
The recording is pitched slightly sharp.
Mendelssohn: *Hebrides* Overture
    4 Nov. 1945, studio 8H: Dante Lys 337 (limited distribution)
Mendelssohn: Symphony No. 3, "Scottish"
    4 Apr. 1941 studio 8H: Music and Arts ATRA 268
Mendelssohn: Symphony No. 4, "Italian"
    14 Mar. 1942, studio 8H: Music and Arts ATRA 268
    28 Feb. 1954, Carnegie Hall: Nuova Era 013.6311* (limited
        distribution)
Mendelssohn: Symphony No. 5, "Reformation"
    8 Nov. 1942, studio 8H: Music and Arts ATRA 268
Meyerbeer: *Dinorah*: Overture, with Metropolitan Opera Chorus
    12 Nov. 1938, studio 8H: dell'Arte 9021; Music and Arts 898
Meyerbeer: *L'étoile du nord*: Overture
    2 Nov. 1951, Carnegie Hall: Music and Arts 898
This is a dress rehearsal of a work dropped from the following day's broadcast.
Mozart, W. A.: Piano Concerto, K. 595, with Mieczyslaw Horszowski
    5 Dec. 1943, studio 8H: Naxos 8.110809*
Mozart, W. A.: *The Magic Flute*: Overture
    1 Feb. 1941, studio 8H: Naxos 8.110829*

Mozart, W. A.: *The Marriage of Figaro*: Overture
    5 Dec. 1943, studio 8H: Naxos 8. 110809*

Mozart, W. A.: Symphony No. 29
    3 Sept. 1944, studio 8H: Grammofono 76544 (limited distribution)

Mozart, W. A.: Mozart: Symphony No. 35
    5 Dec. 1943, studio 8H: Naxos 8.110809*
    2 Nov. 1946, studio 8H: Relief CR 1831
This recording is of a rehearsal for the broadcast of 3 November 1946.

Mozart, W. A.: Symphony No. 41
    20 Apr. 1940, studio 8H: Music and Arts 833

Mussorgsky: *Khovanshchina*: Prelude
    13 Dec. 1953, Carnegie Hall: Relief 1886

Mussorgsky (orch. Ravel): *Pictures at an Exhibition*
    24 Jan. 1953, Carnegie Hall: Nuova Era 013.6311

Paganini: *Moto perpetuo*
    16 Mar. 1940, studio 8H: dell'Arte 9020

Prokofiev: Symphony No. 1
    10 Nov. 1951, Carnegie Hall: Relief CR 1887

Ravel: *Boléro*
    21 Jan. 1939, studio 8H: Music and Arts 898

Ravel: *Daphnis et Chloé*: Suite No. 2
    26 Nov. 1938, studio 8H: Naxos 8.110818*
    27 Apr. 1940, studio 8H: Music and Arts 898

Ravel: *La valse*
    27 Apr. 1940, studio 8H: Music and Arts 898

Roger-Ducasse: *Sarabande*
    7 Apr. 1946, studio 8H: dell'Arte 9020

Rossini: Overtures
The following are on Relief CR 1884:
    Il Signor Bruschino, 8 Nov. 1942, studio 8H
    La Cenerentola, 22 Oct. 1938, studio 8H
    La gazza ladra, 12 Apr. 1941, studio 8H
    La scala di seta, 5 Nov. 1949, studio 8H
    Semiramide, 17 Nov. 1951,Carnegie Hall
    The Barber of Seville, 21 Nov. 1943, studio 8H
    William Tell, 16 Mar. 1940, studio 8H

Rossini: *William Tell*: Passo a sei; Soldiers' Dance
    19 Nov. 1938, studio 8H: Relief 1884

Roussel: *The Spider's Feast*
    7 Apr. 1946, studio 8H: dell'Arte 9021

Rubinstein: *Valse caprice*
   21 Dec. 1940, studio 8H: Relief 1886
Schubert: Symphony No. 2
   12 Nov. 1938, studio 8H: dell'Arte 9022; Dante-Lys 337 (limited
      distribution)
   23 Mar. 1940, studio 8H: Naxos 8.110838*
The Naxos edition is pitched slightly sharp.
Schumann: Symphony No. 2
   29 Mar. 1941, studio 8H: Naxos 8.110836-7*; Dante Lys 337 (limited
      distribution)
   17 Mar. 1946, studio 8H: dell'Arte 9020
Sibelius: *En Saga*
   26 Feb. 1949, studio 8H: dell'Arte 9024
   15 Mar. 1952, Carnegie Hall. Music and Arts 755
The same performance is on the RCA videocassette of the telecast of this
concert.
Sibelius: *Finlandia*
   7 Dec. 1940, studio 8H, Naxos 8.110810*
Sibelius: "Lemminkäinen's Return"
   7 Dec. 1940, studio 8H: Naxos 8.110810*; dell'Arte 9020; Music and
      Arts755
Sibelius: *Pohjola's Daughter*
   7 Dec. 1940, studio 8H: Naxos 8.110810*
This recording duplicates a performance issued by RCA.
Sibelius: Symphony No. 2
   18 Feb. 1939, studio 8H: dell'Arte 9019
   7 Dec. 1940, studio 8H: Naxos 8.110810*
This recording duplicates a performance issued by RCA.
Sibelius: Symphony No. 4
   27 Apr. 1940, studio 8H: Music and Arts 755
Sibelius: "The Swan of Tuonela"
   18 Feb. 1939, studio 8H: Music and Arts 755
Smetana: *The Bartered Bride*: Overture
   26 Nov. 1938, studio 8H: Naxos 8.110818*
Sousa: "The Stars and Stripes Forever"
   4 Apr. 1943, studio 8H: dell'Arte 9024
   25 May 1945, Madison Square Garden: Grammofono 78535/36*
      (limited distribution)
Strauss, R.: *Death and Transfiguration*
   1 Jan. 1938, studio 8H: Music and Arts ATRA 613
   Undated rehearsal for the broadcast of 17 Nov. 1946, studio 8H: AS disc
      308 (limited distribution)

Strauss, R.: *Don Juan*
 14 Oct. 1939, studio 8H: Music and Arts 754
 14 May 1940, Constitution Hall, Washington, D.C., Hunt 538 (limited distribution)
 28 Feb. 1954, Carnegie Hall: Nuova Era 013.6311* (limited distribution)

Strauss, R.: *Don Quixote*, with Emanuel Feuermann
 22 Oct. 1938, studio 8H: Music and Arts ATRA 613

Strauss, R.: *Ein Heldenleben*
 1 Feb. 1941, studio 8H: Naxos 8.110820*; Music and Arts 754

Strauss, R.: *Till Eulenspeigel's Merry Pranks*
 16 Mar. 1940 studio 8H: Hunt 538 (limited distribution)
 5 Mar. 1949, studio 8H: Music and Arts 754

Tchaikovsky: Concerto No.1 for Piano, with Vladimir Horowitz
 19 Apr. 1941, Carnegie Hall: Naxos 8.110807*; Music and Arts 956*

Tchaikovsky: *Manfred* Symphony
 21 Dec. 1940, studio 8H: Music and Arts 956
 10 Jan. 1953, Carnegie Hall: Music and Arts 220

Tchaikovsky: *Romeo and Juliet*: Fantasy Overture
 21 Mar. 1953, Carnegie Hall: Music and Arts 260

Tchaikovsky: Symphony No. 6
 29 Oct. 1938, studio 8H: Naxos 8.110825*
 19 Apr. 1941, Carnegie Hall: Naxos 8.110807*; Music and Arts 956*
 21 Mar. 1954, Carnegie Hall: Nuova Era 013 6322 (limited distribution); Melodram 18014 (limited distribution)

Tchaikovsky: *The Nutcracker Suite*
 17 Nov. 1951, Carnegie Hall: Nuova Era 013 6322 (limited distribution)

Tchaikovsky: *The Tempest*: Symphonic Fantasy
 12 Mar. 1944, studio 8H: Music and Arts 956; Relief CR 1887

Tchaikovsky: *Voyevoda*: Overture
 19 Apr. 1941, Carnegie Hall: Music and Arts 956*; Relief CR 1887
Relief inaccurately identifies this piece as Tchaikovsky's "Symphonic Ballad" Op. 78—of the same name—rather than the Op. 3 overture that Toscanini performed.

Tommasini: *Carnival of Venice*
 29 Mar. 1941, studio 8H: Naxos 8.110836-7*

Vaughan Williams: *Fantasia on a Theme by Thomas Tallis*
 15 Oct. 1938, studio 8H: Relief CR 1888

Verdi: *Aida*: Overture
 30 Mar. 1940, studio 8H: Movimento Musica 051 008 (limited distribution)

Verdi: *Falstaff*
    Extensive rehearsals for the broadcasts of 1 and 8 Apr. 1950, studio 8H:
        Music and Arts ATRA 248

Verdi: *Hymn of the Nations,* with Jan Peerce
    25 May 1944, Madison Square Garden: Grammofono 78535/36*
        (limited distribution)

Verdi: *La traviata*
    Undated dress rehearsals for the broadcasts of 1 and 8 Dec. 1946, studio
        8H: Music and Arts ATRA 271
    Orchestra rehearsal of 5 Dec. 1946, studio 8H: Relief 1812

Verdi: Requiem, with Zinka Milanov, Bruna Castagna, Jussi Björling,
        Nicola Moscona, and the Westminster Choir
    23 Nov. 1940, Carnegie Hall: Music and Arts ATRA 240*

Verdi: *Rigoletto*: Act III
    25 May 1944, Madison Square Garden: Grammofono 78535/36*
        (limited distribution)
This disc duplicates an RCA recording.

Verdi: Te Deum
    23 Nov. 1940, Carnegie Hall, Music and Arts ATRA 240*

Wagner: *A Faust Overture*
    29 Mar. 1941, studio 8H: Naxos 8.110836

Wagner: *Die Meistersinger von Nürnberg*: Prelude to Act I
    7 Mar. 1953, Carnegie Hall: Rodolphe 32490 (limited distribution)
    4 Apr. 1954, Carnegie Hall: Music and Arts ATRA 3008*

Wagner: *Die Walküre*: Act 1, Scene 3, with Rose Bampton and Set
        Svanholm
    Rehearsals of 4 and 5 Apr. and broadcast of 6 Apr. 1947, studio 8H:
        Myto 90316

Wagner: *Die Walküre*: Ride of the Valkyries
    25 May 1944, Madison Square Garden: Grammofono 78335/6* (limited
        distribution)

Wagner: *Götterdämmerung*: Dawn and Siegfried's Rhine Journey
    25 May 1944, Madison Square Garden: Grammofono 78335/6* (limited
        distribution)
    4 Apr. 1954, Carnegie Hall: Music and Arts ATRA 3008*

Wagner: *Götterdämmerung*: Siegfied's Death and Funeral Music
    7 Mar. 1953, Carnegie Hall: Music and Arts ATRA 601

Wagner: *Lohengrin*: Prelude to Act I
    4 Apr. 1954, Carnegie Hall: Music and Arts ATRA 3008*

Wagner: *Lohengrin*: Prelude to Act III
    7 Mar. 1953, Carnegie Hall: Music and Arts ATRA 601

Wagner (arr. Toscanini): *Parsifal*: orchestral highlights
    23 Mar. 1940, studio 8H: Naxos 8.110838*

Wagner: *Parsifal*: Prelude and Good Friday Spell
    9 Apr. 1944 studio 8H: Naxos 8.110817*

This recording is pitched slightly sharp.

Wagner: *Siegfried*: Forest Murmurs
    4 Apr. 1954, Carnegie Hall: Music and Arts ATRA 3008*

Wagner: *Siegfried Idyll*
    7 Mar. 1953, Carnegie Hall: Music and Arts ATRA 601

Wagner: *Tannhäuser*: Overture and Bacchanale
    8 Nov. 1952, Carnegie Hall: Music and Arts ATRA 601

This release duplicates an RCA recording

Wagner: *Tannhäuser*: Overture (Dresden version)
    25 May 1944, Madison Square Garden: Grammofono 78335/6* (limited
       distribution)

Wagner: *Tristan und Isolde*: Prelude and Liebestod
    7 Mar. 1953, Carnegie Hall: Music and Arts ATRA 601
    25 May 1944, Madison Square Garden: Grammofono 78335/6* (limited
       distribution)

Weber: *Oberon*: Overture
    28 Feb. 1954, Carnegie Hall: Nuova Era 013.6311* (limited
       distribution)

Appendix 9

NBC SYMPHONY ORCHESTRA BROADCASTS: THE OTHER CONDUCTORS

In the main, this listing is confined to guest conductors on broadcasts that were part of what NBC called "the regular winter series," which usually ran from early fall to early spring. Also included are the broadcasts led by Leopold Stokowski during his three-year association with the network. For a complete listing of all the radio work involving NBC Symphony personnel, see Donald Carl Meyer's dissertation, *The NBC Symphony Orchestra* (1994).

First Season

2 Nov. 1937: Artur Rodzinski
Weber: *Oberon*: Overture
R. Strauss: *Ein Heldenleben*

13 Nov. 1937: Pierre Monteux
Bach-Respighi: Passacaglia and Fugue in C Minor
Mozart: Symphony No. 35, "Haffner"
Franck: *Psyché*: Psyché and Eros
Debussy: "Ibéria"
R. Strauss: *Till Eulenspiegel's Merry Pranks*

20 Nov. 1937: Pierre Monteux
Handel: Concerto Grosso in D Major
Sibelius: Symphony No. 1: Adagio and Scherzo
Griffes: *The Pleasure Dome of Kubla Khan*
Wagner: *Lohengrin*: Prelude
Ravel: *Daphnis et Chloé*: Suite No. 2

27 Nov. 1937: Pierre Monteux
Franck: Symphony in D Minor
Freed: *Jeux de timbres*: Adagio (conducted by the composer)
Tailleferre: *Overture to an Opéra Bouffe*
d'Indy: *Fervaal*: Prelude
Stravinsky: *Firebird*: Suite

4 Dec. 1937: Artur Rodzinski
Handel–Harty: *Water Music:* Suite
Beethoven: Symphony No. 5
Sibelius: *Pohjola's Daughter*
Debussy: Nocturnes: *Nuages*; *Fêtes*
Albéniz–Arbos: *Triana*

11 Dec. 1937: Artur Rodzinski
Tchaikovsky: *Romeo and Juliet*: Fantasy Overture
Stravinsky: *Petrushka*: Suite
Shostakovich: Symphony No. 1

18 Dec. 1937: Artur Rodzinski
Haydn: Symphony No. 100, "Military"
Brahms: Symphony No. 4
R. Strauss: *Salome*: Salome's Dance

12 Mar. 1938: Carlos Chavez
Rossini: *William Tell*: Overture
Sibelius: Symphony No. 4
Buxtehude: Chaconne in E Minor
Halffter: *Danse de la bergère*
Falla: *The Three-Cornered Hat*: Dances

26 Mar. 1938: Howard Hanson
Locatelli: Concerto Grosso in F Minor
Purcell: *Diocletian*: Overture; Incidental Music
MacDowell: Suite No. 2, "Indian": In War Time; Village Festival
Hanson: Symphony No. 3

2 Apr. 1938: Artur Rodzinski
Beethoven: Symphony No. 1
Barber: Symphony in One Movement
Debussy: *Prelude to the Afternoon of a Faun*
Prokofiev: Symphony No. 1, "Classical"
Dohnányi: Suite for Orchestra

9 Apr. 1938: Artur Rodzinski
Weber: *Oberon*: Overture
Respighi: *Ancient Airs and Dances*: Suite No. 1
Shostakovich: Symphony No. 5
Albéniz: *Ibéria*: "Fête-Dieu à Séville"
Wagner: *Die Meistersinger von Nürnberg*: Prelude to Act III, Dance of the
        Apprentices, and Finale

16 Apr. 1938: Artur Rodzinski
Bach-Wertheim: Toccata and Fugue in D Minor
R. Strauss: *Also sprach Zarathustra*
Schreker: *The Birth of the Infants*: Orchestral Suite
J. Strauss: *Die Fledermaus*: Overture
    Tales from the Vienna Woods

23 Apr. 1938: Hugh Ross
Delius: *A Mass of Life*
Rimsky-Korsakov: *Tsar Sultan*: Suite

30 Apr. 1938: Pierre Monteux
Beethoven: Symphony No. 2
Schumann: *Manfred*: Overture
Dukas: *La péri*
Sibelius: *Valse triste*
R. Strauss: *Don Juan*

7 May 1938: Pierre Monteux
Chausson: Symphony in B-flat Major
Powell: *Rhapsody on Negro Themes*
Davis: *Poem for Orchestra*
Cowley: *Crazy Horse Suite*
Withorne: *Sierra morena*

14 May 1938: Sir Adrian Boult
Busoni: *Comedy* Overture
Beethoven: Symphony No. 7
Walton: Viola Concerto, with William Primrose
Copland: *El salón México*

21 May 1938: Sir Adrian Boult
Vaughan Williams: Symphony No. 4
Holst: Fugal Concerto for Flute, Oboe, and Strings
Butterworth: *A Shropshire Lad*
Elgar: *Enigma Variations*

28 May 1938: Dimitri Mitropoulos
Purcell-Mitropoulos: *Dido and Aeneas*: Dido's Lament
Schumann: Symphony No. 2
Glazunov: *Overture on Three Greek Themes*
Chopin-Lewitzski: *Chopiniana*
    Polonaise in A-flat Major
    Revolutionary Etude

4 June 1938: Bernardino Molinari
Paisiello: *Nina*: Overture
Beethoven: Symphony No. 5
Catalani: *La Wally*: Prelude to Act III
Mendelssohn: *A Midsummer Night's Dream*: Scherzo
Verdi: *I vespri siciliani*: Overture

11 June 1938: Bernardino Molinari
Vivaldi: *The Four Seasons*: Winter
Mozart: Symphony No. 29
Pizzetti: *La pisanelle*
        Intermezzo
Boccherini: Minuet in A Major
Corelli-Pinelli: Suite for Strings
Berlioz: *The Damnation of Faust*: Rákóczy March

18 June 1938: Bernardino Molinari
Tchaikovsky: Symphony No. 6, "Pathétique"
Respighi: *The Fountains of Rome*
Verdi: *La forza del destino*: Overture

25 June 1938: William Steinberg
Mendelssohn: *A Midsummer Night's Dream*: Overture
Mozart: Symphony No. 41, "Jupiter"
Wagner: *Siegfried*: Forest Murmurs
Liszt: *Les préludes*

Second Season

10 Dec. 1938: Artur Rodzinski
Glinka: *Ruslan and Ludmila*: Overture
Tchaikovsky: Symphony No. 5
Starakadomsky: Concerto for Orchestra
Stravinsky: *Firebird*: Suite

17 Dec. 1938: Artur Rodzinski
Weber: *Euryanthe*: Overture
Dvořák: Symphony No. 8
Hindemith: *Mathis der Maler*
R. Strauss: *Till Eulenspiegel's Merry Pranks*

24 Dec. 1938: Artur Rodzinski
Humperdinck: *Hansel and Gretel*: Prelude
Bach-Respighi: Three Chorales
Beethoven: Symphony No. 1
Brahms-Schoenberg: Piano Quartet in G Minor

31 Dec. 1938: Artur Rodzinski
Vivaldi: Concerto Grosso in G Minor
Scriabin: Symphony No. 3, "Divine Poem"
Kodály: *Háry János*: Suite
R. Strauss: *Der Rosenkavalier*: Waltzes

4 Mar. 1939: William Steinberg
Bruckner: Symphony No. 4
Stravinsky: *Fireworks*
Dukas: *The Sorcerer's Apprentice*
J. Strauss: *Emperor Waltz*

11 Mar. 1939: Bruno Walter
Mozart: Divertimento, K. 287
    Piano Concerto, K. 466, with Walter doubling as pianist
    Symphony No. 40

18 Mar. 1939: Bruno Walter
Weber: *Oberon*: Overture
Haydn: Symphony No. 92, "Oxford"
Brahms: Symphony No. 1

25 Mar. 1939: Bruno Walter
Corelli: Concerto Grosso in G Minor
Beethoven: Symphony No. 1
Mason: *Old English Folk Song Suite*
R. Strauss: *Death and Transfiguration*

1 Apr. 1939: Bruno Walter
Berlioz: *Le corsaire*: Overture
    The Damnation of Faust: Minuet of the Will o' the Wisps; Dance of the
        Sylphs; Rákóczy March
    Symphonie fantastique

8 Apr. 1939: Bruno Walter
Wagner: *A Faust Overture*
    Siegfried Idyll
Mahler: Symphony No. 1

15 Apr. 1939: Hans Lange
Bloch: Concerto Grosso for Strings and Piano
Beethoven: Symphony No. 4
Delius: *In a Summer Garden*
R. Strauss: *Don Juan*

22 Apr. 1939: Alberto Erede
Menotti: *The Old Maid and the Thief* (world premiere)

Third Season

9 Dec. 1939: Désiré Defauw
Handel: Concerto Grosso in D Minor
Respighi: *The Birds*
Franck: Symphony in D Minor

23 Dec. 1939: Désiré Defauw
Bach: *Christmas Oratorio*: Sinfonia
Humperdinck: *Hansel and Gretel*: Prelude
Grétry: *Cephale and Procris*: Ballet Suite
Poot: *Overture Joyeuse*
Brahms: Symphony No. 3

30 Dec. 1939: Désiré Defauw
Schumann: Symphony No. 4
Wagner: *Tannhäuser*: Bacchanale
Berlioz: *The Damnation of Faust*: Minuet of the Will o' the Wisps; Dance of
    the Sylphs; Rákóczy March

6 Jan. 1940: Bernardino Molinari
Dvořák: Symphony No. 9, "From the New World"
R. Strauss: *Death and Transfiguration*
Rossini: *Semiramide*: Overture

13 Jan. 1940: Bernardino Molinari
Mendelssohn: Symphony No. 4, "Italian"
Saint-Saëns: *Carnival of the Animals*
Vivaldi-Molinari: Concerto in A Major
Stravinsky: *Petrushka*: Suite

20 Jan. 1940: Bernardino Molinari
Pizzetti: *Concerto dell'estate*
Falla: *La vida breve*: Interlude; Dance
Tchaikovsky: Symphony No. 4

27 Jan. 1940: Bernardino Molinari
Taylor: *Through the Looking Glass*: Suite
Debussy-Molinari: *L'isle joyeuse*
Haydn: Symphony No. 88
Ravel: *Daphnis et Chloé*: Suite No. 2

3 Feb. 1940: Bernardino Molinari
Rimsky-Korsakov: *Scheherazade*
Rossellini: *Canto di Pauledo*
Salvicci: *Sinfonia italiana*
Respighi: *The Pines of Rome*

10 Feb. 1940: Bruno Walter
Haydn: Symphony No. 88
Bruckner: Symphony No. 4

17 Feb. 1940: Bruno Walter
Handel: Concerto Grosso in G Minor, Op. 6 No. 6
Mozart: Symphony No. 35, "Haffner"
Brahms: Symphony No. 2

24 Feb. 1940: Bruno Walter
D'Indy: *Istar Variations*
Ravel: *Rapsodie espagnol*
Schubert: Symphony No. 9

2 Mar. 1940: Bruno Walter
Schumann: Symphony No. 4
R. Strauss: *Don Juan*
Debussy: *Prelude to the Afternoon of a Faun*
Smetana: *The Bartered Bride*: Overture
    The Moldau

9 Mar. 1940: Bruno Walter
Schubert: Symphony No. 5
Mozart: Minuets and German Dances, K. 568 and 605
Tchaikovsky: Symphony No. 5

Fourth Season

12 Oct. 1940: William Steinberg
Weber: *Der Freischütz*: Overture
Berlioz: *Roméo et Juliette*, part 2
Wagner: *Rienzi*: Overture
    The Flying Dutchman: Overture
    Lohengrin: Prelude
Liszt: *Faust Symphony*
    Mazeppa

19 Oct. 1940: William Steinberg
Mozart: Symphony No. 39
Mendelssohn: *A Midsummer Night's Dream*: Intermezzo; Song and Chorus;
    Nocturne; Funeral March; Dance of the Clowns; Scherzo
Stravinsky: *Firebird*: Suite

26 Oct. 1940: William Steinberg
Brahms: *Tragic* Overture
Falla: *Nights in the Gardens of Spain*
Tchaikovsky: Symphony No. 4

2 Nov. 1940: William Steinberg
Schoenberg: *Verklärte Nacht*
Mahler: Symphony No. 7: fourth movement
Verdi: *Otello*: Act III, Ballet Music
Beethoven: Symphony No. 5

9 Nov. 1940: William Steinberg
Dvořák: Symphony No. 7
Copland: *Billy the Kid*
J. Strauss: *Perpetuum mobile*; *Roses from the South*; *Tritsch-Tratsch Polka*

16 Nov. 1940: William Steinberg
Mendelssohn: *Hebrides* Overture
Adolph Busch: *Three Etudes for Orchestra* (world premiere)
Brahms: Symphony No. 2

11 Jan. 1941: Alfred Wallenstein
Beethoven: *Coriolan* Overture
Mendelssohn: Symphony No. 4, "Italian"
Schoenberg: *Verklärte Nacht*
Brahms: *Variations on a Theme by Haydn*

25 Jan. 1941: George Szell
Schumann: Symphony No. 4
Haydn: Symphony No. 97
R. Strauss: *Till Eulenspiegel's Merry Pranks*

8 Mar. 1941: George Szell
Smetana: *The Bartered Bride*: Overture
       String Quartet No. 1 (arr. Szell)
Dvořák: *Carnival* Overture
Smetana: *The Moldau*
Dvořák: *Four Slavonic Dances*

15 Mar. 1941: George Szell
Mozart: Piano Concerto, K. 467, with Hortense Monath
Schubert: Symphony No. 9

22 Mar. 1941: George Szell
Berlioz: *Roman Carnival* Overture
Piston: *The Incredible Flutist*
Beethoven: Symphony No. 3, "Eroica"

Fifth Season

7 Oct. 1941: Dimitri Mitropoulos
Haydn: Symphony No. 80
Beethoven: Symphony No. 4

14 Oct. 1941: Dimitri Mitropoulos
Mozart: *The Marriage of Figaro*: Overture
Chausson: Symphony in B-flat Major
Bach-Weiner: Toccata and Fugue in C Major

21 Oct. 1941: Efrem Kurtz
Lalo: *Le Roi d'Ys*: Overture
Schumann: Symphony No. 4
Bruckner: Symphony No. 9: Scherzo
Tchaikovsky: Suite No. 3: Theme and Variations

28 Oct. 1941: Efrem Kurtz
Glinka: *Ruslan and Ludmila*: Overture
Tchaikovsky: Symphony No. 6, "Pathétique"

4 Nov. 1941: Leopold Stokowski
Bach-Stokowski: Prelude in E-flat Major
Warner: *Sinfonietta*
Brahms: Symphony No. 3

11 Nov. 1941: Leopold Stokowski
Beethoven: Symphony No. 9 (first three movements not broadcast), with
        Anne Brown, soprano; Winifred Heidt, contralto; William Horne,
        tenor; and Lawrence Whisonant, bass

18 Nov. 1941: Leopold Stokowski
Prokofiev: *The Love for Three Oranges*: Infernal Dance; The Prince and the
        Princess; March
Kelly: *Adirondack Suite*: Prelude
Brahms: Symphony No. 4

25 Nov. 1941: Leopold Stokowski
Bach-Stokowski: Harpsichord Concerto, BWV 1056: Arioso
Tchaikovsky: Symphony No. 4
Heufrecht: Two Fantastic Marches

2 Dec. 1941: Juan José Castro
Bach-Castro: Three Chorales
Gianneo: *Children's Comedy* Overture (radio premiere)
Franck: Symphony in D Minor

9 Dec. 1941: Juan José Castro
Maldero: Symphony in B-flat Major
Wagenaar: *Sinfonietta*

16 Dec. 1941: Juan José Castro
Ginastera: *Ballet Suite*: Panandi (world premiere)
Glinka: *Kamarinskaya*
Castro: *Symphony of the Fields*
Mendelssohn: Symphony No. 4, "Italian"

23 Dec. 1941: Sir Ernest Macmillan
Humperdinck: *Hansel and Gretel*: Prelude
Schubert: Symphony No. 9

30 Dec. 1941: Sir Ernest Macmillan
Bach-Macmillan: Chorale Prelude, "In Dir ist Freude"
Tchaikovsky: Symphony No. 5

6 Jan. 1942: George Szell
Dvořák: *Husitska*: Overture
     Symphony No. 8

13 Jan. 1942: George Szell
Weber: *Oberon*: Overture
Haydn: Symphony No. 92, "Oxford"
Smetana: *Wallenstein's Camp*

20 Jan. 1942: Dean Dixon
Weber: *Euryanthe*: Overture
Arnell: *The Land*: excerpts
Prokofiev: Symphony No. 1, "Classical"
Enesco: Roumanian Rhapsody No. 1

27 Jan. 1942: Dean Dixon
Creston: Pastorale and Tarantella
Sibelius: Symphony No. 2

3 Feb. 1942: Frank Black
Shulman: Variations for Viola and Orchestra, with Emanuel Vardi
Cooley: *Caponsacchi*
Spialek: *Sinfonietta*
Cooley and Shulman were members of the NBC Symphony Orchestra.

10 Feb. 1942: Frank Black
Glazunov: *Carnival* Overture
Mozart: Symphony No. 28
Debussy: Nocturnes: *Nuages*; *Fêtes*
Saint-Saëns: *Introduction and Rondo capriccioso* (played by first violins)

17 Feb. 1942: Alfred Wallenstein
Spohr: Symphony No. 2
Levant: Piano Concerto, with Oscar Levant, piano
Ravel: *La valse*

24 Feb. 1942: Alfred Wallenstein
Haydn: *Armida*: Overture
Beethoven: Symphony No. 8
Walton: *Façade*, with Richard Hale, narrator
Tchaikovsky: *Romeo and Juliet*: Fantasy Overture

3 Mar. 1942: Fritz Reiner
Beethoven: *Egmont*: Overture
    Symphony No. 1
Berlioz: *Roman Carnival* Overture
Revueltas: *Janitizio*
Riegger: *New Dance*

10 Mar. 1942: Fritz Reiner
Rossini: *Semiramide*: Overture
R. Strauss: *Don Quixote*

17 Mar. 1942: Fritz Reiner
Beethoven: Symphony No. 7
Borodin: *Prince Igor*: Polovtsian Dances

24 Mar. 1942: Leopold Stokowski
Cooley: *Eastbourne Sketches*: Promenade
Beethoven: Symphony No. 6, "Pastoral"

31 Mar. 1942: Leopold Stokowski
Bach: *St. Matthew Passion*: Concluding chorus
Wagner: *Parsifal*: Good Friday Spell; synthesis of music from Act III
Rimsky-Korsakov: *Russian Easter* Overture

7 Apr. 1942: Leopold Stokowski
Bach-Stokowski: Chorale, "Ein feste Burg ist unser Gott"
MacDowell: Piano Concerto in D Minor, with Frances Nash, piano
Stringfield: *Negro Parade*
Stravinsky: *Firebird*: Suite

14 Apr. 1942: Leopold Stokowski
Still: *And They Lynched Him to a Tree*
Mussorgsky: *Boris Godunov*: Symphonic Synthesis

Sixth Season

27 Sept. 1942: Désiré Defauw
Dukas: *La péri*
Fauré: *Pelléas et Mélisande*: Suite
Debussy: Nocturnes: *Nuages*; *Fêtes*
Chabrier: *España*

4 Oct. 1942: Nicolai Malko
Smetana: *The Bartered Bride*: Overture
Haydn: Symphony No. 94, "Surprise"
Mussorgsky: *A Night on Bald Mountain*
Granados: *Three Spanish Dances*

11 Oct. 1942: Nicolai Malko
Liadov: *The Enchanted Lake*
Shostakovich: Symphony No. 1
Rimsky-Korsakov: *Capriccio espagnol*

18 Oct. 1942: Erich Leinsdorf
Mozart: *The Impresario*: Overture
Haydn: Symphony No. 97
Schubert: *Rosamunde*: Dances
Bruckner: Symphony No. 6: Adagio
J. Strauss: *Roses from the South*

25 Oct. 1942: Erich Leinsdorf
Bach: *St. Matthew Passion*: Chorale
    Suite for Orchestra No. 3 in D Major, BWV 1068
Prokofiev: *Peter and the Wolf*
Copland: *Music for Radio*

15 Nov. 1942: Leopold Stokowski
Triggs: *The Bright Land*
Gould: *Spirituals for Orchestra*

22 Nov. 1942: Leopold Stokowski
Beethoven: Symphony No. 7
Wagner: *Tristan und Isolde*: Prelude and Liebestod

29 Nov. 1942: Leopold Stokowski
Tchaikovsky: *The Drama of Ostrovsky*: Overture
    Symphony No. 5

6 Dec. 1942: Leopold Stokowski
Bach-Stokowski: Chorale Prelude, "Wir glauben all' an einen Gott"
    Adagio, Toccata, and Fugue
Hovhaness: *Exile Symphony*
Lavalle: *Symphonic Rhumba*
Wagner: *Siegfried Idyll*

13 Dec. 1942: Leopold Stokowski
Shostakovich: Symphony No. 7, "Leningrad"

14 Feb. 1943: Leopold Stokowski
Holst: *The Planets*

21 Feb. 1943: Leopold Stokowski
Stravinsky: Symphony in C
Debussy-Stokowski: *Evening in Granada*
Ravel: *Daphnis et Chloé*: Suite No. 2

28 Feb. 1943: Leopold Stokowski
Hindemith: Symphony in E-flat Major
Wagner: *Tristan und Isolde*: Love Music

7 Mar. 1943: Leopold Stokowski
Tchaikovsky: *The Tempest*: Symphonic Fantasy
Prokofiev: *Alexander Nevsky*, with Jennie Tourel (American premiere)

14 Mar. 1943: Leopold Stokowski
Vaughan Williams: Symphony No. 4
Gould: *New China March*
    Red Cavalry March
Debussy: *Prelude to the Afternoon of a Faun*

21 Mar. 1943: Leopold Stokowski
Milhaud: Symphony
Mussorgsky-Stokowski: *Pictures at an Exhibition*

28 Mar. 1943: Leopold Stokowski
Bach-Stokowski: *St. Matthew Passion*: "Es ist vollbracht"
Debussy: Music from *Le martyre de saint Sébastian*
Wagner: *Parsifal*: Prelude to Act I; Prelude to Act III

Seventh Season

12 Dec. 1943: Leopold Stokowski
Bach: Brandenburg Concerto No. 2
Bach-Stokowski: Chorale Prelude, "Christ lag in Todesbanden"
    Toccata and Fugue in D Minor
Schuman: *Prayer, 1943*

19 Dec. 1943: Leopold Stokowski
Russian Christmas Music (traditional)
Handel: *Messiah*: Christmas sections
Vaughan Williams: *Fantasia on Traditional Christmas Music*
Harris: *Folk Rhythms of Today*
Mohaupt: *Concerto for Orchestra on Red Army Themes*

26 Dec. 1943: Leopold Stokowski
Beethoven: Symphony No. 5
Creston: *Chant for 1942*
Taylor: *Raymuntcho*: Introduction; Ballet

2 Jan. 1944: Leopold Stokowski
Wagner–Stokowski: *Tristan und Isolde*: Love Music
Hanson: Symphony No. 4

9 Jan. 1944: Leopold Stokowski
Albéniz: *Holiday in Seville*
Debussy: *Prelude to the Afternoon of a Faun*
Fernandez: *Reisado do pastoreio*: Batuque
Guarnieri: *Brazilian Dance*
        Flower of Trememinibé
        Savage Dance
Copland: *Short Symphony*

16 Jan. 1944: Leopold Stokowski
Tchaikovsky: *Romeo and Juliet*: Fantasy Overture
Skilton: *Sunrise Song*
Thomson: *The Plow That Broke the Plains*
Zimbalist: *American Rhapsody*

23 Jan. 1944: Leopold Stokowski
Wagner: *Lohengrin*: Prelude
        Die Walküre: Magic Fire Music
Hindemith: *Nobilissima visione*

30 Jan. 1944: Leopold Stokowski
Shostakovich: Prelude in E-flat Minor
Tchaikovsky: Symphony No. 6, "Pathétique"

6 Feb. 1944: Leopold Stokowski
Cesti–Stokowski: Arioso: "Tu manchi a tormentarmi"
Schubert: Symphony No. 8, "Unfinished"
Novacek: *Perpetuum mobile*
Schoenberg: Piano Concerto, with Eduard Steuermann, piano (world
        premiere)

13 Feb. 1944: Leopold Stokowski
Butterworth: *A Shropshire Lad*
Debussy-Stokowski: *La cathédrale engloutie*
Antheil: Symphony No. 4

20 Feb. 1944: Leopold Stokowski
Rimsky-Kosakov: *Capriccio espagnol*
Tchaikovsky: *Solitude*
Stravinsky: *Petrushka*: Suite
Amfitheatrof: *De profundis clamavi*

27 Feb. 1944: Leopold Stokowski
Brahms: Symphony No. 3
Bach-Stokowski: Passacaglia and Fugue in C Minor

Eighth Season

25 Dec. 1944: Eugene Ormandy
Corelli: Concerto Grosso No. 8, "Christmas Concerto"
J. C. Bach-Ormandy: Sinfonia No. 3 for Double Orchestra
Berlioz: *L'enfance du Christ*: Repose of the Holy Family
Stravinsky: *Firebird*: Suite

31 Dec. 1944: Eugene Ormandy
Handel-Ormandy: Concerto Grosso, Op. 3 No. 6
Mozart: Symphony No. 35, "Haffner"
Barber: *Essay No. 2*
Wieniawski: Violin Concerto No. 2, with Erica Morini

7 Jan. 1945: Eugene Ormandy
Villa-Lobos: *Bachianas brasileiras*, No. 1
Khrennikov: Symphony in B-flat Major
Mendelssohn: String Octet in E-flat Major: Scherzo
J. Strauss: *Tales from the Vienna Woods*

14 Jan. 1945: Eugene Ormandy
Brahms: *Academic Festival* Overture
    Symphony No. 2

18 Feb. 1945: Sir Malcolm Sargent
Elgar: *Cockaigne* Overture
Dvořák: Symphony No. 7

25 Feb. 1945: Sir Malcolm Sargent
Handel: *Water Music* [probably the Hamilton Harty suite]
Elgar: Violin Concerto, with Yehudi Menuhin, violin

4 Mar. 1945: Sir Malcolm Sargent
Vaughan Williams: *The Wasps*: Overture
Sibelius: Symphony No. 1

11 Mar. 1945: Sir Malcolm Sargent
Holst: *The Perfect Fool*: Ballet
Walton: Viola Concerto, with William Primrose, viola
Ireland: *London* Overture

Ninth Season

9 Dec. 1945: Dimitri Mitropoulos
Mozart: *The Magic Flute*: Overture
Vaughan Williams: *A London Symphony*

16 Dec. 1945: Dimitri Mitropoulos
Bach: Brandenburg Concerto No. 5
Prokofiev: Piano Concerto No. 3, with Mitropoulos doubling as soloist

23 Dec. 1945: Dimitri Mitropoulos
Bach-Boessenroth: Choral Prelude: "Wir glauben all' an einen Gott"
Schoenberg: String Quartet No. 2 (arr. by the composer)
Siegmeister: *Ozark Set*, with Astrid Varnay, soprano

30 Dec. 1945: Dimitri Mitropoulos
Berlioz: *King Lear*: Overture
Berg: Violin Concerto, with Joseph Szigeti, violin
Couperin-Milhaud: *La sultane*: Overture; Allegro

17 Feb. 1946: Erich Kleiber
Mozart: *The Marriage of Figaro*: Overture
Beethoven: Symphony No. 6, "Pastoral"

24 Feb. 1946: Erich Kleiber
Mozart: Symphony No. 33
Schubert: *Rosamunde*: Entr'acte; Ballet Music
Ginastera: *Panambi*: Ballet Suite

3 Mar. 1946: Erich Kleiber
Handel: *Berenice*: Overture
Schubert: Symphony No. 3
Ravel: *Mother Goose Suite*

10 Mar. 1946: Erich Kleiber
Wagner: *Parsifal*: Prelude and Good Friday Spell
Siegfried: Forest Murmurs
Tannhäuser: Overture (Dresden version)

The following programs, although not part of the winter season, are significant.

27 May 1946: Leonard Bernstein
Blitzstein: *The Airborne Symphony*

2 June 1946: Leonard Bernstein
Haydn: Symphony No. 102
Gillis: *Moto perpetuo*
Ravel: Piano Concerto, with Bernstein doubling as soloist

23 June 1946: Vladimir Golschmann
Tchaikovsky: *Francesca da Rimini*
Beethoven: Piano Concerto No. 2, with William Kapell

Tenth Season

15 Dec. 1946: Fritz Reiner
Mozart: Symphony No. 41, "Jupiter"
Bartók: *The Miraculous Mandarin*: Suite
R. Strauss: *Till Eulenspiegel's Merry Pranks*

22 Dec. 1946: Fritz Reiner
Humperdinck: *Hansel and Gretel*: Prelude
Schumann: Symphony No. 2
Kodály: Dances of Galanta

29 Dec. 1946: Fritz Reiner
Debussy: "Ibéria"
Hindemith: *Mathis der Maler*
Wagner: *Die Meistersinger von Nürnberg*: Prelude

5 Jan. 1947: Fritz Reiner
Mozart: *The Impresario*: Overture
Brahms: Symphony No. 4
J. Strauss: *Vienna Life*

12 Jan. 1947: Eugen Szenkar
Copland: *An Outdoor Overture*
Tchaikovsky: Symphony No. 5

19 Jan. 1947: Eugen Szenkar
Villa-Lobos: *Bachianas brasileiras*, No. 4: Prelude
Schumann: Symphony No. 4
Ravel: *Daphnis et Chloé*: Suite No. 2
Wagner: *Die Meistersinger von Nürnberg*: Prelude to Act III and Dance of the
    Apprentices

26 Jan. 1947: Eugen Szenkar
Mozart: *The Marriage of Figaro*: Overture
Berlioz: *Symphonie fantastique*

2 Feb. 1947: Eugen Szenkar
Bach: Toccata and Fugue in D Minor
Brahms: Symphony No. 1

Eleventh Season

20 Dec. 1947: Erich Kleiber
Borodin: Symphony No. 2
Weber: Konzertstück in F Minor, with Claudio Arrau, piano
Falla: *El amor brujo*: Introduction; Ritual Fire Dance

27 Dec. 1947: Erich Kleiber
Corelli: Concerto Grosso No. 8, "Christmas Concerto"
Schubert: Symphony No. 5
J. Strauss: *The Gypsy Baron*: Overture
      Tales from the Vienna Woods

3 Jan. 1948: Erich Kleiber
Dvořák: *Carnival* Overture
Tchaikovsky: Symphony No. 4
Dvořák: Wedding Dance

10 Jan. 1948: Erich Kleiber
Beethoven: *Egmont*: Overture
      Symphony No. 3, "Eroica"

17 Jan. 1948: Ernest Ansermet
Beethoven: *Leonore* Overture No. 2
Martin: *Symphonie concertante*
Ravel: *Daphnis et Chloé*: Suite No. 2

24 Jan. 1948: Ernest Ansermet
Strong: *Paraphrase on a Chorale by Hassler*
Debussy: *Jeux*
Martinů: Symphony No. 5

31 Jan. 1948: Ernest Ansermet
Beethoven: Symphony No. 4
Stravinsky: *Symphonies of Wind Instruments*
Ravel: *La valse*

7 Feb. 1948: Ernest Ansermet
Mozart: Symphony No. 40
Debussy: *Gigues*
Stravinsky: *Petrushka*: Suite

Twelfth Season

18 Dec. 1948: Ernest Ansermet
Bach: Suite No. 3 in D Major for Orchestra, BWV 1068
Honegger: *Horace victorieux*
Ravel: *Rapsodie espagnol*

25 Dec. 1948: Ernest Ansermet
Humperdinck: *Hansel and Gretel*: Prelude
Schubert: Symphony No. 9

8 Jan. 1949: Ernest Ansermet
Bartók: *Music for Strings, Percussion, and Celeste*
Stravinsky: *Firebird*: Suite

15 Jan. 1949: Guido Cantelli
Haydn: Symphony No. 93
Hindemith: *Mathis der Maler*

22 Jan. 1949: Guido Cantelli
Ghedini: *Pezzo concertante*
Casella: *Paganiniana*
Tchaikovsky: *Romeo and Juliet*: Fantasy Overture

29 Jan. 1949: Guido Cantelli
Wagner: *A Faust Overture*
Bartók: Concerto for Orchestra

5 Feb. 1949: Guido Cantelli
Franck: Symphony in D Minor
Ravel: *La valse*

Thirteenth Season

24 Dec. 1949: Guido Cantelli
Handel: *Messiah*: Overture
Bach: *Christmas Oratorio*, Part 2: Sinfonia
Tchaikovsky: Symphony No. 4

31 Dec. 1949: Guido Cantelli
Haydn: Symphony No. 94, "Surprise"
Stravinsky: *Le chant du rossignol*
Wagner: *Rienzi*: Overture

7 Jan. 1950: Guido Cantelli
Mozart: Symphony No. 29
Hindemith: *Mathis der Maler*

14 Jan. 1950: Guido Cantelli
Frescobaldi-Ghedini: Four Pieces
Beethoven: Symphony No. 7

21 Jan. 1950: Ernest Ansermet
Chabrier: *España*
Bach: Brandenburg Concerto No. 3
Bloch: *Concerto symphonique*, with Corinne Lacombie, piano (American
    premiere)

28 Jan. 1950: Ernest Ansermet
Martinů: Concerto Grosso
Debussy-Ansermet: *Epigraphes antiques*
Hindemith: *Nobilissima visione*: Suite

4 Feb. 1950: Ernest Ansermet
Mozart: Symphony No. 36, "Linz"
Debussy: "Ibéria"
Foss: *Recordare* (Second Tragic Ode)

11 Feb. 1950: Ernest Ansermet
Schumann: *Genoveva*: Overture
Bartók: Viola Concerto, with William Primrose, viola
Liszt: *Two Episodes from Lenau's "Faust"*: Nocturnal Procession; The Dance
    in the Village (*Mephisto Waltz No. 1*)

Fourteenth Season

9 Oct. 1950: Milton Katims
Mendelssohn: *Ruy Blas*: Overture
Scott: *From the Sacred Harp*
Milhaud: *Le boeuf sur le toit*

16 Oct. 1950: Milton Katims
Beethoven: Symphony No. 8
Debussy: Rhapsody No. 1 for Clarinet and Orchestra, with Alex Williams,
    clarinet
Kodály: *Dances of Galanta*

23 Oct. 1950: Fritz Reiner
Berlioz: *Béatrice et Bénédict*: Overture
Schumann: Symphony No. 2
Bartók: *Hungarian Sketches*

30 Oct. 1950: Fritz Reiner
Beethoven: *Leonore* Overture No. 2
Mozart: Symphony No. 35, "Haffner"
R. Strauss: *Death and Transfiguration*

6 Nov. 1950: Fritz Reiner
Brahms: Symphony No. 2
Copland: Concerto for Clarinet and Strings, with Benny Goodman (world
    premiere)

13 Nov. 1950: Erich Leinsdorf
Haydn: Symphony No. 88
Debussy: Nocturnes: *Nuages*; *Fêtes*
R. Strauss: *Don Juan*

20 Nov. 1950: Jonel Perlea
Weber: *Der Freischütz*: Overture
Smetana: *The Moldau*
Beethoven: Symphony No. 2

27 Nov. 1950: Jonel Perlea
Enesco: Romanian Rhapsody No. 2
Wolf: *Italian Serenade*
Ravel: *Alborado del gracioso*
Wagner: *Parsifal*: Prelude
    Götterdämmerung: Siegfried's Rhine Journey

4 Dec. 1950: Guido Cantelli
Mozart: *A Musical Joke*
Rossini: *Semiramide*: Overture
Schuman: *Undertow*: Selections

11 Dec. 1950: Guido Cantelli
Milhaud: Introduction and Funeral March
Dallapiccola: *Marcia Suite*
Verdi: *I vespri siciliani*: Overture
Haydn: Symphony No. 93

18 Dec. 1950: Guido Cantelli
Vivaldi: Concerto Grosso in A Major
Busoni: *Tanzwalzer*
Beethoven: Symphony No. 5

25 Dec. 1950: Guido Cantelli
Corelli: Concerto Grosso No. 8, "Christmas Concerto"
Vivaldi: *The Four Seasons*: Winter
Geminiani-Marinuzzi: *Andante for Strings, Organ, and Harp*
Monteverdi-Ghedini: Magnificat

1 Jan. 1951: Guido Cantelli
Rossini: *The Siege of Corinth*: Overture
Bartók: Concerto for Orchestra

8 Jan. 1951: Guido Cantelli
Schubert: Symphony No. 2
Ghedini: *Concerto dell'Albarto* (after Melville's *Moby-Dick*)

15 Jan. 1951: Guido Cantelli
Vivaldi: Violin Concerto in A Minor, with Mischa Mischakoff
Geminiani: Concerto Grosso No. 2
Brahms: *Tragic* Overture
Debussy: *Le martyre de saint Sébastien*: Incidental Music
Stravinsky: *Fireworks*

22 Jan. 1951: Guido Cantelli
Mozart: Symphony No. 29
Gillis: *Portrait of a Frontier Town*: Prairie Sunset
Mussorgsky–Ravel: *Pictures at an Exhibition*

24 Feb. 1951: Bruno Walter
Mozart: *The Marriage of Figaro*: Overture
    Violin Concerto, K. 216, with Joseph Szigeti
R. Strauss: *Death and Transfiguration*

3 Mar. 1951: Wilfrid Pelletier
Beethoven: *Egmont*: Overture; two songs; with Helen Traubel
Haydn: Symphony No. 88
Wagner: *Götterdämmerung*: Immolation Scene, with Helen Traubel

10 Mar. 1951: Walter Ducloux
Weber: *Euryanthe*: Overture
Schumann: Symphony No. 4
Stravinsky: *Firebird*: Suite

17 Mar. 1951: Walter Ducloux
Mozart: Symphony No. 39
Foote: Suite for Strings
Wagner: *Tristan und Isolde*: Prelude and Liebestod

24 Mar. 1951: Milton Katims
Gluck: *Iphigenia in Aulis*: Overture
Larson: *Pastoral Suite*
Sibelius: *King Christian II*: Elegy
Schumann: Symphony No. 1, "Spring"

31 Mar. 1951: Milton Katims
Bloch: Concerto Grosso
Adomian: *Suite for Orchestra*
Thomson: *Louisiana Story*

7 Apr. 1951: Milton Katims
Cimarosa: *Il matrimonio segreto*: Overture
Mozart: Symphony No. 35, "Haffner"
Sibelius: "The Swan of Tuonela"
Mennin: Symphony No. 3

14 Apr. 1951: Milton Katims
Beethoven: Symphony No. 1
R. Strauss: *Salome*: Dance of the Seven Veils
Barber: Symphony No. 1

Fifteenth Season

1 Dec. 1951: Guido Cantelli
Mozart: *The Marriage of Figaro*: Overture
Mendelssohn: Symphony No. 4, "Italian"
Ravel: *Pavane for a Dead Princess*
    La valse

8 Dec. 1951: Guido Cantelli
Geminiani-Marrinuzzi: *Andante for Strings and Organ* (not broadcast)
Vivaldi: *The Four Seasons*, with Mischa Mischakoff, violin

15 Dec. 1951: Guido Cantelli
Brahms: Symphony No. 3
Roussel: *Sinfonietta for Strings*
Berlioz: *The Damnation of Faust*: Rákóczy March

19 Jan. 1952: Fritz Reiner
Debussy: *Petite Suite*
Ravel: *Le tombeau de Couperin*
Bartók: *Two Romanian Dances*
R. Strauss: *Till Eulenspiegel's Merry Pranks*

26 Jan. 1952: Eugene Ormandy
Haug: Passacaglia
Rachmaninov: Symphony No. 2

2 Feb. 1952: Guido Cantelli
Vivaldi: Concerto Grosso in A Minor
Tchaikovsky: *Romeo and Juliet*: Fantasy Overture
Ghedini: *Pezzo concertante*
Verdi: *La forza del destino*: Overture

9 Feb. 1952: Guido Cantelli
Wagner: *A Faust Overture*
Bartók: Concerto for Orchestra

16 Feb. 1952: Guido Cantelli
Gabrieli: Canzone from *Sacre sinfonie*
Monteverdi: *Sonata sopra Sancta Maria*
Franck: Symphony in D Minor

23 Feb. 1952: Guido Cantelli
Ghedini: Partita
Mussorgsky-Ravel: *Pictures at an Exhibition*

1 Mar. 1952: Guido Cantelli
Shulman: *A Laurentian Overture*
Tchaikovsky: Symphony No. 5

Sixteenth Season

29 Nov. 1952: Guido Cantelli
Weber: *Euryanthe*: Overture
Creston: *Two Choric Dances*
Miller: *Procession* (world premiere)
Schumann: Symphony No. 4

6 Dec. 1952: Guido Cantelli
Vivaldi: Concerto in A Minor for Two Violins, with Remo Bolognini and
    Daniel Guilet
Brahms: Symphony No. 1

13 Dec. 1952: Guido Cantelli
Mozart: Symphony No. 29
Bartók: *Music for Strings, Percussion, and Celeste*

20 Dec. 1952: Guido Cantelli
Haydn: Symphony No. 88
Stravinsky: *Jeu de cartes*
Ravel: *Boléro*

27 Dec. 1952: Guido Cantelli
Bach: *Christmas Oratorio*, Part 2: Sinfonia
Cherubini: Symphony in D Major
R. Strauss: *Death and Transfiguration*

3 Jan. 1953: Guido Cantelli
Schubert: Symphony No. 8, "Unfinished"
Britten: *Sinfonia da Requiem*
Wagner: *Rienzi*: Overture

21 Feb. 1953: Guido Cantelli
Rossini: *The Siege of Corinth*: Overture
Tchaikovsky: Symphony No. 6, "Pathétique"

28 Feb. 1953: Guido Cantelli
Haydn: Symphony No. 93
Hindemith: *Mathis der Maler*

Seventeenth Season

8 Nov. 1953: Pierre Monteux
Beethoven: *Leonore* Overture No. 2
Brahms: Symphony No. 2

15 Nov. 1953: Pierre Monteux
Beethoven: *The Creatures of Prometheus*: excerpts
    Symphony No. 7

20 Dec. 1953: Guido Cantelli
Barber: *A School for Scandal*: Overture
Bettinelli: *Two Inventions*
Debussy: *Le martyre de saint Sébastien*
Ravel: *Daphnis et Chloé*: Suite No. 2

27 Dec. 1953: Guido Cantelli
Handel: *Xerxes*: Largo
Schubert: Symphony No. 9

3 Jan. 1953: Guido Cantelli
Frescobaldi-Ghedini: Three Pieces
Franck: Symphony in D Minor

10 Jan. 1954: Guido Cantelli
Beethoven: Symphony No. 1
Casella: *Paganiniana*
de Falla: *The Three-Cornered Hat*: Dances

31 Jan. 1954: Guido Cantelli
Haydn: Symphony No. 88
Hindemith: *Concert Music for Strings and Brass*
Wagner: *Rienzi*: Overture

7 Feb. 1954: Guido Cantelli
Gabrieli-Ghedini: *Aria della battaglia*
Mozart: Divertimento, K. 287
Ravel: *La valse*

14 Feb. 1954: Guido Cantelli
Rossini: *La Cenerentola*: Overture
Tchaikovsky: Symphony No. 4

21 Feb. 1954: Guido Cantelli
Stravinsky: *Le chant du rossignol*
Beethoven: Symphony No. 5

28 Mar. 1954: Charles Munch
Debussy: "Ibéria"
Ravel: *Le tombeau de Couperin*
Roussel: *Bacchus and Ariadne*: Suite No. 2

NOTES

Notes to Chapter 1

1. These include world premieres of Leoncavallo's *Pagliacci*, Boito's *Nerone*, and Puccini's *La bohème, La fanciulla del West*, and *Turandot*; and the first performances in Italy of Tchaikovsky's *Eugene Onegin*, Debussy's *Pelléas et Mélisande*, and Weber's *Euryanthe*. Toscanini also conducted the American premiere of Mussorgsky's *Boris Godunov*. His reforms involve the gradual elimination of encores, raising the standards of orchestral execution in the pit, and introducing the laterally (rather than vertically) opening curtain. Turning off the house lights once a performance began was also a Toscanini innovation. For more about these matters see Harvey Sachs, *Toscanini* (New York: J. B. Lippincott, 1978).

2. Samuel Chotzinoff, *Toscanini: An Intimate Portrait* (New York: Alfred A. Knopf, 1956), 75–80. This anecdote typifies the many faults of Chotzinoff's book, which is neither intimate nor a portrait, but rather a collage of gossipy details that often make Toscanini look foolish. In addition, the book contains errors of detail about the conductor's NBC broadcasts.

3. According to Sachs (256), the article was written by Chotzinoff's friends, Russell and Marcia Davenport, and drew, presumably, upon information supplied by Chotzinoff.

4. "Toscanini on the Air," 65.

5. "Toscanini on the Air," 66.

6. Sachs, 258.

7. *The NBC Symphony Orchestra* (New York, 1938). This 120-page volume features reproductions of charcoal portraits drawn by Bettina Steinke of each member of the orchestra and of Rodzinski, Monteux, and Toscanini. A biographical sketch accompanies each drawing.

8. This performance was given on 7 November 1937. The program consisted of Weber's overture to *Oberon* and Richard Strauss's *Heldenleben*. NBC's use of the tag "dress rehearsal" was, to say the least, quite free, since the Strauss work never appeared on any of the orchestra's programs that season. The Weber was performed under Monteux eleven days later.

9. See B. H. Haggin, *Arturo Toscanini: Contemporary Reflections of the Maestro,* ed. Thomas Hathaway (New York: Da Capo Press, 1989), 32. This book is a reprint in a single volume of Haggin's *The Toscanini Musicians Knew* and *Conversations with Toscanini*. In this edition each volume retains its original title and its own pagination.

10. See Sachs, 269.

11. *The NBC Symphony Orchestra*, 12. Monteux received rather shabby treatment from NBC at this time. As he was preparing to return to San Francisco after his stint with the newly created orchestra, he received a call from the network. According to Monteux, the orchestra was in a panic, aware it was to perform *La mer* under Toscanini within a few weeks. But many of the musicians had never played the work, and they "begged" Monteux to come to the studio and "teach" it to them. As Monteux notes: "An orchestra does not usually beg a conductor to teach them anything, and I knew they feared the outcome of presenting a work to the Maestro ill-prepared and not known by the players. Well, of course, I could not refuse." Monteux spent three hours in this preparation but never received any acknowledgment from NBC for his efforts. See Doris Monteux, *It's All in the Music* (New York: Farrar, Strauss and Giroux, 1956), 196.

12. Marcia Davenport, "All Star Orchestra," *Stage*, December 1937, 79.

13. This is true not only for Joseph Horowitz, but also for many others whose views Horowitz embraces, notably those of Theodor Adorno and Virgil Thomson.

14. For some of Toscanini's benefit concerts such as those of 6 May 1940 and 22 February 1941, this law was ignored; tickets were sold to the public, but both were aired in their entirety. In other instances, however, notably the two benefit concerts of the first season, this law was circumvented: by not broadcasting the first work on the concert of 6 February 1938 (Beethoven's First Symphony) and by transmitting only via shortwave the single work that comprised the concert of 4 March 1938 (the Verdi Requiem).

15. This number is the official figure provided by NBC. Others have estimated the studio's capacity as close to twelve hundred.

16. Horowitz, 186.

17. *New York Times*, 14 November 1937.

18. Many of the performances so preserved feature these conductors in repertory for which they left no commercially released recording. Prime examples include Bruno Walter directing Tchaikovsky's Fifth Symphony, Debussy's *Prelude to the Afternoon of a Faun*, and Ravel's *Rapsodie espagnole*; Leopold Stokowski and Eduard Steuermann in the world premiere of the Schoenberg Piano Concerto; Dimitri Mitropoulos in the Haydn Symphony No. 80; Erich Kleiber leading Schubert's Third Symphony; Ernest Ansermet in the Schubert Ninth; and Guido Cantelli conducting Haydn's "Surprise" Symphony and Stravinsky's *Chant du rossignol*, to cite but a few examples. See Appendix 9.

Notes to Chapter 2

1. Samuel Antek and Robert Hupka, *This Was Toscanini* (New York: Vanguard, 1963, 15–16).

2. Haggin, *Conversations with Toscanini*, 17–18.

3. Sachs, *Toscanini*, 268. Sachs also explodes the notion that Toscanini never fired a musician (207–8) and notes that Toscanini once wished to audition all of the New York Philharmonic's first violins. As an amplification of this point, it should be added that Toscanini did this by having each member of the section sit for a week in the concertmaster's chair. It was, at best, an unfair practice, presenting far greater hazards to some than others, depending on the repertory at hand. For a violinist named E. Täk, it proved disastrous. In what amounted to a musical version of Rus-

sian roulette, Täk drew Dvořák's *Symphonic Variations*, a work having a difficult solo passage whose demands he could not meet. His contract, consequently, was not renewed. Had the repertory been different, he might have survived. One wonders if Toscanini ever learned that Täk, after returning to Europe to join the Amsterdam Concertgebouw Orchestra, was ultimately swallowed up in the Holocaust.

4. Sir Donald Tovey, *Essays in Musical Analysis* (London and New York: Oxford University Press, 122–28).
5. Haggin, *The Toscanini Musicians Knew*, 35.
6. Haggin, *The Toscanini Musicians Knew*, 27.
7. Quoted in George R. Marek, *Toscanini* (New York: Atheneum, 1975), 232–33.
8. Haggin, *The Toscanini Musicians Knew*, 35–36.
9. *Toscanini*, 231. Marek may be confused here. In July of 1941, Toscanini was in South America and could not have been attending rehearsals at NBC. Furthermore, if he had been in New York, his presence at such rehearsals would have been most unlikely in the light of his having resigned his position. Still, it does seem plausible that NBC's choice of a guest conductor may have displeased him.
10. Sachs, 278–79.
11. Sachs, 279–80, and Oliver Daniel, *Stokowski: A Counterpoint of View* (New York: Dodd Mead, 1982), 454–56.
12. Marek, 235.
13. Daniel, 458, and Maxim Shostakovich, " Prénom Maxim," *Le monde de la musique*, January 1986, xiv.
14. Haggin, *The Toscanini Musicians Knew*, 26–27. When Shulman's recollections of the visit were first published in 1967, Stokowski, who was still living, was not identified. But a check of the New York Philharmonic's programs reveals that he was, indeed, the conductor of the Franck symphony for the broadcast of 19 October 1941, which attests to the accuracy of Shulman's memory a quarter of a century after the fact.
15. Stokowski actually completed the cycle in 1931 with a recording of the Fourth Symphony. It was never issued, however, and he produced a second completion of the cycle with another recording two years after.
16. *Maestro* (January–December 1970), 28.
17. Sachs, 281.
18. General Motors published all of Kettering's talks in a book, where they are arranged by topic rather than in chronological order. None of the talks is dated, making it impossible to know on which broadcast a specific talk occurred. See Charles F. Kettering, *Short Stories of Science and Invention* (Detroit, 1955).
19. Horszowski does not mention this detail, but discusses other interesting ones concerning the preparation of this performance. See Haggin, *The Toscanini Musicians Knew*, 104–6.
20. Haggin, *The Toscanini Musicians Knew*, 77.
21. According to Sachs (89), Toscanini read through the score of the Dvořák in 1905 but did not find it appealing.
22. "Symphony Notes" for NBC Symphony broadcasts from 19 November to 17 December 1944.
23. Horowitz, 175.
24. Sachs, 296.
25. Chotzinoff, 129–30.
26. Haggin, *Conversations with Toscanini*, 61–62.

27. Sachs, 292.
28. Dennis Matthews, *Arturo Toscanini* (New York: Hippocrene Books, 1982), 84.
29. Sachs, 286.
30. Haggin, *Conversations with Toscanini*, 88.
31. Haggin, *The Toscanini Musicians Knew*, 33.
32. Haggin, *Conversations with Toscanini*, 88–89.
33. Sachs, 295.
34. Haggin, *The Toscanini Musicians Knew*, 212.
35. Antek, 99–100.
36. Sachs, 300.
37. Marek, 113.
38. Sachs, 304. Sachs also notes: "Both concerts were . . . recorded and could still be heard today [1978] by the public." In 2000, both concerts were issued in superior transfers on two Testament CDs.
39. Sachs, 305.
40. Sachs, 304–5.
41. Sachs, 305.
42. Haggin, *The Toscanini Musicians Knew*, 37.
43. Sachs, 307.
44. Robert C. Marsh, *Toscanini and the Art of Conducting* (New York: Collier Books, 1962), 273.
45. Sachs, 306.
46. Sachs, 307.
47. Haggin, *The Toscanini Musicians Knew*, 37.
48. After his retirement from NBC, Toscanini contemplated leading a production of *Falstaff* that would inaugurate the newly completed Piccola Scala in Milan. It became increasingly clear, however, that he was not up to the task.
49. Haggin, *The Toscanini Musicians Knew*, 136.
50. Chotzinoff, 146.
51. Sachs, 309. Sachs also discusses unpleasant scenes at the last rehearsal.
52. The program comprised Berlioz's *Roman Carnival* Overture, Tchaikovsky's *Nutcracker* Suite, Dvořák's "New World" Symphony, and Wagner's prelude to *Die Meistersinger*.
53. A history of the Symphony of the Air was written by its manager, Jerome Toobin, *Agitato: A Trek through the Musical Jungle* (New York: Viking Press, 1975).

Notes to Chapter 3

1. Joseph J. McLellan, "Of Time Warp and Toscanini," *Washington Post*, 15 April 1990.
2. Note that among the many performances on Toscanini's ten televised concerts (now available on videocassettes), only those of the Brahms Double Concerto and *Liebeslieder Waltzes*, Beethoven's Fifth Symphony, Debussy's *Prelude to the Afternoon of a Faun*, and Verdi's *Aida* were approved by Toscanini for release. His approval for the other televised performances was most likely never sought, as they comprise, in many cases, repertory for which he left an authorized recording.
3. See "Atterberg's Forty-Year-Old Hoax," *Music Journal*, 11 July 1968, 30.
4. *Musical America,* 25 December 1939. In the 3 December 1939 *New York Times*, Olin Downes claimed Ania Dorfmann played "admirably,"

5. Artur Rubinstein, *My Many Years* (New York: Alfred A. Knopf, 1980), 506–7.

6. Sachs, 340–41.

7. See Tobia Nicotra, *Arturo Toscanini* (New York: Alfred A. Knopf, 1929), 9.

8. See Haggin, *The Toscanini Musicians Knew*, 133–34.

9. The only cycle of the 78 rpm era was recorded between 1927 and 1938 by Felix Weingartner. In March 1952 Bruno Walter completed another, the first produced on long-playing records. The following November Toscanini made his second recording of the Eighth Symphony, completing the second cycle of the LP era, begun in 1949.

10. "Legge on Toscanini," *Gramophone* (June 1990): 9.

11. Toscanini programmed the "Eroica" more frequently, but many of those presentations were not broadcast and occurred on the NBC Symphony's 1950 tour. Ironically, the "Pastoral" was included only once on the orchestra's tours.

12. *On the Performance of Beethoven's Symphonies*, reprinted in *Weingartner on Music and Conducting* (New York: Dover, 1969), 171.

13. "Radio Music," printed in Shaw, *How to Become a Musical Critic*, ed. Dan H. Laurence (New York: Da Capo, 1978), 32.

14. See Marek, 62–63.

15. The only 78 rpm recording was made in 1944 by the Boston Symphony under Koussevitzky, with William Primrose as violist.

16. A performance in the late nineteenth century was led in the United States by Walter Damrosch.

17. See B. H. Haggin, *Conversations with Toscanini* (New York: Dolphin, 1959), 141–42. This passage is not reprinted in the new Thomas Hathaway edition used as the main reference throughout this book.

18. Haggin, *The Toscanini Musicians Knew*, 145–46.

19. See Horowitz, *Understanding Toscanini*, 182.

20. See Haggin, *Conversations with Toscanini*, 182.

21. Paul Henry Lang, *Music in Western Civilization* (New York: W. W. Norton, 1941), 864.

22. See George Bernard Shaw, *The Great Composers*, ed. Louis Crompton (London and Berkeley: University of California Press, 1979), 39.

23. *Toscanini and the Art of Conducting*, 184.

24. Haggin, *Conversations with Toscanini,* 40–41.

25. *Toscanini and the Art of Conducting*, 216.

26. See Haggin, *Conversations with Toscanini* (Dolphin ed.), 145. His comments about Toscanini's changing views of the Brahms Third Symphony are not included in the reprint edited by Hathaway.

27. See Goldsmith's informative annotations for the compact disc reissue of Toscanini's recording of the work, RCA 60529.

28. Sachs, 113.

29. See Taubman, *The Maestro* (New York: Simon and Schuster, 1951), 290.

30. Sachs, 231.

31. Sachs, 101.

32. Haggin, *The Toscanini Musicians Knew*, 229.

33. Haggin, *The Toscanini Musicians Knew*, 211.

34. See Sachs, 236.

35. Denis Matthews, *Arturo Toscanini* (New York: Hippocrene Books, 1982), 69.

36. Matthews, 69.

37. Taubman, 22.
38. See note 15 in chapter 2.
39. See Sachs, 109–10.
40. "A Singer's View of Toscanini," *Saturday Review*, 25 March 1967, 58.
41. Haggin, *The Toscanini Musicians Knew*, 58–59.
42. See Marsh, 157.
43. Haggin, *The Toscanini Musicians Knew*, 137.
44. Earlier recordings were made by Howard Barlow and Sir Malcolm Sargent.
45. Donald Tovey, *Essays in Musical Analysis*, vol. 1 (New York: Oxford University Press, 1935), 15–56.
46. Donald Tovey, *Essays in Musical Analysis*, vol. 3 (New York and London: Oxford University Press, 1936), 5.
47. Tovey, *Essays in Musical Analysis*, 1:153.
48. Haggin, *Conversations with Toscanini*, 59.
49. In Turin on 20 March 1896. The concert included the Brahms *Tragic* Overture, the Tchaikovsky *Nutcracker Suite*, the Schubert Ninth Symphony, and the Entrance of the Gods into Vallhalla from Wagner's *Rheingold*.
50. As noted elsewhere, March and Haggin have been two of the strongest proponents of this notion.
51. Reacting to what was probably believed in 1929 to be a copyist's error, Toscanini, in his New York Philharmonic recording, "corrected" the dissonant chording in measure 8 of the minuet, thereby spoiling one of Haydn's wittiest jokes, one that satirizes musicians' inability to get it right the first time through. Upon the passage's immediate repetition, Haydn eliminated the dissonance.
52. See Taubman, 286.
53. Taubman, 286.
54. Sachs, 30.
55. Haggin, *Conversations with Toscanini*, 54.
56. Haggin, *Conversations with Toscanini*, 59.
57. Haggin, *The Toscanini Musicians Knew*, 111, 114.
58. Sachs, 199.
59. Haggin, *Conversations with Toscanini*, 88.
60. Haggin, *The Toscanini Musicians Knew*, 18.
61. Marek, 236.
62. Sachs 115ff.
63. Marek, 113.
64. Sachs, 92–97.
65. Sachs, 97.
66. See Igor Stravinsky, *An Autobiography* (New York: Norton Library, 1962), 129–30.
67. Haggin, *Conversations with Toscanini*, 89.
68. Tovey, 2:85.
69. Haggin, *The Toscanini Musicians Knew*, 134.
70. Haggin, *Conversations with Toscanini*, 136.
71. Haggin, *The Toscanini Musicians Knew*, 125.
72. Sachs, 191.
73. Sachs, 58.
74. Verdi's criticism appeared in published correspondence, and Toscanini underlined it.
75. Sachs, 219–20.

76. Sachs, 219–20.
77. Sachs, 13–14.
78. A nearly complete recording of the 1930 Bayreuth *Tannhäuser* was made in the studio, but with Karl Elmendorff conducting under the supervision of Siegfried Wagner. It is possible that this recording retains some of the features of Toscanini's production.
79. Haggin, *The Toscanini Musicians Knew*, 17.
80. Marsh, 201, 207.
81. Matthews, 55.
82. Haggin, *The Toscanini Musicians Knew*, 137.
83. Sachs, 105.
84. Haggin, *The Toscanini Musicians Knew*, 64.
85. Haggin, *Conversations with Toscanini*, 130.
86. Martin Bernstein, a double bassist in Toscanini's New York Philharmonic, told me that in Siegfried's Rhine Journey, for example, Toscanini, unlike many other conductors, took exceptional care in observing Wagner's indications of marcato. Significantly, too, when he came to Bayreuth in 1930, Toscanini corrected long-standing errors in some of the orchestral parts that German conductors had over-looked.
87. Antek, 143–81.

Notes to Chapter 4

1. "When History Is a Casualty," *New York Times*, 30 April 1993.
2. Sachs, 321–22.
3. These include symphonies by Haydn, Mozart, Beethoven, and Brahms, as well as works by Mendelssohn, Debussy, Wagner, and Richard Strauss.
4. Sachs, 322–23.
5. The terms are Haggin's.
6. Marsh, 93f.
7. Quoted from Sachs, 120.
8. Not until the release of the 1951 recording on compact disc did RCA acknowledge that part of it was drawn from the 1951 broadcast. In fact, the recording comprises mainly broadcast material, preserving, among other flaws, faulty ensemble in outer movements. Why these flaws were not corrected remains a mystery.
9. Antek, 9.
10. "Toscanini as Maestro and Teacher," *Saturday Review*, 25 March 1967, 56.
11. *Über das Dirigieren*, 1869.
12. *Antek*, 12.
13. *Toscanini and Great Music* (New York: Farrar and Rinehard, 1938), 58.
14. *The Maestro Myth* (New York: Birch Lane Press, 1992), 82.
15. Horowitz, 272, 334, 364–66.
16. Antek, 76.
17. Sachs, 312.
18. "The Maestro in Riverdale," *Saturday Review*, 25 March 1967, 60.

BIBLIOGRAPHY

Antek, Samuel, and Robert Hupka. *This Was Toscanini*. New York: Vanguard Press, 1963. Reprint, New York: Random House, 1980.

Bilby, Kenneth. *The General: David Sarnoff and the Rise of the Communications Industry*. New York: Harper and Row, 1886.

Chotzinoff, Samuel. *Toscanini: An Intimate Portrait*. New York: Alfred A. Knopf, 1956.

Daniel, Oliver. *Stokowski: A Counterpoint of View*. New York: Dodd Mead, 1982.

Davenport, John, and Marcia Davenport. "Toscanini on the Air." *Fortune*, January 1938, 78.

Erskine, John. *Philharmonic-Symphony Society of New York: Its First Hundred Years*. New York: Macmillan, 1943.

Ewen, David. *The Story of Arturo Toscanini*. New York: Holt, Rinehart and Winston, 1960.

Frank, Mortimer H. "From the Pit to the Podium: Toscanini in America." *International Classical Record Collector* (Winter 1998): 8.

Frank, Mortimer H. "Toscanini in esilio: gli anni americani." In *Toscanini*, edited by L. Bergonzini. Bologna: Editrice QUEB, 1992.

Frassati, Luciana. *Il Maestro*. Torino: Bottega d'Erasmo, 1967.

Freeman, John W. "Atterberg's Forty-Year-Old Hoax." *Music Journal*, 11 July 1968, 30.

Freeman, John W. "The Maestro in Riverdale." *Saturday Review*, 25 March 1967, 60.

Freeman, John W., and Walfredo Toscanini. *Toscanini*. New York: Treves, 1987.

Gelatt, Roland. *Music Makers*. New York: Alfred A. Knopf, 1953.

Gilman, Lawrence. *Toscanini and Great Music*. New York. Farrar and Rinehart, 1938.

Haggin, B. H. *Arturo Toscanini: Contemporary Reflections of the Maestro*. Edited by Thomas Hathaway. New York: Da Capo Press, 1989.

Haggin, B. H. *Conversations with Toscanini*. New York: Doubleday Dolphin Books, 1959.

Haggin, B. H. *The Toscanini Musicians Knew*. 2d ed. New York: Horizon Press, 1980.

Hoeller, Susanne Winternitz. *Arturo Toscanini: A Photobiography*. New York: Island Press, 1943.

Hirschmann, Ira. *Obligato: Untold Tales from a Life with Music*. New York: Fromm International, 1994.

Horowitz, Joseph. *Understanding Toscanini*. New York: Alfred A. Knopf, 1987.

Hughes, Spike. *The Toscanini Legacy*. New York: Dover, 1969.

Kakutani, Michiko. "When History Is a Casualty." *New York Times*, 30 April 1993.

Katims, Milton. "Toscanini as Maestro and Teacher." *Saturday Review*, 25 March 1967, 56.

Kettering, Charles F. *Short Stories of Science and Invention*. Detroit: General Motors, 1955.

Kolodin, Irving. "The Genius of the Inexplicable." *Saturday Review*, 25 March 1967, 62.

Lang, Paul Henry. *Music in Western Civilization*. New York: W. W. Norton, 1941.

Lebrecht, Norman. *The Maestro Myth*. New York: Birch Lane Press, 1991.

Leinsdorf, Erich. *Cadenza: A Musical Career*. Boston: Houghton Mifflin, 1976.

Lipman, Samuel. *Music and More*. Evanston: University of Illinois Press, 1992.

Lyons, Eugene. *David Sarnoff*. New York: Harper and Row, 1966.

The Maestro. 1969 to 1973. Published sporadically by the American Arturo Toscanini Society [dissolved in 1975].

Marcus, Leonard, ed. *The Recordings of Beethoven*. New York: Charles Scribner's Sons, 1970.

Marsh, Robert Charles. *Toscanini and the Art of Conducting*. New York: Collier Books, 1962. [This is a revised version of the following entry.]

Marsh, Robert Charles. *Toscanini and the Art of Orchestral Performance*. New York: J. B. Lippincott, 1955.

Marsh, Robert Charles. "Toscanini and the Recording Machine." *Saturday Review*, 25 March 1967, 59.

Matthews, Denis. *Arturo Toscanini*. New York: Hippocrene Books, 1982.

McLellan, Joseph J. "Of Time Warp and Toscanini." *Washington Post*, 15 April 1990.

Marek, George. *Toscanini*. New York: Atheneum, 1975.

Merriman, Nan. "A Singer's View of Toscanini." *Saturday Review*, 25 March 1967, 58.

Meyer, Donald Carl. "The NBC Symphony Orchestra." Ph.D. diss., University of California, Davis, 1992.

Meyer, Donald Carl. "Toscanini and the NBC Orchestra: High, Middle, and Low Culture." In *Perspectives in American Music,* edited by Michael Saffle. New York: Garland, 2000.

Monteux, Doris. *It's All in the Music.* New York: Farrar, Strauss and Giroux, 1965.

The NBC Symphony Orchestra. New York: National Broadcasting Company, 1938.

Nicotra, Tobia. *Arturo Toscanini.* New York: Alfred A. Knopf, 1929.

O'Connell, Charles. *The Other Side of the Record.* New York: Alfred A. Knopf, 1947.

Rubinstein, Artur. *My Many Years.* New York: Alfred A. Knopf, 1989.

Sachs, Harvey. *Reflections on Toscanini.* New York: Grove Weidenfeld, 1991.

Sachs, Harvey. *Toscanini.* New York: J. B. Lippincott, 1978.

Sarnoff, David. *Looking Ahead: The Papers of David Sarnoff.* New York: McGraw-Hill, 1968.

Schonberg, Harold. *The Great Conductors.* New York: Simon and Schuster, 1967.

Shore, Bernard. *The Orchestra Speaks.* London: Longmans, Green, 1938.

Shostakovich, Maxim. 1986. "Prénom Maxim." *Le monde de la musique* (January): xiv.

Szell, George. "Toscanini and the History of Orchestral Performance." *Saturday Review,* 25 March 1967, 53.

Taubman, Howard. *The Maestro.* New York: Simon and Schuster, 1951.

Toobin, Jerome. *Agitato: A Trek through the Musical Jungle.* New York: Viking Press, 1975.

Walter, Bruno. *Theme and Variations: Autobiography.* New York: Alfred A. Knopf, 1946.

INDEX

This index covers chapters 1 through 4. The appendices are organized either alphabetically or chronologically.

Aldrich, Richard, 238
Ansermet, Ernest, 40, 89, 92, 189
Antek, Samuel, 43, 96, 248
Atterberg, Kurt, 117–118

Bach, Johann Sebastian, 48, 82, 90, 108, 118–119
Bachman, Edwin, 104, 258
Baker, Bernard, 118
Barber, Samuel, 48, 119
Barzun, Jacques, 132, 243
Bazzini, Antonio, 120
Beecham, Sir Thomas, 184, 196
Beethoven, Ludwig van, 42, 47, 49, 57, 89, 120–131, 236, 237, 238, 239, 243, 244, 245, 249, 251, 252, 254, 259
Bellini, Vincenzo, 131
Berg, Alban, 82
Berlioz, Hector, 42, 59, 85, 86, 89, 131–135, 259
Bernstein, Leonard, 85, 126
Bernstein, Martin,51, 171
Bizet, Georges, 135
Björling, Jussi, 112
Black, Frank, 62, 71, 77, 81, 88
Bloom, Robert, 29, 30
Bodansky, Artur, 255
Boccherini, Luigi, 136
Boito, Arrigo, 136, 259
Bolzoni, Giovanni, 137
Borodin, Alexander, 44, 137

Bossi, Enrico, 137
Boult, Sir Adrian, 52, 156, 173
Brahms, Johannes, 21, 37, 42, 43, 44, 57, 113, 114, 137–148, 241, 242, 244, 248, 251, 255, 256, 259
Brieff, Frank, 109, 255
Burghauser, Hugo, 28, 62
Busch, Adolf, 52
Busch, Herman, 52
Busoni, Ferruccio, 148

Cantelli, Guido, 40, 92–93, 101 113, 257
Carboni, William, 165
Cartier, Edward C., 65
Caruso, Enrico, 25
Casals, Pablo, 52
Castlenuovo-Tedesco, Mario, 148
Catalani, Alfredo, 148–148
Cherubini, Luigi, 44, 96, 149–150, 259
Chotzinoff, Samuel, 23–24, 26, 30, 35 36, 40, 47, 48, 51, 52, 62, 84, 113
Cimarosa, Domenico, 150
Claney, Howard, 36, 48
Cooke, Alistair, 36
Cooley, Carlton, 29, 50, 133, 134, 183, 209
Copland, Aaron, 150
Cornell, Katharine, 106
Creston, Paul, 150

Debussy, Claude, 44, 86, 89, 107, 151–154, 259
Davenport, Marcia, 30
Degeyeter, Pierre, 154
Donizetti, Gaetano, 154
Dorfmann, Ania, 122, 123
Downes, Olin, 34, 36, 58, 74, 156, 252
Dukas, Paul, 96, 154
Dvořák, Antonin, 48, 155–156, 259

Eisenhower, Dwight D., 112
Elgar, Sir Edward, 156–157
Enesco, Georges, 157

Falla, Manuel de, 157–158
Fernandez, Oscar, 158
Feuermann, Emanuel, 52, 209
Fiedler, Arthur, 96, 125
Foroni, Jacopo, 158
Franchetti, Alberto, 158–159
Franck, César, 66, 159–160, 259
Freeman, John W., 117, 257, 258
Fried, Oskar, 215
Furtwängler, Wilhelm, 115, 125, 197, 198, 231, 242, 243, 254, 255, 259

Gershwin, George, 160
Gilbert, Henry F., 161
Gillis, Don, 109, 161
Gilman, Lawrence, 54, 252
Gingold, Joseph, 126, 215, 230
Giordano, Umberto, 161
Glanrz, Harry, 245
Glassman, Karl, 114, 245
Glinka, Mikhail, 161–162
Gluck, Alma, 23, 58, 107
Gluck, Christoph Willibald, 162–163, 259
Goldmark, Karl, 50, 75, 163
Goldsmith, Harris, 146, 186 199, 213
Goodman, Saul, 229
Gould, Morton, 164
Graener, Paul, 164
Grauer, Ben, 65, 67
Grieg, Edvard, 164
Griffes, Charles Tomlinson, 165
Grofé, Ferde, 165
Guilet, Daniel, 114, 127, 210

Haggin, B. H., 44, 92, 112, 133, 144, 147, 178 182, 213, 230, 238, 239
Hall, David, 78
Handel, George Frideric, 165–166
Hamilton, Gene, 48, 52, 54
Harris, Roy, 166
Harty, Sir Hamilton, 197, 198
Haydn, Franz Joseph, 47, 75, 108, 166–172, 238, 241, 242, 359
Hayes, Helen, 105
Heifetz, Jascha, 23, 52, 178
Hérold, Louis Joseph Ferdinand, 172
Hess, Myra, 87, 124
Hitler, Adolf, 46, 47, 235
Hobby, Oveta Culp, 70
Hoffstetter, Roman, 172
Horowitz, Joseph, 30, 252–256
Horowitz, Vladimir, 52, 53, 58, 140, 141, 239, 253
Horszowski, Mieczyslaw, 73, 182
Huberman, Bronislaw, 52
Humperdinck, Engelbert, 172–172
Hunter, Ralph, 101, 149

Johnson, Robert, 77

Kabalevsky, Dmitri, 69, 82, 173
Kakutani, Michiko, 235
Kalinnikov, Vassily, 173
Karajan, Herbert von, 192, 218
Katims, Milton, 88, 92, 96, 107, 109, 152, 243
Kennan, Kent, 174
Kennedy, Joseph, 47
Kettering, Charles F., 71–72, 78, 82
Kipnis, Alexander, 230
Kleiber, Erich, 40, 82, 89, 242
Klemperer, Otto, 147, 259
Knappertsbusch, Hans, 232
Kodály, Zoltán, 174
Koussevitzky, Serge, 86, 133, 185, 196, 242, 245
Krasnopolsky, Michael, 248
Krehbiel, Henry, 162
Kurtz, Edmund, 155

Lebrecht, Norman, 253
Legge, Walter, 257
Leinsdorf, Erich, 49, 67, 92

Levant, Oscar, 160
Levi, Hermann, 230
Levine, James, 42
Liadov, Anatol, 174–175
Liszt, Franz, 175
Loeffler, Charles Martin, 175

Maazel, Lorin, 62
Mackay, Clarence, 23
Maeterlinck, Maurice, 151
Mahler, Gustav, 230, 259
Mancinelli, Luigi, 175–176
Marek, George, 62
Marsh, Robert C., 143,145, 237, 238, 239
Martucci, Giuseppe, 176–177
Massenet, Jules, 176
McLellan, Joseph, 115
Mendelssohn, Felix, 58, 89, 177–180, 237, 241, 242, 243, 251
Mengelberg, Willem, 41, 173, 198, 209
Merriman, Nan, 89, 163
Meyerbeer, Giacomo, 48, 104, 180
Mignone, Francisco, 181
Miller, Frank, 49, 94, 95, 107, 113, 142, 153, 209
Milstein, Nathan, 52
Mischakoff, Mischa, 27, 142, 183, 210
Moldovan, Nicholas, 74
Mitropoulos, Dimitri, 40, 82, 96, 126
Monteux, Pierre, 30, 34, 40, 48, 111
Morgenthau, Henry, 64
Mozart, Leopold, 181
Mozart, Wolfgang Amadeus, 37, 47, 54, 83, 86, 107, 181–185, 237, 238, 244, 245, 249, 258
Mullin, Frank, 69
Mussolini, Benito, 47, 50, 70, 71, 120, 235
Mussorgsky, Modest, 107, 186

Nesbit, John, 102
Newman, Ernest, 156
Nicolai, Otto, 186
Nikisch, Arthur, 259

O'Connell, Charles, 62
Olivier, Laurence, 107
Olivieri, Allesio, 187

Paganini, Nicolò, 49, 187
Patterson, Robert, 70
Peerce, Jan, 112, 188
Pelletier, Wilfrid, 96, 101,127
Ponchielli, Amilcare, 187
Primrose, William, 50, 52, 133
Prokofiev, Serge, 50, 187–188
Puccini, Giacomo, 82, 100, 188–189, 259

Raff, Joseph Joachim, 104
Ravel, Maurice, 56, 186, 189, 259
Reiner, Fritz, 40, 85, 96, 101, 253
Respighi, Ottorino, 75, 190–191
Rieti, Vittorio, 191
Rodzinski, Artur, 28, 30, 40, 48
Roger-Ducasse, Jean, 191
Roosevelt, Franklin Delano, 72
Rose, Leonard, 44
Rossini, Gioachino, 45, 49, 58, 191–193
Roussel, Albert, 193–194
Royal, John F., 28
Rubbra, Edmund, 139
Rubinstein, Anton, 194
Rubinstein, Artur, 123–124
Ruta, Armand, 29

Sachs, Harvey, 47, 64, 88, 102, 107, 110, 115, 176, 210, 236, 237
Saint-Saëns, Camille, 194–195
Sarnoff, David, 23, 24, 26, 27, 28, 40, 47, 60, 65, 91
Scarlatti, Domenico, 195
Schalk, Franz, 242
Schnabel, Artur, 244
Schoenberg, Arnold, 72, 82
Schubert, Franz, 21, 48, 83, 85, 96, 195–198, 237, 242, 251
Schumann, Robert, 85, 96, 198–201, 242, 252
Serkin, Rudolf, 124, 183
Shapiro, Harvey, 57
Shaw, George Bernard, 129, 139
Shaw, Robert, 92
Shostakovich, Dmitri, 64, 66, 201
Shostakovich, Maxim, 66
Shulman, Alan, 29 30, 57, 61, 66, 90, 110, 111
Shulman, Sylvan, 29

Sibelius, Jean, 56, 75, 201–204
Siegmeister, Elie, 204
Sinigaglia, Leone, 205
Smetana, Bedrich, 206
Smit, Kalman, 29
Smith, John Stafford, 205–206
Sousa, John Philip, 206
Spitalny, H. Leopold, 62
Steinberg, William, 56
Steinke, Bettina, 31
Steuermann, Eduard, 72
Stokowski, Leopold, 40, 60, 62, 65, 66, 67, 118, 245, 249, 259
Strauss, Johann, 206–207
Strauss, Richard, 148, 181, 208–211, 259
Stravinsky, Igor, 152, 211
Strong, George Templeton, 211
Suppé, Franz von, 211–212
Szell, George, 40, 57, 230, 242

Taylor, Deems, 64
Tchaikovsky, Peter Ilych, 21, 82, 86, 212–216, 237, 241, 251, 259
Thomas, Ambroise, 216

Thomson, Virgil, 33
Tommasini, Vincenzo, 217
Tovey, Sir Donald, 51, 215
Tyson, Alan, 172

Vaughan Williams, Ralph, 82, 217
Verdi, Giuseppe, 57, 96, 107, 110, 137, 217–224, 237, 259
Vieuxtemps, Henri, 224
Vivaldi, Antonio, 37, 44, 224

Wagner, Friedelind, 52
Wagner, Richard, 21, 40, 42, 48, 51, 76, 82, 86, 224–232, 241, 242, 251, 259
Waldteufel, Émile, 232
Wallenstein, Alfred, 57, 76, 88, 199
Walter, Bruno, 40, 48, 52, 57, 101, 125, 139, 184, 197, 230, 243, 255, 259
Walter, David, 190, 229
Weber, Carl Maria von, 76, 233–234, 242
Weingartner, Felix, 125, 129, 242
Williamson, John Finley, 139
Wolf-Ferrari, Ermanno, 234
Wummer, John, 44